CASES IN CONSUMER BEHAVIOR

HOLT, RINEHART AND WINSTON MARKETING SERIES

Paul E. Green, ADVISER
WHARTON SCHOOL, UNIVERSITY OF PENNSYLVANIA

Philip Kotler, ADVISER
NORTHWESTERN UNIVERSITY

James F. Engel, David T. Kollat, Roger D. Blackwell
CONSUMER BEHAVIOR
CASES IN CONSUMER BEHAVIOR
RESEARCH IN CONSUMER BEHAVIOR

CASES IN
CONSUMER BEHAVIOR

Roger D. Blackwell
James F. Engel
David T. Kollat

THE OHIO STATE UNIVERSITY

HOLT, RINEHART AND WINSTON, INC.

New York   Chicago   San Francisco   Atlanta
Dallas   Montreal   Toronto   London   Sydney

FOREWORD

The Advisory Editors of the Holt, Rinehart and Winston Marketing Series are pleased to publish this collection of cases to supplement *Consumer Behavior* by Engel, Kollat, and Blackwell. This marks the first collection of cases ever published that deals exclusively with situations requiring the understanding, analysis, and prediction of consumer behavior. It meets the demand of instructors for a new type of case that recognizes the behavioral texture that lies at the very heart of marketing processes. Existing cases, in spite of their many merits, generally lack enough behavioral material so that the student can make a sophisticated analysis of consumer needs, wants, and reactions to marketing strategies. This case collection intends to fill the void.

The cases are numerous and remarkably varied in their coverage of types of buying situations, types of consumer research instruments, and types of marketing issues. Pairing this casebook with the text, *Consumer Behavior,* will enable the student to apply significant concepts in realistic action-oriented situations and gain a first-hand sense of their utility.

—*Paul E. Green*
—*Philip Kotler*

PREFACE

Analyzing a real business problem is an exciting and challenging process. It forces the participant to become involved in the realities of business strategy. The competent executive is not one who knows only theory although it is likely that he has thought extensively about the theories and concepts that can be applied to specific problems.

Collections of case materials have played an important role in the development of business education. Some cases are descriptive. They help the student understand what business will be like when he enters the field. Other cases are analytical. They force the student to reason through a situation, to extract the relevant from the redundant, and to create new solutions to old problems. A case experience can be the most challenging and creative aspect of the business student's education. This is true whether the student is an undergraduate still looking toward a career or an experienced executive returning to the campus for an encounter with fresh, new thinking.

The cases in this book deal with the influence of consumer behavior upon management strategy. They present actual management problems in sufficient detail that students can put considerable energy into defining the specific problem and then test his decision-making skills and creativity at solving the problem. A few of the cases present a straightforward problem that will not require a full class period for solution. Most of the cases, however, have enough background and analytical material that the student can become involved in the total process of the company's strategy.

An important trend in modern business is greatly increased reliance upon research findings for decision making. This book was developed on the premise that modern executives must obtain the ability to interpret and use sophisticated research reports. One problem, as we see it, is that researchers are often most concerned with the *sophistication* or *innovativeness* of the research design and managers are often most concerned with the *use* of the same. We believe that there is an important need for a bridge between the research *suppliers* and the research *appliers*. Therefore, we have presented case material in this book so that the persons with a primary interest in conducting research will gain experience in designing and reporting research in terms of its uses.

Too often, executives have been presented with valuable findings and have not known how to apply them. There are many excellent research studies buried in file drawers simply because management avoided or did not have the ability to use the studies their staff had prepared. This book is intended to develop among management the ability to read, understand, and translate into action empirical research findings. After working through the cases in this book, managers should develop an orientation to expect solid research results before making important decisions.

This book covers the gamut of companies and problems. There are large firms and small ones; manufacturers, retailers, and service industries; companies with sophisticated research departments and companies with no research department. There are examples of well-prepared, high-quality research projects and there are reports of limited value. This, unfortunately, parallels actual practice and it is the task of management to separate the good research from the bad research.

This book is designed to be used for a variety of purposes. It is structured to coordinate with *Consumer Behavior* by the same authors and publisher. With that book, this one can be used to develop the managerial applications of the decision process approach presented in the text. Today, there are a number of readings books in consumer behavior with which this book can be successfully used to develop the ability to apply behavioral theories to the solution of realistic marketing problems. The breadth of topics covered in the cases is sufficient that this book can be used by itself by instructors relying heavily on the case approach.

Many instructors will find the book useful in marketing research and managerial marketing classes. The last few years have witnessed a marked increase in interest in consumer behavior in these courses. Many doctoral students coming out of leading graduate programs have concentrated on consumer behavior and have indicated the need for a consumer behavior casebook with a managerial emphasis that can be used in general marketing and marketing management courses.

Because of the emphasis on research for management information, this book can also be used in most contemporary marketing research courses. A few of the cases require considerable statistical sophistication for a thorough analysis but most require no more than a basic course in statistics coupled with an understanding of the behavioral sciences in a marketing context.

When we conceived this book, we thought of it primarily for pedagogical purposes. As we became involved in the collecting of materials for it, however, we began to realize that many of the cases were of value for their research content as well. Many companies made available to us reports never before released outside the firm's management. We believe that executives and students will find that some of the cases provide valuable insights to the research practice and management policies of the industries represented in the book.

Many people contributed to the development of the book. We gratefully acknowledge the contribution of our research assistant and doctoral student at The Ohio State University, John Schlacter. Company executives who graciously offered their time were many and we especially acknowledge the cooperation of the following: Douglas Miller, Director of Marketing Services, Mead Johnson and Company; J. T. Miller, Director of Research, Meredith Publishing Company; Lewis Winters, Research Psychologist, E. I. DuPont de Nemours Company; Arthur DeMoss, President, National Liberty Life Insurance Company; Dr. Homer E. Spence, Assistant Professor, Department of Marketing, University of Washington; J. W. Edgerton, Public Relations Director, W. T. Grant Company; H. J. Aneiro, Marketing Research Director, Eastern Air Lines; Hugh King, Director of Marketing, Charles of the Ritz, Inc.; C. James Whipple IV, Chairman of the Board, Aqua-Craft Corporation; Robert O. Safford, Executive Vice President, Alexander Hamilton Life Insurance Company of America; Thomas P. Carlson, Director of Marketing Research, Munsingwear Corporation; Dr. Thomas Robertson, Assistant Professor of Business Administration, University of California, Los Angeles; James N. Kennedy, Business Research Administrator, Illinois Bell Telephone Company; Dr. Kenneth Davis, Professor of Marketing, Dartmouth College; C. Gordon Jelliffe, President, City National Bank; Robert Glick, President, Glick Furniture, Inc.; The Home Furnishings Marketing and Research Council; Dr. Sidney Levy, Vice President, Social Research, Inc.

Of great value also were the insightful comments of the reviewers of the manuscript: Professor Donald Granbois of Indiana University, Professor Paul Green of the University of Pennsylvania, and Professor Philip Kotler of Northwestern University.

It has become routine to acknowledge the assistance of wives in the preparation of a book. The fact is, in our instance, if they did not perform the difficult so routinely, this book would not have been finished.

We continue to look for someone whom we can blame for the errors in the manuscript. So far, no one comes to mind but ourselves.

—Roger D. Blackwell
—James F. Engel
—David T. Kollat

Columbus, Ohio
March 1969

CONTENTS

PART I

FUNDAMENTAL PROCESSES OF MOTIVATION, PERCEPTION, AND LEARNING

CHAPTER 1

MOTIVATION AND AROUSAL

Mead Johnson and Company (A): Motivation for Purchasing Diet Foods

The affluent American society contains a large number of overweight people. Estimates of the size of the United States' "well rounded" individuals are as high as 40 percent of the population. In addition to these people, there are many others who wish to avoid becoming overweight who are extremely healthy and diet conscious, or who lack time and desire to prepare and consume complete meals and thus are interested in diet foods. Metrecal, marketed by Mead Johnson and Company, is designed for these people.

Background for Metrecal

Prior to 1959, several efforts were made to exploit the market of obese people in the United States. Milk diets, for example, had been in use for years. About 1955, Life Research Corporation began door-to-door selling of a powdered product called Wey-Rite, which was to be mixed with water. The product had very little success. In 1956, the Rockefeller Institute diet became popular for a short time but soon lost popularity. A complaint against it was that it was time consuming and that it was difficult to find all the ingredients the consumer had to mix together. There were also criticisms of the diet on the grounds that it lacked sufficient protein. The institute had suggested, however, that a typical person could live off nine hundred calories a day and lose weight.

Mead Johnson and Company was a manufacturer of pharmaceutical items and had a well-established reputation. Its original research in the field of nutrition was concerned with food supplements for hospitals. As a result of this research, Sustagen was developed in 1953 as a highly concentrated food powder for patients requiring substantial amounts of nutrients. Sustagen could be drunk with water or administered through an intravenous tube.

From Sustagen research, Mead Johnson developed a food powder with adequate nutriments to satisfy what it considered to be a market of 45 million Americans who wanted easily and effectively to lose weight. The product was called Metrecal, meaning "metered or measured calorie." The product could also be used as a supplement for underweight people or as an emergency food supply.

Metrecal is a powdered mixture of skimmed and whole milk, soya flour, sugar, starch, corn oil, coconut oil, yeast, flavoring, vitamins, and minerals. It is drug-free; that is, it contains no appetite depressant and is a true food supply. One day's supply which is approximately 900 calories, provides about 70 grams of protein, 20 grams of fat, and 110 grams of carbohydrates. Upon development of the product, clinical tests were made at the Good Samaritan Hospital in Phoenix, Arizona. The results of these studies showed that 97 out of 100 persons taking the diet drink and eating no other food lost approximately one-half pound a day.

Early Appeals

In October, 1959, Mead Johnson began promotion of Metrecal. In order to differentiate it from previous diet foods and diet gimmicks, the company elected to use its established reputation in the medical field to indicate the healthful qualities and medical acceptance of the product.

Distribution Channels

Approximately 250 detail men were used to call on doctors throughout the United States telling about the new diet product and informing them of the nutritional value and the clinical tests. They would open a can and let the doctor taste it. Many doctors began recommending Metrecal to their corpulent patients.

Meanwhile, salesmen for Mead Johnson began calling on drugstores and drug wholesalers in an effort to have Metrecal on drug counters. The salesmen were able to take advantage of the reputation and good name of Mead Johnson as a well-recognized producer of excellent pharmaceutical products.

Advertising

Metrecal received relatively extensive advertising in the *Journal of the American Medical Association* and other medical journals. The ads stressed the medical need for the product and how it should be administered. These ads were backed up by direct mail pieces to physicians and drugstores and by doctors' samples.

Initial reaction was good, and about eight months after introduction, Mead began to place advertising in consumer magazines. The ads featured serious statements about Metrecal and were prepared to appear as medical statements of what Metrecal could do and what it could not do. The advertising recommended that the consumers consult with their family doctor before taking Metrecal.

The product was immediately so successful that it spawned many cartoons, jokes, and stock market fluctuations. The phenomenal sales success of Metrecal also led to the appearance of many competing but similar products. By 1961, the total market for diet drinks had reached an annual volume of well over $100 million.

Competition

By 1961, the success of Metrecal had attracted at least 75 labels, and by 1965 over 250 labels had appeared on the market. A partial list of products available in December of 1960 is given in Table 1–1. Most of these products were very similar in nature, they received widespread distribution, and many were marketed by major food manufacturers.

At the end of 1960, a survey conducted by *Advertising Age* summarized the nature of the market in major American cities:

Washington, D.C.

A survey of six drug chains indicated that all sold Metrecal plus their own private label and that both had a fairly prominent display. Metrecal was sold for different prices in different stores, but the private brands were always less. The price of Metrecal varied from $.97 to $1.29 for an eight-ounce can of powder, whereas the same amount of the other diet drink powders sold from $.59 to $.98.

Dallas

There were at least twelve brands of liquid weight reducers. Of the seven major supermarket chains, three were handling liquid diet drinks, and at least three of the four major drug chains were handling the product. The competition of various brands was causing prices to be cut sharply.

St. Louis

Fashionable hotels were putting Metrecal on menus, and it was very popular. Sears, Roebuck and food stores were selling these products in the market at a lower price than Metrecal.

Minneapolis

At least eight different labels were offered including Quota, which was manufactured by Quaker Oats, a well-known name in dairy products. Metrecal and Quota were in a price battle, and both used extensive newspaper advertising.

Table 1–1

Partial List of Powdered Formula Product Brand Names
(From a Check of 12 Cities)

Name	Seller
Albacal	Alba Milk Co.
Alocal	Allen Co.
Arcross	Lit Bros.
Bal-Cal	Sears, Roebuck
Borbro	Borbro Labs
Borden's Ready Diet	Borden Co.
Cal-A-Day	Whelan Products Inc.
Caloration	Personal National Labs
Calor-Ease	Nat'l Food Stores
Calorid	Glenbrook Labs (Sterling Drug)
Caltrol	Clay Franklin Inc.
Controcal	Milk Proteins Inc.
Countdown	Slenderella
CPS Calorie Control	Carson Pirie Scott & Co.
Diet-Cal	Sterling Chemical Co.
Diet-Cal 900	Penslar Co.
Dietene, Meritene	Dietene Co.
Dieta-Fair	Preston National Co.
Forti-Cal	Foremost Dairies
Fulvita 900	Pacific Vitamin Corp.
Gimbels	Gimbels
Harris-Cal	Home Products
Horlick food concentrate	Horlick Corp.
J. L. Hudson	J. L. Hudson
Kay-Cal	Vitamins for Health Corp.
Kor-Val	E. J. Korvette
Leader-Cal	Continental Vitamin Corp.
Liqui-Cal	Gold Seal Products
Lo-Cal	Hall Johnson Labs
Lucerne Slenderway	Safeway

Table 1–1 (continued)

Name	Seller
Macy's	Macy's
Macy's Instant Mix	Macy's
Master-Cal	Masters
McKesson 900	McKesson Labs
Metrecal	Mead Johnson & Co.
Minvitine	Wander Co.
Norcross	Famous-Barr
Nutri-Cal, Pro-Cal	Continental Vitamin Corp.
People's Drug	People's Drug
Plan	Plan Foods & Research Co.
Pro-Cal	Signet Co.
P.S. Calorie Control	Aimcee Wholesaling Corp.
Quota	Quaker Oats Co.
Reducal	Leonet Corp.
Regucal, Rencal	Dietary Controls Co.
Rexall diet supplement	Rexall Drugs
Route 900	General Mills
Sealtest 900	National Dairy Products Co.
Sells' low calorie diet	Sells Specialties Co.
Slendz	General Health Corp.
Slim-Shake	Slim-Shake Corp.
Super-Diet	Food Science Corp.
Thera-Cal	Kent Pharmaceutical Co.
Vitacal	Ames Mercantile Co.
Walgreen food concentrate	Walgreen Drug
Wey-rite	Life Products International

SOURCE: Lawrence Bernard, "Calorie Metered Food Sales Grow Fatter as Consumer Gets Slimmer." Reprinted with permission from the December 5, 1960, issue of *Advertising Age*. Copyright 1960, by Advertising Publications Inc.

San Francisco

A price war raged between competing manufacturers. In a famous restaurant, a Metrecal cocktail with rum was listed on the menu at $1.50 and without alcohol at $1.00.

Similar conditions of competition were found in other cities and market areas. Distribution, prices, and promotion were very much in flux. Some cities were in cut-throat price wars while others were fairly stable. Metrecal Liquid was introduced by Mead Johnson in 1960 in six packs of eight-ounce cans (as contrasted to eight ounces of powder that made four glasses).

Sego

The Pet Milk Company introduced Sego in 1961, and it slowly began eating into Metrecal's market share. Most other competitors eventually dropped out of the market, and Sego emerged as the number-one contender with Metrecal. Industry sources estimated Sego's market share to be 2 percent in 1961, 17 percent in 1962, 29 percent in 1963, and 42 percent in 1964. Sego's management preferred to define the market as consisting of liquid products (excluding wafers, cookies, diet dinners, and so forth) and apparently had a larger share of the liquid market than did Metrecal. The President of Pet Milk explained the growth of Sego:

> We like to come out first with a good product and hold onto the lead. That's the ideal. But here we could not be first. Mead Johnson was. I decided we ought to come out with a different product and carefully plan our campaign. So we concentrated on a research plan. The researchers reported that Metrecal and its dairy imitations were excellent products, but that some dieters shortly after drinking a can, felt "those pangs of hunger that spell failure for any dieter." Research also discovered that the limited number of flavors caused monotony and turned many dieters away.[1]

Pet Milk based its strategy upon its research findings. Their product contained nine-hundred calories as did Metrecal, but contained ten fluid ounces to Metrecal's eight, thus giving more volume and $1\frac{3}{4}$ grams more protein to prevent hunger pains. Sego was also offered in more flavors than Metrecal, and, instead of emphasizing the medical problems as did Mead, Pet Milk stressed the benefits of losing weight and treated Sego as a food. Sego advertising emphasized girlish figures, many flavors, and slimming down for summer fashions. Sego's appeals were especially directed to women in their thirties, which researchers reported to be "when the figure starts to go."

Changes in Metrecal Strategy

Mead Johnson undertook numerous changes in an attempt to prevent Sego and other competitors from cutting further into their sales and profits. At first, Metrecal had been distributed through staid pharmaceutical channels,

[1] "The Race Is to the Smart," *Forbes,* October 1, 1964, p. 24.

but this was soon changed to include supermarkets. Prices were also cut. In 1960 the original price of over $2.00 was cut to $1.59 and later to $1.19. Mead also began to use cents-off coupon promotions.

Numerous new products were developed. Additional flavors were added. Diet wafers were added in September of 1961, and diet soups were added in the fall of 1962. The product was placed in vending machines of factories and offices. Diet cookies were added, and testing began for a Metrecal diet dinner with meat and vegetables.

The Problem

In 1964, Metrecal was still using a problem-oriented approach as the primary appeal in its advertising. By Sepember, 1964, however, the sales decline in Metrecal was serious, and Mead Johnson switched the Metrecal account from the Kenyon and Eckhardt advertising agency to Ogilvy, Benson, and Mather. At this time, a careful appraisal was needed of the motivation for dieting and the appeals that should be the foundation of Metrecal marketing strategy. Ogilvy, Benson, and Mather was asked to suggest a new approach to the marketing strategy of the Metrecal account.

Questions

1. What should be the primary "appeal" of Metrecal advertising?

2. What research should be performed or made available to the advertising agency in order to develop a new marketing approach?

3. Prepare a set of policy statements that should be adopted by Mead Johnson for the Metrecal marketing program.

4. What type of system should be instituted to monitor performance of a new approach?

The Dairy Industry: Motivation for Milk Consumption[2]

The Institute for Motivational Research, a New York research firm, undertook a qualitative study of the psychological reasons for consumption or nonconsumption of milk products. It stimulated much interest throughout the dairy industry, because it raised some perplexing issues for marketing strategy.

---

[2] Reproduced with special permission from Ernest Dichter, *Handbook of Consumer Motivations.* New York: McGraw-Hill Book Company, Inc., 1964, pp. 53–58.

Findings

Milk, say respondents in a psychological survey conducted by the Institute for Motivational Research, is the most perfect of all foods. It has most of the ingredients necessary for growth and sustenance. It is nature's bounty, completely nourishing. One respondent said, "I've heard that milk is almost a complete food and not just a beverage. And I believe that. I think a person could live indefinitely on milk."

This aggrandizement of milk which sets it above all other foods is the result of a number of influences:

a. The infant-state milk experience, when milk does indeed provide satisfaction to a great many physical and psychological needs.

b. The effortlessness of drinking milk, a liquid food requiring no chewing and offering no resistances. Even ice cream, while a more exciting food, is less perfect than milk for it offers temperature resistance. Milk in its original state has body temperature.

c. The parental and other educational influences stressing the goodness of milk.

Much evidence of parental and educational influences stressing the importance of drinking milk for its nutritional values was produced by depth interviewing. This was mentioned by nearly all respondents.

Further evidence of the "perfection" of milk is provided by the findings of a special test devised for the purpose of measuring the "fallibility" of milk. Respondents were asked to list what improvements they would like to have made in relation to five food products: apples, bread, roast beef, peas, and milk. The purpose of the question was to determine the relative degree of dissatisfaction, as measured by the number of improvement suggestions made, for each of these five products. The results showed milk to be the least "fallible" of the products tested [see Table 1–2].

Table 1–2

Scale of Product Fallibility

	Number of Improvement Suggestions Made*	Percent of Total	Suggested Improvements per Respondent
Apples	177.4	26.3	1.13
Bread	156.0	23.2	0.99
Roast beef	134.1	19.8	0.85
Peas	129.8	19.2	0.83
Milk	78.1	11.5	0.50
	675.5	100.0	

* Adjusted to common $N = 157$.

The perfection of milk, which sets it above other foods, is not only a function of intrinsic product qualities and of educational influences, it is, more importantly, a function of its psychological symbolism. It was found in our interviews that milk symbolizes motherhood. Above its objective meaning, milk has a psychological meaning, derived from the early association of milk and mother. When people speak of milk, they invariably speak of their childhood and mother, or about their own children. From the infant-mother relationship milk derives new meanings. It comes to signify love, security, warmth, and effortless need-satisfaction. These psychological elements of the nursing situation have long been recognized by psychologists and have influenced modern pediatricians to stress the importance of holding and fondling the infant while feeding him, even when formula milk is substituted for breast milk.

The psychological meaning of milk is a most important determinant of specific milk attitudes, for it is even basic to the milk reactions of adults. We have evidence that, when it comes to milk, people often react on the basic or "infantile" level.

Milk is closely associated with emotional security. This is quite clear in the case of the infant, who derives nourishment from milk and obtains the reassurance of the mother's love and protection while being held and nursed. Less obvious, perhaps, is the fact that milk may symbolize security even to the grown individual. There is ample proof of this in interviews. Respondents who were asked to describe their most satisfying milk drinking experience would tell us that they had particularly craved and enjoyed milk when they were sick or out of the hospital after an operation, when they were hot and tired, or when they were feeling low or lonely. These are all examples of feeling in need of care, in need of "mother," and of deriving emotional security from milk because of its mother symbolism.

Rejection of milk, or of a specific type of milk, was commonly expressed by statements such as "It gags me," "It makes me throw up," or "I can't hold it down." Distaste, in the case of milk, is not expressed in the same manner as is distaste for other foods. It is the expression of distaste employed by the infant, who spits out or vomits foods he dislikes, having no other means of expression.

In spite of the very strong trends toward greater acceptance of the use of formula milk in infant feeding, the feeling still prevails that mother's milk is the most perfect. This feeling is evidenced both by the special pride shown by mothers who nurse their babies and by the strong need for justification felt by mothers who put their babies on formula.

Attributing perfection to mother's milk is, of course, a direct result of the symbolism of milk. Formula milk may be equally nourishing objectively, but it lacks the emotional and psychological attributes of mother's milk. This results in all forms of milk being unwittingly compared to mother's milk, which is the first, most natural and most satisfying of all milks. On the psychological level, unprocessed cow milk, fresh dairy milk, evaporated milk, powdered milk, etc., represent various forms of deviation from mother's milk. Rationally people learn to appreciate the advantages of homogenizing, evaporating, bottling, canning, and so forth. Psychologically they resent these processes because they tend to break down the mother-milk relationship and thus take away from the original perfection of milk.

Society imposes sanctions and precludes the continuation of the mother-infant milk relationship after the infant stage. We might say that weaning is one of the first penalties that society imposes upon the child for growing up. The child is gradually taught to give up the mother as his sole source of security and affection and to find new compensations in the society of which he becomes a member. To effect this transfer, a number of social sanctions operate. Undue attachment to one's mother is often called "sissy" and immature behavior. Ridicule and shame accompany such behavior and tend to inhibit it. With regard to mother's milk, which is the basic object-symbol of the mother-child relationship, social taboos operate to repress and inhibit the primitive desires. Expressions of the social taboos are evident in the strong "taste" reaction of adult individuals to mother's milk. The thought of drinking mother's milk is revolting and repulsive. Often even the sight of a child who is no longer an infant and is still suckling at the mother's breast or from a bottle is revolting to the adult in Western society. One respondent said, "I've even tasted breast milk, I don't know how they drink it, its foul, pretty foul. The doctor ordered it once; it was absolutely terrible."

We have here, then, the first example of ambivalent emotional attitudes toward milk. On the one hand, the longing for the perfection and psychological need-satisfaction derived from mother's milk, and on the other, the strong, socially conditioned rejection of it after the infant stage.

Milk is very often tied up with parental authority. In discussing their childhood and present milk-drinking habits, respondents spontaneously refer to the exertion of parental authority in connection with milk. A few typical remarks are, "My mother always insisted that I drink milk," "I was forced to drink milk every day," and "My parents never forced me to drink milk, but we all liked it and did."

Most respondents assume that parental authority did exert or would have exerted itself to see to it that the child drank an adequate amount of milk. Milk thus has come to represent the acceptance of parental authority. It is a virtuous beverage—if you drink milk, you are a good child.

When there are conflicts in the acceptance of parental authority and rebellion against it, milk may become the target of the conflict. Not drinking and actively disliking milk is often a way of acting out rebellion against parental authority, while drinking and liking milk is often a way of proving one's goodness.

Another important area of conflict in connection with milk is the ambivalent social attitude regarding what people consider natural. We have its first striking example in the acceptance of mother's milk versus fresh dairy milk. The naturalness of mother's milk is acceptable when it is romanticized in the mother-infant relationship. As the infant grows into the child, the naturalness of mother's milk becomes progressively more offensive. Other forms of milk, socially acceptable forms, replace mother's milk.

The ambivalence toward the natural is also found in connection with unprocessed cow milk. This type of milk is often idealized as the richest, most nourishing milk. It also is rejected by many for its very natural qualities: the cow scent, the warmth, and the creaminess, all too closely connected with the animal qualities.

In the romantic view of the natural, the natural is associated with the fresh, the wholesome, the healthy. On the other hand, the natural is also associated with the licentious, the dirty, the animalistic.

Implications

Although the research report did not stress the implications for marketing strategy, management of many dairy firms attempted to reorient marketing activities in accordance with these findings. Others felt that no action could be taken at this time.

Questions

1. What are the purposes of this type of research?

2. Evaluate the research findings. Do the conclusions appear to be sound?

3. What implications emerge for marketing action? Describe in detail.

4. What unanswered research questions still remain, if any? What directions may future research take?

Better Homes and Gardens: Needs Satisfied by Magazine Readership[3]

In 1951, the editorial mission of *Better Homes and Gardens,* a publication of the Meredith Corporation, was to provide help, ideas, and inspiration

---

[3] Although the study reported in this case is several years old, it is of interest because it was a pioneering effort to understand some of the behavioral dimensions of a market.

to consumers so that they could get more enjoyment from their families and homes. This policy was consistent with what Meredith executives perceived to be the needs of their market segment. Management reasoned that because readers were buying a family service magazine they must be interested in family and home. Studies of the demographic characteristics of readers supported this view.

Management felt, however, that demographic data alone did not adequately describe the needs of the market it was serving. This lack of knowledge made it difficult to clarify editorial policies and to enlarge or change these policies. It was concluded that these decisions required qualitative information to supplement the available demographic data. Accordingly, it was decided that research should be undertaken to (1) measure in greater depth the impact of the magazine on its readers and (2) provide more effective guidance for editors and advertisers into the emotional meanings and functions of the magazine in the lives of its readers.

Nature of Study

Social Research, Inc. (SRI), a Chicago based research organization, was contracted to undertake the project because of its excellent reputation for research on consumer motivations and attitudes. Once SRI agreed to conduct the study, it became necessary to spell out specific research objectives. It was decided that the study should answer the following questions:

1.   What habits and attitudes do *Better Homes and Gardens* readers (husband and wives) have toward the magazine?

2.   How do they use it?

3.   What do they think of it as a whole and of its various contents?

4.   What kinds of things do they do with the magazine?

5.   How do these habits and attitudes relate to basic social and psychological realities in subscribers' lives?

6.   How are they molded by these realities?

7.   How do the feelings, beliefs, and concerns of these families affect the ways in which they think about and use *Better Homes and Gardens*?

After defining the objectives of the proposed research, the methodology necessary to secure the desired information was established. The following techniques were selected:

Depth Interviewing
Respondents were encouraged to talk fully about a series of topics of concern to the investigator. The respondents freely volunteered ideas, beliefs, and

feelings and were allowed expression with minimal direct questioning by the interviewer. In this manner, the respondent brought up matters that were significant to him, recounted anecdotes that helped explain his beliefs, and provided the researcher with materials as the respondent saw it, rather than in the artificial light of a stringent question-and-answer procedure.

Projective Techniques

The respondent was presented with some emotionally meaningful stimulus to which he responded with his own ideas and feelings. With such techniques it is possible to investigate systematically specific areas of concern while freeing the respondent to state in his own way his feelings and ideas on the matter. The specific techniques used were (1) sentence completion, (2) cartoon completion, and (3) thematic pictures.

The depth and projective techniques demanded a moderately small sample that could be investigated intensively and economically. Two hundred *Better Homes and Gardens* subscribers from the Chicago metropolitan area were selected. Among these two-hundred people, two major social groups were represented:

Upper Middle Class

The upper middle class was made primarily of professional workers, officials, proprietors, and their families. These were usually leaders in their communities, highly respected, achieving citizens.

Middle Majority Class

The middle majority group was made largely of clerical and white-collar workers, salesmen, craftsmen, and some foremen and small business proprietors. It also included semiskilled workers.

Findings

Readership Patterns

The study revealed some interesting facts about the way the magazine was read. They were

1. The magazine was read all through the month.

2. The entire magazine was read.

3. The wide variety of features the magazine contained provided articles of interest for both husband and wife.

4. The concentrated attention accorded the magazine was demonstrated by clipping and saving habits.

5. The saving of recipes was most common.

6. There was a common pattern of thoroughness in reading the magazine (especially by housewives).

7. Housewives considered reading the magazine a part of their jobs as homemakers. Reading the magazine contributed to a feeling of mastery and knowledge in the field of homemaking.

8. In line with reading the magazine as part of their jobs, homemakers read with a real sense of effort and concentration—not as a simple leisure time activity, nor as something just to be skimmed. They conceived of the magazine as important and gave it the attention an important thing deserves—as seen in habits of reading from cover to cover and of rereading parts of an issue.

The men in the magazine's homes reacted to the magazine in three different ways.

1. There was a fairly stable and substantially large audience of men who read parts of the magazine regularly in accordance with their wives' suggestions or their own particular interests. The reading among these men was more sporadic than that of their wives, but these men did read parts of the magazine and back issues rather thoroughly when a particular project arose.

2. There is a somewhat smaller group of men for whom most of the features in *Better Homes and Gardens* were quite meaningful . . . who read it rather thoroughly. This group of husbands was self-sustaining, and they were enthusitasic readers of *Better Homes and Gardens.* For them, the home was more than a place to relax in, more than simply the domain of the wife. These men took a strong positive interest in the house. They liked to putter around, build, remodel, paint, select furniture, etc. These were the men whose hobby was the house, rather than photography, stamp collecting, baseball, wood carving, or chess. Thus, they gave as much attention as the wife to features on remodeling, handyman hints, color schemes, furniture building, and the like, and read from their own motivation rather than at the suggestion of their wives.

3. A third small group rejected the magazine as unworthy of concentrated attention because it somehow "seemed more of a woman's magazine." Men in this group may stoutly maintain that "no woman's magazine can tell me how to do a man's work." They were "stand-offish" in their attitudes towards *Better Homes and Gardens,* resistant to being swept up in their wives' feeling that *Better Homes and Gardens* was a "wonderful magazine, it has just everything." These men are a minority among *Better Homes and Gardens* subscriber-families.

Needs Satisfied by the Magazine

In studying the relationship between *Better Homes and Gardens* and its husband and wife readers, SRI discovered three kinds of satisfactions that were sought and generally satisfied: practicality, fantasy, ostentation. The appeal of the magazine did not lie in any one of these, nor in their rank order. Rather, it seemed to stem from the formula with which they were combined.

Practicality

Practicality had two phases. It was not only a quality of certain kinds of behavior and judgment; it was also a goal. For example, the middle majority adult prided himself on being realistic and down-to-earth; he or she had little tolerance for the imaginative, whimsical, or irrational. Thus, he (or she) was reluctant to admit admiration for things on irrational grounds and was quick to explain personal preferences as actually being practical.

To middle majority people, all problems were serious ones, and all serious problems involved practical issues. Thus the reference to practicality and usefulness of *Better Homes and Gardens* was two-edged. One side referred to the actual employment of recipes, instructions, and color combinations. The other side referred to the normal value that was placed on practicality and means (roughly): "I like *Better Homes and Gardens* because it is all about homemaking and [so no one can question my right to read it] . . . it is practical."

It was also found that the middle majority group had vague goals about how to make life better, prettier, happier, and more romantic than it is. They had vague fears and ideas about living: disease, depression, storm, accident, old age, and strange neighborhoods. Therefore, both husbands and wives felt that they were being realistic and practical if they had well-formulated ideas of how to master a situation or on how to take advantage of opportunities that might arise.

Fantasy

In connection with the *Better Homes and Gardens* study, *fantasy* meant the functions whereby the reader found satisfaction in just reading and looking at the magazine. It was found that for *Better Homes and Gardens* the colors, the style in which written material was presented, the layout of articles and adverisements, and the familiarity of the reader with the magazine all facilitated the ease with which the reader could project into a fantasy situation.

Reader participation through fantasy was important for the readers of *Better Homes and Gardens.* Much like practicality, fantasy often resulted in action at a later date, and this possibility justified the reader's pleasure to a great extent. The ideas and images that the reader developed during reading became part of a reservoir of attitudes and information and influenced later judgments and behavior. At a later date, if a need arose or an opportunity to use a *Better Homes and Gardens* item occurred, the information came out of the reader's memory and thus influenced action. The following quotation typifies such a train of thought: "There was an article on 'How to Launder.' It was about criss-cross curtains, about a year ago. I haven't any criss-cross curtains, but when I finally get them, I'll at least know how to launder them. I've wanted some for a long time and hope to get them."

Ostentation

In the Middle Majority (even more than in some other social groups) alertness to the views of outsiders was a pervasive attitude influencing judgments from child care to bedspreads. *Better Homes and Gardens* served an important need in providing the reader with material about such things as styles in living, taste in homemaking, and standards for judgment of others. As one woman said, "Lots of times we have ideas about what we want to do, but we don't dare try them out until we look at *Better Homes and Gardens.* If it has a picture like our idea we know it's O.K."

The *Better Homes and Gardens* reader showed concern with the home as the setting of the most important living experiences and interpersonal relations and desired to make the setting of his life as attractive, comfortable, and esthetically pleasing a place as possible. This kind of interest was part of what was grouped under *ostentation.* For example, typical questions of interest might be

What does a well-set table look like?

What colors are good for a living room?

How can chipped furniture be easily repaired?

What furniture is in style this year?

All these are related to ostentation in that they tapped the individual's social awareness and his or her desire to emulate standards of appropriateness and "smartness" in homemaking. In addition, personal taste was strongly influenced by self-awareness with all its social ingredients.

The study found that the material in *Better Homes and Gardens* was very relevant to the ostentation need and was regarded as a dependable aid to the homemaker. If the reader was uncertain about taste, it was a guide to how to do things "right" and it presented standards as well as ideas. The magazine was thought to provide concrete examples that assisted in deciding whether or not "that's for me." The magazine was found to be particularly useful to the person who was desirous of moving up in social status, who wanted to appear increasingly sophisticated and "up and coming."

By studying the magazine, a reader typically felt that she could bring her home into conformity with her own conceptions of social elevation without risking *faux pas* of ignorance or extreme individuality. In this way the forward-and-upward looking husband and wife would be able to communicate to others their social and personal competence.

The three functions of *Better Homes and Gardens*—practicality, fantasy satisfaction, and ostentation—were not divisible. While one reader might emphasize useful tips more than socially oriented guides, another would place "pure pleasure" ahead of household helps. In the reader's strivings, however, all played a part; they were fused into motivation to read the magazine.

The study revealed that the magazine as a whole, without regard to the nature of its separate parts, loomed largest in the minds of its readers. Some readers had favorite sections, but there was no consensus on this point. In general, the kinds of needs and attitudes discovered referred to the magazine as a whole. The research indicated that the positive feelings about the magazine were derived from what was regarded to be its overall excellence in satisfying the needs of the reader.

Action-Impact of the Magazine

It was found that readership of *Better Homes and Gardens* resulted in specific reactions to many sections of the magazine. These sections, as well as the magazine as a whole, had considerable impact upon the attitudes and behavior of the readers. These findings are summarized as follows:

Food and Recipe Articles (and Ads)
Were Prominent for Their Immediate Usefulness

For concrete, immediate, practical usefulness, recipes and food information represented an attraction of the magazine for its housewife readers. Here the magazine always paid off right away, without delay. Although the housewife recognized the more diffuse, long-term gains from reading other features, she was happy to have something she could put to use immediately.

Home Building Articles (and Ads) Were of Interest

Home building articles and ads were at the opposite end of the time continuum to food articles and recipes. Many people never build a house, and most husbands and wives who do, build only one during a lifetime. Yet the articles and ads on this subject were of perennial interest.

Remodeling and Furnishing Features Combined Fantasy and Action Appeals

Next to recipes, the collection of remodeling and furniture articles was found to occur most frequently.

Gardening Features, as Recipes, Had Immediate Use

Gardening features provided information likely to be utilized immediately, either in planting something new or in augmenting the gardener's technical knowledge.

Better Homes and Gardens Had Value in All Areas of Homemaking

The magazine was found to have immediately useful things like recipes, spring gardening features, and trends in decorating; potentially useful things like how-to-do-it's, remodeling ideas, and child care articles; and, finally, emergency solving tips and facts giving help and information for new, acute situations around the house, such as when a storm door blows off and when a faucet springs a leak and the plumber is too busy to make a call.

The Shopping Guide and the How-to-Do-It Tips Were Frequently Used
Use of the shopping guide and how-to-do-it tips were similar to the immediate, concrete use given recipes. Housewives look to the shopping guide for information on new products and, frequently, for gift ideas, while how-to-do-it and handyman tips were read with interest by both husbands and wives.

Housewives Selected Articles for Their Husbands to Read
The housewife, in selecting articles for her husband to read, expressed by her action her feeling of the importance of the husband-wife relationship to the well-being of home and family.

Better Homes and Gardens Was an Old Friend to Its Readers
The readers knew the magazine and were familiar with it. Its content was predictable from month to month and season to season, not necessarily in terms of particular features and articles, but in spirit, slant, and style of its editoral and advertising material. Because *Better Homes and Gardens* was regarded as an old friend, readers approached it with confidence, anticipating useful and pleasant experiences.

Readers Felt That Better Homes and Gardens Was
"Right for Our Economic and Social Level"
The feeling that the magazine was right for their own economic and social level was characteristic of husband-wife readers from both the upper middle and the middle majority groups. Apparenty both, and with equal ease, found material in the magazine that conformed with their ideas of what is appropriate for their own economic and social position. The style, taste, and general feeling of the magazine illustrations were suitable for people in these social class groups. They read into them their own standards and desires.

There Was an Attitude of Trust in the Adequacy and
Excellence of the Information Contained in the Magazine
There was widespread feeling among readers that both articles and advertisements could be depended upon. As one housewife put it,

> *Better Homes and Gardens* helps people to improve their homes in less expensive ways. It shows you how to plan meals, helps you to learn to decorate your house better. It helps people afford things they wouldn't be able to otherwise have, for by planning you can save a lot of money and effort. It makes you more efficient.

Advertising and Editorial Material Were Equally Valued

The attitudes of consumers toward advertising in general were complex and differed considerably in particular social classes. The upper middle class was somewhat uniformly critical of advertising, making blithe assumptions about the ulterior motives of advertisers, the cost of it reflected in the purchase price of merchandise, and so on. The middle majority group was considerably more tolerant and pragmatic but quick to protest the general "sinfulness" of advertising whenever a particular ad was displeasing. Most persons regarded the ads in much the same way as they regarded the editorial material.

The attitudes of readers toward ads had the same positive-feeling tone that characterizes attitudes toward the editorial material. Indeed, many husbands and wives did not differentiate between the two when they discussed the magazine topics that interested them most. Frequently, the husband and wife seemed to have decided what to buy from the editorial material and then learned what brand to buy and where to look for it from the advertisements.

Questions

1. Evaluate the methodology used in the study.

2. What specific needs does *Better Homes and Gardens* satisfy?

3. What are the implications of the study for the magazine's editorial content and special features?

4. Prepare a proposal outlining how the study can be used to convince advertisers to use this vehicle.

CHAPTER 2

PERCEPTION

Kookmar versus American Homes: Customer Design Perceptions

The Kookmar Glass Works of Buffalo, New York, manufactures a line of products made of Amperstam, a trademark for a material with a low co-efficient of thermal expansion and a high resistance to mechanical impact. This material was originally developed for the nose cones of space vehicles, but by 1959 Kookmar had test marketed a line of cookware that could be taken from a freezer and placed directly on top of an open flame or electric burner. The product was introduced nationally in May, 1960. The saucepans were white and had somewhat the appearance of porcelain or china, or fine ceramic. On the side of the saucepans was a blue floral design, a cluster of three flowers.

Kookmar introduced a number of new products in the years that followed, and by 1969 the product line numbered about 31 items. These included various sizes of saucepans, percolators, serving dishes, and related items. By 1968 the company included the blue floral design on the side of many of the products they marketed. They also used the design in advertising materials and in sales promotion brochures.

Background

In 1964 Kookmar decided to apply to the United States Patent Office for registration to protect the blue petalburst design. This application was opposed by the American Homes Glass Corporation of Cleveland, Ohio. Extended legal activity followed to determine if Kookmar should be granted trademark protection of the petalburst.

Kookmar's Trademark Application

The president of Kookmar, Tracy Reinhard, testified to the reasons why Kookmar should have trademark protection of the blue petalburst design:

It had become very obvious from our experience that the consumer was largely relying on this insignia to identify "Kookmar Ware" and to specifically associate "Kookmar Ware" with the claims which we had made for the product. It was also becoming obvious that other people were making quite exact copies of this and applying it to material which did not have the characteristics that our products have.

We felt that this could lead to substantial confusion and possibly to some unfortunate experiences for consumers.

In additional testimony, Reinhard stated that Kookmar would object to the use by another company of "anything which could be confused or so close as to be confused in its use of our insignia."

American Homes' Opposition

The American Homes Glass Corporation opposed the trademark registration application of Kookmar. Their position was that the blue petalburst was an ornamentation or a pattern and not a distinctive mark symbolizing the resource or manufacturer involved in the products.

In cross-examination of Kookmar executives, legal counsel for American Homes determined that Kookmar produced numerous products of Amperstam which did not include the blue petalburst design. Some of these were plain white and had no design. Percolators and other products were marketed with a black petalburst design. American Homes counsel also produced evidence that Kookmar Ware was marketed in the State of Washington with a floral design other than the blue petalburst. This design was called a wheat design.

Once a trademark is granted, the owner can sometimes prevent any other company from using a design that may tend to cause confusion in the minds of consumers. Thus, a company that produced white dishes similar in appearance to the Kookmar Ware products conceivably could be prohibited from employing a floral design on the side of their product.

Problem

The Lanham Act of 1946 specifies the nature of trademarks and the manner of registering them. In Section 45 of that act a trademark is defined: "The term trade-mark includes any word, name, symbol, or device or any combination thereof adopted and used by a manufacturer or merchant to identify his goods and distinguish them from those manufactured or sold by others."[1]

The problem at issue was whether the petalburst serves to distinguish the products of Kookmar from other manufacturers or whether it was only an ornamentation. Court cases provided precedents that the trademark must be

[1] Public Law 489, approved July 5, 1946, by the 79th Cong., 60 Stat. 427.

added to a product that would otherwise be complete without the trademark. That is, a symbol that is an integral part of the design of the product was considered to be primarily a design feature rather than a mark used purely to identify the manufacturer.

The question became one of determining whether the majority of consumers perceived the petalburst as identifying the products of Kookmar or whether they perceived them to be merely part of the design or ornamentation. Also, the application by Kookmar requested registration of the petalburst without regard to color. American Homes vigorously opposed the application for a trademark by Kookmar; and American Homes' opposition was watched closely by other major manufacturers of glass cooking and kitchen products.

Mail Survey Study

As part of the evidence supporting their application, Kookmar presented the results of a mail survey that had been conducted by Hess Testing Institute, Inc. (HTI) in late 1967. Kookmar ordered this survey to try to establish that a substantial part of the potential market associated the petalburst design with Kookmar. The advertising manager of Kookmar testified that the potential market was all females over eighteen years old.

Sample

HTI maintains a consumer panel that is mailed questionnaires and other items periodically. The panel is a carefully controlled quota sample. That is, proportions of the total panel are kept approximately in proportion to the total population characteristics on certain control variables. Those control variables are income, geographical region, age of housewife, population density, education of housewife, and size of family.

The president of HTI, David Samuels, on May 2, 1968, testified that this sample represented about 90 percent of all families in the United States. The groups not included, Samuels testified, were single persons, Negroes, foreign-speaking people, and families with extremely low income or extremely high income. Because the panel was questioned with the written word, HTI was unable to include groups with a high proportion of illiterates.

When asked how the names are selected to be included in the panel, Samuels testified:

> In as random a fashion as we can develop. Thus, names are taken from surveys that have been made in person by organizations that are friendly to us, or that are asked to do so by mutual clients.
>
> Panel members frequently are asked to give us the names and addresses of friends or relatives living a distance away from where they are.
>
> We will purchase lists frequently from people like McIntyre, Pope or

> Donnelley . . . . In the true acceptance of the word, they are as random as they can be on a developed basis.

In cross-examination, Samuels was asked what proportion of those asked agreed to serve on the panel. The testimony follows:

Q. In other words, they have previously been asked if they were willing to serve on occasion, and they are people who have answered affirmatively?

A. Yes.

Q. So that you have eliminated by that process those who either don't answer your invitation or definitely don't want to serve. Is that right?

A. Yes.

Q. Do you have any approximate figure or percentage of the people who accept your invitation as opposed to those who don't answer or turn it down?

A. Depending on the list, it would run anywhere from 10 to 25 percent who will send their registrations.

HTI maintains 26 panels of a thousand housewives. Each panel is selected with the same process and is a quota sample so that results between two panels can be compared to each other or any number of panels can be combined to achieve a desired sample size. In the Kookmar study, two panels were used giving a sample size potential of two-thousand housewives.

On September 3, 1967, two-thousand questionnaires were mailed to housewives in the HTI panels concerning the Kookmar design. October 6, 1506 of the questionnaires had been returned by panel members, and it was on the basis of these returns that Kookmar made its conclusions about perception of the cornflower design.

HTI does not pay the housewives who participate in its panel, although they do receive free gifts, usually of limited value. Samuels testified as to the motive for participation in the panel:

> Primarily, we impress on the housewives and through them their family members that they are members of a very select group, that what they have to say matters to many of the major manufacturers in the country, that their voice is important in telling what products should or should not be made, in telling manufacturers what they want in certain products, in determining in many cases whether or not certain television programs will continue on the air or even get on the air in some cases.

Samuels testified that panel members who did not fill out the questionnaires carefully or who habitually failed to return the questionnaires were dropped from the panel. Panel turnover, for these and other reasons, amounted to 10 to 15 percent a year. Several of the panel members who responded to the questionnaire later gave depositions verifying their response and permitted cross-examination. Of those who testified, most had been members of the panel for a number of years, and some had been members for fourteen or fifteen years. The members testified that they responded to questionnaires from HTI several times a month.

Questionnaire

The questionnaire used in the HTI survey was a postcard containing the blue petalburst (in both the form used on saucepans and the form used on percolators and other "vertical" merchandise) and three questions (see Exhibit 2–1). The questions asked with what company and with what products the respondent associated the blue symbol and whether the respondent owned the products bearing the symbol.

Exhibit 2–1

HTI Questionnaire

Dear Member:

Today I have for you just a couple of quick questions that will take only a moment of your time to answer.

Without checking or asking anyone else, I would like you to tell me what company and what products, if any, you associate with the symbols on the other half of this postcard. I would also like to know whether you own any products that have these symbols on them and, if you do, specify what products these are.

Would you take a minute right now while you are thinking about it to answer these questions and return the card to me right away. Your prompt reply will be much appreciated.

Cordially,
Carolyn Betts, Director

1. With what *company,* if any, do you associate the symbols on the left?

2. With what *products,* if any, do you associate the symbols on the left?

3. (a) Do you own any products that have these symbols on them?

     Yes ☐   No ☐

   (b) If "Yes," what products? (be specific)

Kookmar Results

The results of the HTI panel survey are presented in Tables 2–1 and 2–2. Table 2–1 shows that 789 of the 1506 panel members who responded mentioned Kookmar in some fashion as associated with the blue petalburst. There were 115 associations with companies other than those having Kookmar in

Table 2–1

Companies Associated with Petalburst Symbols
(Hess Testing Institute Panel Results)

Response	Number	Percent*
Responses mentioning Kookmar		
Kookmar Ware	537	36
Kookmar	110	7+
Kookmar Glass	83	5+
Kookmar Glass Works	26	2−
Kookmar Glass Ware Co.	12	1−
Jones Kookmar	12	1−
Smith Kookmar	9	1−
TOTAL KOOKMAR	789	52
Responses mentioning other associations		
Scott	32	2
Pyrex	19	1
Hudson	14	1
Kleenex	11	1
Gala	8	1
Others	31	2
TOTAL OTHER ASSOCIATIONS	115	8
Do not know	509	34
Not reported	93	6
TOTAL RESPONSES TO QUESTIONNAIRE	1506	100

* Percentages were calculated on total questionnaires returned, not on the total sent out.

their name and 509 who reported no association. Table 2–2 shows the distribution of associations with various products. Testimony was given to indicate that about half of the tabulated questionnaires had been returned within two weeks of the date of mailing.

The president of HTI was questioned by American Homes legal counsel about the appropriateness of this survey method for a trademark recognition study. His response was given in testimony:

. . . I would say that a vast majority of marketing research people would agree that this is a reasonable, honest effort to determine a recognition of this symbol, illustration, whatever you want to call it, on the parts of many hundreds of housewives in all parts of the country.

That there are other ways to do it, there is no question. I would suggest, at least within the competence of ourselves and the Kookmar marketing research organization, the fact that this study was not done in other ways would indicate everybody's conclusion that it was soundly conceived and well executed.

Table 2–2

Products Associated with Petalburst Symbols
(Hess Testing Institute Panel Results)

Response	Number	Percent*
Responses mentioning product		
Kookmar Ware	330	22
Cooking utensils, ware	210	14
Casseroles, baking ware	155	10
Pots, pans	82	5
Frying pans, skillets	30	2
Teapots	26	2
Dishes	63	7
Heat & Serve dishes	59	7
Coffee pots or percolator	123	8
Other products	173	11
No association with product	433	29
Not reported	36	2
TOTAL RESPONSES TO QUESTIONNAIRE	1720	

* Percent was calculated on basis of 1506 questionnaires returned. Responses total more than 1506 because multiple responses were permitted.

Personal Interview Study

In May, 1968, American Homes contacted a university professor of marketing research and asked him to review the Kookmar survey. The professor evaluated the mail-panel survey and reported what he considered to be major methodological flaws in the study. American Homes then requested that he prepare a research design that would provide an accurate measure of the proportion of consumers who perceived the cornflower as identifying the products of Kookmar. In October of 1968 the professor testified in this case.

He described the research design that was prepared and reported results from the survey as it was actually conducted. The testimony describing the study was nearly a thousand pages; only the most salient points are described here.

Design

The professor recommended that considerable attention be given to defining the problem and developing a better methodology to solve the problem. He testified that the major problems in the Kookmar survey were the methods of selecting respondents and the interviewing situation. Specifically, a recommendation was made that respondents be selected on a probability basis, that a personal interview be used rather than a mail questionnaire, and that certain changes be made in the questionnaire.

Sample

The sample size was established at three hundred. In a random sample of attributes, 50 percent of the respondents were to recognize the petalburst design. This would yield an estimate within $\pm$ 6 percent with a 95 percent level of confidence.

Kookmar sales were distributed throughout the United States, although figures were obtained to indicate some concentration in the Pacific area, the Eastern Seaboard and the East North Central area. A list of cities was prepared in these areas from which sampling might be done. The cities were selected from those believed to be good test cities—that is, representative of the population in general—and which would be available economically to Smith Marketing Research of Cleveland, the firm selected to do the interviewing. The cities listed in the Pacific area were Los Angeles and San Francisco; in the East North Central area, Cincinnati, Dayton, and Indianapolis; in the Eastern Seaboard, Atlanta, Buffalo, and Philadelphia. The cities finally included were to be selected at random. When the study was undertaken, one hundred respondents were sampled from the Buffalo, Cincinnati, and San Francisco areas.

The actual selection and interviewing of respondents was done by Smith. The following instructions were given for selecting respondents from each city:

1. Select five Census tracts from the metropolitan area of the city by listing all Census tract numbers and choosing five with a random number table. Eliminate tracts that are primarily business areas.

2. Determine from Census tract data the number of households in each tract.

3. Allocate the number of respondents to be chosen in each tract by dividing the number of households in each tract by the summation of households in all five tracts.

4. Multiply the fraction that represents the households in each tract to total tracts times eighty, the sample size to be selected from urban areas of the city, and select that number of respondents from each tract.

5. Determine a random starting point within the Census tract and sample every ninth householder. (Detailed instructions were provided that neighbors or households "across the back fence" would not be sampled.)

6. Interview the first adult (over seventeen) that answers the door.

7. Treat units within apartment houses as separate households except that no more than two units are to be selected from one apartment house.

The sampling plan also provided that rural households be included, a rarity in personal interview marketing studies. Instructions for selecting twenty respondents from rural areas surrounding each city were stated in the following manner:

1. Let 1 represent North, 2 represent Northeast, 3 represent East, and so forth.

2. With a random number table, select a number to represent the direction of respondents from the central city.

3. Let the next two-digit number from the table represent the number of miles to travel in that direction.

4. Trace that number of miles from the nearest highway paralleling that direction and select the city with population under 2500 nearest that point.

5. In that (small) town, select a random starting point and sample every ninth respondent. Use the procedures developed for the urban sample until ten respondents are sampled.

6. Follow the sample procedure to select another city. Within that city, choose a rural postal route with random numbers.

7. Select a box number with random numbers and sample every fifth household on that rural route until ten respondents are interviewed.

In this manner, one hundred respondents were selected in each of the three metropolitan areas and the rural areas within a ninety-nine mile radius of each city.

Black Study

Kookmar applied for a trademark for the petalburst irrespective of color, even though Kookmar's primary use had been with a blue design. When panel members had given depositions, American Homes counsel asked some of them if the blue color was important in their identification of the design. Some answered that it was very important. Consequently, it was decided that the American Homes study should also investigate if a nonblue color affected the proportion of consumers perceiving the design as an identification of Kookmar.

A separate study was conducted identical to the one using the blue design. The questionnaire and interview procedures were exactly the same except that the questionnaire contained a black petalburst rather than a blue petalburst. The respondents to the black petalburst questionnaire were selected by taking households immediately adjacent to those sampled with the blue petalburst questionnaire. This insured that the black petalburst sample would be as nearly like a control group as possible for the blue petalburst sample. The only difference would be the color of the petalburst design. The questionnaire used for both studies is given in Exhibit 2–2.

Exhibit 2–2

Consumer poll

The results of this poll will be presented as statistical averages. Please give your sincere and honest answers to the questions. Please answer each question before going to the next. Your help is very much appreciated.

Please do not turn the page until instructed

1. For you, do these designs identify the products of a particular company or not?

   Yes _____   —1
                                                (1)
   No   _____   —2

Please do not turn the page until instructed

2. (If you answered "Yes" to Question 1, please answer the following questions. If you answered 'No," please skip to Question 6.)

   With what company do you identify products having these designs?

   _____   (2) _____

   _____   (3) _____

   _____   (4) _____

   _____   (5) _____

Please do not turn the page until instructed

3. Specifically, with what *products* do
   you identify these designs?

_____   (6) _____

_____   (7) _____

_____   (8) _____

_____   (9) _____

_____   (10) _____

_____   (11) _____

_____   (12) _____

Please do not turn the page until instructed

4. Do you identify these designs with
   the products of any other companies?

   Yes   _____   —1   (13)

   No   _____   —2

5. If yes, what companies?

_____   (14) _____

_____   (15) _____

_____   (16) _____

_____   (17) _____

Please do not turn the page until instructed

6. Please look at the following list of products and think of those
   that you own. Place a checkmark beside each product that you own
   or normally have in your home.

   General Electric toaster   _____   —1   (18)
   Scott towels or paper products   _____   —2
   Revere pots and pans   _____   —3
   Libbey glasses   _____   —4
   Kookmar Ware   _____   —5
   Del Monte canned goods   _____   —6
   Kleenex tissues and paper products   _____   —7
   Hoover sweeper   _____   —8

_____   _____
        (Name)   (Street Address)

_____   _____
        (City)   (State)

Thank you very much

```
Time of interview _____:_____AM/PM
Investigator Name _____
Investigator Number _____                                    (19–22)
```

Panel:	Black	−2	
	Blue	−1	(23)
Respondent Sex:	Male	−1	(24)
	Female	−2	
Date:	_____/_____/_____		(25–30)
Interviewing City:	Buffalo	−005	(31–33)
	Cincinnati	−010	
	San Francisco	−057	
Interviewing Place:	Urban	−1	(34)
	Rural—Nonfarm	−2	
	Rural—Farm	−3	
(If Urban) Census Tract Number _____			(35–38)
(Office Use Only) Respondent Number _____			(39–41)

Interviewing

Courts traditionally have been reluctant to accept survey evidence on the basis that it represents hearsay evidence and is therefore inadmissible. The interviewing plan specified special procedures so that both a written record of the respondent's answers would be maintained (and could therefore be entered as evidence) and that the interviewer would observe each response so that she could testify to what she saw as well as to what she heard. The instructions for interviewing procedures are given in Exhibit 2–3.

Exhibit 2–3

Instructions to interview supervisors

The greatest of care should be given to these interviews. They may be entered as evidence in an important legal case and the degree to which the court can rely on them is heavily influenced by how carefully the interviewers follow instructions and obtain representative respondents. Please do not tell the interviewers that the questionnaires will be used in legal proceedings but try to impress upon them the unusual need for obtaining every item requested in precisely the form requested.

1. Please assign your most qualified and stable interviewers to this project. It is probable that some of them will be called as witnesses to testify about the questionnaires. Interviewers who have had continuous employment for several years and are likely to be with agency in the future are the only ones who should be assigned to these interviews.

2. Please verify that the random sampling plan is strictly followed. The quality of this survey depends on random sampling procedures and supervisors will probably be asked to testify in court proceedings that the random sampling plan was followed.

3. Please instruct interviewers to try to obtain the cooperation of all who are contacted regardless of their attitudes toward surveys. THE CLIENT

IS VERY INTERESTED IN OBTAINING RESPONSES FROM PEOPLE WHO ARE DISINTERESTED IN THIS SURVEY AND WHO MAY INITIALLY REFUSE TO BE INTERVIEWED. Please instruct interviewers in how they can obtain co-operation if people initially refuse. Such phrases as "This is an extremely short survey—just a few questions." "We would really appreciate your opinions and this will take just a few moments," or "we are selling nothing; your opinions are just as important as anyone else; won't you take just a few moments to help?" are phrases that may be used to induce cooperation. If only cooperative people are included in the survey, the results may be biased and this is the reason for the extreme importance put upon inducing people to answer the questions.

4.   Please instruct interviewers to read the questions aloud and *actually observe* what the respondent writes on the questionnaire. The inter-viewer must be prepared to testify that she observed the respondent write down the answer given on the card in response to interviewer's question.

5.   Please instruct the interviewers to prevent respondents from changing answers to the first questions after reading later questions. This question-naire seeks the *spontaneous reaction* of the respondent.

6.   Please instruct interviewers to get the respondent to write (sign) her name and address on the final page of the questionnaire. This is essential.

7.   After the interview is finished, please instruct the interviewer to write the time and date of the interview and sign her own name to the top of the questionnaire.

8.   Please instruct the interviewer to keep a separate record of the interviews and after each interview, to record a few simple facts about the interview that might help her to remember that particular interview—such as whether the respondent was cooperative, friendly, physical features, some-thing about the house, etc. The supervisor should collect these records (a separate sheet of paper listing each interview and pertinent facts is adequate) and attach them to the questionnaires and other records.

9.   If the slightest suspicion should develop that falsification is occurring or that the procedures of a particular interviewer are leading to biased results, please eliminate that interviewer from this project and delete any interviews that she might have collected.

Result

The results of the personal interview study were that 86.3 percent of re-spondents did not identify the black petalburst design with Kookmar and that 75.3 percent of the consumers did not identify the blue petalburst with

Kookmar. Table 2–3 gives the tabulation of the other answers that were received for the "black" sample and Table 2–4 gives the tabulation for the "blue" sample.

Table 2–3

(Responses to Questions 2 and 3 of the Consumer Poll—300 Personal Interviews)

Response	Number
Companies identified with black petalburst design	
Kookmar Ware, Kookmar Glass, Kookmar	41
Procter and Gamble	4
Libby	1
Owen	1
Gala Towels	1
Edging to Bounty Towels	1
Teflon	1
Scott Towels, Scott products, Scotties	15
Dru-Ware	5
Kleenex	1
Paper company	1
Stationery company	1
Nursery	1
Noritaki Company	1
Cereal company	1
Wallpaper company	1
Products identified with black petalburst design	
Coffee percolator, coffee pot, coffee maker, etc.	18
Toilet paper	3
Saucepans, pots, pans	12
Cooking ware, oven ware, cooking dishes, etc.	9
Baking dishes	2
Teapots, teakettles	6
Face soap, soap	3
Kookmar Co., Kookmar Ware	1
Baked foods, cookies	2
Don't know, don't remember	12
Dishes, dinner ware, china, plates, etc.	11
Gala towels, paper towels, Bounty paper towels	9
Paper products	2
Serving spoon and forks	1
Paper tissues, facial tissues	2
Air freshener	1
Dutch oven	1
Dixie cups	1
Paper napkins	1

Table 2–3 (continued)

Response	Number
Products identified with black petalburst design	
Casserole	16
Skillet, frying pan	3
Salt and pepper shakers	1
Roasting pan	2
Butter	1
Kitchen ware	2
Johnson's talcum powder	1
Bowls	1
Flowers	1
Paper place mats	1
Cereal	1
Electric frying pan, small appliances	2
Utensils	1
Silk	1

Table 2–4

(Responses to Questions 2 and 3 of the Consumer Poll—300 Personal Interviews)

Response	Number
Companies identified with blue petalburst design	
Kookmar Ware, Kookmar Glass, Kookmar	74
Toilet paper company	1
Procter and Gamble	3
Bounty towels	1
Don't know or don't remember	31
Scott towels, Scott products, Scotties	7
Cookware	1
Dru-Ware	1
Carnation	2
Delsey toilet tissue	1
Paper company	1
Betty Flowers Shop	1
Artex Painting	1
Post or Kellogg	1
"Something" ware	1
Modess	1
Soap company	1
Desco Ware	1
Crown Zeller	2
Pyrex	2

Table 2–4 (continued)

Response	Number
Products identified with blue petalburst design	
Coffee percolator, coffee pot, coffee maker, etc.	39
Toilet paper	6
Saucepans, pots, pans	15
Cosmetics	1
Cooking ware, oven ware, cooking dishes, etc.	27
Baking dishes	9
Teapots, teakettles	11
Face soap, soap	4
Kookmar Ware	3
Baked foods, cookies	1
Don't know, don't remember	15
Dishes, dinner ware, china, plates, etc.	12
Cooking products	3
Serving products	1
Toothpaste	1
Gala towels, Bounty paper towels	17
Paper products	3
Polish	1
Paper tissues, facial tissues, Kleenex	10
Dutch oven	5
Paper cups	1
Paper napkins	2
Casserole	27
Skillet, frying pan	13
Salt and pepper shakers	1
Roasting pan	4
Carnation milk	2
Butter	1
Kitchen ware	1
Pyroceram ware	1
Johnson's talcum powder	1
Pyrex dishes	1
Bowls, serving dishes, etc.	6
Flowers	1
Painting	1
Freezing ware	1
Broiler tray, pan	2
Cereal	1
Electric frying pan	1
Modess	1
Pitcher	1
Cakepans	1

Question 6 was included in the study to determine if persons owning Kookmar Ware responded differently from nonowners. The proportion of Kookmar owners in both the blue and the black sample was slightly in excess of 50 percent. The owners of Kookmar products had a much higher identification of the products with Kookmar than did nonowners.

Conclusion

The Trademark Trial and Appeal Board had the task of determining whether Kookmar should be granted registration for the petalburst design and, if granted, whether it should be only for a blue design or for any color of design. Many factors enter into this decision, but it became apparent that the question of which survey was valid was of great interest in this case. Some of the issues that were examined in detail in cross-examination of witnesses was whether the questionnaires measured what they should measure, whether respondents were selected to be representative of the potential users and purchasers of Kookmar, whether men had any influence on the purchase decision (and consequently whether they should be included in the survey[2]), and whether valid conclusions could be drawn from the survey.

Questions

1. What criteria should the Trademark Trial and Appeal Board use in determining whether consumers perceive the petalburst design primarily as a design or primarily as a symbol identifying the resource or manufacturer?

2. How should the Board evaluate the surveys that were entered as evidence?

3. What additional factors should enter into the decision on the trademark question other than those presented in the surveys?

Twink: Perception of Taste

A large bottler of soft drinks introduced a new cola product, Twink, on a test market basis in a major metropolitan area in the southern part of the United States. Formulated specifically for stated taste preferences in the region, it was anticipated that the brand would attain at least a 6 percent share of the market after seven months of test marketing. The actual share, however, proved to be much less than that, and management felt that the product

[2] The Kookmar survey included no men. The American Homes survey included about 18 percent men. The American Homes position was that men had some influence in the purchase of Kookmar Ware and should therefore be included, although to a lesser extent than women.

taste may be at fault. It was intentionally formulated to be stronger than competitive products and more highly carbonated. Therefore, a taste test was authorized, and the results are summarized here.

Taste Test

There are a number of brands of cola on the market, but only three were felt to be of sufficient importance to warrant their inclusion in the test. Brand A had 38 percent of the market; Brand B, 18 percent; and Brand C, 11 percent. A marketing research firm was hired to compare the taste of these four brands.

Research Design

It was felt that the taste test should first be run without the brands being identified. Then the test could be repeated with brand names stated to see if knowledge of the brand influenced a taste rating. Therefore, a decision was made to present the branded samples first to half the group followed by unbranded and then to reverse the order with the remaining respondents.

It was feared that the order in which the samples are consumed might bias findings. Therefore, it was necessary to specify that each brand was consumed first, second, third, or fourth an equal number of times. The resulting research design is shown in Table 2–5, and it will be noticed that eight test groups are required. A total sample of 320 was selected, giving 40 in each subgroup.

Table 2–5

A Diagram of the Research Design

Order of identification	Brand Presented First			
	A	B	C	Twink
Identified, not identified	1	3	5	7
Not identified, identified	2	4	6	8

Female respondents were recruited from names and addresses filled out in four stores in a supermarket chain in connection with a drawing for a new automobile. Eighty names were selected from each of the four stores. Respondents then were randomly assigned to the eight test groups, and the experiment was conducted in one evening in a small ballroom at a local hotel.

Each product sample was presented in an opaque glass, and great caution was exercised to guarantee identical amounts and temperatures. Plain glasses were used when the samples were unidentified, and labels with typed brand names were added for the remaining tests.

Each respondent took several sips from the sample glass and then rated the taste on a ten item scale using the standard semantic differential procedure (See Figures 2–1 to 2–4). Each scale dimension was presented in the form

FIGURE 2–1. Median ratings for Brand A[a]

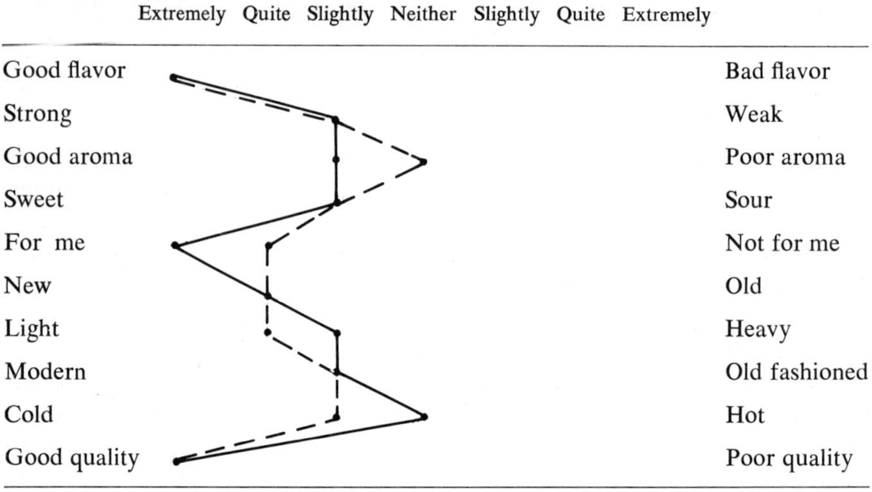

Extremely Quite Slightly Neither Slightly Quite Extremely

Good flavor	Bad flavor
Strong	Weak
Good aroma	Poor aroma
Sweet	Sour
For me	Not for me
New	Old
Light	Heavy
Modern	Old fashioned
Cold	Hot
Good quality	Poor quality

[a]Each point plotted represents the median rating score for all respondents. Ratings are not significantly different ($p = .05$).

———————Brand not identified

– – – – Brand identified

FIGURE 2–2. Median ratings for Brand B[a]

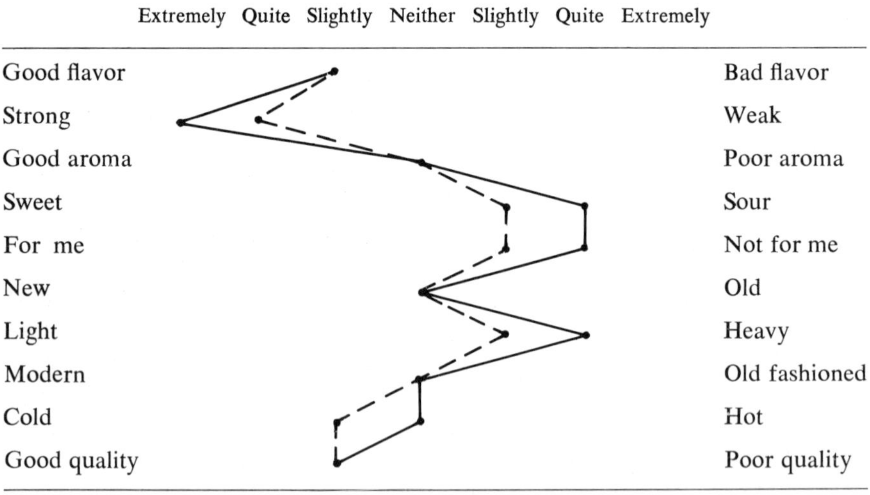

Extremely Quite Slightly Neither Slightly Quite Extremely

Good flavor	Bad flavor
Strong	Weak
Good aroma	Poor aroma
Sweet	Sour
For me	Not for me
New	Old
Light	Heavy
Modern	Old fashioned
Cold	Hot
Good quality	Poor quality

[a]Each point plotted represents the median rating score for all respondents. Ratings are not significantly different ($p = .05$).

———————Brand not identified

– – – – Brand identified

FIGURE 2–3. Median ratings for Brand C[a]

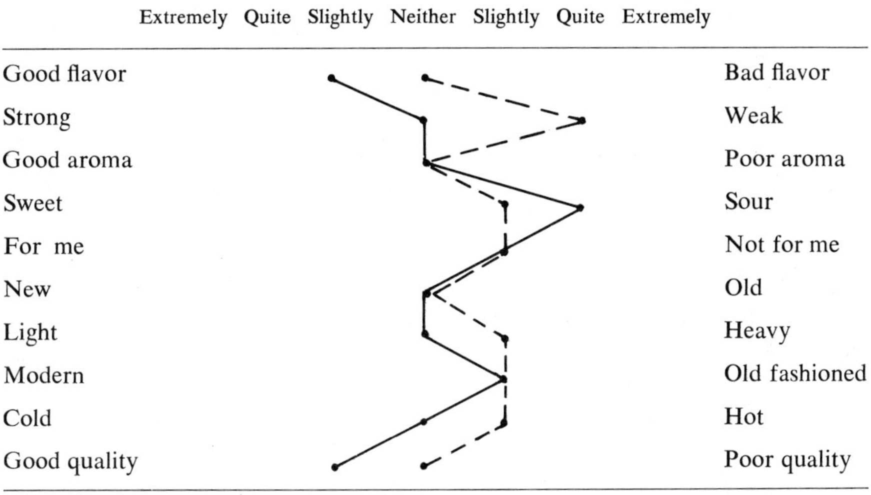

Extremely Quite Slightly Neither Slightly Quite Extremely

Good flavor	Bad flavor
Strong	Weak
Good aroma	Poor aroma
Sweet	Sour
For me	Not for me
New	Old
Light	Heavy
Modern	Old fashioned
Cold	Hot
Good quality	Poor quality

[a]Each point plotted represents the median rating score for all respondents. Ratings are not significantly different ($p = .05$).

——————Brand not identified

– – – – Brand identified

FIGURE 2–4. Median ratings for Twink[a]

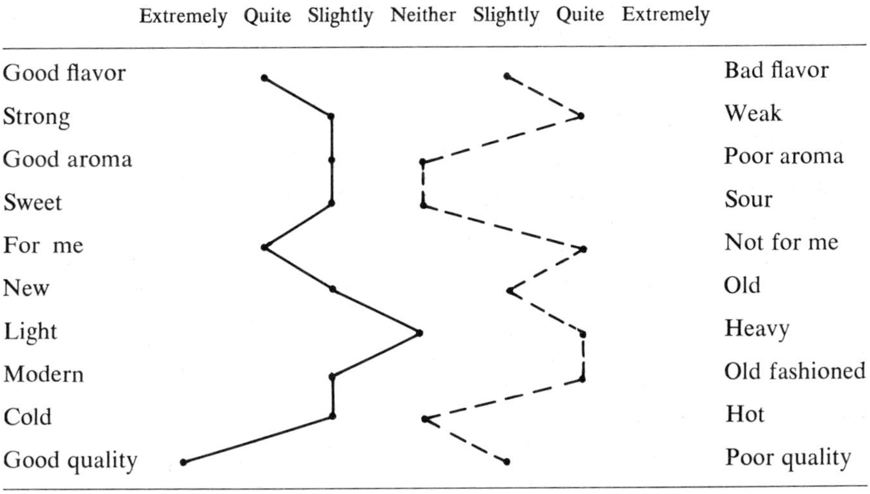

Extremely Quite Slightly Neither Slightly Quite Extremely

Good flavor	Bad flavor
Strong	Weak
Good aroma	Poor aroma
Sweet	Sour
For me	Not for me
New	Old
Light	Heavy
Modern	Old fashioned
Cold	Hot
Good quality	Poor quality

[a]Each point plotted represents the median rating score for all respondents. Ratings are not significantly different ($p = .05$).

——————Brand not identified

– – – – Brand identified

of paired adjectives, and the respondent then checked which of seven positions best represented her rating for that item.

A small piece of bread was consumed after one sample was rated, and the respondent proceeded to the next. This was repeated until each of the four samples was consumed. Then a period of one half hour intervened, after which the experiment was repeated again with the samples either identified by brand or not identified, depending upon what was done in the first test. Respondents were paid $2.50 for participating.

Data Analysis

The ratings given by each respondent were tabulated, and the median rating was computed for each item on the scale. In turn, the medians generated when brands were identified were compared with those in the opposite situation, and a statistical test was made. Because the data are ordinal, it was felt that analysis of variance and other tests designed for interval data should not be used. Therefore, the median test was utilized, with a .05 level of significance specified. If a significant difference was produced, it would mean that the median ratings for a given brand differed depending upon whether or not the brand was identified, and in ninety-five out of one hundred experiments that were run using the same procedure a difference that large would not be produced because of chance fluctuations.

The ratings for each of the four brands appear in Figures 2–1 to 2–4. It will be noticed that there is a statistically significant difference in only one case—Twink. With the other three brands, the differences introduced by identifying the sample are not greater than would be expected by chance.

Interpretation

Management was puzzled by the ratings. It appears that Twink scores quite well on the flavor when the brand is not identified. In fact, the ratings are quite comparable to those for brand A—long the market leader with a current share of 38 percent. This fact, in itself, was gratifying and seemed to verify the decision to make Twink somewhat stronger than competitive alternatives. No other brand, however, showed significant differences in ratings between the two situations. Some felt that the findings must be in error and that the test should be repeated. Others felt that this test shows that the problem of slow market growth does not reside in the taste but most likely is accounted for by the advertising program. According to this point of view, it is clear that the name Twink brings forth connotations that are decidedly unfavorable and that are sufficiently strong to change the taste ratings, even though the samples consumed are identical.

Questions

1. Critically evaluate the research design used. Was proper precaution exerted to control bias?

2. What conclusions should be drawn from the data, if any?

CHAPTER 3

LEARNING

Kingston Cigarettes: Learning of a Social Practice

Kingston cigarettes, the fictionalized name of a major marketer of king-sized cigarettes, sold about 8 percent of all filter cigarettes in the United States. Surveys conducted periodically by the firm indicated Kingston smokers were among the most brand loyal of any cigarette, were among the heaviest smokers of any brand, and tended to be less likely to quit smoking for health reasons than smokers of other filter brands.

Problem

Because of rising concern about the health hazards in smoking cigarettes, the major cigarette firms accepted voluntary restrictions on advertising cigarettes in ways that would appeal specifically to persons under twenty-one years of age. Among other things, these restrictions provided that young persons could not be portrayed using cigarettes, that programs could not be scheduled where the audience was more than 50 percent young people, and that appeals could not be used stressing sports or subjects of special interest to young people.

This produced no immediate effects on sales of Kingston cigarettes, nor did it seem to affect most other brands. Even though the surgeon general of the United States released a report relating smoking to cancer in 1964, health warnings were placed on cigarette packs in 1965, and repeated health warnings had been released by various organizations, sales of cigarettes continued to increase. Occasionally, an important news release affected sales temporarily, but the trend was toward higher sales.

The management of Kingston cigarettes was concerned, however, about the long-run effects on sales of not advertising with appeals directed toward youth. Management's concern was that the proportion of cigarette smokers in the future may be significantly lower if they were not exposed to advertising that they found appealing during their youth. The question was posed, *"When do individuals begin smoking and why do they begin to smoke?"* The company also wanted to know if failure to smoke in the teens would carry over into later years and result in a lower proportion of smokers or if beginning to smoke would simply be delayed a few years.

Research Methodology

In April of 1967 a study was authorized by the Kingston manager to determine the influence of the early years on later smoking patterns. The study was undertaken by Indero, Inc., an independent research organization in a major northern Ohio city. Although the study was conducted in only one city to conserve expenses, management was willing to consider a national study if the results indicated a more extensive study was needed.

A total of 1240 personal interviews were conducted in various areas of the metropolitan area. A quota sample was used to include specified proportions of the population stratified on demographic variables and to include an equal number of smokers of the major cigarette brands. Of those interviewed, 1024 were smokers, and the rest were nonsmokers or former smokers. A smoker was defined as one who smoked at least ten cigarettes a day. The survey included many questions; only those relating to the beginning of smoking are included here.

Results

Respondents were asked the age when they first began smoking. Table 3–1 shows that 57 percent of smokers began smoking before age sixteen. Kingston smokers were about average. Only 10 percent of smokers began after age twenty-one.

Table 3–1

Age of Initial Smoking ("How old were you when you first started smoking?")

	Kingston	Kent	Winston	Marl-boro	L & M	Non-filter	Total Smokers
16 years or under	55%	54%	59%	60%	50%	65%	57%
17 to 21 years	35	37	33	35	41	27	35
Over 21	10%	9%	8%	5%	9%	8%	8%
BASE	(162)	(171)	(176)	(186)	(161)	(168)	(1024)

Table 3–2 shows that young smokers generally keep their mother from knowing of their smoking much more than they do their father. About 31 percent of the parents of Kingston smokers did not realize (in the perception of the smoker) that their child was smoking at the time he first began. In the clear minority of instances did smokers believe both their parents were aware when the children began smoking.

Table 3–2

Incidence of Parental Smoking ("Did either of your parents smoke at that time?")

	Kingston	Kent	Winston	Marl-boro	L & M	Non-filter	Total Smokers
Neither parent	31%	40%	29%	24%	29%	32%	31%
Father only	40	36	40	39	40	46	41
Mother only	7	7	7	9	6	7	7
Both parents	22	17	24	28	20	14	21
Don't remember	–	–	–	–	1%	–	–*
BASE	(162)	(171)	(176)	(186)	(161)	(168)	(1024)

* Less than 0.5 percent.

Table 3–3 reveals the attitudes smokers perceived their parents to exhibit at the time the children started smoking. Of the brands represented in this study, the parents of Kingston smokers appear to have a more tolerant attitude toward children starting smoking than did parents of other brand smokers. Only 19 percent of Kingston parents were very much against their children smoking compared to 26 percent for all smokers.

It became clear to the management of Kingston that this research was provocative but lacked enough detail to answer the questions they had raised. There were a number of other studies published in behavioral science journals to indicate that cigarettes had many ritualistic functions in the teenage years. When young people meet a new acquaintance, start out on a date, or enter a room filled with strange people, the cigarette becomes a means of bridging social barriers. In some cases it may be used as a symbol of attaining a certain level of maturity or social position.

One set of studies at the University of Wisconsin indicate that heavy smokers are more likely to have unhappy childhoods than light smokers or nonsmokers. These studies also indicate a negative relationship between academic achievement and smoking among youth: "In both high school and college, smoking reflects a lack of involvement in the scholastic program and an attempt to obtain satisfactions outside the school environment. The educational system is perhaps not meeting the needs of the smoking student."

Table 3–3

Parental Attitude toward Smoking ("How did your family feel
about your starting to smoke?")

	Kingston	Kent	Winston	Marl-boro	L & M	Non-filter	Total Smokers
Very much against my smoking	19%	28%	23%	36%	27%	23%	26%
Somewhat against my smoking	23	17	16	21	20	26	20
Not against my smoking	23	23	34	24	23	27	26
Didn't have anything to say about it	35	32	27	19	29	23	28
Don't remember	–	–	–	1%	–	–	–*
BASE	(162)	(171)	(176)	(186)	(161)	(168)	(1024)

* Less than 0.5 percent.

There were indications that, generally, young people had an unpleasant experience with their first cigarette and that a taste for cigarettes had to be acquired over time, through repeated smoking.

Strategy Implications

The question of a strategy to be followed by Kingston raised a number of ethical questions as well as strategy decisions. Kingston concluded from the pilot research conducted by Indero that adolescence was a critical time for the establishment of smoking habits in general and perhaps specific brand preference. Management also believed that about 50 percent of all high school males and 25 percent of all high school females were smoking by their senior year.

In view of the voluntary restrictions related to advertising to youth and the threat of much more severe government regulation, Kingston believed it impossible to advertise overtly to teenagers. However, it might be possible to undertake innovative types of educational programs directed toward high schools (such as scholarships or films and study guides). It might be possible also to develop their regular adult promotion program in such a way that it would also be effective in reaching the youth market.

The management of Kingston felt that the most creative and mature thinking possible was needed to answer some very basic questions about influencing the smoking patterns of young people and the long-range ramifications these strategies might have on Kingston sales. In 1968, the firm considered engaging a consulting firm specializing in the application of behavioral science techniques to the solution of basic marketing problems. Kingston management had to decide if the consulting firm should be retained and what they would expect the consulting firm to do for them.

Questions

1. Do the results of the 1967 study indicate the need for a broader investigation of the learning process involved in the formation of a smoking habit?

2. What should be investigated by the consulting firm if they are engaged?

3. How would the consulting firm's research be likely to be useful in developing marketing strategy for Kingston?

4. Until the consulting firm is engaged and results are obtained, Kingston must continue to develop their current marketing strategy. What should they do about promoting Kingston cigarettes among youth markets at the present time?

5. If Kingston should discover that promotion directed toward youth is instrumental in forming life-long smoking patterns and brand preferences, they might wish to direct some of their promotional resources to the youth market. Considering the ethical dimensions of this problem, should Kingston attempt to find legal ways of circumventing the industry code and government regulations in order to appeal directly to young people?

Boni, Vinson and Bailey: Measuring Response to Advertising

The Boni, Vinson and Bailey (BVB) advertising agency in New York is among the largest in the United States, with annual billings in 1968 in excess of $280 million. The agency was established in 1922 by Kenneth Boni, who continued to serve as chairman of the board, although his participation was limited because of his advanced age. His desire to have the firm be a "complete" agency still permeated the organization, however, and along Madison Avenue, BVB was highly regarded for its well-rounded creativity, organization, and research.

In 1968 the agency was contemplating the purchase of new equipment and employing additional staff to begin using some research methods designed to measure the learning process of consumers responding to advertisements.

Another large agency on Madison Avenue had recently announced the opening of a behavioral laboratory that contained equipment and used methods emphasizing physiological measurement of consumer response. The advertising industry, in general, noted the new laboratory methods with a considerable interest but also with a considerable skepticism about their reliability and validity. In the advertising industry, differences of opinion were often found about the value of research. Some advertising men maintained that creativity was of supreme importance and that about the only value of research was to evaluate the effectiveness of advertising that had already been produced and placed in the market place. Others, however, maintained strongly that research results should be an integral part of the creation of advertising themes and campaigns.

Problem

The top management of BVB, with the advice of the vice president in charge of research, Dr. Paul Rowley, was considering budgeting for 1969 an amount sufficient to purchase and operate equipment for measuring the learning effectiveness of advertising by using the operant behavior technique. The exact amount required was difficult to determine because the equipment had to be custom designed and because substantial remodeling and support areas were required in order to use effectively the equipment and methods. Dr. Rowley estimated that a preliminary budget of forty-thousand dollars was needed for purchase of the equipment and necessary remodeling and that an equal amount should be budgeted for direct expenses connected with operation of the facility. These figures were necessarily rough, and management recognized that flexibility would be necessary in the research budget. The total research budget of BVB in 1968 was approximately $800,000. The general administrative and support facilities of the operant behavior equipment as well as the direct expenses would draw from the overall budget.

If management approved the purchase and operation of the new equipment, approximately four months lead time would be necessary to design and install the equipment, and at least three to four months of testing would be necessary before the results could be used to investigate actual problems of major accounts. In making their decision about whether to budget for the acquisition, management asked Dr. Rowley to prepare a detailed description of the equipment that would be needed and to present evidence that results using it would be valid and reliable for clients.

CONPAAD

The application of operant behavior techniques for the measurement of advertising was pioneered by the E. I. DuPont de Nemours Company. In

1964, they developed equipment called CONPAAD (Conjugately Programmed Analysis of Advertising). The original developer was Ogden R. Lindsley, a student of the Harvard behavioral psychologist B. F. Skinner, who had used operant behavior techniques since 1931. Operant behavior theory is the reverse of the typical stimulus-response theory; that is, operant behavior is defined in terms of the stimulus to which it leads rather than in terms of one that precedes it. An important feature of operant behavior is that the operant response is reinforced by the stimulus to which it leads. The rate of operant response also is reinforced by the stimulus to which it leads. The rate of operant response to a stimulus by a human subject (Skinner originally used rats) theoretically measures the reinforcement or reward value of that stimulus or the interest of the person in what he is seeing or hearing. By placing the respondent in a situation where his interest in a stimulus can be measured by the operants emitted, the experimenter is able (1) to obtain discrete, quantifiable units of behavior and (2) to record behavior in a manner that allows small segments of it to be observed.

Equipment

Dr. Rowley investigated the equipment that had been designed for CONPAAD by DuPont. Although the equipment considered by BVB would not be identical (because changes were constantly being made), it would be sufficiently similar that a description of CONPAAD would be an accurate description of that proposed for BVB.

Figure 3–1 is a schematic representation of CONPAAD. The operant behavior procedures are conducted in a specially designed room, and a chair is provided for the respondent. Immediately in front of the chair are two foot pedals. A motion picture screen is mounted on the wall directly in front of the chair. A speaker is mounted on the wall behind the respondent. A motion picture projector is used to present both the auditory and the visual stimuli.

Foot pedals control the intensity of the stimuli. One pedal controls the brightness of the visual stimulus; the faster this pedal is pressed, the brighter the picture becomes on the screen. If the respondent slows down, the picture then becomes dimmer; if the pedal is not pressed at all, the picture becomes barely perceptible. In the same manner the other pedal controls level of sound; the faster the pedal is pressed up and down, the louder the sound becomes.

The rate of response to the commercials is indicated on recording paper by an upward movement of the recording pen. As a result, the rate of response is indicated by the slope of the resulting graph, and the graph is interpretable without further analysis. The auditory and visual responses are recorded as separate graphs. Further analysis is usually made, however. Scores for ads and commercials are expressed in percentage terms—the percentage of bright-

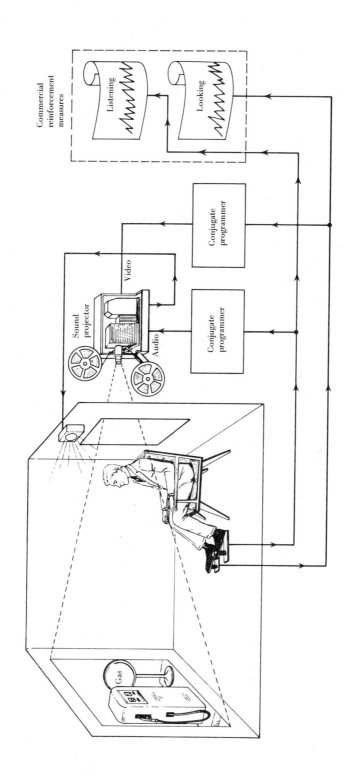

FIGURE 3–1. Schematic representation of arrangements for viewing film and recording responses.

ness (loudness) that, on average, accrued for each ad or commercial with 100 percent being maximum.

When viewing filmed commercials, respondents must work foot pedals to get varying levels of brightness or loudness (one foot pedal for each). The image at first is slightly above the brightness threshold and below the sound threshold. The commercials are embedded into a short show.

When viewing print ads, respondents obviously control only the video. Therefore, one foot pedal is needed to increase brightness. A print ad (or editorial), in the form of a 35mm slide, comes on fully bright for one second and then fades in brightness. The respondent must continue to work a foot pedal to keep the slide (page) visible. The faster the respondent works, the brighter the slide becomes. When the respondent stops pressing, the page fades and in two seconds the next page (slide) comes into view.

Reliability

DuPont not only pioneered the development of CONPAAD but also devoted considerable resources to evaluating the reliability, validity, and sensitivity of the method. The following findings were obtained from studies conducted by DuPont or Associates for Research in Behavior, a Philadelphia firm that operated the equipment for DuPont and, at times, for other firms.

One study employed 192 males (twenty-one to sixty-five years old). Each respondent viewed nine print ads. Some of these same ads were used in a second study using ninety-six females (twenty-five or younger). In this second study each respondent viewed a total of ten ads. A third study also had ten ads and employed ninety-six males (eighteen to sixty-five years old). Finally, a fourth study was done with eleven ads and ninety-six respondents (70 percent male and 30 percent female, between twenty-five and sixty-five years old). The overlapping ads in these four studies are shown in Table 3–4 with

Table 3–4

Advertising Ratings in Four CONPAAD Studies*

Print Ad	Study 1	Study 2	Study 3	Study 4
A	———	40.2 (10)	60.1 (5)	65.3 (3)
B	63.0 (2)	61.2 (4)	60.0 (6)	72.1 (2)
C	88.5 (1)	65.0 (2)	———	75.9 (1)
D	54.8 (7)	67.4 (1)	53.0 (9)	62.6 (5)
E	51.7 (8)	54.9 (5)	57.5 (8)	59.2 (6)
F	———	———	59.5 (7)	47.4 (10)
G	56.0 (6)	44.9 (9)	60.2 (4)	53.7 (9)
H	62.1 (3)	61.5 (3)	65.1 (1)	63.8 (4)
I	58.7 (5)	50.7 (6)	62.2 (3)	55.6 (8)
J	60.0 (4)	48.0 (8)	62.9 (2)	58.4 (7)
K	37.2 (9)	48.3 (7)	49.0 (10)	42.6 (11)

* 100 percent effort is predetermined; fractional effort to see each ad is averaged over the pool of respondents.

Table 3–5

Correlation Between Four CONPAAD Studies

Study to Study		Correlation	P
I	II	+.26	
I	III	+.74	.02
I	IV	+.80	.01
II	III	−.28	
II	IV	+.43	
III	IV	+.28	

their CONPAAD scores and ranks in parentheses. A rank correlation on all possible pairs of studies is shown in Table 3–5.

Five of the six correlations were positive, two at significant levels. These latter two correlations were between somewhat similar population groups. Group I and Group III each had males and similar age distributions. Group I versus Group IV had an all-male versus a 70 percent male sample. Group II were all females and had a restricted age range. This group showed mostly low correlations with the other three (male) groups.

The data in Table 3–4 are rate scores expressed as a percentage of the respondent's maximum rate of pedal pressing. The maximum is determined prior to testing and, of course, is different for different respondents, but is usually 3 or 4 presses per second.

A few reliability studies have been done using television commercials. In two studies, four beer commercials were compared with each other by two separate groups of male beer drinkers. The ranks of the four commercials were identical in both studies. Two of the four were tested in a third study, and they scored in the same order relative to each other as they had in the previous two studies.

In another study the same people saw the same commercial twice, and their scores on both observations were correlated. The group was small ($n = 12$), but the correlation was .85, which is significant at .02. In still another study using the split-half reliability test, ten commercials were administered to a split group. The correlation between the average scores of the two groups who saw the same commercials was .87, which is significant at $p = .02$. The group was larger in this study ($n = 100$ per commercial).

Validity

Validity studies frequently are difficult to accomplish in advertising research because of the inadequacy of criterion variables. Several studies have been undertaken by DuPont or Associates for Research in Behavior, however, and the results are presented below.

Readership

In the first study reported here, six articles of editorial matter of equal length were randomly placed within print advertisements in two individual studies. These articles were purposefully included to measure the validity of the CONPAAD technique. The articles had previously been tested for female readership.

The first study employed forty-eight females, ages eighteen to fifty-five. The second study used 96 females, mothers under age twenty-five.

Table 3–6 indicates a comparison of the readership ranks and CONPAAD time[1] score ranks from both studies. The two studies in Table 3–6 replicated readership results almost perfectly for the best and worst articles.

Table 3–6

CONPAAD* and Readership Ranks for Six Articles

Articles	Readership Rank	Study I Rank	Study II Rank
A	1	1	1
B	2	3	2
C	3	4	4
D	4	2	5
E	5	6	6
F	6	5	3

* Scores based on the amount of time spent reading each article.

Article A, the best article in readership, generated the highest CONPAAD time scores, and the worst article in readership, Article F, also received the lowest CONPAAD time score in Study I. The rank correlation between article readership and Study I is +.77, significant beyond the .02 level of significance. The rank correlation between readership scores and Study II is positive, but not significant at +.66. It is possible to get time scores using CONPAAD equipment.

In another study, a pair of commercials for soft drinks were compared with each other, and one was found to be much more effective in the CONPAAD test than the other. These commercials were used in the marketplace in a coupon redemption campaign; thus, measures of sales effectiveness of the commercials were available. When the commercials were tested in the laboratory, CONPAAD successfully predicted the sales measures for the commercials.

The soft drink commercial study was replicated, however, with results that were originally confusing. In the replication study using CONPAAD, the "bad" sales commercial received the highest rating. Upon reanalyzing the data, however, researchers found that the content that preceded the commercial affected its response level considerably. In the study, each commercial had been placed in two spots an equal number of times. Figure 3–2 shows the results of the reanalysis. On the left-hand side of each group of two bars are the results of the commercial placed in an "exciting" spot, and on the right-hand

[1] The CONPAAD time score is a score of the amount of time a respondent presses the "video" pedal to keep the article (ad) on the screen. The intensity of brightness is therefore not considered in this score.

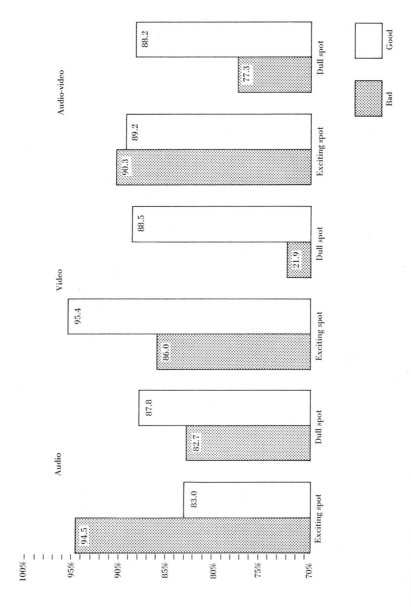

FIGURE 3–2. Averaging commercial-prescore for soft drink commercials following exciting and dull preperiod.

side are the results from being placed in a "dull" spot. This figure shows that there are interaction effects between the commercial and the particular spot in which it is placed. Note also that the scores here are in terms of work to see (or hear) a commercial over work to see that portion of the show just before the commercial. Using this fraction still does not control for the effect of the pre-period. For audio-video combined, a commercial following an "exciting" spot seems about equal whether it's "good" or "bad." Following a "dull" spot a "bad" commercial suffers most.

Recall

A number of other validity tests were conducted by comparing CONPAAD scores with other measures of advertising effectiveness. These were, of course, subject to the fact that the other measures often were not validated. With recall measures, CONPAAD scores (for both storyboard and finished ads) predicted the best commercial and the worst but erred on middle scores. The results are shown in Table 3–7.

Table 3–7

Relation Between Recall and CONPAAD Results

		CONPAAD	
Commercial	Recall	Storyboard	Finished
A	1	1	1.5
B	2	3	1.5
C	3	2	3
D	4	4	4

Learning Scores

In another study, CONPAAD scores were compared to learning scores. (A learning score technique was developed by John Dollard at Yale University in conjunction with DuPont and is based primarily on a learning-and-motivation theory approach to persuasive communications. A series of ratings are made of several aspects of a commercial. These are then pooled into an overall score on effectiveness of the commercial.) Twelve pairs of commercials were available with learning scores. In every case but one, there was good agreement with the CONPAAD scores.

Information Theory

From a theoretical perspective, CONPAAD results should coincide with what would be predicted from varying hypotheses developed in the behavioral sciences. One principle is that consumers like, seek, and work for information. Therefore, a commercial that contains a moderate amount of information should be responded to more on CONPAAD than a commercial that contains a low amount of information. Table 3–8 shows a significant difference between the CONPAAD scores for high and low information commercials, both on audio and video.

Table 3–8

Average Difference Scores for High and Low Information Commercials*

Mode	High Information Scores	Low Information Scores
Audio	+10.9%	
Video	+10.9%	

* These scores represent work for commercial over work for the period of the show immediately preceding commercial placement, balanced for pre-period effects.

Conditioning Theory

Another study was based on conditioning theory. It would be expected that consumers would eventually extinguish or satiate to a message that contained little or no information. Failure to satiate would be taken as negative evidence of CONPAAD's sensitivity. In the study, a commercial was created that consisted primarily of numbers running backwards (10, 9, 8, 7, 6, 5, 4, and 3) and repeated six times. The response rates were plotted over time to this pseudo commercial. The subjects show a steady decline, and 85 percent of the subjects eventually reached the criterion of satiation.

On the basis of these and other studies, Dr. Rowley recommended that BVB budget the necessary amount to purchase operant behavior equipment similar to CONPAAD. To do so, of course, meant that money budgeted for other types of research had to be curtailed somewhat, but Rowley felt that the new equipment should receive a high priority. The top management of the agency held the responsibility for making the final decision.

Questions

1. What issues in learning theory, attitude change, or other areas of consumer psychology could effectively be investigated with the equipment proposed by Dr. Rowley?

2. What criteria should the top management of an advertising agency use in evaluating the value of the proposed equipment?

3. Is the evidence presented in the text sufficient to justify confidence in CONPAAD type equipment?

4. Should BVB budget the amount required to purchase the proposed equipment?

5. What effect do you think this equipment will have on creative-research deportment interaction? Should the equipment be used primarily prior to, during, or after commercial production?

PART II

NATURE AND INFLUENCE OF
INDIVIDUAL PREDISPOSITIONS

CHAPTER 4

PERSONALITY CHARACTERISTICS

National Liberty Life Insurance Company: Personality and Direct Mail Buying[1]

In 1959 Arthur DeMoss, a veteran insurance man with a flair for marketing, developed a new approach to merchandising insurance by mail. Being an abstainer from alcohol, DeMoss knew that nondrinkers constitute a select group from the standpoint of health hazards. He also knew something else: total abstainers in the United States are numbered in the millions, and they tend to be serious-minded people.

Aiming directly at this special market, DeMoss created the Gold Star plan of hospitalization insurance, capitalizing on the fact that abstainers are less accident prone and on the whole enjoy better health than people who drink. Instead of starting by recruiting and training a sales force from scratch, an expensive and time-consuming project, the Gold Star Plan made its offering by direct mail merchandising under the slogan *special plans for special people.*

The combination of an attractive policy (which pays the insured $100 a week in cash while he is in the hospital, which is noncancellable, and which requires no medical examination), plus the appeal to a select market and the use of direct mail for efficiency in pinpointing market targets, all contributed to take the Gold Star plan from a standing start in 1959 to an annual renewal premium income well in excess of $21 million a year by the end of 1967. As the premium product of the National Liberty Life Insurance Company, the Gold Star plan accounts for most of the young company's business.

---

[1] Taken in part from *Perceived Risk: The Case of Mail Order Buying Versus Non-Mail Order Buying,* a doctoral dissertation completed by Homer E. Spence at The Ohio State University under the direction of the authors in 1967.

The Problem

Although National Liberty's management was convinced that the potential in the total abstainer market had barely been tapped, the rate of response generated by direct mail offerings had diminished with time. Management felt that market penetration had to be increased, even though the size of this market segment relative to the total United States population was decreasing.

In light of the advantages the company offers, growth should continue at record speed. Gold Star plans are offered at a price lower than identical policies for a mixed group of drinkers and nondrinkers. Company research documents this price advantage with proof that nondrinkers spend about 20 percent less time in the hospital than those who drink.

Management had examined many possible explanations for the diminishing direct mail response rate. One strong possibility was that dramatic growth had been achieved by "skimming the cream" off the market. It may also have been that many in the target market feel that their present hospitalization insurance coverage, group or otherwise, was adequate without the addition of another policy.

Still another possibility was that people perceived high risk in purchasing insurance by mail and hence avoided purchase of this type of policy for that reason alone. If that was the situation, then the company had to drastically evaluate its entire marketing program. Therefore, a decision was made to evaluate risk perception and direct mail purchase to determine whether or not a barrier to purchase existed from this source.

Methodology

Concept of Perceived Risk

Perceived risk, as an influence on buying behavior, has received considerable comment in the recent literature. Its primary advocate, Raymond Bauer, points out the role of perceived risk in this manner: "Consumer behavior involves risk in the sense that any action of a consumer will produce consequences which he cannot anticipate with anything approximating certainty, and some of which at least are likely to be unpleasant."[2] In this study, *perceived risk* was defined as "the amount of risk an individual says that he feels or sees to exist in a given act or object." If this risk is high, it would be expected that he would be reluctant to buy by mail, because mail shopping would appear to be a riskier shopping strategy than other alternatives.

It appears to be that the basic personality trait of "desire for certainty"

[2] Raymond A. Bauer, "Consumer Behavior as Risk Taking," in Robert S. Hancock (ed.), *Dynamic Marketing for a Changing World*. Chicago: American Marketing Association, 1960, p. 390.

underlies the tendency to perceive high risk in a buying situation.[3] Those who are unable to tolerate ambiguity or uncertainty should be more likely to perceive high risk in relatively ambiguous buying situations such as purchasing by mail.

The following hypotheses were investigated based on the theoretical analysis:

1. There is a greater degree of perceived risk in the act of purchasing a product by mail than in purchasing it from a store or a salesman.

2. There is a greater degree of perceived risk in the act of purchasing hospitalization insurance by mail than in purchasing it from a salesman.

3. Persons who exhibit a lower tolerance for ambiguity will perceive a correspondingly lower degree of risk in the act of purchasing by mail than of purchasing from a store or a salesman than will persons who have a high tolerance for ambiguity.

Sampling Procedure

Those interviewed were members of one of the three following groups:

1. All persons in Columbus, Ohio, who presently are National Liberty policyholders.

2. Members of the approximately ten-thousand persons in Columbus who are on company mailing lists.

3. All persons in Columbus, Ohio, not included in the above groups.

A sample of one hundred was chosen from each group. Policyholder and prospect samples were chosen by random means, and the third sample, the control sample, was matched geographically to the prospect sample. Whenever an interviewer completed an interview with a prospect, he immediately selected another household in the same block using a predetermined procedure.

Questionnaires

All respondents were personally interviewed in their homes. Some of the questionnaires used appear in Appendix A; and comment is included here on only three basic instruments: (1) the perceived risk scale, (2) the desire-for-certainty test, and (3) the socioeconomic questionnaire.

Perceived Risk Scale

This instrument was designed to measure the relative amount of risk a respondent feels in one buying situation as opposed to another. The scale,

[3] Orville G. Brim, Jr., "Attitude Content Intensity and Probability Expectations," *American Sociological Review,* 20 (1955), 68–76.

which appears in its complete form in Appendix A, is a paper-and-pencil test. The respondent was instructed to rate a series of twenty products individually with respect to the amount of risk he felt there was in the act of purchasing each product in one of two buying situations. He was then asked to rate each of the products in the same manner, but with the buying situation being the second of the two situations. He evaluated the amount of risk perceived using a five-point scale ranging from 1 (very high risk) to 5 (very low risk).

The products to be rated were presented as a product type, and not a brand name, described by using such phrasing as *well-known brand* or *unfamiliar brand* in an attempt to manipulate risk. Here are some examples:

1.   19-inch TV set: well-known brand, $99.

2.   Tulip bulbs: $1.50 per dozen.

3.   Hi-Fi record album: unfamiliar brand, $1.98.

Half the time the respondents were instructed to rate the amount of risk present if the product were purchased through the mail and then to rate the product again in terms of purchase from a store or salesman. In the remaining instances the order of mail versus store-salesman was reversed.

The scale was scored by assigned weights of 5, 4, 3, 2, and 1 for each response category. The total score generated by a respondent for each of the twenty products was evaluated, and a difference score was then computed for each product by subtracting the store situation score from the mail situation score. This score was then summed across all respondents, and a mean difference score was computed that reflected differences in the way respondents rated a product under the mail-buying and store-salesman buying situations.

Similarly, a respondent's perceived risk score was computed by summing the scores for each of the twenty products and assessing differences between the two buying situations.

Desire-for-Certainty Test

The desire-for-certainty test was used to assess a respondent's ability to tolerate ambiguity. This test is based on the assumption that those with a strong desire for certainty evidence this tendency by claiming a high certainty that something definitely will happen (probability near 1) or will not happen (probability near 0). Thirty-two commonplace situations are presented, and probability values are filled in by the respondent. Maximum uncertainty is demonstrated by probability values around .5.

The test is scored by determining whether a probability estimate given for a particular situation is closer to 0 or 1. The distance from the closest of these figures is then computed, and this figure is measured by the respondent's certainty value (that is, confidence estimate of weight of 1 for "very sure" through 5 for "not sure at all.") Scores for the thirty-two situations are summed and averaged. This produces an average score falling between 0 and 250. Following this procedure yields scores with numerical values inversely related to desire for certainty.

Socioeconomic Questionnaire

A standard questionnaire was used to gather pertinent socioeconomic data such as age, sex, income, and religion. The questionnaire was administered by using direct questions such as "Do you own your own home?"

Results

Perceived Risk and Direct Mail Purchases

It was hypothesized that there is a greater degree of perceived risk in the purchase of a product by mail than in purchasing it from a store or a salesman. The data in Table 4–1 indicate that this hypothesis was not verified.

Table 4–1

Average Total Perceived Risk Difference Scores for All Respondents

Sample Group	$\bar{D}$*
Policyholders ($n = 100$)	10.42†
Prospects ($n = 101$)	12.54
Control ($n = 100$)	13.16
TOTAL ($n = 301$)	12.04

* The sum across all twenty products of differences between mail buying situation ratings and store-salesmen buying situations ratings divided by sample size (n).

† Read as: The policyholder sample perceived an average difference of 10.42 out of a total possible difference of ±80 between mail buying and store-salesman buying. The positive score indicates that this sample saw a greater amount of risk in the mail situation than in the store-salesman situation.

It cannot be said that there is greater risk in a mail purchase than in other situations. A total difference score was computed for all respondents as follows:

$$\bar{D} = \frac{\text{total } D}{\text{total sample size}} = \frac{3626}{301} = 12.0465$$

A *t* test was computed to determine whether or not 12.0465 was significantly greater than 0, a condition that must hold if the hypothesis is to be accepted. The value of *t* was found to be

$$\begin{aligned}
\text{computed } t &= .8996 \\
\text{critical value of } t &= 1.645 \text{ (one-tailed)} \\
\text{degrees of freedom} &= 300 \\
n &= 301
\end{aligned}$$

The significance level was .05. For a finding to be statistically significant, this would mean that a difference this large between 0 and 12.0465 would not occur by chance in 95 out of 100 times. Such a conclusion could not be made, however, in this case.

Perceived Risk in Purchase of Hospitalization Insurance

Of special interest to National Liberty was the degree of risk perceived in purchase of hospitalization insurance by mail. It was hypothesized that risk would be greater in that situation, but this was again not verified by the data (Table 4–2).

Table 4.2 shows that the average total perceived risk difference score for hospitalization insurance is $\overline{D} = 0.6678$. Once again a t test was performed, and the difference was not significant. Similar results were found for the other twenty products in Table 4–2.

Tolerance of Ambiguity and Risk

It was hypothesized that persons showing a high desire for certainty and hence a lower ability to tolerate ambiguity would show less perceived risk when buying by mail than those with lower desire or certainty. A product moment correlation coefficient was computed between the perceived risk $\overline{D}$ scores and respondents' scores on the Brim desire-for-certainty test. The computed value was $r = .032$. This correlation coefficient, in turn, was not statistically significant, which means that it could easily have occurred simply because of chance. Therefore, the hypothesis was not supported. There appears to be no demonstrable relationship between perceived risk and desire for certainty.

A related question of interest is whether or not members of the three different samples varied in terms of desire for certainty. Of particular interest are possible differences between policy holders and prospects. The data in Table 4–3 show that differences are quite small, and they are not statistically significant.

Variations in D Scores between Samples for Hospitalization Insurance

Table 4–4 shows that $\overline{D}$ for hospitalization insurance appears to differ among the three sample groups. To determine whether or not this difference is sufficient to verify that results were not simply due to chance, a single factor analysis of variance was performed (or one-way ANOV). The data in

Table 4–2

Average Total Perceived Risk Difference Scores on All Products
Ranked in Order of Magnitude of Difference

Product and Rank	$\overline{D}$*	t†
1. Fresh strawberries	1.3654‡	.898
2. Children's shoes	1.0332	.690
3. 19-inch TV set	0.8339	.614
4. Power lawn mower	0.7508	.556
5. Ready-made drapes	0.7475	.602
6. Hospitalization insurance	0.6678	.582
7. Bourbon whiskey	0.6412	.471
8. Metal lawn chair	0.6179	.512
9. Aluminum siding	0.5581	.509
10. Christmas cards	0.5515	.421
11. Stationery	0.5050	.422
12. Mutual fund	0.5017	.410
13. Tulip bulbs	0.4850	.396
14. Double-bed sheet	0.4684	.403
15. Hi-fi album	0.4452	.405
16. Monopoly game	0.4452	.325
17. Life insurance	0.4319	.409
18. Sewing machine	0.3821	.363
19. Vitamins	0.3621	.315
20. Aspirin	0.2525	.205

* $\overline{D}$ = the sum across all respondents of the difference in perceived risk ratings between the mail buying and store-salesman buying situations divided by sample size.

† t = computed test statistic t where $\overline{D}$ was tested against zero to see if a significant difference existed. The critical value of t at the .05 level of significance (one-tail) is 1.645 with 300 degrees of freedom. None of the t tests were significant.

‡ Read as: For all respondents, the average difference in perceived risk between the mail buying and store-salesman buying situations for fresh strawberries was 1.3654 out of a total possible of ±4. The positive score indicates that more risk was perceived in the mail buying situation.

Table 4–5 indicate that the differences were not significant, meaning that policy holders, prospects, and controls do not differ in the risk assigned to purchase of hospitalization insurance by mail versus a store or salesman.

Raw Product Risk Rating Scores

All of the data examined thus far are in the direction hypothesized, yet results are not statistically significant. One reason may be that the perceived risk scale is inadequate for its purposes. It was thoroughly pretested, but one cannot be certain of its validity. One further analysis helps to shed light on its utility.

One would expect certain situations to be more risky than others without

Table 4–3

Average Desire-for-Certainty Scores for Policy Holders, Prospects,
and Control Respondents

Sample Groups	Desire-for-Certainty Score*
Policyholders ($n = 100$)	86.84†
Prospects ($n = 101$)	84.08
Control ($n = 100$)	80.02
TOTAL ($n = 301$)	83.33

* Scores can range from 50 (lowest desire for certainty) to 250 (highest desire for certainty).

† Read as: The average desire-for-certainty score for the policy holder sample was 86.84.

Table 4–4

Average Perceived Risk Scores for Hospitalization Insurance
for Each of the Three Sample Groups

Sample Groups	$\bar{D}$ for Hospitalization Insurance
Policyholders	.5400*
Prospects	.7129
Controls	.7500

* Read as: The average perceived risk difference score for the policyholder group on hospitalization insurance was .5400 out of a total possible ±4.

Table 4–5

Summary for the Analysis of Variance Testing the Significance of the Differences
in $\bar{D}$ for Hospitalization Insurance among the Policyholder, Prospect
and Control Sample Groups

Source of Variation	Sum of Squares	d.f.	Mean Square	F
Between groups	2.5141	2	1.2571	0.9950*
Within groups	392.2632	298	1.3163	
TOTAL	394.7773	300		

* The critical value of F at the .05 level of significance is 3.87; hence F was not significant.

examination of the mail or store-salesman buying situations. Life insurance, for example, should be perceived as more risky and fraught with consequences than, say, purchase of a Christmas card. The data in Table 4–6 verify that, in general, this proves to be true, thus providing further evidence that the perceived risk scale is discriminating properly.

Table 4–6

Level of Risk Perceived in Purchasing from a Store or Salesman and by Mail
for Each Product in the Perceived Risk Scale, Ranked in Descending Order
by Level of Perceived Risk in the Store-Salesman Situation ($N = 300$)

Product and Rank in the Store-Salesman Situation	Average Perceived Risk Rating Score		Rank in the Mail Situation
	Store-Salesman Situation	Mail Situation	
1. Life insurance*	4.12†	4.55	1
2. Sewing machine	3.88	4.26	2
3. Vitamins	3.70	4.06	4
4. Aluminum siding	3.56	4.11	3
5. Aspirin	3.40	3.65	11
6. Mutual fund	3.34	3.84	6
7. Hi-fi album	3.30	3.74	7
8. Hospitalization insurance	3.22	3.89	5
9. Bourbon whiskey	3.04	3.69	9
10. Ready-made drapes	2.97	3.71	8
11. Monopoly game	2.91	3.36	15
12. Power lawn mower	2.85	3.40	14
13. Tulip bulbs	2.77	3.26	17
14. 19-inch TV set	2.74	3.57	12
15. Metal lawn chair	2.66	3.28	16
16. Stationery	2.61	3.11	19
17. Christmas cards	2.58	3.13	18
18. Children's shoes	2.54	3.57	13
19. Double-bed sheet	2.44	2.93	20
20. Fresh strawberries	2.36	3.67	10

* Read as: Life insurance was ranked first, that is, highest in perceived risk of all the twenty products for the store-salesman buying situation.

† Read as: Life insurance received an average perceived risk rating score in the store-salesman situation of 4.12 out of a total possible of 5, where 1 = very low risk, and 5 = very high risk.

The data in Table 4–6 indicate that the range of average product perceived risk was 1.76 in the store-salesman situation and 0.88 in the mail situation. This seems to indicate that the respondents tended to discriminate among product risk levels to a considerably greater degree in the store-salesman situation than in the mail buying situation. Table 4–6 also indicates that the relative levels of risk perceived at the extremes were fairly stable. Note that four out of five products receiving the highest perceived risk ratings in store-salesman situations are among the five highest in the mail buying situation. At the same time, three out of the five lowest store risk ratings are in the same group in the mail situation. This may offer a partial explanation of why the perceived risk $\overline{D}$ scores were so low.

The data also show that of the six products ranked in the five lowest perceived risk $\overline{D}$ score rankings (there is a tie for fifteenth position), four are in
the five highest perceived risk ratings for the store-salesman situation and
three for the mail situation. These products are life insurance, sewing machine, and vitamins for the mail situation, plus aspirin in the latter situation.
One might interpret this as an indication that as the degree of risk perceived
in a product itself increases, the importance of the situational risk factor
declines in importance. This is merely a proposition that requires further
study.

Differences in Raw Rating Scores for the Three Sample Groups

Additional analysis focused on differences in perceived risk rating scores in
the mail buying situation and in the store-salesman buying situation for each
of the three samples. This showed once again that there were no statistically
significant differences.

Desire or Certainty and Total Perceived Risk Scores

Finally, a product moment correlation was computed between total perceived risk scores (store plus mail) and scores on the Brim test scores. The
resulting correlation coefficient of -0.15 was significant at the .05 level (a
correlation coefficient this large would occur by chance less than five times
out of 100).

This finding tends to support a proposition that persons who have a low
tolerance for ambiguity generally see more risk in buying situations. One
must note, however, that the correlation coefficient yields an r^2 of only
0.0225. In other words, the desire-for-certainty or tolerance-for-ambiguity
personality variable accounts for only 2.25 percent of variance in total perceived risk scores.

Conclusions

None of the major hypotheses could be supported, and secondary analyses
yielded little in the way of additional data that would invalidate a major
conclusion that there is no reason for believing that people perceive significantly more risk in buying by mail as opposed to buying from a store or a
salesman. In addition, the personality variable of desire for certainty (tolerance for ambiguity) was not related in any significant way to the findings.
Therefore, it may be concluded that National Liberty need not consider a
change away from a basic marketing strategy of selling by mail. The reasons
for a slowdown in response rate to direct mailings must be sought elsewhere.

Questions

1. Do the findings indicate any major reason why National Liberty should not continue selling by mail?

2. What other questions might have been investigated to shed light on the basic underlying problem?

3. Were the research methods used realistic in light of the company problem? What suggestions do you have for future research?

Appendix A: Perceived Risk Sale

Product Risk Questionnaire

We all know that there is a certain amount of risk involved in the purchase of goods and services. Everybody sees different kinds and amounts of risk when buying different products.

For example, if you are thinking about buying a car you may be faced with the risk that the model you are interested in may not be built as well as a competitor's model. Or there is the risk that the price you pay may not be the lowest one possible. Then there is the risk that the car may not perform as well as you expect it to. Perhaps if you buy a large expensive car you will be faced with the risk that your friends may think you are trying to put on airs or be a social climber.

On the following pages you are asked to think about the amount of risk that you personally see in a number of buying situations.

> *Example:*
> Suppose you are on a shopping trip and you have decided that you need to buy some milk. One of your choices on the shelf at the store is a half gallon of an unfamiliar brand of milk selling at 49 cents. How much risk do you feel there would be in the purchase of this product? You can indicate the amount of risk you see in the purchase by circling one of the following choices.
>
> Very High   High   Moderate   Low   Very Low
>   Risk   Risk   Risk   Risk   Risk

You should consider all kinds of risk in making your choice, such as the risk that the milk is spoiled, the risk that another brand may be better or the risk that the milk may be priced higher than another brand at another store.

Remember, the important thing is to circle the amount of risk that you think there is in purchasing the product.

Directions: Assume that you have already decided to buy each of the following products through the mail. Assume that you have seen a picture of each product and have read a description of it in an advertisement. Please circle the amount of risk that you think exists in the purchase of each one of the products *through the mail.*

1.	Double-bed sheets: well-known brand, $3.98	Very High Risk	High Risk	Moderate Risk	Low Risk	Very Low Risk
2.	Life insurance: unfamiliar company	Very High Risk	High Risk	Moderate Risk	Low Risk	Very Low Risk
3.	Power lawn mower: well-known brand, $99	Very High Risk	High Risk	Moderate Risk	Low Risk	Very Low Risk
4.	Ready-made drapes: $15 per pair	Very High Risk	High Risk	Moderate Risk	Low Risk	Very Low Risk
5.	19-inch TV set: well-known brand, $99	Very High Risk	High Risk	Moderate Risk	Low Risk	Very Low Risk
6.	Hi-fi record album: unfamiliar brand, $1.98	Very High Risk	High Risk	Moderate Risk	Low Risk	Very Low Risk
7.	Christmas cards: $2 per box of 25	Very High Risk	High Risk	Moderate Risk	Low Risk	Very Low Risk
8.	Metal lawn chair: $5.98	Very High Risk	High Risk	Moderate Risk	Low Risk	Very Low Risk
9.	Tulip bulbs: $1.50 per dozen	Very High Risk	High Risk	Moderate Risk	Low Risk	Very Low Risk
10.	Monopoly game: $6	Very High Risk	High Risk	Moderate Risk	Low Risk	Very Low Risk
11.	Children's shoes: well-known brand, $8.99 per pair	Very High Risk	High Risk	Moderate Risk	Low Risk	Very Low Risk
12.	Bourbon whiskey: well-known brand, $5.95 per bottle	Very High Risk	High Risk	Moderate Risk	Low Risk	Very Low Risk
13.	Hospitalization insurance: pays $100 per week in cash while you are hospitalized, costs $7 per month	Very High Risk	High Risk	Moderate Risk	Low Risk	Very Low Risk

14.	Fresh strawberries: 49¢ per quart	Very High Risk	High Risk	Moderate Risk	Low Risk	Very Low Risk
15.	Stationery: $2 per box	Very High Risk	High Risk	Moderate Risk	Low Risk	Very Low Risk
16.	Aspirin: unfamiliar brand, 17¢ per bottle of 100 tablets	Very High Risk	High Risk	Moderate Risk	Low Risk	Very Low Risk
17.	Vitamins: unfamiliar brand, $3.49 per bottle of 100	Very High Risk	High Risk	Moderate Risk	Low Risk	Very Low Risk
18.	Aluminum siding: well-known brand, $75 per square foot installed	Very High Risk	High Risk	Moderate Risk	Low Risk	Very Low Risk
19.	Sewing machine: unfamiliar brand, $75	Very High Risk	High Risk	Moderate Risk	Low Risk	Very Low Risk
20.	Well-known mutual fund: $15 per share	Very High Risk	High Risk	Moderate Risk	Low Risk	Very Low Risk

Now, suppose that you had the chance to buy each of the products or services *from a store or from a salesman*. Please circle the amount of risk that you think exists in the purchase of each product. Remember, you are going to buy from the store or salesman that you would normally buy the product or service from rather than going to by mail.

1.	Stationery: $2 per box	Very High Risk	High Risk	Moderate Risk	Low Risk	Very Low Risk
2.	Power lawn mower: well-known brand, $99	Very High Risk	High Risk	Moderate Risk	Low Risk	Very Low Risk
3.	Aluminum siding: well-known brand, $75 installed	Very High Risk	High Risk	Moderate Risk	Low Risk	Very Low Risk
4.	Hi-fi record album: unfamiliar brand, $1.98	Very High Risk	High Risk	Moderate Risk	Low Risk	Very Low Risk
5.	Fresh strawberries: 49¢ per quart	Very High Risk	High Risk	Moderate Risk	Low Risk	Very Low Risk

6.	Aspirin: unfamiliar brand, 17¢ per bottle of 100 tablets	Very High Risk	High Risk	Moderate Risk	Low Risk	Very Low Risk
7.	Metal lawn chair: $5.98	Very High Risk	High Risk	Moderate Risk	Low Risk	Very Low Risk
8.	Ready-made drapes: $15 per pair	Very High Risk	High Risk	Moderate Risk	Low Risk	Very Low Risk
9.	Monopoly game: $6.00	Very High Risk	High Risk	Moderate Risk	Low Risk	Very Low Risk
10.	Tulip bulbs: $1.50 per dozen	Very High Risk	High Risk	Moderate Risk	Low Risk	Very Low Risk
11.	Life insurance: unfamiliar company	Very High Risk	High Risk	Moderate Risk	Low Risk	Very Low Risk
12.	Children's shoes: well-known brand, $8.99 per pair	Very High Risk	High Risk	Moderate Risk	Low Risk	Very Low Risk
13.	Bourbon whiskey: well-known brand, $5.95 per bottle	Very High Risk	High Risk	Moderate Risk	Low Risk	Very Low Risk
14.	19-inch TV set: well-known brand, $99	Very High Risk	High Risk	Moderate Risk	Low Risk	Very Low Risk
15.	Vitamins: unfamiliar brand, $3.49 per bottle of 100	Very High Risk	High Risk	Moderate Risk	Low Risk	Very Low Risk
16.	Well-known mutual fund: $15 per share	Very High Risk	High Risk	Moderate Risk	Low Risk	Very Low Risk
17.	Double-bed sheet: well-known brand, $3.98	Very High Risk	High Risk	Moderate Risk	Low Risk	Very Low Risk
18.	Hospitalization insurance: pays $100 per week in cash while you are hospitalized, $7.00 per month	Very High Risk	High Risk	Moderate Risk	Low Risk	Very Low Risk
19.	Sewing machine: unfamiliar brand, $75	Very High Risk	High Risk	Moderate Risk	Low Risk	Very Low Risk
20.	Christmas cards: $2 per box of 25	Very High Risk	High Risk	Moderate Risk	Low Risk	Very Low Risk

CHAPTER 5

ATTITUDE FORMATION AND CHANGE

Armour Company: Attitude Change

In 1962, the Armour Company, one of the largest meat packers, placed a series of twelve advertisements in *Better Homes and Gardens* magazine. The objective was to increase subscriber knowledge and improve subscriber attitudes toward the company and its products. Representative advertisements appear in Figure 5–1.

Armour management was very much interested in the success of this campaign. Therefore, the research division of Meredith Publishing Company, the publisher of *Better Homes and Gardens,* was authorized to conduct a survey to measure the effects of the campaign on both awareness of the product and its benefits and the attitudes toward it.

Research Design

Researchers concluded that two possible research designs could be used, both of which had both advantages and disadvantages. The first alternative involved the use of two samples, one to be tested before exposure and the other to be tested after exposure, plus a nonexposed control group. The second alternative involved the use of the same group of subscribers subjected to both "before" and "after" measurements.

The second alternative was chosen for a number of reasons that are discussed following.

Limitations of the First Approach

A multiple-sample research design has two basic limitations:

1. It would require the use of a control group of nonsubscribers to the magazine. The problem is that such a control group could be exposed to the advertising through newsstand purchase or "pass-along" readership.

☆ ARMOUR
REPORTS
TO THE
CONSUMER
☆ Number 7 in a Series
☆ Reading Time 3 Minutes

NEVER UNDERESTIMATE THE POWER OF A HOT DOG

Most people regard the hot dog (or frankfurter if you like) as a not too nourishing but expedient snack or meal.

The truth about Armour Star Franks is that they are nourishing. In fact, they have complete protein, iron, calcium, niacin, thiamine and riboflavin - enough to provide a balance of nutrition equal to *their weight in sirloin steak.*

This is because Armour Star Franks are made of pure beef:

chuck, flank, round and other cuts - pure pork, including whole hams and bacon squares. These are flavorful, succulent meats.

Chopped fine, seasoned, smoked and cooked the Armour way, they become a delicious *meat* meal. An economy meat meal you need never feel guilty about serving your family, even though it is easy to prepare.

∞∞∞∞∞∞∞∞∞∞∞∞∞∞∞∞
*The meats that wear
the Armour Star are the meats
the butcher brings home.*
∞∞∞∞∞∞∞∞∞∞∞∞∞∞∞∞

ARMOUR STAR

WHY DOES ARMOUR STAR PORK SAUSAGE IN FT. WORTH TASTE DIFFERENT FROM THAT IN BOSTON?

Blame it on the weather if you like. Better yet, blame it on the climate. The warmer the climate the spicier the people like their sausage. The cooler the climate the less spicy they like it.

For example, cayenne pepper is used in the Southwest where it is a favorite, but not in New England where the citizens regard it too hot. Sage is not as popular in Kansas City as elsewhere, so they get more instead.

Armour makes every attempt to cater to different tastes.

In one way though, Armour Star Pork Sausage is the same. It is all made from Government inspected pork and ground fresh daily.

BRINGING UP BACON

The most desirable bacon, the bacon that is tender and has the flavor most people enjoy, should have a reasonable amount of fat. About ⅔. If the bacon has less fat than this, it is likely to be tough and stringy. More fat will make it oily and diminish flavor.

Ideal bacon comes from those young porkers that have been raised solely on hard grains. Only one in four pigs brought to market is of this kind, and Armour selects from them for Star Bacon.

If you are looking for a bacon that will fry crisp, yet be tender and flavorful, look for the Armour Star brand.

The bacon that's brought up right.

SOME CUTTING REMARKS ABOUT HAM

The thinner you slice ham, the better it will taste.

This is because in cutting, the knife releases delicious juices in the meat. The more slices, the more juices. And the thinner the slivers you cut, the greater the basting effect of these juices.

Start with a sharp knife and the canned ham that's juicy to begin with, the "Ham What Am" by Armour.

FIGURE 5–1A.   Examples of Armour advertisements.

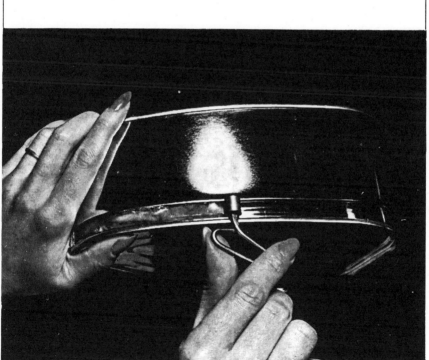

FIGURE 5–1B. Examples of Armour advertisements.

2. A potential hazard is represented by variations between the "before" and "after" samples.

Advantages of the Second Approach

Reinterview of the same group after a period of time offers these advantages:

1. The danger of variations between samples is removed. Hence, a control group is not required.

2. Even though the same sample is exposed to the "before" and "after" measurement, there is little possibility that the sample group will be conditioned or changed by the exposure:

   a. The type of purchase (meat products) is not in the nature of a major purchase decision.

   b. The study was presented to interviewees as one about meat packers in general, not Armour.

   c. The study made no reference to advertising of any sort. Even the interviewers were not aware of the sponsor of the study.

   d. The time interval of a year between the "before" and "after" measurements should have reduced respondents' memory effect to a minimum.

Survey Design

The field work for the study was handled over the telephone by the Research Division of Western Union. Interviews were made by specially trained operators. Detailed instructions for interviewing were provided by the Meredith research staff.

The sample consisted of names and addresses of *Better Homes and Gardens* subscribers. Names appear on IBM cards filed in trays with several trays to a cabinet. In turn, these cabinets are arranged by region, state, city, and postal zone. Fifty cabinets were chosen at random. Then, within each cabinet, the principal city was chosen. These vary in population, but each one selected was sufficiently large to have a Western Union office with a research interviewing staff. In each of three cases another city in the same area had to be substituted to meet this requirement. From each of these cities, fifty names of married women were chosen by random methods.

The first phase began in October, 1962. For the "before" study, telephone calls were made to the persons named in the list just described until seven interviews were completed in each city—a total of 350 interviews.

The "after" study was undertaken in November, 1963. Telephone calls were made to all of the 350 persons called previously. Some had moved and could not be traced. A few had changed their telephone numbers to unlisted ones. Other persons were out of the city and could not be reached, and a few refused to be interviewed for one reason or another. Calls were completed with 267 of the original sample of 350.

The questionnaire used appears in Exhibit 5-1. Each of the answers were compared item by item from the answers given in the earlier study, and any similarities or differences were noted.

Exhibit 5–1

The Questionnaire Used

This is the Survey Department of Western Union. We are conducting a survey for a national client. I'd like to ask you a few questions about some different *brands* of meat products—products like *bacon, hot dogs, canned hams, and the like.*

1. First of all, what *brands* of this kind of meat products do you know of? What others? (BE SURE TO PROBE)
2. Now, I'd like to know some of your preferences for brands of meat. Not just the brand you buy now, but the brand you would prefer to buy if all brands costed the same and all brands were available where you shop.
   a. If all brands were available to you, and all were priced just the same, what *brand* of *bacon* would you prefer to buy?
   b. If all brands were available to you, and all were priced just the same, what *brand* of *hot dogs (frankfurters)* would you prefer to buy?
   c. If all brands were available to you, and all were priced just the same, what *brand* of *canned hams* would you prefer to buy?
   d. If all brands were available to you, and all were priced just the same, what *brand* of *luncheon meats* would you prefer to buy?
   e. If all brands were available to you, and all were priced just the same, what *brand* of *pork sausage* would you prefer to buy?
3. Now, for a few items* I'd like to have you rate some meat packers as average, below average, or above average.

   Let's start with Armour. Compared to all the meat packers whose names you know, would you say Armour is *average, above average,* or *below average* for (pick up items on answer sheet)

   Note: If the respondent says she has never heard of Armour, or indicates she is unable to rate Armour, note this on the answer sheet and terminate the interview.

(Be sure the respondent understands what is being asked of her. If she doesn't, repeat the question.)

   *Quality of products, etc.

Survey Results

Three important analyses emerge from the data: (1) changes in awareness of the Armour brand, (2) changes in brand preference, and (3) changes in the Armour image.

Awareness

As the data in Table 5–1 indicate, there were some changes in awareness

Table 5–1

Changes in Awareness of the Armour Brand

	Percent Naming Brand		
	Without Probe	Added with Probe	Total
1962			
Brand X*	40.1	16.9	56.9
Armour	34.8	20.6	55.4
1963			
Armour	49.8	15.7	65.5
Brand X*	46.8	12.7	59.5

* Top brand awareness in 1962 and 1963.

of the Armour brand. Total awareness jumped approximately 10 percent, but of special significance is that awareness without probe, an indication of strength of awareness, increased from 34.8 percent in 1962 to 49.8 percent in 1963.

Brand Preference

Brand preference also increased from 1962 to 1963, although the gains were less dramatic. Luncheon meats especially showed a pronounced increase, although bacon and certain other products remained roughly the same (Table 5–2).

Table 5–2

Changes in Brand Preference for Armour

	Percent of Change		Comparative Industry Position	
	1962	1963	1962	1963
Armour luncheon meats	4.9	10.1	3	1
Armour pork sausage	3.4	6.4	3	1
Armour hot dogs	7.9	9.4	3	1
Armour canned hams	18.4	20.2	1	1
Armour bacon	12.7	12.7	2	2

Brand Image

Table 5–3 contains a detailed analysis of the ratings given the Armour Company along a number of attributes. Respondents were asked to rate the

Table 5–3

Changes in the Armour Image*

	Percent of Total Homemakers				
Attribute Rated	Higher Rating 1963	Highest Rating (both studies) †	Other Ratings (no change)	Lower Rating 1963	Net Higher Rating Minus Lower
Products consistently good	29.6	9.7	49.8	10.9	+18.7
Value for the money	27.7	4.9	57.3	10.1	+16.6
Modern	30.3	3.8	50.2	15.7	+14.6
Concerned with consumers	28.5	3.3	53.2	15.0	+13.5
Improving their products	28.1	3.7	52.1	16.1	+12.0
Friendly	22.4	1.1	65.6	10.9	+11.5
Helpful	26.6	2.6	55.5	15.3	+11.3
Quality of products	23.6	15.0	48.3	13.1	+10.5
Variety of products	24.7	6.8	52.8	15.7	+9.0
Convenient packaging	22.5	5.6	55.4	16.5	+6.0

* Order of rating: "above average," "average," "don't know," "below average."
† Rated above average in both the first (1962) and the second (1963) interview.

company on each dimension in terms of "above average," "average," "don't know," and "below average." Of special significance is the last column in the table labeled *net higher rating minus lower*. It provides a clearcut indication of changes from 1962 to 1963, and a consistent favorable pattern emerges. Product value and customer concern apparently were strongly communicated by the twelve advertisements, because changes along these dimensions are pronounced.

Conclusion

Management was pleased over the favorable outcome of the research project. It now remained for management to decide whether or not to introduce a similar campaign on a broader scale in a variety of other media.

Questions

1. What can be concluded from these research findings?

2. Should this campaign be continued and expanded in the future?

W. T. Grant Company (A): Attitudes toward
a Retail Chain

The W. T. Grant Company, a large retail chain, until 1964 confined all advertising efforts to local promotions sponsored by individual stores. In the meantime, however, Sears, Roebuck began to advertise nationally on a major scale, and it became apparent that annual expenditures of $5 million or more had succeeded in establishing the image of Sears as a modern, highly competitive retailer. Grant management considered the advisability of a similar campaign, and in 1965 a national advertising program was undertaken for the first time.

Company History[1]

The W. T. Grant Company was founded by William Thomas Grant about 1906 with the opening of a 25 cent variety store in Massachusetts. This operation was highly successful, and stores were very shortly opened in Waterbury, Connecticut, and Bridgeport, Connecticut. Expansion continued throughout New England and into the Middle Atlantic and near Middle Western states. By 1967 the company was operating well over a thousand store units.

Expansion was characterized by a steady trend upward in pricing limits: from 25 cents to $1, then to $5. At the present time there is no price limit on the goods sold, particularly in the larger units. Appliances, garden implements, and several other categories, for example, now run up into the hundreds of dollars.

Until the mid-thirties, the Grant chain was considered as variety stores. Since that time they have moved steadily (even more than Kresge and other of the variety chains) into more direct competition with Sears, Montgomery Ward, J. C. Penney, and, in some measure, the discount stores.

The postwar population shift and changes in buying habits stimulated a store location evaluation program in which the older downtown stores were being closed and larger stores were being opened in local and regional shopping centers. Grant was the first of the variety chains to make the move that later turned out to be a mixed blessing. Although they hedged the population shifts, many of the earlier shopping center units were too small and were incapable of adapting themselves to the mushrooming of merchandise lines and big ticket items.

In addition to trading up to bigger ticket items in these stores, the store

---

[1] For more background, see James F. Engel, Hugh G. Wales, and Martin R. Warshaw, *Promotional Strategy*. Homewood, Ill.: Richard D. Irwin, Inc. 1967, pp. 531–538.

attempted to increase credit sales. At the present time, about 24 percent of the sales are made on credit.

Retail Operation

Grant changed from a a small downtown store selling variety items to what it today describes as a "nationwide chain of general merchandise stores—not a chain of variety stores." Variety items now account for only 15 to 20 percent of total sales. Management has increasingly turned to private-brand items of high quality. The Bradford line of appliances provides an outstanding example of this new emphasis.

The trend has been toward rapid opening of new and modern stores. Today nearly 70 percent of Grant's stores are in shopping centers, and these stores account for 60 percent of total volume. Management predicts that the percentage of volume accounted for by suburban stores will continue to increase.

Marketing Objectives

The basic marketing objective that Grant hoped to achieve with its national campaign was an updating of the Grant image. Research indicated that an image lag existed between what Grant formerly was and what it is today. Therefore, corollary objectives designed to fulfill Grant's marketing need were developed.

1. Management felt that Grant must create an image of itself as a general merchandise store rather than as a variety store.

2. It should attempt to attract new customers and encourage current customers to shop more of the entire store.

3. It was deemed necessary to develop greater consumer awareness of Grant.

4. Sales of higher ticket items were to be pushed.

Consumer Research

It was recognized by Grant executives that the implementation of the basic image objective and its corollaries through the 1965 advertising campaign and those that would follow were circumscribed greatly by Grant's lack of knowledge concerning its markets and customers. Therefore, Grey Advertising, Inc., was asked to undertake the first of a series of annual studies planned for Grant to measure and evaluate changes in (1) the profile of the Grant shopper and (2) consumer attitudes toward Grant. The main objective of the first study was to establish a point of reference for future comparisons in these areas.

A secondary objective, however, was of more timely concern. That was to check the validity of three current hypotheses about Grant:

1. Is Grant perceived more as a variety store than as a general merchandise store?

2. Do shoppers tend to buy low ticket items at Grant and high ticket items elsewhere?

3. Is the Grant customer typically middle-class, young, married, with young children, and suburban?

Method and Sample

For the Grey study 1500 personal interviews were drawn from the agency's national probability sample of the total United States. One thousand of these interviews were conducted within the Grant trading area, while five hundred took place outside this area. The preponderance of interviews within the trading area was felt to be necessary in order to provide adequate representation of both Grant "A" and "B" stores (see following). From this sample certain interesting comparisons and contrasts between Grant areas and the total United States could be drawn. The areas, for instance, were similar in age distribution, size of household, and education. Differences were also apparent, however. There was a slightly higher proportion of families in the under $5000 a year income category in the total United States than in the Grant areas. Also, Grant areas were more predominant in the East and in metropolitan areas of one million or over than they were in rural locales.

Basic Definitions

Certain definitions necessary to the interpretation of data resulting from the Grey research are included at this point.

Primary shopper: The person in the household who does most of the shopping for that household.

Regular Grant shoppers: Shoppers in the Grant trading area who have patronized Grant at least once a month during the past year.

Occasional Grant shoppers: Shoppers in the Grant trading area who have patronized Grant at least once during the past year, but less frequently than once a month.

Non-Grant shoppers: Shoppers in the Grant trading area who have not patronized Grant during the past year.

Grant A stores: Grant stores with an annual sales volume of one million dollars or more.

Grant B stores: Grant stores with an annual sales volume of less than one million dollars.

Findings—Shopping Experience and Grant Customer Profile

A profile of Grant shoppers:

1. About two thirds of the shoppers living in the Grant area patronized Grant in the past year—28 percent were regular shoppers and 33 percent were occasional shoppers.

2. The incidences of shopping at Grant were about the same in Grant A and B store areas.

3. Grant regular shoppers tended to be patrons of long standing. Almost half of the regular shoppers first visited Grant before 1950.

4. In comparison with all shoppers living in the Grant area, the regular Grant shopper tended to be younger, to have a large family, to be middle-income, to have the household head be a skilled laborer, and to live in suburban areas and in the East.

Awareness of Grant and competition:

1. Grant was well-known among all shoppers living in both Grant A and B store areas.

2. Total awareness of Grant in the United States was slightly under that of Sears, Penney, and Woolworth, but far above J-Mart.

3. The best-known Grant services were "easy returns" and availability of charge accounts. Other Grant services—repair service and home delivery—were less known.

4. The use of charge accounts at Grant was not yet widespread. Even among regular Grant shoppers, only one in ten had a charge account at Grant.

Knowledge of store merchandise and related buying behavior

1. Knowledge of the lower-priced items of merchandise carried by Grant was extremely high among the shoppers living in the Grant area.

2. Shoppers were generally less knowledgeable about Grant's higher-priced merchandise, although Grant's regular shoppers showed greater awareness of these items than did occasional and non-Grant shoppers.

3. Grant was preferred to all other stores by its regular shoppers for shopping for the lowest-priced items. For the higher-priced items, even among Grant's regular shoppers, Grant received a low degree of store preference. Among competitive stores, for these items, Sears was the most preferred store, especially for hardline items.

4. Purchase of items in the past year followed the same pattern: low-priced items were most often bought at Grant by regular and occasional shoppers, but the incidence of purchase was very low for the higher-ticket merchandise.

5. Purchase of low-ticket items dominated the last shopping trip to Grant: more than half of Grant's regular customers spent less than five dollars on their last visit.

Findings—Consumer Attitudes toward Grant

In order to measure the attitudes of Grant customers, Grey chose to compile a comprehensive list of characteristics of the store, its merchandise and services, and its related consumer benefits. It then interviewed consumers to obtain evaluations of these attributes in the "ideal" general merchandise store and used a rating scale from "extremely desirable" to "not at all desirable."

Finally, through the process of factor analysis on an electronic computer, the minimum number of independent attitude factors necessary to enable consumers to evaluate a store completely were isolated and linked to the phrases that characterized them. The factors and phrases used to identify them follow.

1. *Confidence as related to*
    Sales people
        One can trust the sales people.
        The sales people are friendly; they don't act as if they're doing you a favor.
    Value
        The store always gives you value for your money.
        It takes returns any time you're unsatisfied. No fuss.
        It represents its merchandise values honestly.
    Quality
        It carries good quality merchandise.
    Advertising
        One can believe what it tells you in its advertising.
    Style
        One can find every color and size in stock.
        Its merchandise styling is well accepted.
    Price
        It has a number of different price lines for each item of merchandise.
        It will always match competition on a price.

2. *Shopping convenience*
        It is easy to get around the store and is a convenient place to shop in.

3. *Feeling of belonging*
        One gets a feeling of belonging when shopping there.

4. *Children's wear*
        It is a good store to buy teenage clothing.
        It is a good store to buy children's and infant's clothing, such as coats and hats, shoes, shirts and pants, and dresses and suits.

5. *Women's articles*
        It is a good store to buy women's dresses and coats.

It is a good place to buy women's articles, such as bras and foundation garments.
It is a good store to buy inexpensive cosmetics and beauty aids like nail polish, bobby pins, hand lotion, and hair nets.

6. *Men's wear*
It is a good store to buy men's slacks and jackets.
It is a good place to buy men's work clothes.
It is a good place to buy men's apparel, such as underwear, socks, and shirts.

7. *Hardlines*
It is a good store to buy small electrical appliances such as toasters, irons, mixers.

8. *Family store*
One can find just about everything you want for every member of the family.

Results—Attitudes of Grant Shoppers toward Grant

The overall image of Grant in its trading area was good: one out of three shoppers gave Grant a highly favorable rating ("excellent" or "very good"). One in ten shoppers gave Grant an "excellent" rating.

Grant's regular shoppers had an even better opinion. One in five rated Grant "excellent" on an overall basis.

Grant's image on specific attitude factors showed the greatest strengths to be in shopping, convenience and women's articles (specifically, women's cosmetics and beauty aids).

Consumers' attitudes toward Grant with respect to confidence in the store showed that Grant is rated the highest on sales people and value and the lowest on style and price.

Regular shoppers rated Grant more favorably than did occasional and non-Grant shoppers on all specific attitude factors.

Conclusions

Although the main research objective of this first study was to establish a point of reference for future comparison, it was possible nevertheless to check the validity of three hypotheses regarding Grant, that is, (1) that the Grant shopper is typically young, middle-class, suburban, married, with children; (2) that the shoppers tend to buy low-ticket items at Grant and high-ticket items elsewhere; and (3) that Grant is viewed more as a variety store than as a general merchandise and apparel store. *The conclusion of this first study was that these three hypotheses were entirely valid.*

With a clearer profile of the Grant customer in mind, management could now turn to the task of devising advertising and marketing strategies designed to implement the basic marketing objectives of that company.

Questions

1. What strengths and weaknesses were discovered through this research?

2. What are the implications for marketing strategy?

W. T. Grant Company (B): Attitude Change through Advertising

As is pointed out in the preceding case, the W. T. Grant Company, a large variety store chain, started national advertising in 1964. The overall objective was to change the image of the firm from that of a "higher-priced Wool-worth's" to one that corresponds with the vastly changed merchandising policies of the company. Grey Advertising, Inc. designed a campaign to change the image; and, consistent with agency policy, a series of copy research studies was undertaken. This case includes the results of a research analysis of the effectiveness of the "Girlswear-Easter" advertisement. The data included here come from the research report prepared for Grant's management in March, 1966, by the Grey marketing and research department.

Method

This test of the Grant Girlswear-Easter advertisement was conducted in the following cities: New Haven, Connecticut; Portland, Maine; St. Paul, Minnesota; Buffalo, New York; and Long Beach, California. A total of 236 females were interviewed from February 7 to 18, 1966.

Research Design

The test ad was inserted in a magazine so that respondents were exposed to it in a normal reading situation. The magazine was *Today,* a fictitious publication created by Grey. *Today* contained editorial material, the test ad, and other advertising and was printed in the format of an actual consumer magazine. To the reader, *Today* appeared to be a new publication of general interest.

Interviewers visited qualified respondents in their homes on the pretext of getting opinions of the new magazine. A copy of the magazine was left with each respondent. No mention of any advertising was made at the time of placement. On the following day telephone interviews were conducted with respondents who qualified as readers, that is, those women who had read the magazine the day before and could prove readership by identifying at least one of the editorial features.

The first part of the interview was designed to determine whether readers remembered the Grant ad. If they could not voluntarily identify it, a product prompt was given ("Do you remember seeing an ad for a retail store?"). If necessary, a brand prompt also was used ("Do you remember seeing an ad for W. T. Grant?"). At this point respondents who claimed to have seen the ad were asked what they remembered about it.

The second part of the interview dealt with respondents' attitudes toward Grant and the general merchandise store at which they shopped most frequently. Using a six-point scale, they rated both stores on a series of phrases representing product benefits and attributes.

A different group of respondents—who were familiar with Grant but who had not been exposed to the ad—were also questioned about their attitudes toward the firm. Using the same six-point scale, they rated the brand on the same series of phrases as the exposed group.

Analysis

The effectiveness of an ad was measured in these areas: impact (which includes attention, interest, comprehension, and impact) and attitudes.

Impact Measurement

Impact was measured as in the following manner:

1. *Attention and interest:* determined by the related recall score, or the percent of total readers who can give: (1) aided or unaided identification of the brand and (2) some playback of the ad (either some specific detail or a general correct description).

2. *Comprehension and impact:* based upon the communication of the copy recall objectives. These are the major buying incentives and supporting product information the ad is designed to convey.

3. *Sample size:* includes all those who were exposed to the ad. In this case the number was 236 respondents.

Attitude Measurement

The Grey attitude shift scoring technique evaluates the changes in attitudes (toward a retail store) after exposure to a piece of advertising. Attitude shift measurement is contingent on prior development of a series of phrases that represent the key dimensions or factors (product benefits and attributes) underlying consumers' total evaluation of retail stores. For Grant, these key dimensions and the phrases which represent them were derived from a factor analytic study of consumers' attitudes toward general merchandise stores ("W. T. Grant Company, [A]").

To analyze the changes in attitudes associated with exposure to test advertising, two techniques are used; both define attitude shift but differ in the
method of analysis. The standard technique is usage weight score analysis;
the other method, presently used only on an experimental basis, is called
difference score analysis. Both are based on ratings obtained using a six-point
scale labeled from "excellent" to "poor." A description of each method
follows.

Usage Weight Score Analysis

The usage weight score analysis evaluates changes in attitudes toward
Grant based on ratings that have been weighted to reflect the probabilities
of becoming a shopper at the store. Grey has found, through experimentation,
that this technique yields an extremely sensitive and reliable measure.

For both the exposed and unexposed groups, usage weighted ratings on key
evaluative dimensions (factors) are combined into a calculated overall rating
of the store. By using a regression equation built on the unexposed group, it is
possible to predict how the exposed group would have rated had they not
been exposed to the test advertising. The difference between this predicted
score and the actual rating score (obtained from the exposed group) con-
stitutes a measure of attitude shift. The evaluative factors used appear in
Table 5–4.

Use of an unexposed-exposed research design makes it necessary to match
the two samples as closely as possible to insure that the effects of advertising
alone are being measured, not the effects of extraneous variables. Usage
weight scoring allows a matching of samples on a large number of important
variables. This matching is accomplished by using the regression equation.

Difference Score Analysis

Difference score analysis, like usage weight score analysis, also consists of
determining whether or not a calculated overall rating increases or decreases
as a function of exposure to a piece of advertising. This evaluation is based,
however, on the difference between ratings of Grant and ratings of its competition. Using the six-point scale, respondents rate both Grant and the
general merchandise store at which they shop most frequently.

Difference score analysis embodies all the sensitivity of usage weight scoring
and adds the advantage of measuring in a competitive environment. The latter
makes it possible to register decreases in favorableness toward competitive
stores as improvement in attitudes toward Grant.

Respondents' usage-weighted ratings of the general merchandise store at
which they shop most frequently are subtracted from their usage-weighted
ratings of Grant's. The resultant difference scores are then combined to
produce a calculated overall rating for each group (exposed and unexposed).

Table 5–4

Phrases Representing the Individual Factors

General Rating

On an overall basis.
My personal opinion of the store.

Confidence

It takes returns anytime you're unsatisfied without any fuss.
You can trust its sales people.
It always gives you value for your money.
It represents its merchandise values honestly.
It carries good quality merchandise.
You can believe what it tells you in its advertising.

Shopping Convenience

It is a convenient place to shop in.

Men's Wear

It's a good store to buy men's wear, such as work clothes, jackets, shirts, and underwear.

Women's Wear and Accessories

It's a good store to buy things for women, such as dresses, coats, undergarments, or cosmetics and beauty aids.

Feeling of Belonging

It gives people a feeling of belonging when shopping there.

Children's Wear

It's a good store to buy teenage and children's clothing.

Hardlines

It's a good store to buy small electrical appliances, such as toasters, irons, and mixers.

Family Store

You can find just about anything you want for every member of the family.

Customer Associations

Most of its customers are women.
Its customers are mostly young adults.

As in usage weight score analysis, by using a regression equation built on the unexposed group, it is possible to predict a pre-exposure rating for the group exposed to the test advertising. The difference between this predicted score and the actual score obtained from the exposed group provides a measure of attitude shift.

Conclusions and Recommendations

Research Conclusions

The Girlswear-Easter ad can be considered extremely effective. Its performance in the impact area was excellent. Even more important is the fact that, with only one exposure, the ad improved readers' attitudes toward Grant.

Attitude Shift

Readers became more favorable in their opinion of Grant after exposure to the ad. Their attitudes toward the store improved, not only on an absolute basis but also in relation to competitive stores as well.

Usage weight score analysis (the absolute measure) showed an overall attitude shift of $+1.4$, while difference score analysis (the ratings of Grant versus competition) indicated a shift of $+1.9$. Both shifts were statistically significant at better than the .05 confidence level.

Impact

The ad succeeded in attracting the attention of a large number of readers and in conveying to them the idea that "real values on children's clothes and other merchandise are available at Grant."

The Girlswear-Easter ad received a related recall score of 86 percent, the highest score obtained by any ad tested via the same method in *Today* magazine. Scores for sixteen single-page ads tested in the female issue of

Table 5–5

Related Recall Data

	Total %
Related recall score	*86*
Mentioning some aspect of the benefit: value	72*
Savings (total mentions)	(67)
On children's clothes	60
On family clothes	13
On other merchandise (general)	47
Childs outfit a bargain at $12	20
Outfit costs $12	5
Quality (total mentions)	(42)
Attractive outfit and fashions	21
Good quality and well-made merchandise	18
Up-to-date and modern styles	10

* Includes 36 percent who mentioned both savings and quality.

Today have ranged from 27 percent to 58 percent, with an average of 40 percent. Experience with double spreads is more limited, because only two have been tested, which scored 50 percent and 57 percent, respectively. The data on related recall appear in Table 5–5.

Grant's primary buying incentive, the "value" story, was well communicated. Over three quarters of those recalling the ad mentioned either one or both aspects of the idea: "You save at Grant" and "Grant offers quality merchandise." Most people connected the savings idea with children's clothes, although a sizeable number generalized these economies to include other merchandise. References to quality were somewhat less numerous but indicated good communication of the idea.

Table 5–6

Effectiveness of the Execution Devices

	Total %
Mentioning the execution devices	*84*
Girl in outfit (total mentions)	(78)
Yellow/yellow and white outfit	65
Portions of outfit or accessories	52
Old-fashioned picture (total mentions)	(27)
Girl and mother	16
General	11
Layout design/girl in diagonal	21

As the data in Table 5–6 indicate, the execution devices employed in the ad generally received good mention; almost everyone in the related recall group talked about at least one element. More than three quarters remembered the girl in her outfit, and most identified the outfit by its color.
The old-fashioned picture of the mother and daughter was less memorable; about a third of the related recall people mentioned it, some of them describing it specifically, some in general terms.

Diagnostic Implications

The level of success achieved by the Girlswear-Easter ad in both the Impact and Attitude areas appears to have resulted from a particularly effective combination of all the elements rather than from any one element. All of the visual components of the ad, its bright color, unique layout, the cute model, and the old-fashioned picture, seem to have acted to arrest the reader's eye and draw it to the sales message. The quality aura of the execution and the savings idea, stated explicitly and supported by the price, would seem to be the primary factors responsible for both the excellent communication of the value benefit and the improvement of attitudes toward Grant.

Questions

1. Critically evaluate the methodology used to assess attitude change. Are you willing to accept the conclusions as they are given?

2. What implications emerge for marketing planning?

Eastern Air Lines: Attitude Change

In 1953, Eastern Air Lines had just completed its twenty-sixth straight profitable year, showing a net gain of nearly $15 million. By 1963, that profit had turned into a loss of nearly $20 million. Almost as bad as the loss situation was the image projected to the public. It had become so bad that in 1963 WHEAL ("We Hate Eastern Air Lines") clubs had been informally organized by businessmen who traveled on Eastern Air Lines.

Background

In 1963, the airline was in a crisis position with its very survival threatened. Drastic action was indicated to instigate a turn-around in the company's profit and image situation. A new, young President of Eastern Air Lines was appointed in 1963. His assessment of the company's situation follows.

> . . . ominous signs had begun to appear. Beginning in the mid-1950's, the gates were opened to let competition into Eastern's profitable green and once-protected pastures. In the early 1960's, many airlines, caught in a new jet tide of overcapacity and competition, were navigating in red ink. This time Eastern was engulfed.
>
> Sharing all the industry's ills, Eastern also suffered from a complexity of ailments of its own. The bitter jurisdictional dispute between pilots and flight engineers over which union was to control the third seat in jet cockpits finally brought the airline to the ground completely in mid-1962. Its short-range route structure, designed for piston power, had only one 2,000 mile run for the long-range jets—the once-a-day trip between New York and Mexico City. On its major revenue-producing routes, where passengers were demanding turbine speeds, Eastern was outgunned four to one by competitors' jets. Ironically, the early DC-8's Eastern cancelled were claimed by its arch competitor in the South. Its principal competitor in the East leased Boeing 707's to move in on the Florida run. Swiftly,

now, its rivals took the lead in a new race in which Eastern was to fall farther and farther behind.

There was an even more crippling blow to come. The long cherished hope for a Southern Transcontinental route was shattered when both of these lucrative routes went to its two chief competitors. All of Eastern's rivals, now, were coast-to-coast carriers. Cut off from the West, it had access to but one of the seven largest domestic air markets. In other areas, where it once had the reign of productive skies, it now had to contend with from three to six jet-powered competitors.

To get more jets, a purchase-and-lease-back plan financed 15 Boeing 720's. These would bring jet capacity to scarcely half strength. Even before it had financing completed, Eastern joined with United Air Lines to launch Boeing's production of the medium-range 727. An order was placed for 40 of these jets with the three engines mounted in the rear. But this help was more than two years away and time was running out.

Born in these desperate days was the concept of the Air Shuttle, every-hour-on-the-hour schedules between New York and both Boston and Washington with no reservations required. To back its promise of a guaranteed seat, Eastern has, to date, operated sixteen flights for that single passenger who was at the gate when the regular flight was filled.

The public service record of the Air Shuttle, now operated with prop-jet Electras, and soon to have pure jets, is unequalled anywhere. In its four years it has carried nearly 10 million passengers. It has flown as many as 160 extra sections to carry as many as 21,000 passengers in a single 24 hours. Although there is a wide variety of other services offered by Eastern and seven other airlines between New York and Boston, and the eight between New York and Washington, eight out of ten who travel by air between these three cities choose the Air Shuttle.

But in 1963, Eastern needed more than the Air Shuttle's help. After a plan to merge with American Airlines was debated with competitors before the Civil Aeronautics Board for 17 months, the application was withdrawn. By then, Eastern was fast running out of flying speed. Of eleven trunk carriers, it ranked tenth in on-time performance. Less than one fourth the seats it could offer were in jets. Personnel were cut back, standards of service sagged. Once loyal passengers deserted in droves. It had taken 18 long, hard years to build up an earned surplus of $63 million. In four short years, it had lost that much—and more. But something more important than dollars—the morale that had made Eastern great—was being lost.[2]

Floyd Hall, when he was appointed as president, brought to Eastern a new

[2] Floyd D. Hall, "Sunrise at Eastern" (Address to the Newcomer Society, December 2, 1965), pp. 20–23.

management team that set about to accomplish drastic changes in the attitudes held toward Eastern by air travelers. These changes were of two basic types:

1. Drastic "mechanical" improvements related to functional problems such as improved reservation services, less lost baggage, increased jet fleet, improved on-time service and maintenance.

2. An image improvement program.

The mechanical improvements were accomplished first and involved a major expenditure of capital funds. These changes are not described here but they were drastic and were designed to give the consumer the aspects of flying service that he considered most important. In part, these were based upon an extensive report on air travel prepared by the Bureau of Advertising of the American Newspaper Publishers Association[3] and in part on Eastern's own consumer research activities. Among other things, this report indicated that the business travel market is dominated by "heavy users." It was found that 20 percent of the business flyers account for 68 percent of all business trips. Among nonbusiness flyers, however, the market is dominated by persons who fly only once a year. Only 20 percent of business flyers in this sample also fly for nonbusiness purposes and only 30 percent of nonbusiness flyers also fly for business. This study indicated that time saved and time lost were the most important component of attitudes toward flying. Comfort is also an important component, even more among business flyers than nonbusiness flyers.

Attitude Research

At the same time that Eastern was striving to correct the mechanical problems, they were planning for an image campaign that would be implemented as soon as the mechanical problems were corrected. The head of the Consumer Research Department, Doreen Wilkins, expressed the importance of image for Eastern:

> We are a service industry, that is, we exist to serve the public. If the public likes us, we prosper, individually and collectively. If the public doesn't like us, either individually or collectively, we are nothing. It is basic to our very existence, then, that we stand well with the people we serve. Our image, in short, is what our public thinks of us, and we care because our livelihood depends on it.

To help accomplish the image objectives of Eastern, a new advertising agency was engaged. This agency, Young and Rubicam, assisted in conducting an attitude study of air travelers in New York, Chicago, and Wash-

[3] This report is described in the case "Evaluating Alternative Modes of Travel," in Chapter 11 of this book.

ington, D.C., primary service areas of Eastern. In measuring Eastern's image, Young and Rubicam was concerned with such subjects as the extent to which Eastern's name is known, the extent to which it is preferred over competition, whether its routes and destinations are associated with its name, and whether its name signifies such desirable attributes as punctuality, courtesy, dependability, safety, modernity, and progressiveness.

The results of the Young study are described below. In general, the following conclusions were reached:

1. American Air Lines is first in the mind among New York and Washington air travelers. Eastern is second.

2. United Air Lines is first in the mind in Chicago with American second, and Eastern third.

3. In all cities in the sample, the proportion of air travelers liking Eastern is considerably less than the proportion actually flying on the airline.

The advertising agency also cross-tabulated the studies to determine attitudes toward Eastern by particular market segments and in reference to specific components of the image. Among all flyers in New York, Eastern was rated higher or lower than competitive airlines on the items shown in Table 5–7.

Table 5–7

Comparison of Eastern with Other Air Lines by All Flyers

Relatively Higher	Relatively Lower
Flight availability	Safety record
Extensive route	On-time performance
Baggage, reservations	Efficient hostesses
Help with children	Good food in flight
Comfortable terminal facilities	In-flight information

Among business flyers in the survey, the agency found that Eastern rated lower than competitive airlines on many aspects of service and higher on only a few (Table 5–8).

The agency also determined attitudes toward Eastern by the most frequent flyers of all types. Eastern compared with competitive airlines in the way shown in Table 5–9.

Finally, the agency provided ratings by nonbusiness flyers about Eastern compared with competitive airlines and found that nonbusiness flyers rated more items relatively higher than competitive airlines than did business flyers (Table 5–10).

On the basis of these surveys, researchers at Eastern concluded that consumers—especially business flyers—were flying Eastern out of necessity. That

Table 5–8

Comparison of Eastern with Other Air Lines by Business Flyers

Relatively Higher	Relatively Lower
Flight availability	Flight crew competency
Reservations	Safety record
Help with children	Efficient maintenance
	On-time performance
	Neat, clean plane and seats
	Newest equipment
	Comfortable seating
	Baggage handling
	Pre-flight information
	Helpful ground personnel
	Efficient hostesses
	Good food in flight
	In-flight information

Table 5–9

Comparison of Eastern with other Air Lines
by Most Frequent Flyers

Relatively Higher	Relatively Lower
Flight availability	Safety record
Baggage/reservations	On-time performance
Help with children	Newest equipment
Comfortable terminal facilities	Comfortable seating
Efficient hostesses	Pre-flight information
	Food in flight
	In-flight information

Table 5–10

Comparison of Eastern with other Air Lines
by Nonbusiness Flyers

Relatively Higher	Relatively Lower
Passenger safety	On-time performance
Flight availability	Friendly ground personnel
Extensive routes	
Speed	
Baggage/reservations	
Helpful with children	
Comfortable terminal facilities	

is, Eastern had frequent, convenient flights; and consumers desired this, so they flew Eastern. Given a choice, however, they would have flown other airlines, and, on competitive flights, they were doing exactly this. Basically, attitudes toward Eastern were unfavorable.

Attitude Change Program

As soon as Eastern was reasonably along its way to correcting the mechanical problems (through additions to the jet fleet, computerized reservations and flight control, and employee morale-training programs), full-scale attention was given to changing the image of Eastern.

The attitude change program was carefully planned and programed. Clearcut objectives for customer satisfaction, leadership, and corporate citizenship

Table 5–11

Eastern Air Lines' Strategic Plan "In Support of Customer Satisfaction"

Purpose	Strategy

To provide an air transportation service that meets the needs of the traveling and shipping public	*Safety*
	    Promote safety consciousness
	
	Convenience
	    Adequate capacity
	    Timely schedules
	    Ticketing procedures/reservations
	    Sales office locations
	    Check-in procedures
	    Terminal design
	    Baggage handling
	
	Reliability
	    On-time performance
	    Schedule reliability
	
	Comfort
	    Passenger cabin facilities
	    Food service
	    Seating design and arrangement
	    Other in-flight services
	
	Economy
	    Lowest possible rates consistent with sound economics
	
	Sincerity
	    Improve employee attitudes and responsiveness to customer needs

Table 5–12

Eastern Air Lines' Strategic Plan "Return to Leadership"

Purpose	Strategy
To return Eastern Air Lines to a position of leadership in the U.S. air carrier industry	*Management reorganization* Development of organization plan Staffing of the new organization *Establishment of modern management concepts* An objectives program Performance standards Management training program Management appraisal program Effective compensation program Management succession plan *Development of a new corporate image* Remodelling of facilities Refurbishing of flight equipment A new corporate symbol A coordinated styling plan

were formulated to coordinate with the image program. The specifics of these programs (called the strategic plan) are presented in Tables 5–11 to 5–13.

One of the first items in the image program was the design of a new Eastern symbol. The industrial design firm of Lippincott and Margolis was commissioned to present a bold new symbol intended to connote speed, modernity, and the jet age. A modern color scheme of Ionosphere and Caribbean blue was designed for the exterior of all Eastern planes, both the new jets and the older prop fleet. Inside the planes, stewardesses and pilots appeared in smart, tailored uniforms created by a famous designer. A new musical theme was created and sung by the sultry "Girl from Ipanema."

Great attention was given the food service. The most famous restaurants in the cities that Eastern served were employed to prepare meals for first class service. The food service became truly gourmet meals with fine wines, appetizers, and desserts as a regular part of each meal. Color photographs of these meals were featured in Eastern advertising. Also featured were photographs of the most attractive of the Eastern stewardesses in their new uniforms, the new corporate symbol, and pictures of the fine china and crystal that became a standard part of first-class service. Similar improvements were brought about in coach service with careful attention to color and style coordination.

A new advertising program, particularly advanced for the airline industry was developed by Y and R, and every city served by Eastern was billed as

Table 5–13

Eastern Air Lines' Strategic Plan "In Support of Good Corporate Citizenship"

Purpose	Strategy
To be a good corporate citizen	*Improved employee satisfactions*
	Compensation
	Recognition
	Pride
	Environment
	Stability
	Challenge
	Advancement
	Labor peace
	Improved relationships with regulatory agencies
	Personal introductions
	Understanding of each other's view points
	Improved relationships with the financial community
	Development of timely and factual reports
	Development of cooperative attitudes
	Improved relationships with society as a whole
	Participation in federal, state and community affairs
	Acceptance of opportunities to tell "Eastern Air Lines' Story"

"home city." Training films stressing the new look at Eastern were developed and presented to employees. These emphasized the marketing concept or total customer satisfaction, and ticket agents and other support personnel were trained to understand the importance of giving customers complete satisfaction, even when they were traveling on an airline other than Eastern. Agents tried to become especially helpful at finding alternative flights to cities that Eastern did not serve and for making reservations on other airlines when Eastern flights were full.

Effects of Program

Eastern began receiving phone calls, letters, and personal comments relating satisfaction with the "new" Eastern. Flights began filling up, and

Eastern set new boarding records for several months consecutively. In cities where Eastern had not been very strong, special attention was given. In Atlanta, which was the home city for Delta Airlines, Eastern came slowly from behind to surpass Delta in total boardings. Passengers and revenues rose sharply.

Profits for the company began to rise rapidly and by 1965 had reached a level of $29,671,000. Mr. Hall was pleased as were the other officers and stockholders of the corporation. It appeared that consumers had changed from a set of unfavorable attitudes to a set of favorable attitudes.

Questions

1. What factors account for the dramatic change in attitudes that appears to have occurred toward Eastern Air Lines?

2. What research should Eastern take now to evaluate the success of the program?

3. In this case, attitude research was apparently precipated by a crisis situation. Design a research program for an airline that would have indicated the nature of their problems before it reached the crisis stage.

4. Assume one of the competitive airlines such as United or National has lost customers to Eastern because of this program. What steps would you recommend to the competitor to regain lost customers?

PART III

SOCIAL INFLUENCES IN MARKETING

CHAPTER 6

CULTURAL INFLUENCE

Schneiderman's Funeral Homes: Cultural Influences on Marketing Policies

Schneiderman's Funeral Homes was established in 1908 in Westerville, Ohio by Fred C. Schneiderman. The firm was successful and became well-known throughout the central Ohio area. In 1926, Fred Schneiderman and his son Timothy decided to move the business to nearby Columbus, a much larger city than Westerville. They retained the Westerville branch when they constructed a new facility in downtown Columbus. Both facilities were operated successfully, and in the latter part of the 1950s another branch was located in the far western area of Columbus, an area that had experienced rapid growth in population during World War II and that now contained a high proportion of middle-aged persons. In 1964, another branch was opened in Upper Arlington, an affluent suburb on the northwest side of Columbus. The firm had been owned and operated by the Schneiderman family throughout this period. In 1968 it was operated by two Schneiderman brothers, grandsons of the founder of the firm.

Throughout this period, changes had occurred in the funeral service field. While Schneiderman emphasized personal service, the firm had emerged as a sizeable operation with gross receipts estimated to be well in excess of $1 million, and it was the largest funeral firm in Columbus. Many changes appeared to be occurring in the funeral field, however, and in 1968 the firm was considering some basic changes in its pricing policy and promotion strategy. The Schneiderman brothers felt that it was important to assess the cultural influences on these decisions.

Background on the Funeral Industry

A brief look at the development of the funeral service in the United States will set the stage for comment upon current conditions.

When society itself was relatively simple, the family and friends of the deceased were usually able to handle the details of the funeral. The local cabinet-maker was called upon to build a coffin, and, because there were no means of preservation available, burial took place in the village churchyard as soon after death as was practicable.

As towns and villages grew into cities, it became less desirable to use urban churchyards as burial grounds. Cemeteries came to be placed at the out-skirts of town and to be separated from particular religious denominations. The necessity for transportation from church or home to cemetery brought the livery man into the scene.

The Civil War, a cause of many social and technical innovations, was responsible as well for a major change in funeral practices. In order to return the remains of war casualties to their homes, the practice of embalming was revived and improved. Embalming is believed to have been introduced by ancient Egyptians who believed that the body would be reinhabited by the departed spirit at some future time. In modern times, of course, embalming is seen primarily as a health measure.

These changes gave rise to a new pattern of funeral service in the late nineteenth and early twentieth centuries. Funeral establishments emerged, in cities at first but spreading eventually to all parts of the country, offering embalming, transportation, and burial services, combined with arrangements for wakes in the home or in facilities provided by the undertaker.

Over time, the concept of disposal of the dead was replaced by a concept of service to the living. The "undertaker" became the "mortician" or the "funeral director," and funeral services in general took on a more professional tone. Increased understanding of the psychological implications of the funeral service led to efforts to "degloom" the funeral and to transform it into a genuinely helpful experience for the bereaved. The funeral director has come to assume the role of aiding and counseling the survivors in appropriate ways in addition to handling the essential details of preparation and burial of the remains.

The funeral service has, however, retained its close religious association. At the 1959 convention of the National Funeral Directors Association, Robert L. Fulton presented the findings of a study of the clergy's attitudes toward modern funeral practices. On the whole, clergymen expressed satisfaction with current arrangements, although Protestant ministers were somewhat dissatisfied as compared with Catholic priests. This is perhaps due to the different views of the funeral taken by the two groups. The Catholic priest, for example, sees the funeral as a service of prayer for the salvation of the soul and as a ceremony honoring the memory of the deceased. It also serves to remind the living to prepare for death and judgment. Protestant ministers, on the other hand, view the funeral in terms of the peace and understanding that it can bring to the survivors. To this group, the purpose of the funeral is to comfort the bereaved and to emphasize the hope of a future life. Interpretations aside, however, the religious aspects of funerals continue to play an important role in modern funeral practices.

Beginning in the early 1960s, a great deal of criticism of the funeral industry arose, exemplified by Jessica Mitford's caustic book *The American Way of Death*. This widely read work advanced the thesis that the American funeral is an extravagant and excessively sentimental affair designed to extract maximum profit for the funeral industry. Although some of the public criticism was deserved, a great deal of the furor was based on erroneous or misleading information that tended to be more sensational than accurate.

The funeral industry in general reacted to the criticism in a somewhat passive manner, failing to mount a systematic, unified rebuttal of critical charges. Such defenses as were offered were limited, sporadic, and sometimes conflicting.

Research Design

Because Schneiderman was the largest funeral firm in central Ohio, the Schneiderman brothers felt that they should take the lead in assisting the image of local funeral directors and innovating policies that would lead to improved community relations. In addition, they were interested in expanding the market share and profitability of their firm, and they hoped to uncover ways in which this could be done. Accordingly they engaged a marketing research group to perform a funeral attitude study in the Columbus metropolitan area.

Sample

The study consisted of a probability sample of 310 consumers in Franklin County (in which Columbus and suburbs were located). The respondents were selected from the Columbus telephone book with strict adherence to selection using a random number table. The first adult answering the phone was interviewed. More than 98 percent of all persons who were reached on the phone agreed to the interview and completed all questions.

Technique

Respondents were called on the phone by trained interviewers and asked a "warm-up" question. The questions progressed to more sensitive areas including attitudes toward funeral services offered by local funeral firms, attitudes toward cremation, opinions on governmental regulation of the funeral industry, estimates of perceived prices of funerals, and demographic information including income and religion.

Results

The results of several important areas are presented here. These data relate to pricing, product offering, promotion, and general attitudes.

Pricing

One of the views held by some spokesmen within the funeral industry is that an important reason for negative attitudes toward funeral directors is the pricing system used. Prices of Schneiderman, like all other funeral firms in the area, were established on the basis of the casket. When a person came to Schneiderman to arrange a funeral he was taken into the display room and allowed to look at a number of caskets. Each casket was marked with a price ranging from $240 to $4800. There were available special-order caskets of high quality hardwood at prices in excess of $1000 and there were metal and cloth-covered wood caskets considerably less than $1000.

Consumers were told that the price quoted included the casket, the complete services of the funeral director, and the use of the firm's facilities. Schneiderman provided excellent facilities that included an air-conditioned, carpeted chapel and a fourteen-thousand dollar Cadillac hearse and a limousine. The funeral director assigned to a particular "case" attempted to provide every reasonable service a surviving family might need. This included arranging for an organist and clergyman (although separate fees were charged by these personnel), arranging flowers, embalming, lining up cars, directing the service and many auxiliary services such as providing special equipment, and meeting relatives at the airport. Some firms provided a list of the services typically offered to a family, and the list often included over a hundred items. Once a price had been selected for the casket, however, all other services were included without additional fees with the exception of the advances paid to clergymen, cemeteries, and others.

Table 6–1 presents the findings of what consumers in the Columbus market believed funeral prices to be. The question was worded in the following

Table 6–1

Price Estimate of Metropolitan Columbus Ohio Area Consumers
of an Average Funeral, June 1967

Item	Number
Average estimate	$1140
Highest estimate	$9999
Lowest estimate	$ 100
SAMPLE SIZE	310

Table 6–2

Distribution of Actual Funeral Prices

Price	Percent
$ 0–199	19
200–499	14
500–799	35
800–999	21
$1000 and over	11

manner: "Funerals cost different prices, but what would you estimate to be the average price paid for a complete funeral? This would include the casket and service, but not the cemetery lot or a vault."

Table 6–2 presents the actual prices charged by Schneiderman's during the period of their last thousand funerals. It is readily apparent that a sizeable discrepancy exists between what Schneiderman is charging (and their prices are close to those of other major firms in the area) and what consumers perceive prices to be. Consumers believe Schneiderman is charging more than they actually are.

One hypothesis is that the reason for the incorrect perception of funeral prices and also for negative attitudes toward funeral prices is that people believe funeral directors are charging primarily for a casket and believe that the price is too high. Actually, the casket is a minor part of the funeral price; consumers are paying primarily for services and facilities, and caskets are only a minor part. Schneiderman's cost records indicate that the breakdown of actual costs for components of the service provided is as follows: casket, 10 percent; funeral home and facilities, 38 percent; professional services, 31 percent; profit, 12 percent. The perceptions of consumers about the components of funeral prices are somewhat different. Table 6–3 shows how respondents to the survey perceive the breakdown to be.

Table 6–3

Estimates of Percent of Total Funeral Price by Component*

Component	Average Estimate	Highest Estimate	Lowest Estimate
Casket	42.15%	99.99%	3%
Physical facilities	16.19	65	0
Professional services	17.69	75	0
Profit	23.79	80	0

* The respondents made replies in dollars based on a $1000 funeral price and this was converted to a percent in order to compare it to actual cost data.

Cremation

Schneiderman had no cremation facilities in their present locations. In one of the locations that Schneiderman contemplated opening the next year, however, the possibility existed of adding a crematory. This area of the city was a suburban area on the north side of Columbus containing a high proportion of university and other professional families. This was an area with a fairly high concentration of "liberal" religions such as Unitarians and oriental religions. About one fourth of this area was Catholic, however.

Cremation facilities could be added for about twelve-thousand dollars, which Schneiderman did not consider a heavy expense. Cremations typically had lower prices, however, because consumers tend to purchase less expensive caskets for cremations than for earth interment. The possibility existed that the presence of a crematory on the premises might lead to a higher proportion of cremations than would occur if it were not so convenient. On the other hand, the largest competitor operated a branch funeral home in this area and had a crematory in it. Cremation facilities were available from most of the major cemeteries in Columbus for a fee of $100 which was charged to the consumer in addition to the normal funeral fees. Table 6–4 shows, by religious groupings, the numbers of respondents favoring cremation.

Table 6–4

Cremation

Religion	Total	Favor	Against	Favoring, %
None stated	16	5	11	31.2
Catholic	59	5	54	8.4
Nonlisted Protestant	42	3	39	7.1
Baptist/Disciples	36	7	29	19.4
Lutheran	25	3	22	12.0
Methodist	53	8	45	15.0
Presbyterian	24	4	20	16.6
Episcopal	15	5	10	33.3
Judaism	5	1	4	20.0
Other	35	9	26	25.7
TOTAL	310	50	260	

Choice of Firm

Funeral firms traditionally have advertised very little. Exceptions to this statement exist in southern California, Missouri, and certain other areas of the nation. Primarily, however, aggressive promotion of any type has either been prohibited by the state licensing boards that control funeral service or has been considered culturally unacceptable because of the nature of the service. Funeral firms and the organizations that associate them with one another have opposed advertising or any type of aggressive marketing strategy on the grounds that funeral directing is a profession and that it is therefore unethical to advertise, other than to use a "card" type of placement in yearbooks, obituary pages, and the like.

Most of the funeral firms in Columbus did some advertising, and Schneiderman had a fairly substantial commitment to billboards and newspaper advertising. Both media involved institution types of ads for Schneiderman. Schneiderman did offer to pay civic and religious groups one dollar a member who toured the facilities of Schneiderman. Schneiderman felt that this was a successful public relations approach to overcoming the lack of knowledge most people had about what went on inside a funeral home and also that this familiarized potential customers with the outstanding facilities maintained by Schneiderman.

Traditionally, funeral firms had attracted business on the basis of long-established friendships or service relationships. Increasingly, the management of Schneiderman believed, this would change because of the increasing mobility of consumers. As they moved between various areas of the city and between cities more rapidly, Schneiderman felt, there would be less knowledge of funeral firms through personal sources of information with a corresponding need for increasing advertising on the part of funeral firms that wished to obtain new service relationships. Respondents in the survey were asked what local funeral firm they would recommend if a friend asked them for advice.

Table 6–5

Respondents' Reasons for Recommending a Particular Funeral Firm

Reasons	Number	% of Sample	% Giving a Reason
Experience with firm	105	33.87	46.88
Personal			
Friend			
Viewed persons there			
Reputation of firm	45	14.52	20.09
Friend of director's family			
or employee	30	9.68	13.39
Location of firm	18	5.81	8.04
Advertising	10	3.23	4.46
Personality of funeral director	7	2.25	3.13
Reasonableness of price	5	1.61	2.23
Religious preference of funeral			
director	4	1.29	1.78
Subtotal	224	72.26	100.00
No reason given	86	27.74	0
TOTAL	310	100.00	100.00

(Schneiderman received the highest number of recommendations, management was glad to find.) The respondents recommending a firm were asked to indicate the reason for their recommendation, and Table 6–5 presents the results of this question.

Service Satisfaction

Respondents were asked to rate the service of funeral firms and the ratings were cross-classified by the customers who had recent (last three years) experience with funeral arrangements and those who had no recent experience. Table 6–6 displays the finding that consumers who have actual

Table 6–6

Rating of the Services of a Funeral Director as a Function of Experience

Rating	With Experience	No Experience	Total
Excellent	45	50	95
Good	15	144	159
Fair	1	46	47
Poor	–	5	5
Bad	2	1	3

experience tend to be even more favorably impressed with the service of funeral firms than those who have no experience. Using a Chi-square analysis, there was less than one chance in one hundred of this relationship occurring by chance.

Another measure of satisfaction with the funeral industry, perhaps, was secured by asking respondents if they thought the government ought to regulate the funeral industry. The responses were: opposed, 190; in favor, 111; no opinion, 9. This shows that about 36 percent of respondents favored some type of regulation.

Managerial Decisions

The data were analyzed by the Schneiderman brothers, and they attempted to decide what actions should be taken in their marketing strategy.

One item given a high priority was to change their pricing method. The practice of pricing on the basis of the casket had developed in the nineteenth century because of the fact that casket builders (cabinet-makers, furniture manufacturers) had been the first funeral directors. After funeral directors began offering additional services such as embalming, they priced their funerals by making the funeral at three times the cost of the casket.

This was one time for the cost, one time for services rendered, and one time for profit. This system had been largely retained, although the multiple was now between three and five.

Schneiderman was considering switching to a "professional" (also called functional) pricing system that had been tried successfully by some funeral firms in other cities and states. Basically this meant that the funeral director decided on an amount to charge for his professional services (perhaps four hundred dollars), an amount to charge for his facilities (probably average overhead) and then sold caskets as merchandise with mark-ups appropriate for the turnover and risk costs in similar fields. This had the effect of raising prices for a complete funeral at the low end (where the majority of funerals were purchased) but lowering prices at the high end. However, Schneiderman management felt that substantially more high quality caskets would be sold under the professional system to people who now were forced to purchase less than what they really wanted because of the very high price for caskets in the upper ranges. They were quite unsure, however, about the acceptance of an innovation such as this in a field that had been marked by cultural stability.

Schneiderman also desired to make a decision immediately about whether they should budget for a crematory in their new location.

Overall, Schneiderman felt that more aggressive advertising strategy was warranted as the population became more mobile. However, they were unsure whether the data in this study justified switching to a more aggressive advertising policy. They did desire, however, a complete review of the promotion they should be doing both to gain a specific advantage for their firm and to promote in general the image of the funeral industry.

Questions

1. Should "professional" pricing approach be adopted?
2. Should a crematory be included in their new branch location?
3. What kind of a promotion program should Schneiderman be undertaking?
4. What additional research should Schneiderman schedule in order to be ready for the stiff competition that they anticipate in the future?

Mead Johnson (B): Cultural Influences on the Use of Diet Foods

Metrecal, a liquid diet drink, was originally introduced and promoted using a "medical" approach.[1] In 1964, Mead Johnson switched the Metrecal

---

[1] For the background to this case, the reader should carefully review the case "Mead Johnson (A)" in Chapter 1 of this book.

advertising account from Kenyon and Eckhardt to Ogilvy, Benson, and Mather. The medical approach had begun to lose its sales effectiveness, and it had become apparent that Mead Johnson needed a new market approach if it was to continue to "live off the fat of the land."

Metrecal-for-Lunch Bunch

The Ogilvy revised approach emphasized a "join the Metrecal-for-lunch bunch" theme. The campaign developed by Ogilvy was sometimes referred to as a "Pepsi generation" campaign. It displayed attractive people in elegant dinner settings, active scuba diving scenes, or other situations made possible because the people consumed Metrecal at lunch.

The new advertising approach for Metrecal dropped the medical approach completely and stressed the desirability of Metrecal as a food. Typical copy (see Figure 6–1) referred to Metrecal in "a glorious lineup of 19 wickedly rich, creamy milkshake flavors." Some ads displayed people having fun while others primarily described the product. In addition to the advertising for the liquid Metrecal, which constituted the majority of sales, Metrecal also began advertising in 1964 of their line of diet solid foods. Figure 6–2 presents an introductory ad. Copy in other advertisements suggested, "Today you can fill up on hearty meals like chunky chicken with noodles, vegetables and gravy twice a day and still lose two to four pounds the very first week."[2]

Metrecal Customer

In 1964, Mead Johnson completed a survey of their customers to determine which groups within the American society were among its best customers. Although the methodology of this study was not reported, the following groups were defined as the primary customers of Metrecal.

1.   Married women

2.   Metropolitan area residents

3.   Middle to upper social classes

4.   Above average income within social class

5.   Higher than average education

6.   More likely than the general public to be a new product innovator

7.   A spender as opposed to a saver

8.   Age group thirty-five to forty-nine

   [2] "Mead Johnson Tests New Line of Diet Dinner," *Advertising Age*, **35** (February 24, 1964), pp. 1 ff.

FIGURE 6–1. New advertising approach stressing the desirability of Metrecal as a food.

New Metrecal® Real Meals

Hot, hearty, and delicious—a complete, nutritious meal with only 225 calories.
Vegetables & Beef...Tuna & Noodles...Rice & Chicken...Chili Beans 'n Beef

FIGURE 6–2. Ad typical of Metrecal's campaigns for its line of solid foods.

Mead Johnson realized that its primary market was presently achieved in the middle-age groups, but it believed that the young adults (age fifteen to thirty-five) represented significant markets that had not been adequately reached. Taking into consideration their research on market characteristics, Mead Johnson began extensive advertising on television as well as in print media. By 1967 they were maintaining a significant television schedule.

Types of Dieters

Besides the problem of determining which groups in a culture were most likely to be dieters, an additional problem exists of determining *how* these groups diet. Some prefer "crash" diets of unusual foods. Some prefer carefully regulated, extended diets of normal foods. Some prefer very rapid but carefully controlled diets for short periods of time. Others prefer to supplement their regular eating patterns with low-calorie foods that help *prevent* weight gains. Another group appears to like to diet even though they are not overweight. It is obvious that the eating habits that belong to various cultural groups will influence who will buy Metrecal and how the product will be consumed after it is purchased.

A number of psychologists and anthropologists have studied the problem of dieting and, more broadly, the topic of eating in a culture. From various reports issued by these researchers, a summary statement was compiled describing cultural influences on dieting. Some of the salient points of this summary are described in the following pages.

Medical Dieters

Medical dieters are those advised by a physician or other medical sources to reduce weight. They tend to be concentrated among middle and higher income groups and frequently have high cholesterol levels. The combination of overweight and fatty deposits in the blood are believed by medical experts to lead to heart trouble and other ailments.

It was to this group that Metrecal originally directed its appeals. The evidence continued to accumulate that excess weight leads to reduced life expectancy, gastric disturbances, decreased vitality, and other serious problems. The current marketing program of Metrecal, however, makes no reference to obesity in its advertising.

Deprivational Dieters

One group of dieters are those who find diets psychologically desirable. These persons, some psychologists believe, punish themselves with a diet either to prevent *perceived* indulgnce or to atone for it. These persons include those who have feelings of guilt about many subjects and purge these feelings by depriving themselves of something (in this case, food). This practice has a striking similarity to the religious practice of fasting.

Attention Attracters

Another influence on some dieters is the desire to attract attention through dieting. These people may not actually be obese. Usually, this group is found among high school or college students or other young people, who are susceptible to the acceptance of fads and other types of conformity. Reference group influences are very strong among this group, and the norms of the group include slim figures and, often, fad diets. Diets occasionally include eating only cottage cheese, only bananas, only boiled eggs and toast, or some other unique arrangement of foods. It is not unusual for a fad diet to become accepted throughout a housing group or some other reference group.

This type of influence is classified as an attention-getting technique for two reasons. It attracts attention to the fact that the participant is upholding the norms of the reference group. It also can be a device for the person who is not overweight or who is just slightly overweight to attract the attention of parents or friends. A subconscious desire may exist for the dieter to be reassured by other persons that her appearance is good and that no need exists for her to be dieting.

Social Interaction Dieters

When people interact with one another, there is a natural interest in appearance of the body and of the clothing that adorns it that results in interest in dieting. There is no innate reason why obese persons should be considered unattractive and in some cultures, where scarcity of food is normal, obesity is considered a sign of prosperity and very desirable. In modern Western culture, however, the slender figure is considered appropriate for the person concerned with social interaction.

The reasons for preferring the slender figure are not clear. Perhaps they include the modern bathing suits, stretch pants, or the "lean, executive look," or they may be manifestations of some deeper cultural trait. Whatever the explanation, a slender personal appearance is sufficiently exalted that corporations demand executives keep trim, military organizations order their officers to a low-calorie mess, secretarial schools offer grooming courses that feature special diets, and women enter reducing plans several weeks before attending special social events. The cultural norm is a slender figure, and acceptance of this norm often means dieting.

Cultural Patterns for Eating

Socialization and acculturation determine what people like to eat, when they eat, and how they eat. Thus, if Metrecal is to be accepted in a culture, consideration must be given to how and when this product will be eaten and which groups will find the least "cultural shock" in accepting it.

The average-sized, moderately active man needs about three thousand calories a day. He can obtain these in many ways. Some of the choices available are thirty-four pounds of turnips, thirty pounds of carrots, twenty-four ounces of sugar, two hamburgers with french fries, or two large milkshakes. Assuming that necessary vitamins and minerals can be suppiled in supplemental form, man could choose any one of these selections. However, people learn that certain product choices fit into the norms of the culture surrounding them and consequently learn to prefer certain items over others.

With only a few exceptions, the desirability of a food in the Western culture is inversely proportional to its calorie count. Thus, when confronted with the choice of pecan pie (five hundred calories) or a portion of green beans (thirty calories), most persons will prefer the former. Why this relationship should be true is in itself an intriguing question.

This relationship appears to hold true on a cross-cultural basis. In many cultures, however, the ability to satisfy the craving for high-calorie inputs is not sufficient for the supply, with the result that the typical consumer subsidies on significantly less than three thousand calories each day. For Americans, however, the acquired taste for calories is easily satisfied for the majority of people with the result that extra calories store up as fat. This creates the problem of the overweight American consumer.

Typically, the reason for accumulating excess flesh arises from fairly normal (as defined by the culture) eating patterns. People maintain weight just eating a normal diet. As the standard of living in a culture improves, however, more "desirable" foods become common and activity decreases. Both of these trends occur for the entire society and are accentuated in the life cycle of particular families and individuals. Dieting, therefore, for the majority of consumers is a departure from preferred forms of eating. To reverse the weight-building eating patterns, the consumer must unlearn what he has learned over a period of years or must find a way (such as substituting synthetic sweeteners or other low-calorie "normal" foods) for continuing existing patterns without weight buildup.

Cultural patterns are known empirically to greatly affect the market for low-calorie liquid foods. For example, between Thanksgiving and New Year, use of liquid diet food drops markedly. During this time, cultural patterns apparently are so strong that consumers are unwilling to forego the pleasures and pressures involved in consumption of high-calorie foods. During this period, stimulating sales of liquid diet foods is so difficult that advertising efforts are abandoned until after the period is over.

Marketing Strategy

Mead Johnson in 1968 was faced with the problem of determining how Metrecal should be used in the American culture. The company had long ago abandoned the medical motivation for using the product and had switched to the food approach. One major competitor, Pet Milk Company, promoted Sego as "great fun to lose pounds by" and a way to "put sweet adventure in your diet." One study indicated that about two thirds of Sego customers were not overweight but used the product to *prevent* overweight.

The major competitor, however, on the basis of number of meal replacement servings sold (as differentiated from dollars) was the Carnation Company with its product called Slender. This was a mix-with-milk powder and was increasing rapidly in popularity along with Metrecal's own Metrecal Shake and Pet's Sego Instant. The mix-with-milk products had doubled in popularity in a year and in 1968 constituted approximately half of all servings sold.

The dynamics of the dietary food market suggested that some very basic questions faced the management of Mead Johnson in developing marketing policies for Metrecal:

Questions

1. Should the product be promoted as a total diet or as a supplementary diet aid?

2. Could promotion strategy be successful in getting consumers to accept this product as desirable and tasty in its own right rather than an inferior substitute to what they really preferred to eat?

3. How should the product be promoted to gain cultural acceptance? What times of the day should it be used? How should it be served? What combinations of food should be recommended with it? Could it be promoted as a food to be served in social situations?

4. At present, primary promotion effort is directed to the liquid diet program. Should this be shifted to the solid food products?

5. Should Mead Johnson consider expanding the Metrecal product line? If so, what new types of diet products should be considered?

6. What research is needed by Mead Johnson and their advertising agency to determine what *uses* of Metrecal products will be accepted by the consuming public?

Miss Ritz Cosmetics (A):   Promoting a Contest in a University Subculture

The Miss Ritz line of cosmetics was introduced in 1966 to appeal directly to young women in the eighteen to twenty-eight age group. The cosmetics were of high quality and moderately priced, but in 1967 they had not achieved much awareness from young women. To date the Miss Ritz line has been distributed in almost the same manner as the older, established Charles of the Ritz cosmetics line from the parent company. The company is experimenting, however, with new marketing approaches for the Miss Ritz line.

Background

Charles of the Ritz, Inc., is a well-established, high quality cosmetics firm. The company developed a makeup and treatment line in the 1920s and has continued over the years to innovate makeup ideas and add new products developed by its laboratory. The line is comprised of makeup, treatment, and fragrance items.

Present Market

Because of its price, quality, and distribution channels, the Charles of the Ritz line appeals mostly to an age group of women well above college age. The company realizes that they are currently getting a very small portion of the youth market's cosmetic dollar.

Distribution Channels

Charles of the Ritz holds a substantial position in the better department and specialty stores, and its line is sold exclusively in those stores. An attempt is made, usually successfully, to have Ritz products displayed in the finest department store of each major city.

Each salesclerk in the Ritz display counter is specially trained in New York by makeup experts so they can sell the exact item and shade that a woman needs. Powder is custom blended to match the complexion of each customer. This custom blending process has been tried by other companies, but Charles of the Ritz believes none has been able to successfully duplicate it. The blended powder and the Revenescence Cream and Liquid comprises a good portion of the sales for Charles of the Ritz.

It is because of the custom blending process that Ritz management believes they cannot sell through drugstores or other stores college women might find more convenient than a department store. Ritz is aware college women are prone to purchase cosmetics in campus drugstores or bookstores, but Ritz believes that the line can have sufficient appeal to cause a substantial market segment to go to a department store to buy the Miss Ritz line.

The company is fairly rigid in its belief that it should not change its present distribution channels and cites the following reasons for this belief:

1. The fashion image of the better department store has a proven appeal to the college market in the allied fields of ready-to-wear and fashion accessories.

2. The marketing strength of the parent company has derived largely from its prestige image maintained through highly select and limited distribution.

3. There are reasons to believe that an important segment of the college and

career girl market is ready for a similar fashion and sophisticated appeal in skin care and makeup, which a too ready expansion of channels could preclude for Miss Ritz.

Problem

In order to achieve a significant market position among the college and career market, the Miss Ritz line was developed. It was custom designed and formulated as was the Charles of the Ritz line and contained some of the makeup items that the Charles of the Ritz line contained. This was an additional reason causing management to believe the present distribution plan should be retained for the new Miss Ritz line. If the Miss Ritz line did not contain the exact shade of a product, it could be supplemented by the Charles of the Ritz line. The Miss Ritz line was marketed at lower prices than the Charles of the Ritz line in deference to the limited budgets of college women.

Ritz management undertook a series of "Sleeping Beauty" contests to achieve awareness of their products. These contests were held on major university campuses and had the following objectives:

1. To achieve awareness of the Miss Ritz line of cosmetics among young women.

2. To differentiate Miss Ritz cosmetics from the regular Charles of the Ritz lines that management believed college women associated with women of their mother's age group.

3. To achieve sufficient interest in beauty and custom blending of cosmetics that young women would be willing to travel to a department store for cosmetic assistance rather than to buy at a campus bookstore or drugstore.

Sleeping Beauty Contest

At the end of April, 1967, Ritz management selected The Ohio State University as a test center for the Sleeping Beauty contest, to serve as a proving ground for further contests at other universities. Besides promoting its product, the company wished to generate research information about student buying patterns and prejudices and to make an analysis of channels of distribution.

A questionnaire was also distributed to two thousand women students, but it was prepared and distributed too late to be useful in developing the contest. It did serve, however, to make some women students aware of the Miss Ritz name and perhaps to make them more interested in the Sleeping Beauty contest. A sample of Miss Ritz lipstick was given to each student who completed the questionnaire.

The operation of the contest was the responsibility of a marketing student who was called "Miss Ritz on Campus." An attractive female marketing student, well known among sorority leaders, had been previously selected for this position. Another female marketing student assisted her in making arrangements, and a marketing professor was available for consultation on problems that might arise. Both students were awarded scholarships for assuming responsibility for the promotion.

Prizes

The grand prize for the girl selected as the Sleeping Beauty at Ohio State was a one-day, all-expenses-paid trip to New York. In New York, the girl was to receive a complete beauty treatment and makeup at the Vidal Sasson–Charles of the Ritz salon. There were nine other prizes for the runners-up consisting of Charles of the Ritz merchandise.

Beauty Seminars

During the week of May 15, Ritz conducted beauty seminars in sorority houses and campus dormitories. The purpose of these seminars was twofold. First, they served to attract the interest of young women in the contest. Second, they provided the actual vehicle for entering the contest. At each seminar a makeup expert from New York gave each girl who wanted to enter the contest a personal makeup. Following the makeup, a Polaroid color photograph was taken of the girl, and this photograph was part of the basis for judging the contest.

Beauty Clinics

During the week following beauty seminars at the housing units, a series of beauty clinics was held downtown at the major store in the city, Lazarus department store. At these clinics girls who attended the beauty seminars were invited for more detailed instruction in how to make up themselves. The women entering the contest were required to make up themselves at one of the clinics and have another Polaroid color photograph made.

Entry to the contest was on the basis of both photographs plus a hundred-word statement describing how she used makeup to maximize her best features and minimize her poorer ones.

Fashion Show

The conclusion of the contest was on June 3 (also the final week of the quarter at the university) and featured a fashion show at Lazarus. The fashion show also featured a lecture by the makeup expert and an announcement of the winners. The show was held in the executive dining room with refreshments supplied by Lazarus. Arrangements were made to accommodate 150 guests at this fashion show.

Results

The contest had some beneficial results but in general fell far below what Ritz management expected. Planning for the contest had not begun until late in the spring, and the week of the beauty seminars coincided with initiation week for the sororities. The central housing association of the domitories approved the contest and seminars in ample time, but no one realized that approval was required from each individual dormitory association until it was too late for some of the domitories to be included in the seminars. In spite of these difficulties, attendance was high at the seminars. Ritz management had the makeup expert, two Miss Ritz girls (traveling representatives) from New York, and Miss Ritz on Campus at the beauty seminars, and these representatives reported that response to the seminar was generally good.

The attendance at the beauty clinics held downtown was extremely low. One clinic was cancelled because only three girls were there. Very few who attended the beauty seminars on campus came again to the beauty clinic at the department store, and very few of those who attended entered the contest. On the day before the fashion show, only eight women out of the 38,000 students at Ohio State had submitted pictures and statements. Because there were more prizes than entrants, all who entered the contest received a prize of Ritz merchandise, and the remaining two prizes were awarded to two girls by drawing names from those who had attended the clinics. Although facilities were available for 150 girls, only 15 actually attended the final lecture and fashion show.

Ritz management was concerned about whether the program should be repeated on other campuses and desired to analyze the difficulties. The student selected for the promotion at Ohio State was capable, well known, and worked very hard at making the program a success. A considerable amount of money was spent on advertising in the student newspaper and on posters for the dormitories.

The possibility existed that one of the goals for the contest—awareness of the Miss Ritz line—had been achieved, even though response to the contest was low. As an aid in evaluation, about one hundred students were intensively interviewed after the contest was underway. This was a convenience sample, but it represented a cross-section of female students. About 10 percent were aware of the contest, and typical comments follow.

> I did read about the contest in the *Lantern* [the campus newspaper]. It doesn't seem like that great a deal.
>
> I saw the on-campus demonstrations and didn't like them. They were too extreme, too thick for every-day wear. The basic concepts of what to wear is probably right, but they put too much on; too gooey. They go too much on one particular trend and make all of the girls up the same way.

I've heard a lot about Miss Ritz on campus lately but not in any of the stores.

I had never heard of Miss Ritz cosmetics until recently when I saw the information about the Sleeping Beauty contest in my dorm.

I had never heard of Miss Ritz until recently when a demonstration was held in our sorority house. My views about the demonstration were somewhat negative because the makeup they used on a couple of my sorority sisters did not look good.

I sat in on a demonstration of the Miss Ritz line of cosmetics and was not impressed. The demonstrator used the makeup too extensively on the models. The point that it is exclusively for the college girl is a gimmick.

Questions

1. On the basis of the Ohio State experience, should Ritz expand the Sleeping Beauty contest to other campuses?

2. What characteristics of the university subculture probably affected the operation of this promotion?

3. If you believe this program was not satisfactory, develop an alternative plan for achieving the stated objectives of the Sleeping Beauty promotion.

CHAPTER 7

SOCIAL CLASS

Griffith Insurance Agency: Social Class Influences on Planning

Avery Griffith, C.L.U., successfully sold life insurance as a broker for several medium-sized life insurance companies for seven years. He worked out of a small office in Evanston, Illinois, and served a broad range of clients. In the past three years, since he had become a Chartered Life Underwriter, the nature of his clients had begun to shift until high income, high social class persons constituted the largest share of his business. Accordingly, he was more involved in complicated trust and business insurance than ever before.

Griffith decided that he could continue to expand his volume only if he were to start an independent agency in which other salesmen and service personnel could assist in the work. This would allow Griffith to assign salesmen to develop smaller accounts and would permit him to concentrate on the large accounts himself. After investigating several locations for a new insurance agency, Griffith selected Lake Forest, Illinois. He contracted for 1750 square feet of space in Market Square, a fashionable shopping center located in the center of Lake Forest. Market Square was a prestige area containing small shops and offices and a Marshall Field department store. The Marshall Field branch was very small and was rumored to exist primarily for the personal convenience of the Field family who lived in Lake Forest and of their close friends of similar status. Actually, however, the store was a favorite shopping place for many Lake Forest residents.

Griffith Insurance Agency

Griffith decided that the new agency would incorporate some advanced concepts into its design. First, it would offer a complete insurance planning service as well as numerous additional financial services. Second, it would be designed to appeal to the specific social classes who dominated the area.

Staff

The complete insurance service was achieved by Griffith's personal qualifications in life insurance. He was a broker for several companies, having available a wide variety of policies. In addition, his C.L.U. training had prepared him for assisting with trust arrangements, and he had continued to study special tax arrangements and other problems involved in the insurance programs of high-income clients. As his vice president, Griffith employed Alan Williams, a Chartered Property and Casualty Underwriter (C.P.C.U.) who, after graduating from college, had worked two years in the underwriting department of a major casualty insurance company. Williams had also begun study toward achieving the C.L.U. in addition to the C.P.C.U. In addition to salary, Griffith gave Williams a 10 percent interest in the business with an option to purchase a greater interest in the future. Williams' duties, in addition to relieving Griffith in his absence, included supervision of the office, research on new developments in the insurance field (especially tax situations), and responsibility for educating Griffith and the rest of the selling staff in technical aspects of insurance and new developments. Williams was confident of his technical knowledge about insurance but was somewhat apprehensive about how his background would integrate with the clients in Lake Forest. Williams' father was a textile factory worker in Tennessee. His father had been an active union steward, and Williams had developed a political philosophy that usually was classified as "ultraliberal." He had attended a large state university in the South. Initially, two salesmen were employed. Edwin P. Corkin was a middle-aged salesman for a local heating and air-conditioning firm. Corkin was slightly grayed and distinguished looking. He was active in civic organizations and respected by many people. The other salesman employed by Griffith was the son of a socially prominent family in Lake Forest, Jonathon T. McCormick. McCormick was twenty-two and had just been graduated from Yale University with a major in history. Academically, McCormick had just barely made it through Yale, but he was personable, and he viewed the insurance field as an attractive career. Griffith intended to hire additional salesmen as growth of the agency warranted such action.

Services

The Griffith Insurance Agency (GIA) planned to provide complete planning and service for all types of insurance. Griffith was considering using the slogan "The North Shore's most comprehensive insurance and financial planning service" to express the agency's desire to service totally the needs of its clients. Griffith and Williams had developed several innovations to accomplish their objectives. One of these was a computerized service that took basic information about the client and, with additional inputs from the agent, projected the total insurance needs of a client with costs at varying ages, projected payout options, and identification of other financial programs that would be needed. The agency planned to lease a remote station for eighty dollars a month and use the time-sharing facilities of a major computer company so that the projections could be developed within a matter of minutes.

Griffith planned to add additional services in the future. First, he intended to sell mutual funds. One of the insurance companies for which the agency was a broker, owned a mutual fund, but Griffith also considered selling other mutuals. He also expected to form a separate firm to handle common stocks, Griffith Investment Brokers (GIB), which would be housed in the same building and employ the same salesmen as GIA. The actual transactions would be handled by a large brokerage firm that would in return provide technical information to Griffith. There was considerable question about the legality of this arrangement at the present time, but Griffith expected this to be cleared up in the near future. This would permit Griffith to become a truly complete financial counseling service.

Social Class Target

Griffith felt that most insurance agencies were directed toward the middle-class markets but that the highest potential existed among the upper social classes. In the Lake Forest market, he felt this was especially true. Consequently, Griffith wanted to develop the image of the agency as one that served the upper social classes in a particularly effective way. He believed that this should affect the services offered, the personnel employed, the advertising, and the physical surroundings of his agency. In arriving at decisions about the marketing mix of the agency, Griffith had given considerable attention to the type of market in which he would be located.

Market

GIA was located in Lake Forest but served both the village of Lake Forest and the adjacent village of Lake Bluff. These were two of the more than 250 suburbs that surrounded Chicago and were part of the North Shore, a series of high-income suburbs extending along Lake Michigan from Evanston to Waukegan. The 1960 Census showed Lake Forest to have a population of about 10,000 and Lake Bluff of about 2,500. Both of these had increased substantially since the 1960 Census. Highland Park, the first suburb south of Lake Forest, had a population in excess of 25,000. Griffith expected that he might draw some clients from Highland Park and from Libertyville, west of

Lake Bluff, but doubted that he would draw from North Chicago, which was much more oriented toward Waukegan.

Status Rankings

Both Lake Forest and Lake Bluff were areas of very high income. Griffith verified that by studying Census data and various issues of the *Sales Management Annual Survey of Buying Power*. Griffith felt that income was not as reliable an indicator of social class as other measures.

Chicago's Community Renewal Program published a ranking of the most desirable communities on a socioeconomic basis using the criteria of percent of professional workers, average years of schooling, and family income. In a recent year, Lake Bluff ranked third out of the 250 Chicago suburbs in both education and percent of professional workers and ranked twentieth in family income. On a weighted scale, this provided a ranking of fourth in the Chicago area of the most desirable "status" suburbs. Lake Forest had higher family income but a considerably lower rating on education and was fifty-third in percent of professional workers. This gave Lake Forest a status level of thirty-second in the Chicago area.

Griffith felt that these data were not completely revealing because he felt Lake Forest to be among the highest status level in the Chicago area and higher by a considerable margin than Lake Bluff. Griffith felt that the true situation was at deviance with the situation indicated by the data because Lake Forest was a much more heterogeneous community. He cited the discrepancy between average income and percent of professional workers as evidence of this. He felt that family income in Lake Forest was a leptokurtic, positively skewed distribution with some families maintaining extremely high incomes—in the millions. Also, there were significant numbers of domestics, clerks, school teachers, and service workers in Lake Forest serving the high-income, invested-wealth families. In Lake Bluff, however, the distribution of all three variables was apparently fairly platykurtic with lesser skewness.

Griffith studied the real estate situation as further evidence of the social class situation in the two communities. He found considerable heterogeneity of living areas and housing types in Lake Forest and relative homogeneity in Lake Bluff. Most houses in Lake Bluff were selling between $35,000 and $45,000, with few deviations. In Lake Forest, however, there was a great deal of deviation, and sales prices ranged from $12,000 to $200,000 and more. The building permits issued in Lake Forest indicated that the average cost of new homes was $51,000, with much less deviation than among the older homes of the community.

Griffith felt that Lake Forest was one of the highest status suburbs in Chicago, but he was somewhat troubled by the fact that other suburbs ranked higher in status from a statistical perspective. As a further check on his beliefs, Griffith examined each issue of the Chicago *Daily News* for the past two years. The "Social Chatter" page contained feature articles about parties and other social events among the upper-uppers of the Chicago Metropolitan area. Griffith found that Lake Forest was mentioned as the site of parties or as the home of persons attending important social events almost every day and mentioned more than any other suburb of Chicago.

Promotional Strategy

For the first few months of operation GIA was based in a temporary office in Highland Park. Because Griffith used this period for establishing contacts, orientation of sales force, and planning, there had been no advertising or other promotional effort and GIA was generally unknown among Lake Forest–Lake Bluff residents, although the personnel were known as individuals by quite a few people. Griffith was now ready to move into the new quarters in Market Square and wanted to prepare a promotion program to announce the opening, to create awareness of the agency, and to establish its image.

Griffith stated that the policy for all promotion would be to connote that this agency was designed for the upper-middle, lower-upper, and upper-upper social classes. He hoped not only to reach this market directly but also to serve other social classes in the area. Griffith believed that if the image were attractive to upper classes, the middle classes would also want to do business with the agency. If he designed it as a middle-class agency, however, he believed that the upper classes would not be attracted to the agency. To accomplish this goal, an introductory promotion program was prepared.

Campaign

Griffith believed that most insurance agencies had very few distinctive features to advertise or to talk about in their advertising. He decided, therefore, to establish a series of seminars to run for ten weeks on personal financial planning that would be of interest to local residents. Griffith doubted that attendance would be high, but he felt that it would cause readership of his advertising, create awareness of the agency, inform the public of GIA's intention to be a complete financial service, and provide a vehicle for establishing an image for the agency.

Griffith arranged for a series of ten distinguished seminars on timely financial topics of interest to high-income people. The speakers included a well-known tax consultant speaking on the Keogh bill, a Northwestern University professor presenting his short-term forecast of economic conditions with an analysis of how this affected personal investment decisions, a University of Chicago professor presenting an analysis of the relative performance of the major mutual funds, an investment broker forecasting the stock market, a representative of the Continental Illinois Bank describing the basics of the bond market for private investors, the president of the local bank describing changes in bank services, the senior vice president of a major insurance company speaking on variable annuities, and Williams and Griffith describing recent innovations in insurance offerings. The series was to be entitled "The Grand Opening Seminar Series," and each ad would have some space alloted to telling about the GIA, its policies, and its personnel.

Media

A twelve-week, local advertising schedule was to be used to inform the public of the seminar series and of the opening of GIA. Primary media were the *Lake Forester* and *Lake Bluff Review,* weekly suburban newspapers, and WEEF and WEEF-FM, radio stations located in Highland Park, serving the North Shore area. A preseminar meeting was to be advertised by direct mail consisting of a carefully selected mailing of engraved invitations to the social elite of Lake Forest. The first seminar was to be an overview of the entire series and an explanation of the agency's intention to provide them with a personalized, comprehensive insurance service. This preseminar was the direct responsibility of McCormick, who selected the guests, arranged for an appropriate meeting place (the Onwentsia Club), and arranged appropriate refreshments and the program.

The circulation of the *Lake Forester* reached 89 percent of the households in Lake Forest, and the circulation of the *Lake Bluff Review* was 95 percent of Lake Bluff households. WEEF and WEEF-FM were new radio stations, and Griffith was unsure of their reach. The schedule for the newspapers included two half-pages before the series began, with pictures of all speakers, and included quarter-page ads each week featuring the speaker for that week. The radio stations featured five minutes of business news each evening at 6:15, and Griffith contracted to sponsor the Wednesday newscast for twenty-six weeks, beginning three weeks before the seminar series.

Creative Strategy

Griffith wanted the artwork in the advertisements to connote an upper social class image. Accordingly, a highly respected Chicago advertising art studio was employed to prepare high-quality cuts far above the quality of the typical newspaper ad. The tone of the ad was formal, the type was light, and there was a great deal of white space. Photographs of each speaker were the prominent feature of the ad and were lined up horizontally through the middle of the space.

The headline stated in formal type, "You are cordially invited to attend a series of seminars presenting ten distinguished speakers from leading financial institutions. . . ." Phrases such as "considering the subject" were used instead of "speaking on," and the copy was as formal as might be expected on an invitation from an important government officer to attend a formal reception. The use of the GIA name was not blatant; it was not included in any heads or subheads. It was mentioned in the copy so that anyone reading the ad would learn something about the sponsor. The ad also included a contemporary but subdued logotype in the lower right corner of the ad, with the inclusion of the phrase "Comprehensive financial services."

Perhaps the most interesting aspect of the advertisement was its nonconventional use of lower-case type. Only a few key words contained capital letters, and these were words of unusual importance in the overall ad. Griffith believed that this would connote an image of progressiveness and of doing things differently that was to be true of the agency. Yet the overall image was formal and reserved, which Griffith believed appropriate for the community.

The entire tone of the ad was not pushy; rather it held the promise of a cordial invitation to attend a distinguished series of seminars on topics obviously of interest mainly to upper-class people. The overall effect of the ad was to connote a reserved, dignified image. Griffith felt the advertising art studio had performed well the task he assigned them and that the advertisements developed exactly the image he wanted for the Lake Forest–Lake Bluff area.

Problem

Griffith showed the advertising plans to a friend who was an account executive for a Chicago advertising agency. The account executive reacted strongly and told Griffith he felt that he was making a big mistake. His analysis of the situation was that the upper classes preferred to purchase their life insurance from long-time associates and college friends and that Griffith was unlikely to get much of their business. Griffith responded that he realized that he would have difficulty in getting upper-class business but that he felt he eventually would get it because of his superior and comprehensive service. He also stated that he would be satisfied to receive the middle groups in Lake Forest–Lake–Bluff because these people represented in themselves a group far above average in their insurance needs. Also, Griffith pointed out that 30 percent of the population in these two suburbs moved each year so that he expected to have new potential customers moving into the area in large numbers, which would enable him to compete with existing agencies.

The account executive stated his belief that the upper-class image created by Griffith would be interpreted to be a "snob" appeal by the rest of the residents and that they would not want to patronize Griffith for fear that they were not really wanted and that they would feel uncomfortable with Griffith personnel. The campaign, the account executive predicted, would not reach the upper groups and would alienate the middle groups and should therefore not be undertaken.

Griffith was not sure what to do. He had already contacted the speakers, although he believed the series probably could still be cancelled without expense to him. He was considering not only changing this particular advertising but also of reevaluating his whole approach to the market. Griffith had planned, for example, to recruit and train salesmen who would have language patterns compatible to upper-class patrons and who would move easily in upper-class social affairs. He decided that he had better give this more thought and planning.

Questions

1. Should Griffith proceed with the series designed to interest high-income families?

2. Should the proposed advertising be run?

3. What policies should be adopted by Griffith with respect to the facilities in his office, the personnel recruited and trained, and the segmentation strategy of the agency?

4. What research would be useful and economically feasible for Griffith to conduct in evaluating his decisions?

5. Criticize the relevance of the social class concept in terms of Griffith's planning.

CHAPTER 8

REFERENCE GROUPS

Flower Power Fashions: Reference Group Influences on Purchasing Decisions

In 1964 Sam Smart was promoted to Assistant Director of Marketing for Durham Industries with responsibility for product planning. Durham Industries was an old-line garment manufacturer and marketer that had maintained a reasonably profitable position in the extremely competitive women's ready-to-wear industry. The firm had annual sales in 1967 of $23 million. Of these sales, about $10 million were derived from sales under the labels owned by Durham and about $13 million were derived from private label merchandise manufactured on contract for numerous retailers.

The lines carried by Durham were moderately priced or slightly higher than average. The brands were respected by retailers as ones that women frequently repurchased and that commanded a fair amount of loyalty from women who had worn them before. They were not nationally advertised except in trade magazines, although the company did offer some limited cooperative advertising on the basis of volume to some of the more important outlets for the higher priced lines of Durham. No advertising allowances were given on the private-brand merchandise.

In 1965 the company had expanded its product offering to include sportswear. The process of entering the marketing of sportswear had occurred almost by chance. Durham had produced a complete line of cotton skirts for several years. In 1964 they began offering culottes, and this caused a reorientation in the sales force because the buyer of culottes was often a different person than the other ready-to-wear lines traditionally carried by Durham. The culottes had been so successful, however, that Durham expanded its line to include bermuda shorts. In 1966, Durham had purchased a plant from another manufacturer in Macon, Georgia, especially suited to the production of blouses. By 1967 the company had developed a complete line of sportswear and had found it to be the fastest growing of their product lines. Most of the sales had been for private-label distribution, and among the outlets with which Durham had especially high success were several small chains of women's specialty stores that served college and university areas. These typically were chains of four to ten regionally located stores that normally served university areas of similar character.

In 1967 Smart attended a seminar sponsored by a garment manufacturers' association where he heard a professor from The Ohio State University discussing market segmentation and the new marketing concept. Among the topics discussed by the professor was the "exploding youth market." The professor stated that the under twenty-five age group was the fastest growing group and that they had rapidly rising incomes as well. In addition, this group spent a disproportionately high proportion of their income on clothing, compared to older groups. Smart felt that these trends were consonant with Durham's own sales success in the sportswear line. Although no market studies had been undertaken, he was fairly confident that the sportswear line was sold primarily to younger consumers.

After the seminar, Smart began thinking of ways that Durham might capture a greater share of the youth market. Although the sportswear line had been particularly successful, most of the other lines were oriented to the middle-aged housewife and had no strong appeal among the college-age consumer. Smart began thinking about this problem, and within a few weeks, developed the idea of a new line of dresses, jumpers, and coordinated outfits to be marketed under the label of "Flower Power Fashions."

Because Durham had no formal marketing research department, Smart flew to Columbus, Ohio, to talk with The Ohio State University professor who had been the stimulus for the idea in the marketing seminar. The professor gave Smart a number of reference sources that described changes in the culture of America, reference group influences, and fashion development. Later, when reading these, Smart felt that they confirmed his premise that the *avant-garde* in fashions might be accepted and actually purchased by the masses of young people much more readily than in previous eras.

In talking with the professor, Smart disclosed that design work for the Flower Power line had already begun but that the higher executives at Durham were skeptical and wanted to test the concept of an *avant-garde* line of apparel before committing themselves to major design, production, and marketing expenses. Durham stressed efficiency in production and that, if the new line did not have sufficient appeal to attract substantial numbers of young college-age women, the line either could not be produced or would have to be sold at substantially higher prices than were currently typical of Durham merchandise. In addition, there was considerable concern among Durham executives about the distribution patterns that would be needed for such a line. Durham had excellent relationships with most of the major department stores in the United States and felt that if major promotional assistance would be needed for Flower Power Fashions, that the most likely source of cooperation would be the department stores. Department stores were experienced at promoting fashion items and special lines, and, in addition, most department stores maintained a competent advertising department that would be needed to prepare layouts and sketches, because Durham had limited experience in this activity. On the other hand, some executives felt a unique line such as this might need to be in small specialty shops located near university campuses in order to be successful.

Problem

The events just described occurred early in 1967, and the conversation with the professor occurred in February. Smart felt that if a new line were to be introduced, the best timing for it would be in late summer and autumn in order to hit the college market at a peak purchasing period. However, in order to be ready for even limited distribution at that time, a decision would have to be reached in the next two weeks to either "go" or "not go." If a decision was made to introduce the line, even on an experimental basis, an approach would have to be made immediately to the retailers involved. Smart asked the professor if there was any way that research could be conducted within the next two weeks that would help the company make a decision about Flower Power Fashions.

Research

The professor revealed that a study by a noncompetitive but related manufacturer was underway at Ohio State and that it might be possible to insert a question about clothing fashions into this study. This study was a series of one hundred depth interviews of young women living in the university area. The sample was not a probability sample but was selected to include a cross-section of the area, including those who lived in the area but were not actually students. The sample included a wide range of majors, years, and types of girls. The professor indicated that Ohio State probably would be an acceptable test site because its characteristics represented almost a stereotype of American universities. Clothing fashions, the professor indicated, would be more conservative than many Eastern and West Coast universities but would probably be well above the average university or college in America.

The professor indicated that the depth interviews would average between thirty and forty-five minutes with each young lady and that a researcher could abstract the parts of the interview that pertained to clothing fashions to be used by Durham. The interviews were conducted by trained interviewers and were recorded in detail so that a fairly comprehensive insight might be possible into the thinking of young women at Ohio State about fashions.

Market

Smart was happy at the prospect of this research and reported that Durham had already considered possible test markets and that Columbus, the home of The Ohio State University, was one of their choices. The Columbus Metropolitan Area contains approximately one million people and is above average in education and income because of its educational and governmental institutions. In addition to containing Ohio State, it is the site of Capital University, Franklin University, Otterbein University, and Dominican College. There are also several business and vocational schools, including an area technical college, Bliss University, Columbus Business University, and many others. Because Columbus is a center of state and Federal government offices, there is also a high concentration of employed, single persons.

Ohio State women students have available two basic sources of clothing. Near the University, along North High Street, is a series of about a dozen women's shops, specializing in college fashions. The largest of these are the University Shop, the College Girl, the Villager, and Jeanne's. The major department stores—with locations downtown and in branches—are Lazarus, the Union, and the Fashion. Madison's is a large women's specialty store with branches throughout the city. The major store, however, is Lazarus, which dominates Columbus retailing. It was founded by the Lazarus family, principal stockholders in Federated Department stores. Lazarus does more department store business in the Columbus area than all other department stores combined and has high acceptability among central Ohio residents. One of its many features is the Collegiene Shoppe, a separate section of the store that successfully caters to sportswear and fashion preferences of young women. The downtown department stores are located about five miles from the Ohio State campus area but are reasonably accessible by bus. There is a large modern, shopping center (Northland) on the northern edge of the city that contains complete units of all the major downtown stores, including Lazarus.

Results

Highlights from some of the hundred depth interviews are presented in Appendix A. They were air mailed to Smart, and he was to review them and present recommendations to Durham management. The professor cautioned that this should be regarded only as exploratory research and that the company should consider a full-scale national study if it wanted a more conclusive answer to their problem. Smart, however, realized that such a study would take several weeks and that, and if a decision were not made within one week after receiving the results of the Ohio State study, the company would be unable to increase production for the following season and thus would probably have to wait a full year before introducing Flower Power Fashions.

After reviewing the results, Smart began to be apprehensive about the original concept for Flower Power. Originally, he had conceived of the line as truly *avant-garde* with emphasis upon flamboyant designs, bright colors, and many of the new fabrics such as plastic and coated materials. The dresses, jumpers, and some other items were well within the production capabilities of Durham, although Durham planned to subcontract to other suppliers some of the accessories necessary for coordination.

Smart felt strongly that Durham needed to take definite and immediate steps to exploit the youth market, but he was unsure of what action the company should take now.

Questions

1. What action should Durham take regarding introduction of Flower Power Fashions for the following year?
   a. Should Smart recommend a strategy based upon the exploratory research just described or should he wait another year for better research?
   b. Whether Durham elects for immediate introduction or postpones a decision, what additional research is warranted? Prepare a proposal that Smart might submit to Durham management.

2. If Durham test-markets a line of fashions directed to the college-age market in the near future, what distribution channels should they use? Specifically, in Columbus, what stores should they use?

3. What marketing policies should be formulated for Durham in order to exploit the youth market. Prepare a one-year plan and a five-year plan.

Appendix A: Verbatim Interviews

Interview 1

In Katy's opinion, there are too many coeds wearing Mod clothing who do not look right in these styles. She thinks that the majority of the girls on campus dress neatly and that most wear sporty styles for classes. In line with this trend, she said that sporty clothes are the most appropriate for classes.

Katy thinks that most clothing is bought by coeds when they go home, especially major purchases such as suits and formals. According to her, coeds visit campus clothing stores when they are just looking around and that they occasionally purchase clothing at these stores.

Interview 2

Carole's initial reaction when asked for her opinions on campus clothing was "I hate saddle shoes." She continued to be very definite in her dislikes, which included miniskirts, lacy hose worn to classes, and fancy hairdos. She also dislikes seeing jeans and sweatshirts on campus. In general she said that "a girl should look like a girl." In her opinion, clothing stores around campus are too expensive and cater mostly to sorority girls. Carole is formerly from Columbus and said that nearly all town girls and many others buy their clothes downtown.

Interview 3

Respondent 3 thinks that the girls at Ohio State dress themselves down: "They don't like to get dressed up, they like to dress down." She doesn't approve of slacks or shorts in class. "A girl should look like a lady while attending classes." She feels that most girls dresses are too plain. She thinks that too many girls try to follow fads instead of finding and wearing what they look good in. "I always wore dresses and heels when I went to class because I look good in them and I feel this is what girls should wear to class." She shops at Jeanne's and Lazarus, but mostly at Verla's. She likes cleancut clothes—Jackie Kennedy style.

She doesn't read many magazines—sometimes *Vogue*. She chooses clothing that she thinks looks good on her. "Clothing—what you can wear—depends on hair style, hair color, and general build."

Interview 4

Respondent 4 feels that most girls on campus do not know how to dress. "Some of these girls look ridiculous in the clothes they wear. Can you imagine a two-hundred pound girl in a miniskirt?" She doesn't approve of slacks and shorts in classes. "I'd rather wear a skirt and sweater or something like that." She doesn't go for the fad clothes but prefers plain, simple outfits. She keeps away from clothing that she "can't" wear, even if everyone else is wearing it. Nevertheless, she says that girls ought to wear whatever they like.

She shops mainly in the University Shop, the Villager, the College Girl, Lazarus, and Madison's. She feels that the shops on campus cater more to the college student, and therefore she buys most of her clothing there.

Interview 5

She likes most of the clothes that girls wear on campus, but she does not go for the fad clothing. She does wear slacks and shorts because "I like to feel comfortable in class and I don't see what difference it makes." However, most of her school clothes consist of skirts and simple dresses.

She does not shop much on campus and buys most of her things at home. But she has shopped at the College Girl and at Lazarus.

Interview 6

"Clothes and makeup definitely make a person" were the opening comments. "I feel that without the right clothes to wear, matching skirts, sweaters, shoes and things like that that make an outfit go together, that a girl is at a distinct disadvantage with boys." She felt the boys on campus and the ones she knew personally would not take a second look unless she was dressed "properly." She also thought too many girls on campus looked like they had just walked out of a closet with whatever was in their hand to wear. She felt that although "I like to feel comfortable, I think that it is important how I look in other people's eyes. Not everybody has the same things to work with, but you should definitely do the best with what you have."

Interview 7

The respondent likes clothes that are simple but stylish. She looks to women that wear clothes that suit their figures and overall appearance. She said that some women go out and buy clothes that look expensive and nice on other women but that they do not consider how the clothing will look on them. She likes the new style of short skirts as long as the person has the figure and so forth to go with them. She prefers sporty looking clothes. She buys most of her clothes at Lazarus because she works downtown and can keep an eye on the new fashions. Lazarus has a variety of prices, and this price consideration is very important because she is a newly wed. Lazarus has enough different shops that one can find clothes that one can wear to work and clothes that one can wear around the house. Lazarus also has more expensive clothes that one can buy for special occasions. She feels that Lazarus' prices are fairly reasonable, but if one wants something of a high quality he has to pay for it.

Interview 8

The respondent indicated that she was not too impressed about "high fashion" clothing. She is more interested in plain clothes, and they do not have to be expensive or flashy. She hesitates to try some of the newer fashions because she feels that they are too flashy, mainly due to the colors. The places where she buys her clothes is important because the "right place" has all the types of clothing she likes; she likes almost everything that the store has. If she finds another lower priced store handles the same brand, she would purchase her clothing there. However, she likes certain stores because she knows that they will have what she likes. She is not interested in buying outwardly expensive clothes because she thinks that the important criteria is neatness and acceptance by her friends. She likes the "Village Store" and Lazarus. She likes Lazarus because they have everything that she might want, but they have fairly high prices.

Interview 9

On the whole, girls dress with good sense here—fads are not that popular here. Most of the girls stick to basic established styles that tend to be very practical, although some do not tend to be. There are always some students who wear the latest wayout fads, to get attention mostly, she thinks. The female student likes particular things for different reasons. She thinks the teenage mod look is terrible, and she dislikes mini's definitely. The mini-tent is repulsive to her.

Interview 10 and 11

The following interview was conducted at the same time because both girls wanted to respond. The girls were Rhonda (R) and Marsha (M).

Q.   Discuss clothing fashions at Ohio State.

R.   Minidresses are fine if you don't have to sit down. You must have very good legs to wear them. Should wear stockings, not hose, since hose tops look terrible.

M.   Mod clothes are cute because they've colorful.

R.   Comfortable.

M.   Not tight.

R.   I like Sta-Prest because they're easier to take care of.

M.   Bonded fabrics are good too. I love pants suits. Slacks aren't good everywhere, but pants suits are. Hip huggers look great on some kids, but you have to be the right person.

Q.   In what stores do you buy your clothes?

M. and *R.*   Lazarus; shoes at Bakers; accessories at College Girl and campus shops, Lazarus when they have sales.

R.   Gloves at the Fashion.

M.   I'm never any other place when I'm downtown other than Lazarus or the Fashion. The campus shops are too expensive, especially for summer clothes. I can't afford their name-brand summer clothes.

R.   I buy Hane's hosiery at Jeanne's on campus because I'm a bug about Hanes hose.

Q.   Advice?

M. and *R.*   Roommates, boyfriends, dates.

R.   I used to get advice from magazines.

M.   I don't read magazines any more.

Interview 12 and 13

The following interview is also a joint interview.

Barb feels that dress at Ohio State is too conservative because she is from New York City and has seen the miniskirt fashions for over a year, although they have just started to be seen on this campus this quarter. Charlotte agrees that all fashions in the Mid West are like this and everyone here looks alike. Girls are either beat or buy their clothes at the University Shop. Barb would rather wear something that is non-ivy-league, nonsorority looking, and something that looks good on her regardless of what other people are wearing. Charlotte would rather wear clothes that are more classic and older looking because her skirt and sweater combinations will not be very practical when she gets out of school.

Interview 14

College kids dress for utilitarian purposes. There are fads in colors, but, if they're inconvenient, the kids won't wear it. There aren't too many miniskirts. Skirts are shorter. They've gone up two inches. Guys without socks is another sign they want comfort. I think it's nice people wear clothes.

I buy sports clothes in Lazarus, formal wear in Akron at Mrs. Randalls, shoes from Lucky's (Akron) who carry Sadler and Weejuns.

I get advice on clothes from roommates who are usually willing to tear me down. I also listen to other kids, my Mom once in a while, and I observe what others are wearing.

Interview 15

(D = Interviewer. K = Respondent.)

D.   What we want to talk about: we want to discuss ideas about fashion, and beauty, and appearance, and how a girl can make herself beautiful.

K.   Ha!

D.   We'll just assume the average coed at Ohio State.

K.   She has to be well groomed, and her hair has to be pretty. I think she has to feel like she knows how to take care of herself properly and know what's the latest style and all the new looks.

D.   Appearance-wise?

K.   She has to look natural, not gaudy, like with too many things distracting from her best features—not too much makeup.

D.   What about clothes?

K.   Clothes have to be in style, and fit well.

D.   And?

K.   Fairly modern.

D. So there are probably style leaders around Columbus, either people we can turn to, or . . . .

K. Advertising. And she talks to other people. She can, but she doesn't have to. She can look at other fashions and the other colors they're wearing. And what she sees in the stores . . . advertising, I guess.

D. Her friends?

K. If it is something she really likes, then it doesn't make any difference. Well, a little.

D. Where do coeds buy clothes, do you think?

K. Not as much at the shopping centers as downtown. They don't have cars. You can just hop on a bus and go downtown anytime you want. They can go to Lazarus, and the Fashion, but not the Union as much because it's too far away. (*Pause*) From Lazarus.

Interview 16

(*D* = Interviewer. *K* = Respondent.)

D. When a girl looks for clothing, what does she look for?

K. What looks good on her . . . . I don't know . . . style.

D. Style?

K. How they look on me. Whether they flatter me or not.

D. What else?

K. It's the type of outfit, too. Like casual. For class . . . at this time of year, a dress. Or in the winter, a sweater and skirt. The same on dates.

D. What . . . kinds of clothes do you find unappealing?

K. (*Long pause*) Things that are too dressy. Like, some things are just too dressy for class. It's just something that's not casual . . . to me, something that looks uncomfortable.

D. Does where you live matter?

K. Oh, yes. Girls in apartments dress more sloppy. You know, more slacks. You get up late, you eat when you want to, you just put on the first thing you see . . . you don't take as much time as if you were living in a dorm.

D. Hm-m-m . . . .

K. It's just what appeals to you, I don't know. Pleasing color, the way it fits, style.

D.   Where do college girls get their clothes?

K.   You mean specific stores? Oh, the College Girl, the University Shop, downtown . . . Lazarus. I'd much rather buy downtown.

D.   Downtown?

K.   Because campus has a crummy selection . . . everything is just alike . . . they're all the same thing.

D.   Uh-huh.

K.   You don't buy something exactly like somebody else's unless it's something very basic, like a white blouse . . . or a dark skirt.

Interview 17

(*D =* Interviewer. *J =* Respondent.)

D.   We would like to discuss beauty and how clothing and/or cosmetics influence the typical Ohio State University coed's appearance.

J.   The average girl, I think, who is capable of improving her appearance (I mean one who is not overweight or slovenly or "beat") pays the most attention to her clothes and her hair style.

D.   How does she buy clothes, for instance?

J.   You never really see anything new. Everything has been so exposed and so advertised, like miniskirts, that finally seeing one seems more like a novelty than an innovation . . . . Black turtlenecks and sandals and culottes have always really been here, but you didn't wear them so . . . publicly. I think it's part of this general permissiveness.

D.   Permissiveness?

J.   More casual clothes . . . slacks and sweatshirts. People are beginning to think dressing up's not really fun anymore. And, at least part of the time, more people don't care what they look like, or what people think in general.

D.   I think that's important . . . whose opinion counts . . . .

J.   I think you find the worst situation in sororities . . . where you have to maintain a certain dress standard . . . or you're ostracized. Even in the dorms, they voted to abolish dress standards for Sunday dinner . . . the Deans didn't like it.

D.   Was that a protest, so to speak?

J.   It was more like most people didn't care, but a few pushed very strongly and managed to get a referendum.

D. What stores are big here? I mean, can you buy everything at one place?

J. Lazarus, of course. Everyone I know shops at Lazarus. You think of them having unique, way out fashions besides just everyday school needs. But I sometimes shop around campus too, just to compare what they have . . . .

Interview 18

Tent dresses are becoming very popular for evening wear. They are shorter than the regular dresses.

There are no fashions that typify college girls. Each girl dresses the way she likes to. Girls like to have attention, so they try to look good when they go to class. Most girls only wear pants and sweatshirts to class when the weather is bad or when they are having a midterm exam and they do not feel like wearing anything else.

Girls are very brand conscious. They buy clothes by brand name for the purpose of impressing other girls. They also buy clothes that do not have brand prestige, but only when they feel sure that other people will not know that the outfit is of lesser quality.

Girls generally do not know good quality clothes, so they buy clothes with a well-known brand name and pay a high price. They feel that if they buy something at a high price, they are getting good quality, but it doesn't always turn out this way. Sometimes you get lower quality at high prices, but if you go on brand name, you can pretty much count on quality. Sometimes I buy brand names to be sure that I am getting good quality.

Clothes definitely add to the beauty of a girl. A person many times looks completely different with a different outfit on. I have a friend who goes to Oberlin College, and I visited her a couple weeks ago. The girls at Oberlin just wear bermudas and shirts to class and leave their hair straight, but in the evening or weekends they get dressed up for their date and they really look different.

Interview 19

The fashion at school is traditional or ivy-league clothes for school. Although a few of the kids wear nonconformist clothes, most of them are very concerned about styles and dress the way that other people are. Some of the brands that I like are Pace Setter and Bobby Brooks.

You can't really tell an individual's personality by the clothes that he wears, but you can get a general idea what he is like. I have been fooled many times by judging a person by the clothes that he wears.

I regularly read some of the fashion magazines like *Glamour* and *Seventeen* to get information about styles. I don't like the way-out high-society clothes, but I like the more conservative clothes. My favorite outfit is a "little boy" type suit.

Boys like girls who are dressed nice but not too wild. In other words, an overall appearance that is pleasing to the eye.

Interview 20 and 21

The following is a joint interview with Sue and Eileen.

Both respondents agreed on most aspects of fashion. Because they are both nursing students and have to wear a uniform to class every day, they feel that their needs in clothing are below that of the average college coed. They both agreed that specialty shops were very expensive and that they did not do much shopping in them. Eileen stated she would usually browse through Jeanne's a couple of times a week but that she rarely bought anything. She said their selection was very limited.

Sue stated her requirements for clothing fashion were comfort and suitability. She frowned on the use of certain clothes as an overt act of impressing anyone. Eileen felt that certain clothing fashions were not indicative of her as a person, that is, miniskirts. Both are conservative in dress and bought things that could be used often. The larger department stores, Lazarus for one, were the most appealing to them, and both felt they bought most of their clothes at school. They also agreed that they bought mostly when they needed something and that they as a general rule were not impulsive buyers. They thought they adopted styles that were here to stay for some time. Eileen stated that her manner of dress was influenced by what other people thought.

Interview 22

This young lady expressed interest in many of the new-type fashions but was strongly opposed to certain items such as the miniskirt. She stated she had seen some younger girls (under twenty) with skirts about one to two inches above the knee that looked "cute" but stated that on the average she did not think the miniskirt-type fashions improve many girls appearances. She definitely thought that girls should not wear such fashions on campus and that older women (over thirty) look extremely foolish in them.

She stated that, regardless of the contemporary fashion, any dress, skirt, or similar article of wear should be chosen in accordance with the girl's figure. She stated clothing to complement one's particular figure is essential for good appearance.

The respondent said that price is not the determining factor when she buys clothing. If she finds something she likes, she will pay the price unless it's entirely beyond her economic reach. She generally equates price with quality;

the higher the price, the better the quality, but not always. She is aware that crafty marketers sometimes use this notion to exploit customers.

She usually purchases her clothes at Penney's or Lazarus, the latter being her least favorite. Lazarus sales personnel she feels are sometimes rude and impersonal and their quality of clothing is not always best. On the other hand she finds Penney's usually courteous and in general prefers this store to any others. She states that most of her friends at Ohio State feel generally the same as she (or at least she thinks they do).

Interview 23 and 24

The following is a joint interview with a home economics major and an arts major.

One girl felt that to a large degree most of the styles were conservative as compared to other places that she had been. The other girl felt that Ohio State was behind the Eastern schools based on a trip she had taken East (the girls there were dressed somewhat differently) and that after a while she had noticed some of the styles at Ohio State. Both girls agreed that, to a certain degree, the different colleges on campus set the styles. Examples given were that in the College of Home Economics the girls were more or less expected to be dressed well and were to use good taste, whereas in the Arts College the students could wear about anything. They seem to think the professors favor the freedom in dress. They both agreed that there is a difference between senior women and freshmen women in their dress and in the way they take care of themselves. The freshmen women are very "fady," meaning that when they go to college they usually have a new wardrobe and will get up early enough to make sure they are neat in their appearance before going to classes. The senior women are more relaxed and usually are not as careful in their appearance and dress (as they put it, "they have learned the ropes").

They felt themselves in the in-between stage for magazines as far as dress and styles go. *Seventeen* and *Glamour* are for younger girls and *Vogue* and *Harpers Bazar* are for the older women. They both agree that to a large degree the girls on campus dress to suit the fellows.

Interview 25

I feel that everyone has the freedom to wear whatever they want to. I buy the clothes that I like even though they may be considered "different" by some people. My main interest is basic clothes; you know, skirts and blouses and sweaters. I have a few loud, bright clothes, but most of them I would consider to be plain. The only people who I try to look "sharp" for are the important people in my life, such as my steady boyfriend and other people close to me.

The clothes that a person wears are very important for making a first impression on a person, but after you get to know the person, clothes aren't very important. I wear "sharp," nice-fitting clothes because I feel more comfortable and self-confident when I feel that I look good.

We were just discussing in psych class this week how you can tell a person's personality by the clothes that he wears. If the clothes are loud and bold, the person is likely to be an extrovert. If the clothes are dark and plain, he is probably an introvert.

Interview 26

It is very important to dress well on campus. I like the short skirts and the accessories that are worn with them where you buy your clothes.

I buy most of my clothes at the University Shop. I know that they always carry the styles that are accepted on campus, so I buy my clothes there. I also think that the prices are reasonable, and they allow me to have a charge account.

Interview 27

Respondent 27 is style conscious and likes to keep up with the latest styles in clothing, however she is not particularly fond of some of the wilder styles such as the tent dresses and some of the tight-fitting types of apparel. She reads *Glamour* and *Mademoiselle* magazines, and she looks to these magazines for advice. She makes a lot of her clothes; but what she purchases, she purchases at home, near Cleveland.

Interview 28

Respondent 28 is somewhat conservative and sticks to latest fashions. She believes that tent dresses only look good on certain people. She purchases most of her clothes around campus at the University Shop and the Villager. She also reads *Glamour* and *Mademoiselle* magazines for advice on fashions.

Interview 29

This respondent felt that most college females decided what to wear on the basis of what everybody was wearing. She felt that it was the more "liberal" or "radical" female students that introduced new clothing fashions to the campus and then that this was picked up and accepted by the other students.

She felt that most of the new fashions were from New York or the West Coast. She felt that the common occurrence of fashion changes was good because people soon get tired of wearing the same thing. It was stated that most of her shopping was done from nearby campus stores because they had almost everything she wanted. Also she did not want to take the time to go downtown and fight the traffic and the people. As she stated, "I do not have any charge cards, so it really does not make any difference where I buy."

This respondent believes that the accepted dress for women in general is becoming more liberal and that this trend will continue into the future.

She felt that her own ideas in the choice of clothes was of primary importance, although other factors such as peer group and male opinion were important.

Nothing in this interview was mentioned about brand names, but she mentioned that she liked to be a leader in a particular style when it was introduced, if she liked it.

Interview 30

This respondent feels that fashion magazines and the College Boards pretty well dictate what will be worn.

She states that she buys primarily what she likes but that her decisions are influenced significantly by what peers think. She stated that she felt men's ideas were important in her manner of dressing but that her own opinions were of primary importance.

She feels that most female students just wear what everybody else is and that they do not consciously think of fashion changes.

She believes that quick changes in fashions are perpetrated by certain key people in an effort to maintain high sales and profits. She stated that she did not feel that branded merchandise was generally superior and that it made little difference to her whether merchandise was a national brand name or not.

Interview 31

This respondent decides what to wear primarily by what everybody else is wearing. She feels that most of the stores carry almost the same merchandise and that most girls prefer to wear skirts, blouses, and sweaters to class.

She feels that most fashion changes are picked up by female students through magazine ads and articles. She mentioned no specific type of person that began a fashion change, but she felt that it was more or less a spontaneous occurrence.

She stated that she does practically all her clothes shopping at Lazarus because her mother has a charge plate there and also because Lazarus has so much merchandise that it is possible for her to do all her shopping there and to not have to stop anywhere else.

This respondent stated that if she was in a hurry to buy some clothing she would buy from campus stores (Jeanne's specifically), but that this was the exception.

She stated that she preferred to buy brand-name goods, not because of what other people thought but rather because she felt that quality was assured.

She also stated that if you buy brand-name goods you do not see so many other people wearing the same thing because the stores do not carry so much duplicate stock of brand goods.

She stated that men's ideas do affect her type of purchases but that she buys for herself first and for her boyfriend second. She feels that most girls buy what other girls think are right in terms of style, looks, and acceptance. She stated that Ohio State girls buy almost entirely casual clothes because there are so few occasions on which to wear more formal clothing.

Interview 32

Campus is not the place to wear miniskirts. Only freshmen and sophomore girls wear them on campus. A modified miniskirt is okay under certain conditions; that is, it is okay to wear a miniskirt if it is not too short and if you are the type of girl that can wear one. Only trim girls should even consider wearing a miniskirt. Slacks also have their place on campus. They should only be worn to big lecture classes. There is a tendency for the girl to feel too relaxed in slacks. The same thing applies to shorts. Shorts and slacks should not be worn to small classes, especially where there is close contact with the professor. The professor tends to get the wrong impression of the girl when she wears slacks and shorts.

Interview 33

The respondent felt one should be able to wear anything she wants to go to class. If the person feels good in shorts, slacks, or miniskirts she should wear them. Although she said anybody could wear shorts, slacks, and miniskirts, she felt that the heavy-set girls did not look good in them. She said she dressed the way she felt when going to class—if she was tired from studying from a test, she might wear shorts or slacks. She didn't think the majority of professors cared what the girls wore to class. She likes bright color combinations in her outfits. Quite often she wears miniskirts to class.

Interview 34

Miniskirts are okay in moderation; they should not be too short because then it becomes ridiculous. This is maybe just a "passing fad." The trend will be toward a more covered up look because then "there is more to guess about."

She favored more conservative standard collegiate clothes.

She didn't like the mod styles. She thought it was more prevalent in the high schools, not near as much in the colleges. She does not like wide belts or wild paisley shirts; she definitely did not approve of the extremely long hair. "Extreme dressers are not sure of themselves; they try to find their own group—not necessarily outcasts, but not confident around the majority of the people."

People are perhaps really too "clothes conscious"; there is too much emphasis on current trends; people think if they do not conform they will be looked down upon.

The respondent liked the bright colors (although she said the brighter colors were not for her); she felt they added a "little spark" to some people.

She felt there is a tendency to compete with other people in the clothing aspect. Some people say "women dress to please other women, not the men."

She said that pierced ears are not really new and that fashions repeat themselves anyway. It is probably just a passing fad and is "barbaric" in a way. People naturally like a change. The trends now seem to be for the males to become more feminine.

She did not like girls to wear neckties. Men have always worn them. It seems to go back to the same old idea of wanting change of trying to be something you are not.

Interview 35

This respondent expressed a strong feeling against any far-out fashions for coeds. She seems to view the coed as a lady rather than a fashion model, to use her own words. She feels that attire such as miniskirts and other such mod-wear is simply not suitable for the coed in her day-to-day activities. She favors the conventional type clothing, a simple skirt-and-sweater combination, suit, or neat-fitting dress. She thinks slacks are all right for coeds to wear, especially during the cold months.

The respondent considers herself somewhat conservative with respect to new fashion and clothing in general and tends to believe that most coeds feel the same way she does. She states that although most coeds are interested in fashion and the far-out fashions that are on the market, they still dress themselves in a conservative manner. She states, "After all, how many women do you see walking across the Oval [square on campus] in a miniskirt." The respondent feels that, although as many as 30 per cent (her estimate) of today's women dress wildly (by this she meant bold prints, spiral design, zebra design, tent dresses), the general way to classify fashion at Ohio State would be as "conservative."

Interview 36

This Ohio State coed is all for the new fashions. She considers this generation to be one of revolution and the miniskirts, pop-art clothes, and other such styles to be very effective means of stressing the rebellious image. She states that she has two miniskirts and wears them occasionally but never to class.

The respondent characterizes her buying of clothes as impulse, opposed to going through a logical process of "do I need this or not" analysis. She states that she has a large wardrobe (would like more, of course) and that this is probably why her buying is of an impulsive nature—because she really does not need any new clothes. She often finds herself buying some new article of clothing when she is depressed.

She usually purchases her clothes in surrounding campus shops mainly because of their proximity. She realizes the prices are high in many of these shops, but she feels the quality is much better. She tends to equate price with quality in almost every situation.

She feels that men in general like the new fashions, especially the miniskirts. She qualifies this by saying men like to look at women in miniskirts, but, when it comes to a husband buying his wife a miniskirt or letting her wear one, the reaction would probably be a negative one.

Interview 37

Most fashion at Ohio State is up-to-date (fairly progressive) the respondent felt. She added that too many girls wear the wrong clothes for their figures. She said the campus stores offer a good variety of clothes for almost every figure, but the students do not take advantage of it. They wear whatever the in-group wears regardless of their figures. The respondent shops at the University Shop and the College Girl, depending on whether she wants something faddy or conservative. She indicated that the University Shop is more conservative. She buys at these shops because they are on her side of the campus. The University Shop is the place to go if you want to browse. The girls (clerks) there give one confidence because they dress well and are willing to give one honest advice. They usually like to know what one is buying for and help one pick something appropriate.

Interview 38

The respondent felt there were four groups of fashions: (1) The half-in-and-half-out group, usually freshmen and sophomores. They still have to wear their high school clothes, but they are building a more collegiate wardrobe. (2) The way-out's. They wear the wild earrings, funny shoes, and lots of men's clothes. (3) The typical college girl. They wear Ladybug's, Gant's, and all coordinated clothes. (4) The students that are out-of-it. They wear old high school clothes and have no interest in fashion or being "cool."

The respondent buys at the University Shop; never Jeanne's or the College Girl—they are too crowded. She likes to have room to look around.

Interview 39

The respondent felt girls here are relatively fashionable, but still conservative. There are not too many miniskirts, but most skirts are very short. Then she stated that they have the "weirdo's" who look like they just stepped out of a magazine. She said they look out of place; they are too extreme.

Interview 40

When discussing what the important components that make up a fashionable woman were, the respondent replied that neatness, dress, accessories, figure, makeup, and hair style were important, with neatness being crucial. The subject also identified a fashionable woman as one who is striking and who leaves a pleasing impression. It was also noted that a fashionable person is also attractive. The criteria seemed to be "doing the most with what you have."

She derives fashion information from magazines through advertisements, editorials, and pictures in general. Other fashion information sources mentioned were association with other women through observation and discussion, from shopping trips, and finally, from other media (radio, TV, newspaper).

Interview 41

The coeds at Ohio State are basically well dressed, however they are more conventional in their dress than on some of the other Ohio campuses. They seem to stick with fashions, but in more of a modified form. You do, however, find extreme fashions on a few people, but the majority of the coeds are not trend setters. I try to keep up with fashion, but budget-wise I am forced to buy more modified forms, basic styles, and not go to extremes. I would, however, consider myself fashion conscious yet not a trend setter.

A majority of my friends buy their clothes at home unless they are from a smaller town, in which case they tend to buy more of their clothes here at school. I buy most of my clothes at home because there are many very adequate stores there.

Interview 42

I feel that a little bit more than half of the girls here at Ohio State actually care how they are dressed and are well dressed while the rest of the coeds are not. However, most of the girls who are well dressed are up on fashion except for those fashions that are way-out. Only a few girls follow these fashion trends. I try to keep up with fashions, although not the way-out ones, and consider myself fashion conscious, but I surely don't consider myself a trend setter.

Most of my friends buy their clothes at home, although sometimes they will buy things here at school. I buy about half of my clothes at home and the other half here in Columbus; however, many of my clothes I make myself.

Interview 43

I like miniskirts, patterned hose, pierced earrings, sweatshirts, cut-off levis, tailored shirts, v-neck sweaters, loafers, knee socks, tent dresses, pant suits, and hip huggers especially well. I don't like saddle shoes, patterned hose, and bloomers. Sweatshirts and cut-off levis are tops, however.

Interview 44

Skirts are more revealing and flashy today than in the past. I believe that this is aimed at creating increased sex appeal. Today's college fashions are pretty faddish and of little value to the girl after graduation from college. I don't like tent dresses, because they don't show a girls figure. Many of today's clothing fashions are useful for only the girl with a good figure. I don't like fish-net hose.

Interview 45

She does not always go along with trends of campus fashion. She goes more by what she likes. She does not like many of the way-out styles popular today, such as the miniskirt. She does keep track of the styles by watching newspaper ads and by observing the fashions being worn on campus. She often shops alone at campus stores and downtown and buys on impulse whenever she sees something she likes. She feels that campus girls are not distinctive enough and that they try to look alike and dress alike.

Interview 46

She does not always wear what is collegiate but pays close attention to what is being worn by other people on campus. She thinks that fashion starts with sororities and that the rest of the campus follows. When she sees something that she really likes or that she thinks she would look good in, she buys it. Sometimes she buys from what appears in fashion magazines (*Glamour*) or from asking wearer the point of purchase. It is very important that a person be stylishly dressed by wearing the clothes that are right for her.

Interview 47

Q. According to the styles of college girls, what do you consider as an appropriate everyday class outfit?

A. A girl should dress according to what best suits her build and what she personally likes. I don't like miniskirts, real long straight hair, fish-net hose. A person can succeed in being an individual without having to conform to fads. I prefer styles that have a long, thin, flaired look, vests, long-sleeved silk blouses. I prefer tans or plain colors, especially blues.

Q.   Where do you think college girls buy their clothes?

A.   Lazarus or Jeanne's or the College Girl. I never can figure out why girls buy clothes around the campus area, especially at Jeanne's, because they are overpriced; probably they buy the label or status associated with it.

Interview 48

Q.   What do you think of the fashions girls are wearing?

A.   The plaids, stripes mixed with polka dots, miniskirts are fine for college campuses but not in the business world. I like variety and wild colors, but I think miniskirts are to be short lived.

Q.   Where do college kids buy their clothes?

A.   The average coed buys mainly at home or downtown Columbus and may make an occasional purchase around the university area, but university located shops are too expensive.

Interview 49

Q.   What do you think of the fashions girls are wearing?

A.   I don't really pay attention to the clothing fashions here at school. I wear exactly what I want to wear when I want to wear it.

Q.   Where do you buy most of your clothes?

A.   At the Army Navy Store.

CHAPTER 9

FAMILY INFLUENCES

Family Participation and Influence in Purchasing Behavior[1]

The role of influence of family members in purchasing behavior has long been recognized as an important consideration in designing marketing strategies. Although many studies of the roles of family members have been conducted, most have been concerned only with role structure as it relates to the physical act of purchasing a product or brand. The Life study reported here is one of the few attempts to study the influence of family members at several stages in the decision-making process. This broader conceptualization of the impact of role structure is more realistic and generates additional insights that are useful in designing product, promotion, price, and channel strategies.

Life Study

Nature of Study

In the Life study, role structure was measured for several stages in the decision-making process. The stages used were defined as follows:

1. *Planning-prepurchase stage*
    a. *The initiator.* The one who originally gets the idea to look around, to change past behavior. The one who starts the process going.
    b. *Suggestor of type or style.* The one who sets broad requirements within a product class, who specifies the type or style of product.
    c. *Suggestor of brand.* The one who has a specific requirement within a product class, who specifies the brand.
    4. *The budgeter.* The one most concerned about the cost of the item, the budget, and so forth. The one who specifies the general price level for expenditure.

[1] The study reported in this case was conducted during 1965 for *Life* magazine by Jaffee and Associates, Inc.

2. *Information-seeking stage*
    a. *Information gatherer (people).* The one who finds out from *people* about the product, price, style.
    b. *Information gatherer (media).* The one who uses various *media* as sources of information about the product.

3. *Buying stage*
    a. *The shopper.* The one who goes to the marketplace, either alone or with a spouse, to check what is available to satisfy the consumption needs of the household.
    b. *The purchaser.* The one who makes the actual purchase.

4. *Postpurchase stage*
    a. *The consumer (satisfied).* The one whose needs for the product have been satisfied.
    b. *The consumer (dissatisfied).* The one whose needs for the product are not fully satisfied.
    c. *The process validator (satisfied).* The one who thinks the entire process was right and would repeat it the same way the next time.
    d. *The process validator (dissatisfied).* The one who thinks that something in the process was wrong and would change some aspect of the process the next time.

The study involved interviews with husbands and wives in 301 middle and upper-middle income households in Hartford, Connecticut; Cleveland, Ohio; and Seattle, Washington.

Role structures for each of the above stages in the decision-making process were determined for the following products: (1) automobiles, (2) refrigerators, (3) vacuum cleaners, (4) coffee, (5) frozen orange juice, (6) toothpaste, (7) pet food, (8) rugs and carpets, and (9) paint.

The questioning began with a joint interview with both husband and wife. For each product, the husband and wife identified the role he or she played for each decision-making stage. In the second phase, husbands and wives were interviewed separately. For each product, each spouse was asked what role he or she performed and what each considered to be the role performed by the other spouse at the planning and buying stages.

Findings

Table 9–1 presents the findings of the study. The percentages are based on each spouse's self-appraisal. Appendix A compares self-appraisal roles with the roles reported by the other spouse.

Questions

1. Evaluate the methodology used in the study. What are the specific strengths and weaknesses? (Be sure to include Appendix A, which follows, in your analysis.)

Table 9-1

Life Study of the Roles of Husbands and Wives in Purchasing Decisions

	Refrigerators		Vacuum Cleaners		Automobiles		Pet Foods		Frozen Orange Juice		Rugs and Carpets		Paint		Coffee		Toothpaste	
	H	W	H	W	H	W	H	W	H	W	H	W	H	W	H	W	H	W
Planning																		
Initiator	71.4	89.0	35.7	83.1	92.8	38.7	15.8	33.3	31.4	82.0	49.3	93.5	60.0	74.2	40.0	43.8	20.9	39.3
Suggestor (type or style)	32.7	69.9	31.0	79.2	80.4	28.7	–	–	–	–	20.3	82.2	58.2	89.3				
Suggestor (brand)	32.7	45.2	35.7	62.3	75.3	20.7	39.5	71.9	–	–	14.5	53.3	74.5	53.4	42.9	91.8	53.5	64.3
Budgeter	34.7	45.2	47.6	50.6	73.2	17.3	–	–	–	–	26.1	58.9						
Information seeking																		
Information gatherer (people)	91.8	84.9	76.2	87.0	79.8	80.7	–	–	20.0	44.1	68.1	81.3	70.9	63.5				
Information gatherer (media)	59.2	54.8	26.2	42.9	56.7	43.3	–	–	41.4	48.6	55.1	65.4	21.8	28.7				
Buying																		
Shopper	87.8	86.3	50.0	74.0	95.9	72.7	–	–	–	–	75.4	94.4	72.8	62.4				
Purchaser	71.4	79.4	54.8	81.8	93.8	52.0	39.5	93.0	38.6	93.7	58.0	91.6	70.0	47.2	28.6	89.0	34.9	89.3
Postpurchase																		
Consumer (satisfied)	69.4	67.4	66.7	61.0	54.6	61.3	89.5	93.0	94.3	96.4	34.8	41.1	90.9	95.5	94.3	98.6	93.0	98.2

Table 9-1 (continued)

	Refrigerators		Vacuum Cleaners		Automobiles		Pet Food		Frozen Orange Juice		Rugs and Carpets		Paint		Coffee		Toothpaste	
	H	W	H	W	H	W	H	W	H	W	H	W	H	W	H	W	H	W
Postpurchase																		
Consumer (dissatisfied)	16.3	21.9	23.8	32.5	43.3	30.0	2.6	3.5	4.3	2.7	31.9	38.3	6.4	3.9	0	1.4	2.3	1.8
Process validator (satisfied)	71.4	64.4	78.6	66.2	54.6	61.3	78.9	87.7	71.4	79.3	66.7	63.6	82.7	84.8	74.3	72.6	76.7	83.9
Process validator (dissatisfied)	20.4	30.1	9.5	27.3	40.2	29.3	10.5	10.5	24.3	18.9	24.6	34.6	14.5	14.0	20.0	23.3	18.6	12.5

Appendix A: Comparison of Self-Appraised Roles with the Roles Reported by the Other Spouse for the Planning and Buying Stages of the Decision-Making Process

Product and Source Used to Obtain Role	Planning Stage				Buying Stage		
	Initiator	Suggestor of Type or Style	Suggestor of Brand	Budgeter	Shopper (Alone)	Shopper (Together)	Purchaser
Refrigerators							
Husband							
Own report	71.4	32.7	32.7	34.7	16.3	81.6	71.4
Wife's report	67.1	35.6	30.1	38.4	13.7	76.7	76.7
Wife							
Own report	89.0	69.9	45.2	45.2	21.9	76.7	79.4
Husband's report	87.8	67.3	46.9	38.8	18.4	81.6	81.6
Vacuum cleaners							
Husband							
Own report	35.7	31.0	35.7	47.6	16.7	35.7	54.8
Wife's report	18.2	13.0	18.2	26.0	11.7	46.8	46.8
Wife							
Own report	83.1	79.2	62.3	50.6	36.4	46.8	81.8
Husband's report	78.6	71.4	57.1	45.2	33.3	35.7	73.8
Automobiles							
Husband							
Own report	92.8	80.4	75.3	73.2	55.7	67.0	93.8
Wife's report	90.0	83.3	78.0	81.3	40.0	70.0	92.0
Wife							
Own report	38.7	28.7	20.7	17.3	8.0	70.0	52.0
Husband's report	29.9	24.7	23.7	13.4	4.1	67.0	38.1

Appendix A (continued)

Product and Source Used to Obtain Role	Planning Stage				Buying Stage		
	Initiator	Suggestor of Type or Style	Suggestor of Brand	Budgeter	Shopper (Alone)	Shopper (Together)	Purchaser
Pet food							
Husband							
Own report	15.8		39.5				39.5
Wife's report	8.8		33.3				31.6
Wife							
Own report	33.3		71.9				93.0
Husband's report	26.3		71.1				89.5
Orange juice							
Husband							
Own report	31.4						38.6
Wife's report	24.3						26.2
Wife							
Own report	82.0						93.7
Husband's report	80.0						91.4
Rugs/Carpets							
Husband							
Own report	49.3	20.3	14.5	26.1	7.2	71.0	58.0
Wife's report	49.5	26.2	19.6	39.3	9.3	67.3	61.7
Wife							
Own report	93.5	82.2	53.3	58.9	41.1	67.3	91.6
Husband's report	85.5	71.0	47.8	44.9	29.0	71.0	89.9

Appendix A (continued)

Product and Source Used to Obtain Role	Planning Stage				Buying Stage		
	Initiator	Suggestor of Type or Style	Suggestor of Brand	Budgeter	Shopper (Alone)	Shopper (Together)	Purchaser
Paint							
Husband							
Own report	60.0	58.2	74.5		36.4	36.4	70.0
Wife's report	58.4	48.3	68.5		28.1	38.2	68.0
Wife							
Own report	74.2	89.3	53.4		24.2	38.2	47.2
Husband's report	74.5	90.0	50.9		15.5	36.4	37.3
Coffee							
Husband							
Own report	40.0		42.9				28.6
Wife's report	16.4		39.7				21.9
Wife							
Own report	43.8		91.8				89.0
Husband's report	48.6		77.1				88.6
Toothpaste							
Husband							
Own report	20.9		53.5				34.9
Wife's report	16.1		48.2				41.1
Wife							
Own report	39.3		64.3				89.3
Husband's report	30.2		74.4				86.0

2. Select one of the products included in the study and indicate the implications of the role structure for product, pricing, promotion, and channel strategies.

3. Select another product and repeat the procedure specified in Question 2. Prepare an outline indicating the ways the marketing strategy implications of role structures vary from one product to another.

Aqua-Craft Corporation (A): Determining Purchasing Influences

Background

The Aqua-Craft Corporation was founded in 1927 by Claude Whipple and Richard Hull. Whipple and Hull first met in 1920 at a major eastern university where they were teammates on the football team. In 1924 both men were graduated from college with degrees in engineering. Hull accepted employment with a major steel manufacturer, and Whipple joined a professional football team. By 1927 both men had decided to change occupations. Whipple had sustained several football injuries, and Hull was not encouraged over the advancement opportunities at the steel company. During a fishing trip, the men explored the possibility of starting a business together. Several months later they decided that a boat company was the best available way of utilizing their respective skills. Whipple's reputation in athletics would be advantageous in promoting the line of boats to dealers and sporting enthusiasts, and Hull could utilize his experience in metals technology and production.

The company was incorporated in 1927 and began producing galvanized steel fishing boats in its factory located in Gary, Indiana. Hull supervised the company's production while Whipple handled the sales side of the business. A former teammate, Robert Smothers, was persuaded to leave a Chicago certified public accounting firm to become the firm's chief financial executive.

By the summer of 1929, the firm was making substantial progress, and the decision was made to go public. Several thousand shares of common stock were issued, but the company remained closely held, with Hull, Whipple, and Smothers owning 60 percent of the outstanding shares. The men planned to use the additional funds to expand the company's production facilities, but these plans were abandoned when the Great Depression hit in the fall of 1929.

From 1929 until 1942 the company barely survived. However, in the spring of 1943, the company was awarded several Government contracts to manufacture water craft for the war effort. During the 1943 to 1946 period, the company's sales volume increased 700 percent, and considerable experience was gained, particularly in manufacturing. When the war ended, management was faced with major decisions about the future direction of the company. Several months of analysis led to the conclusion that the firm should again concentrate on the recreation boat market.

Since 1947 the company's sales have grown steadily. In 1950 sales were $5.2 million; in 1955, $6.5 million; in 1960, $10.2 million; in 1965, $18.5 million; and in 1967 they were $21.7 million. By 1967, the company operated manufacturing facilities in Southern California, Kansas, Louisiana, and Indiana.

Product Line

The rapid increase in sales was made possible partly by a greatly expanded product line. By the spring of 1968, the company produced fifty different boats, thirty-five of which were aluminum construction and fifteen of which were fiberglass. Models include cruisers, runabouts, canoes, sailboats, utility boats, and fishing boats. The company also produces boats for sale under private brands to several major retail chain organizations. Private brands account for approximately 20 percent of the company's sales.

Channels of Distribution

Aqua-Craft distributes its line of boats through 1500 dealers located throughout the United States. These dealers are contacted by the company's own sales force and by the salesmen of forty-five independent distributors. The company also has a national accounts manager who has responsibility for sales to national and regional retail chains.

The independent distributors have been a major factor in the company's success to date. They are responsible for establishing and controlling dealerships and assisting the dealers' sale programs. The company feels that distributors can provide better service and maintain closer contact with the dealers. The distributors also decrease or simplify the company's storage, financing, and credit requirements.

Promotion

The company's advertising budget amounts to approximately 1.5 percent of sales. Consumer magazines, trade papers, farm publications, business publications, and direct mailings are the major media that are used. Specific vehicles that are used include *Field and Stream, Yachting, Popular Science, Popular Mechanics,* and *Motor Boating.*

Past advertisements have concentrated heavily on product features. Boating is often shown as a quiet, restful sport—especially fishing or cruising—or as a social activity involving water skiing and young girls.

Aqua-Craft provides its distributors with point-of-purchase displays, brochures, and other types of sales promotion materials. These materials are then distributed to dealers by the distributors. Dealers must advertise at their own expense because the company does not offer advertising allowances.

Pricing

Aqua-Craft's prices are competitive with comparable models produced by major competitors—Chrysler, Johnson, Traveller, and Glastron. Prices range from $149 for a nine-foot flat bottom to $4495 for an inboard-outdrive cruiser. In general, the company's prices and product line are designed to appeal to the mass boating market as opposed to the high-priced luxury market being served by firms like Chris Craft.

Current Problems

By the spring of 1968, management was growing increasingly concerned about their lack of information about the characteristics and behavior patterns of the market they were attempting to penetrate. Management knew that its sales to various occupational groups followed the experience of their segment of the industry. Skilled workers accounted for 23.6 percent of sales followed by semiskilled workers with 19.3 percent and professionals with 16.9 percent.

In addition, the company's advertising agency recently conducted a study to determine the reasons people buy boats. The results of the study were[2]

Reasons	Percent
Cruising	53
Fishing	41
Hunting	8
Skiing	62
All other	6

The lack of information about buyer behavior and purchasing influences came to a head when the company was finalizing its media schedule for 1968. The advertising agency proposed that the company use the same media and vehicles that had been used in the past (see "Promotion" section of this case). The account executive for the advertising agency put it this way: "Our media strategy has been effective in generating a dramatic increase in sales, and there is no reason to believe conditions have changed. How can you argue with success?"

Bill Whipple, the company's new advertising manager and son of Claude Whipple, and several other executives objected to the media schedule on the

[2] The figures exceed 100 percent because several buyers mentioned more than one reason.

grounds that it was not reaching the people who influence the decision to purchase a boat. Bill Whipple argued:

> It's quite obvious, at least to me, that teenagers are becoming more important. Several of our competitors are designing their boats to have a sports car look in order to appeal to them. And another thing, I'm not so sure housewives aren't important too. Let's face it, boating is a family affair for a lot of folks. It costs a lot of money—maybe $3000 or $4000. With that much money involved, wives are certainly going to have something to say about whether or not a boat is purchased.
>
> I think we better find out who is involved in the decision to purchase a boat before we go any further.

Questions

1. Prepare a proposal outlining the way Aqua-Craft should go about determining the roles of family members in purchasing boats. Your proposal should include
    a. Statement of the problem
    b. Research design
        (1) Type of design and rationale
    c. Sampling
        (1) Definition of universe
        (2) Sampling unit
        (3) Sample size
        (4) Respondent selection procedure
    d. Questionnaire and/or other data collection instrument(s)
    e. Interviewing procedures
    f. Plan of analysis

2. Indicate the specific ways that the results of the study could be used in designing marketing strategies.

PART IV

CONSUMER DECISION PROCESSES

CHAPTER 10

PROBLEM RECOGNITION

Lectromatic Corporation: Analyzing Problem Recognition— Purchasing Relationships

The Lectromatic Corporation, a large manufacturer of electrical appliances, was organized on July 15, 1925, as the result of the merger of two companies with complementary technological expertise. The Thomas W. Wilson Company had been founded in 1884 for the purpose of developing an electrical light. The Charles B. Bronson Company was organized in 1915 in order to adapt refrigeration processes to household use.

The company's growth has been steadily upward with the exception of the depression years. By 1929, it had attained a sales volume of $150 million. By 1933, however, sales had dropped to $43 million, and the company, like many others in the industry, did not recover until the end of the decade. By 1968, the company's sales volume had grown to $4.3 billion.

The company produced all its appliances for the United States market from its manufacturing complex in Georgia. Major subsidiaries include Lectromatic-Canada and Lectromatic-Europe. United States facilities for many consumer goods are currently being expanded in anticipation of long-term growth. The company also plans to intensify distribution in Asia and South America by 1970.

The company's financial condition compares favorably with its major competitors. Like many other companies in the industry, Lectromatic's profit margin has declined in recent years. Net profit as a percent of sales was 4.8 percent in 1967 compared with 5.9 percent in 1965.

Marketing Strategy and Organization

Product Line

Lectromatic enjoys a reputation for high-quality appliances. The company has pioneered improvements in its existing product line, and, particularly since the 1950s, has developed many new small electrical appliances.

The company produces approximately thirty different types of appliances. Major appliances produced include refrigerators, freezers, washers, dryers, ranges, dishwashers, waste disposals, room air conditioners, and other commercial appliances. The company manufactures both black-and-white and color television sets as well as electric radios, phonographs, tape recorders, mixers, blenders, knives, irons, hair dryers, blankets, toasters, coffee makers, skillets, waffle irons, toothbrushes, and clothes and shoe brushes.

Each appliance comes in a variety of models, price ranges, and colors. For example, the company manufactures twenty-seven models of refrigerators, thirty-two different ranges, thirty-one washer and dryer models, twelve different dishwashers, and thirty-two different types of air conditioners. The total product line, excluding color availabilities, consists of slightly over seven hundred models.

Pricing Strategy

Lectromatic follows a regionally oriented, rather than a standardized, pricing policy. Prices to retailers vary from region to region, according to the costs involved in servicing the region and according to other considerations.

Retail prices also vary by region and type of retail outlet. Each individual retailer sets his own prices based on what he pays for the product and on the markup that he needs to implement his particular retailing strategy. The company has not actively pursued a retail price maintenance policy because of the problems and costs involved in enforcement. Generally, retail prices of Lectromatic appliances are either competitive or slightly higher (5 percent) than those of competing brands.

Promotional Strategy

In the past, the company's advertising expenditures have varied between .5 percent and 1.5 percent of sales. In 1968, the advertising budget totaled $29,875,000. In 1966, when the company's sales were $3.9 billion, it spent $27,300,000 on advertising. By contrast, the 1966 advertising expenditures of major competitors were (1) General Electric, $22,901,166; (2) Radio Corporation of America, $14,540,513; (3) Zenith, $5,140,644; and (4) Motorola, $5,989,277.[1]

The company advertises in a variety of media. In 1968, 28.2 percent of the budget was invested in newspapers, 32.3 percent in magazines, 24 percent in network television, 7.5 percent in spot television, 2 percent in network radio, and 6 percent in spot radio. Major competitors typically spend a smaller percentage in newspapers and spot television and a larger percentage in business publications. This is primarily because of the fact that many competitors produce products for the industrial market.

[1] *National Advertising Investment,* January-December, 1966.

The company also has a cooperative advertising program with its dealers. The terms are fifty-fifty—the dealer and the company split the cost of the dealers advertising—provided that the dealer meets certain standards established by the company and that the dealer submits acceptable proof of the advertising. Most competitors have a comparable cooperative arrangement with their dealers.

Channels of Distribution

Appliances are shipped from the company's manufacturing facilities in Georgia to five regional, company-owned, distribution centers located throughout the United States. Domestic, nonprivate-brand appliances are sold through twenty-five zone sales offices. The products are distributed through department stores, furniture stores, appliance stores, discount department stores, television and radio shops, and television repair shops. The company also produces private-brand merchandise for several chain organizations. This merchandise is shipped directly from the firm's plant or a regional distribution center to the chain's warehouse.

Marketing Organization

The marketing department is organized on a functional-product basis (see Figure 10–1). The directors of advertising and sales promotion, product planning, field sales, private brands, marketing intelligence, and two product group directors report to the marketing vice president, Jack A. Wilson. The regular force is organized on a regional basis except for quantity sales to business and institutional customers, and national accounts that handle sales of regular merchandise (nonprivate brands) to retailers operating in several geographic areas. Ten product managers are responsible for making certain that their products receive the proper amount of research, advertising, and sales effort. All research activities are coordinated by the director of marketing intelligence, Harold Wilcox. Bruce Hansen is responsible for the consumer behavior research program.

Consumer Research Program

Background and Problems

In the fall of 1965, Wilcox asked Hansen to critically evaluate the company's consumer research program and submit recommendations outlining the ways that it could be improved. In a meeting that lasted nearly three hours, Wilcox outlined some of the problems to Hansen.

> Last week Jack Wilson asked me to review my operation and re-evaluate the role that marketing intelligence should play. Jack is under a lot of pressure, you know. Since our profit margin has declined, top man-

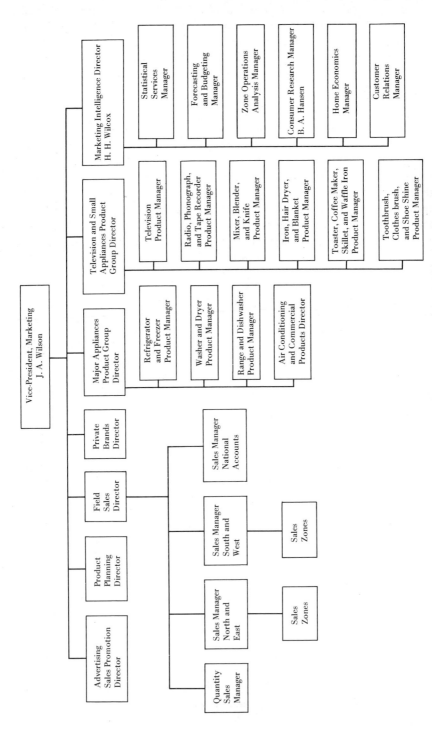

FIGURE 10–1. Lectromatic Corporation—Marketing Department

agement is looking for ways to tighten up expenses. That huge advertising budget of ours is a prime candidate. Wilson's ability to sell the budget in the future is going to require more hard facts than we've had before.

There are other problems too. The product managers say they aren't getting the kind of information they want in time to make decisions. The advertising and sales promotion manager says he needs more information. And, of course, in our own shop, we either don't have the right kind of information or don't know how to use what we have, or both, because our sales forecasts get worse each year. At any rate I want you to really look into this thing. You've got six months.

Hansen, a young Ph.D. from a large midwestern university, took the request seriously. He and his assistants interviewed every member of the marketing department in order to determine the amount and type of information needed and when it was needed. They reviewed journal articles, attended professional meetings, conferred with advertising and marketing research agency executives, and contacted research departments of noncompeting firms that Hansen thought might face similar types of problems.

Six months later Hansen submitted his report. It concluded that the current consumer research program was not meeting the needs of the organization. By depending almost entirely on outside data collection and research groups, operating managers were not getting the kind of information that they needed. Even the useful information commonly reached managers too late.

The report continued by stating that an information system that meets the collective needs of the company has to have several characteristics. First, it must be efficient, that is, capable of providing answers to questions in time for managers to use the information before it becomes obsolete. Second, it must be flexible enough to answer the variety of questions that the organization asks. Finally, it must produce relevant and valid results. With respect to the latter requirement, the report stated:

> Our entire research program utilizes what many psychologists, sociologists, and marketing-behaviorists refer to as a distributive strategy of inquiry. In plain English, this means that we are analyzing only the purchase itself—trying to find out how Lectromatic buyers differ from consumers buying other brands.
>
> While this is a legitimate concern, it has certain limitations. First, we must infer why consumers buy or do not buy our products. If they don't buy we don't know why and if they do buy we still don't know why. This suggests the second limitation; namely that our approach generates limited insights about how our operating managers can go about convincing more consumers to buy our product. It seems to me that a far more useful approach would be to determine, or simply describe if you will, the steps that consumers go through in purchasing appliances. In

other words, instead of focusing only on the purchase itself, we should find out what happens *before* that time. For example, what activities and events result in consumers recognizing that they need an appliance? What sources of information are used to learn about different brands? What is the relative importance of these sources? What features are they looking for? Which features are most important? Answers to these questions will provide relevant data for management decisions. This is called a decision process approach and I recommend that we initiate a research program based on this point of view.

The final conclusions of the report were

If we are to effectively service the consumer behavior information requirements of the organization, and if we are to initiate a Decision Process Research Program (DPRP), and the other programs that will overcome our current deficiencies, our internal organization must be expanded. Outside organizations simply do not presently do the kind of research that we need.

Excerpts of Hansen's report were included in Wilcox's report to Wilson. In May of 1966 Hansen was directed to initiate a DPRP and was authorized 90 percent of the additional personnel, facilities, and financial resources that he had requested.

Lectromatic's Decision Process Research Program[2]

Research Design

The research needs of the company as well as the logic of decision-making itself led Hansen to the choice of a longitudinal design rather than a cross-sectional survey. Hansen justified his selection of longitudinal design as follows:

Longitudinal analysis of reinterview data is the best available method for understanding *changes* that occur over *time*. The span of time that we are concerned with is the time that it requires an average buyer to reach a decision regarding the purchase of one of our products. This time span begins with the emergence of an *intention* to purchase a product and ends with a *decision* to purchase or not to purchase.

A national probability sample of 7500 households was designed. Personal interviews were conducted by a New York based interview firm with an established reputation for quality research. Precautions were taken to minimize the possibility that respondents would know that Lectromatic was sponsoring the study.

2 Only selected parts of this program are reported in this case.

Each respondent was interviewed once each three months over a two-year period. During each interview, respondents were shown a list of household appliances (those produced by Lectromatic) and asked whether or not they planned to buy any of them some time during the next year. Respondents planning to buy were asked when they anticipated acquiring the item and the brand that they thought they would purchase. During each reinterview, each respondent was asked whether the appliances that he had previously stated he intended to purchase had actually been purchased. Respondents purchasing appliances without previously stated purchase intentions were asked to describe the circumstances and events that led them to buy. Selected findings from the study are discussed below.

Length of Planning Period

The time span between purchase intentions and a decision to purchase varied considerably across products (see Table 10–1). Clothes dryers have

Table 10–1

Average Length of Planning Period of Selected Appliances

Appliance	Average Length of Planning Period (Weeks)*
Clothes dryer	17
Electric range	14
Tape recorder	12
Refrigerator	11
Room air conditioner	5
Electric iron	3
Electric skillet	2
Radio	1

* *Planning period* is defined as "the period of time between a stated purchase intention and a purchase."

the longest planning period (seventeen weeks) while many appliances have average planning periods of one week or less.

Relationships between Market Share and Purchase Intentions

The respondents intending to purchase an appliance during the next three months were asked to indicate which brand they thought they would purchase. The percentage of respondents intending to purchase Lectromatic appliances was computed and compared with the firm's current market share in each product category. This type of comparison is made available to product managers, advertising personnel, and other interested managers every three months.

Table 10–2

Relationships between Lectromatic's Market Share and Share of Intentions

Appliance	Market Share	Share of Purchase Intentions
Refrigerators	12	21
Freezers	14	19
Washers	10	14
Dryers	8	12
Ranges	14	17
Dishwashers	13	16
Room air conditioners	18	19
Television: Black-and-White	21	18
Television: Color	17	23
Radios	22	14
Tape recorders	23	31
Mixers	19	20
Blenders	22	14
Knives	21	27
Irons	20	21
Hair dryers	23	28
Blankets	21	6
Toasters	17	12
Coffee makers	18	24
Skillets	17	18
Waffle Irons	26	10
Toothbrushes	24	34
Clothes Brushes	27	12

Table 10–2 shows the relationship between market share and share-of-purchase intentions from the latest survey. Wide variations exist across products; in some instances purchase intentions exceed market share, although for other product categories the opposite relationship exists.

Relationships between Buying Intentions and Purchasing Behavior

Overall, 46 percent of the respondents fulfilled their purchase intentions by buying a brand in the product category for which they had purchase plans. However, as Table 10–3 indicates, wide variations in fulfillment rates were found. Of those respondents intending to purchase a Lectromatic appliance, only 40 percent actually purchased any brand. Fulfillment rates for respondents originally preferring other brands was much higher—48 percent. Lectromatic also had a lower brand-preferred/brand-purchased rate. Of the respondents originally preferring Lectromatic, only 37 percent eventually purchased the brand. In contrast, on the average, 45 percent of the re-

Table 10–3

Relationship between Buying Intentions and Purchasing Behavior

Purchase Intention	Purchasing Behavior	
Lectromatic	40 percent purchased the appliance	37 percent purchased the brand intended
	60 percent did not purchase the appliance	63 percent changed brands
Average for all other brands	48 percent purchased the appliance	45 percent purchased the brand intended
	52 percent did not purchase the appliance	55 percent changed brands

spondents originally intending to purchase other brands actually purchased them.

Net Gain and Loss Analysis

Although the percentage of respondents who switched away from a particular brand is important, it reveals only part of the behavior that is relevant for management decisions. A more comprehensive, and hence more germane, measure is *net change for a brand*. For example, of those who originally intend to purchase Lectromatic, some will fulfill their intentions, some will purchase another brand, and some will not purchase at all. Similarly, of those originally intending to purchase other brands, some will purchase the brand that they originally preferred, some will purchase another brand (perhaps Lectromatic), and some will not purchase at all. The statistic—net gain or loss—includes the intenders who originally planned to purchase Lectromatic but who actually purchased another brand, as well as the respondents who originally preferred another brand but actually purchased Lectromatic.

Table 10–4 itemizes net gains and losses from stated brand intentions for each of the products produced by Lectromatic. It is again clear that Lectromatic products differ widely in the net percentage that they gain or lose from original brand intentions.

Unplanned Purchase Analysis

Before reinterviewing respondents, interviewers reviewed the purchase intentions obtained during the previous interview(s). During each reinter-

Table 10–4

Net Gains and Losses Resulting from Switching from Stated Brand Intentions*

Product and Brand	Number of Respondents Switching to Lectromatic and Other Brands for Each 100 Respondents Switching from the Brand	Net Percentage Gain or Loss
Refrigerators		
Lectromatic	60	−40
Average for other brands	95	−5
Freezers		
Lectromatic	90	−10
Average for other brands	99	−1
Washers		
Lectromatic	86	−14
Average for other brands	103	+3
Dryers		
Lectromatic	87	−13
Average for other brands	106	+6
Ranges		
Lectromatic	95	−5
Average for other brands	103	+3
Dishwashers		
Lectromatic	97	−3
Average for other brands	101	+1
Air Conditioners		
Lectromatic	99	−1
Average for other brands	99	−1
Television: Black-and-White		
Lectromatic	110	+10
Average for other brands	106	+6
Television: Color		
Lectromatic	94	−6
Average for other brands	101	+1
Radios		
Lectromatic	113	+13
Average for other brands	104	+4
Tape recorders		
Lectromatic	92	−8
Average for other brands	97	−3

Table 10–4 (continued)

Product and Brand	Number of Respondents Switching to Lectromatic and Other Brands for Each 100 Respondents Switching from the Brand	Net Percentage Gain or Loss
Mixers		
Lectromatic	101	+1
Average for other brands	104	+4
Blenders		
Lectromatic	107	+7
Average for other brands	102	+2
Knives		
Lectromatic	90	−10
Average for other brands	104	+4
Irons		
Lectromatic	98	−2
Average for other brands	104	+4
Hair dryers		
Lectromatic	92	−8
Average for other brands	98	−2
Blankets		
Lectromatic	112	+12
Average for other brands	102	+2
Toasters		
Lectromatic	107	+7
Average for other brands	103	+3
Coffee makers		
Lectromatic	91	−9
Average for other brands	102	+2
Skillets		
Lectromatic	101	+1
Average for other brands	101	+1
Waffle irons		
Lectromatic	114	+14
Average for other brands	97	−3
Toothbrushes		
Lectromatic	85	−15
Average for other brands	102	+2

Table 10–4 (continued)

Product and Brand	Number of Respondents Switching to Lectromatic and Other Brands for Each 100 Respondents Switching from the Brand	Net Percentage Gain or Loss
Clothes brushes		
Lectromatic	113	+13
Average for other brands	98	−2
Average for all products		
Lectromatic	92	−8
Average for other brands	102	−2

* Purchasers only.

view, respondents were shown a card itemizing the products produced by Lectromatic and were asked whether or not they had purchased any of these products since the last time they were interviewed. If the respondent purchased one or more of the products but had not previously expressed a purchase intention, he or she was asked, "During our previous conversations you expressed no intention of buying (*insert product*). Would you please tell me the conditions or circumstances that led you to purchase (*insert product*)?"

Purchases without previously stated purchase intentions were classified as *unplanned*. Table 10–5 summarizes the reasons for these unplanned purchases cross-classified by whether the appliance is a necessity or a luxury.

Table 10–5

Reasons for Unplanned Purchases

Reason(s) Given	Type of Appliance†		All Purchases
	Necessity	Luxury	
Old appliance not available	47%	13%	35%
Dissatisfied with old appliance	10	3	8
Wanted or needed it	21	57	36
Special opportunity to buy	10	18	14
All other reasons	25%	28%	26%

* Responses total more than 100 percent because many respondents gave more than one reason.

† Appliances classified as necessities include (1) refrigerators, (2) washers, (3) ranges, (4) black-and-white televisions, (5) radios (regular, not FM or transistor), (6) irons, (7) toasters, and (8) coffee makers. The luxury classification includes (1) freezers, (2) dryers, (3) dishwashers, (4) air conditioners, (5) color television, (6) FM and transistor radios, (7) tape recorders, (8) mixers, (9) blenders, (10) knives, (11) hair dryers, (12) blankets, (13) skillets, (14) waffle irons, (15) toothbrushes, and (16) clothes brushes.

Questions

1. Evaluate the methodology used in the study and the data presented in the case.

2. Assume that the methodology is sound. According to the data and the other information presented, what are Lectromatic's marketing problems? Prepare a report indicating how you would recommend that the company overcome these problems. (Be sure to carefully analyze Tables 10–1 to 10–5.)

3. Evaluate the usefulness of the types of data discussed in the case. Give specific examples of how each type of information can be used in formulating marketing strategy.

4. Describe the characteristics of the firms that you feel should adopt this type of consumer research program.

CHAPTER 11

ALTERNATIVE DEFINITION AND EVALUATION

Evaluating Alternative Modes of Travel[1]

In 1961 the airline industry suffered the worst financial year in history. The airlines' load factor was only 57 percent, and the industry as a whole had a net loss of $30 million. It was clear that air travel was no longer a "sellers market." If the airlines wanted more customers, they would have to go out and get them.

Several programs were initiated in an attempt to stimulate demand. Many promotional fares such as family plans, air bus and shuttle service flights, were developed. Several airlines began sponsoring consumer-type research studies in order to learn more about the air travel market. The study reported below was designed to investigate the behavior and attitudes of the segments of the population most likely to be diverted to air travel—the families with an annual income of $7000 or more. In 1961 this group represented 33 percent of the United States population and 60 percent of the airline passengers.

Evaluating Alternative Modes of Travel

Study Objectives

The purpose of the phase of the study reported here was to determine how consumers evaluate alternative ways of traveling. Three approaches were used:

1. Attitudes toward flying per se were measured without reference to other forms of transportation.

2. Attitudes toward flying were measured by comparing it with its major competitor, the automobile.

3. Attitudes toward different aspects of air travel were measured.

[1] Adapted from *The Air Travel Market: Present and Prospective*, Bureau of Advertising, American Newspaper Publishers Association, February, 1963.

The first method was desirable in order to obtain some idea about the most salient "meanings" associated with air travel. The second method was used to gain some insight into why a person chooses or does not choose a particular mode of transportation, such as flying, instead of some other means, such as traveling by auto. The third method is helpful in determining why a consumer chooses a particular airline or flight rather than some other.

Research Procedures

The field work for this study was handled by Home Testing Institute, Inc. (HTI) of Manhasset, Long Island, New York. This organization conducts a series of continuing consumer studies with cross-sectional panels of families, in all walks of life, in every section of the country.

The HTI cross-section is composed of 13,000 families and is constantly updated so that it approximates known Census data on a variety of key characteristics, such as geographic distribution, age, occupation, and income.

On April 6, 1962, a screening questionnaire was sent to all HTI families with an annual *family* income of $7000 or more. Usable responses were obtained from 2268 families.

The respondents were then classified according to the flying behavior of the male head of the household, and four groups were established:

1. *Business flyers.* Families in which the male head of the household had flown in the past year for business purposes.

2. *Nonbusiness flyers.* Families in which the male head of the household had flown in the past year, but not for business purposes.

3. *Former flyers.* Families in which the male household head had flown but not in the past year.

4. *Nonflyers.* Families in which the male head of the family had never flown for any reason.

On May 10, 1962, the main questionnaires were mailed to 250 families in each of the four groups, or to 1000 families in all. This mailing included a questionnaire for the male household head and a shorter version for the housewife.

Whenever possible, families included in the final mailing were selected from the cross-section. However, only 202 nonbusiness flyers responded to the first screening questionnaire. Consequently, it was necessary to add forty-eight more families to the study from the HTI "reserve."

Final tabulations began when usuable questionnaires from 850 families were obtained. Only the families in which both the male head and the housewife returned completed questionnaires were included in the results.

In addition to grouping respondents according to their flying behavior, all respondents were also classified into three social status groups, according to their income and occupation, as follows:

I.   *White collar workers:* $10,000 or more in family income.

II. *White collar workers:* $7000 to $9999 in family income.

III. *Blue collar workers:* $7000 or more in family income.

Classified as white collar were (1) professional, technical, and kindred workers, (2) managers, officials, and proprietors, (3) clerical and kindred workers, and (4) sales workers.

Classified as blue collar were (1) craftsmen, foremen, and kindred workers, (2) operatives and kindred workers, (3) private house workers (domestics), (4) service workers, (5) farmers and farm managers, (6) farm laborers and foremen, (7) laborers (except farm), and (8) others (retired, unemployed, Armed Forces).

The size of each of these three groups, as estimated from the 1960 Census figures is

Status Group	Size (in millions)	Percent
I	4.1	26
II	3.9	25
III	7.6	49
TOTAL	15.6	100

It should be noted that the just given figures represent all United States families with an income of $7000 or more, not just the 93 percent who have both parents present in the household. Although the "both parents present" subgroup is the most relevant, the Census Bureau figures are not presented in such a way as to make this sort of a breakdown possible. Therefore, the above data—based on the total number of families—is the best estimate of how the "both parents present" group distributes among the three status levels.

Status Group I (the $10,000 white collar worker) is considered by many to be the best customer for air travel. The subdivision makes it possible to check this belief and to ascertain the degree to which the other status groups are also good markets—current and potential—for air travel.

Findings

Attitudes toward Air Travel

The questionnaire included identical open-ended questions for husbands and wives about their likes and dislikes about air travel. The question was worded so as to allow the respondent as much room as possible to say what he or she wished to say.

As Table 11–1 indicates, the most salient positive association was the time saved on air trips. From 70 to 90 percent of all groups mentioned this. Comfort was a distant second, and safety and expense received almost no votes as things a person likes about air travel.

Table 11–1

What People Like about Flying

	What Is Liked by			
	Business Flyers	Nonbusiness Flyers	Former Flyers	Nonflyers
Time saved	88%	89%	80%	70%
Comfort	38	28	33	20
Pleasure	8	9	10	9
Service	7	5	6	2
Safety	5	3	2	3
Less expensive	2%	—	1%	1%
Percent mentioning likes	(98)	(97)	(92)	(81)
No specific likes mentioned	2%	3%	8%	19%
BASE	(208)	(196)	(226)	(220)
	What Is Liked by Wives of			
	Business Flyers	Nonbusiness Flyers	Former Flyers	Nonflyers
Time saved	88%	86%	90%	82%
Comfort	36	38	36	24
Pleasure	14	15	15	16
Service	8	10	9	5
Safety	3	2	2	1
Less expensive	2%	2%	3%	1%
Percent mentioning likes	(98)	(98)	(96)	(92)
No specific likes mentioned	2%	2%	4%	8%
BASE	(208)	(196)	(226)	(220)

What do people dislike about flying? Time lost and fear (or lack of safety) were the most salient factors (Table 11–2).

Time lost ranks first by a fairly wide margin for the husbands and their wives in all cases except that of the nonflyers. Business flyers are much more concerned with time lost than with safety. Fifty-six percent of the business flyers mention time lost, whereas only 11 percent of them mention fear. For the nonflyer, on the other hand, fear is the primary negative association with flying, with approximately 27 percent of the men and 41 percent of their wives mentioning accidents, storms, being afraid of heights, or being off the ground.

Table 11–3, taken from data in Table 11–2, indicate that the wives are less concerned with time lost and more concerned with the safety angle than their husbands. It should also be pointed out that fear is an admitted factor for

Table 11–2

What People Dislike about Flying

	What Is Disliked by			
	Business Flyers	Nonbusiness Flyers	Former Flyers	Nonflyers
Time lost	56%	33%	39%	23%
Discomfort	10	9	7	3
Lack of enjoyment	5	7	8	10
Poor service	12	6	4	1
Fear (lack of safety)	11	10	14	27
Too expensive	8%	8%	14%	9%
Percent mentioning dislikes	(78)	(64)	(73)	(68)
No specific dislikes mentioned	22%	36%	27%	32%
BASE	(208)	(196)	(226)	(220)

	What Is Disliked by Wives of			
	Business Flyers	Nonbusiness Flyers	Former Flyers	Nonflyers
Time lost	40%	30%	34%	21%
Discomfort	11	17	15	9
Lack of enjoyment	12	8	15	14
Poor service	9	9	7	1
Fear (lack of safety)	25	25	28	41
Too expensive	9%	7%	13%	10%
Percent mentioning dislikes	(81)	(81)	(84)	(82)
No specific dislikes mentioned	19%	19%	16%	18%
BASE	(208)	(196)	(226)	(220)

Table 11–3

Analysis of the Importance of Time Lost and Fear by Sex and Type of Flyer

	Percent Mentioning	
	Time Lost	Fear
Business flyers	56	11
Nonbusiness flyers	33	10
Former flyers	39	14
Nonflyers	23	27
Wives of		
Business flyers	40	25
Nonbusiness flyers	30	25
Former flyers	34	28
Nonflyers	21	41

only one out of every ten men who flew for business or nonbusiness reasons in the past year.

In passing, it seems somewhat paradoxical that time should be so prominent as both a positive and a negative factor. However, a closer examination of the responses indicates that the positive time association refers primarily to in-flight speed while the negative time association refers primarily to the time lost getting to and from the airport and to delays because of schedules and weather conditions.

Air Travel Compared with Auto Travel

In the previous section details were reported on how respondents react to flying per se; that is, what they like or dislike about flying when queried without any direct reference to other modes of transportation. This section reports their opinions about flying when it is compared directly with an external referent, using the major mode of transportation, the automobile. All subjects, both husbands and wives, were asked to compare air travel to traveling by automobile on a trip of two-hundred miles or more. They were asked to do so on a series of eight semantic scales.[2]

As the data in Table 11–4 indicate, speed is the primary advantage of air over auto travel. From 81 to 90 percent of the respondents rated air travel as much faster, and less than .5 percent rated it as much slower than auto travel. Comfort was the number-two advantage, with from 51 to 69 percent rating air travel as much more comfortable and with only from 1 to 3 percent rating it as much less comfortable than auto travel. Expense is the major disadvantage. Only 1 to 6 percent rated air travel as much less expensive and from 28 to 34 percent rated it as much more expensive than auto travel. The two modes of transportation were rated about even on reliability.

Husband-Wife Differences

There were no significant differences in the way in which husbands and wives rated air versus auto travel with respect to speed, expense, or reliability. However, in general, the husbands gave air travel a better rating on comfort, pleasantness, and safety (Table 11–5).

On the other hand, as Table 11–6 indicates, the women gave air travel a much better rating on glamour and excitement.

[2] Each of the eight scales was arrayed on a five-point continuum. The scales used were:
1. much faster/much slower
2. much more glamorous/much less glamorous
3. much more comfortable/much less comfortable
4. much less expensive/much more expensive
5. much safer/much more dangerous
6. much more exciting/much duller
7. much more pleasant/much more unpleasant
8. much more reliable/much less reliable

Table 11-4

Attitudes toward Air and Auto Travel

	Flying Behavior							
	Business Flyers		Nonbusiness Flyers		Former Flyers		Nonflyers	
Air Travel Is	Husband	Wife	Husband	Wife	Husband	Wife	Husband	Wife
Much faster than auto	85%	90%	90%	89%	81%	87%	82%	84%
Much slower than auto	*	–	–	–	–	*	*	–
Much more comfortable	69	58	61	57	57	51	53	51
Much less comfortable	1	1	1	1	2	1	3	2
Much safer	35	23	30	18	22	15	15	8
Much more dangerous	1	2	2	3	2	3	9	4
Much more pleasant	47	40	47	39	44	33	32	25
Much more unpleasant	3	3	1	1	2	3	5	4
Much more glamorous	29	43	34	43	33	36	33	42
Much less glamorous	1	1	3	1	4	1	5	3
Much less expensive	5	1	5	5	6	*	3	4
Much more expensive	28	31	29	31	33	34	32	29
Much more exciting	27	36	32	44	26	42	32	44
Much duller	4	4	1	1	4	2	3	3
Much more reliable	12	8	16	14	10	6	9	11
Much less reliable	6%	3%	2%	3%	3%	4%	5%	5%
	(208)	(208)	(196)	(196)	(226)	(226)	(220)	(220)

* Less than .5 percent.

Table 11–5

Husband and Wife Evaluations of Comfort, Pleasantness and Safety

| | Percent Saying Air Travel Is . . . than Auto Travel | | |
Flying Behavior	Much More Comfortable	Much More Pleasant	Much Safer
Business flyers	69	47	35
Wives of business flyers	58	40	23
Nonbusiness flyers	61	47	30
Wives of nonbusiness flyers	57	39	18
Former flyers	57	44	22
Wives of former flyers	51	33	15
Nonflyers	53	32	15
Wives of nonflyers	51	25	8

Differences between Flying Behavior Groups

Comfort, pleasantness, and safety are the only scales on which the differences between flyers and nonflyers are large and consistent enough to be considered statistically significant (Table 11–7). In general, business flyers gave air travel the best ratings on these aspects. The ratings by the wives parallel those of their husbands.

Effect of Lowering Price

Price appears to be a major deterrent to air travel. If you make price attractive, how many people would still be unwilling to fly? To obtain some

Table 11–6

Husband and Wife Evaluations of Glamour and Excitement

| | Percent Saying Air Travel Is . . . than Auto Travel | |
Flying Behavior	Much More Glamorous	Much More Exciting
Business flyers	29	27
Wives of business flyers	43	36
Nonbusiness flyers	34	32
Wives of nonbusiness flyers	43	44
Former flyers	33	26
Wives of former flyers	36	42
Nonflyers	33	32
Wives of nonflyers	42	44

Table 11–7

Evaluations of Comfort, Pleasantness and Safety by Flying Behavior Group

	Percent Saying Air Travel Is . . . than Auto Travel		
Flying Behavior	Much More Comfortable	Much More Pleasant	Much Safer
Business flyers	69	47	35
Nonbusiness flyers	61	47	30
Former flyers	57	44	22
Nonflyers	53	32	15
Wives of			
Business flyers	58	40	23
Nonbusiness flyers	57	39	18
Former flyers	51	33	15
Nonflyers	51	25	8

clues to this, the men in the sample were asked the following question: "Suppose you were making a long trip (over 1000 miles) and flying was the cheapest way to get there. Would you fly or use some other means of transportation?"

Almost nine out of every ten of the former flyers said they would go by air, and two out of three nonflyers said they would do so. Thus, there appears to be a sizeable number of people not currently in the market who might be lured in if the price were right (Table 11–8).

Choice between Flights

Having decided to fly instead of to make a trip by some other means, what factors influence such matters as the choice of the flight to take or the choice of an airline? The data on choice between flights will be reported first.

Table 11–8

Effect of Lowering Price

If Flying Were Cheapest Way	Business Flyers	Nonbusiness Flyers	Former Flyers	Nonflyers
Would fly	95%	92%	86%	64%
Would use auto	2	4	7	23
Would use bus	–	–	*	1
Would use boat	–	1	2	*
Would use train	1	2	5	11
Not reported	2%	1%	–	1%
BASE	(208)	(196)	(226)	(220)

* Less than .5 percent.

Table 11-9

Percent Rating Various Factors in Determining Flight Choice as Very and Quite Important and as Very and Quite Unimportant

	Business Flyers	Nonbusiness Flyers	Former Flyers
Cost of flight			
Very or quite important	72%	78%	70%
Very or quite unimportant	3	1	*
Safety record of airline			
Very or quite important	74	84	74
Very or quite unimportant	2	2	2
The airport			
Very or quite important	69	65	64
Very or quite unimportant	4	4	2
Type of plane (jet, prop, etc.)			
Very or quite important	62	67	49
Very or quite unimportant	3	3	3
Meal service			
Very or quite important	31	39	28
Very or quite unimportant	11	8	6
Drink service			
Very or quite important	5	6	4
Very or quite unimportant	61	62	57
Time of departure			
Very or quite important	67	66	54
Very or quite unimportant	2	1	4
Inflight time			
Very or quite important	77	73	65
Very or quite unimportant	2	2	*
Number of stops			
Very or quite important	81	73	60
Very or quite unimportant	2	–	2
Duration of layovers			
Very or quite important	91	89	81
Very or quite unimportant	1	1	1
Time of arrival			
Very or quite important	70	68	55
Very or quite unimportant	2	6	4
	(208)	(196)	(226)

* Less than .5 percent.

All the male respondents who have flown at some time in their life were asked to rate a series of eleven items on a seven-point scale, ranging from very important to very unimportant.[3] Table 11–9 reports the percent of each group who said that a particular item was very or quite *important* in determining which flight he chooses and the percent of each group who said that a particular item was very or quite *unimportant*.

As Table 11–9 indicates, the duration of layovers ranks at the top of the list while meal and drink service are at the bottom of the list in terms of importance. From 81 to 91 percent of the flyers rate duration of layovers as very or quite important. One third of them rate meal service in this fashion, and only from 4 to 6 percent rate drink service in this manner. In addition, 57 to 62 percent of the sample rate drink service negatively, saying that it is very or quite unimportant. Of course, somewhat different results might have been obtained if it had been possible to isolate the people who did not take the kinds of flights on which drink service was a possibility.

Differences Related to Flying Behavior

All three flying groups were highly concerned with the duration of layovers. However, concern with other time-related factors was related to flying behavior, and it appears that the more a person flies, the more likely it is that time is highly important to him. Business flyers were much more concerned with time than were nonbusiness or former flyers. A higher percent of the business flyers than of the other two groups felt that the number of stops and in-flight time were very or quite important. In addition, more business flyers felt that these time-related factors were important than felt that safety and cost were important in choosing a flight. The nonbusiness and the former flyers, on the other hand, ranked safety and cost ahead of the number of stops and in-flight time in importance, as Table 11–10 indicates (abstracted from Table 11–9).

Airline Preferences

All flyers were asked questions about their airline preferences. They were asked if there were "any airlines that you particularly like to use" and if there were "any airlines that you particularly do not like to use."

[3] The eleven items were
1. Amount of time between departure and arrival of flight.
2. The airport from which the flight leaves, or at which it arrives.
3. The type of plane (such as jet or prop).
4. Whether or not there will be meal service.
5. Whether or not drinks are served.
6. The number of stops.
7. The duration of layovers.
8. The cost of the flight.
9. The time of day (or night) of arrival of the flight.
10. The safety record of the airline.
11. The time of day (or night) of departure of the flight.

Table 11–10

| Flying Behavior | Percent Rating Factor as Very or Quite Important | | | | |
	Duration of Layovers	Number of Stops	In-Flight Time	Safety	Cost
Business flyers	91	81	77	74	72
Nonbusiness flyers	89	73	73	84	78
Former flyers	81	60	65	74	70

The data indicate that more than half of the business flyers and four out of ten nonbusiness flyers do have a particular preference for an airline (Table 11–11).

Table 11–11

Degree of Preference for a Particular Airline

Flying Behavior	Percent Who Prefer Using a Particular Airline
Business flyers	55
Nonbusiness flyers	42
Former flyers	30

The major reasons given for preferring a particular airline is good or courteous service, and reliability. At this juncture, safety is not an important factor and is mentioned by only 4 to 6 percent of each flying group.[4]

The data also indicate that relatively few flyers have any prejudices against a particular airline, except the business flyers, where two out of ten said there was some airline that they do not like to use (Table 11-12).

Table 11–12

Degree of Preference against Using a Particular Airline

Flying Behavior	Percent Who Prefer Not Using a Particular Airline
Business flyers	22
Nonbusiness flyers	9
Former flyers	9

In general, the prejudices parallel the preferences, with a lack of courteous service and a lack of reliability being mentioned most often as reasons for

---

[4] "Pretty hostesses" is mentioned almost as often as safety.

Table 11–13

Airline Preferences*

	Business Flyers	Nonbusiness Flyers	Former Flyers
Why prefer using airline			
Good, courteous service	33%	19%	15%
Reliable, no delays	15	12	7
Flight schedules	12	5	5
Good equipment	10	3	5
Comfort, accommodations good	8	6	3
Good food, meals, cocktails	6	2	3
Safety record	5	6	4
Type of plane (jet, prop, etc.)	4	2	1
Convenient, airfield close	2	6	1
Rates lower, economical	1	1	1
Personnel (pretty hostesses)	3	2	4
Total Who Prefer Airline	(55%)	(42%)	(30%)
Why prefer not using airline			
Lack of courteous service	10%	3%	4%
Not reliable	8	3	3
Poor equipment	7	2	2
Flight schedules	4	1	1
Transferring, bumping	3	1	1
Type of plane (DC's, etc.)	3	1	1
Poor safety record	2	1	†
Poor food	1	–	1
Too many stopovers	1	–	†
Total Who Prefer Not Using Airline	(22%)	(9%)	(9%)
BASE	(208)	(196)	(226)

* Percents total more than 100 because some subjects gave more than one reason.
† Less than .5 percent.

preferring not to use an airline. Again, safety record is a minor factor at this choice point. Tables 11–13 and 11–14 summarize both preferences and prejudices in choosing an airline.

Questions

1. Evaluate the methodology used in the study.

2. Assume you are a consultant to the airlines industry. Prepare a report outlining your recommendations for future marketing strategies.

Table 11-14

Summary of Factors Affecting Preferences for Air Travel

Factor	Flying per se	Air versus Auto	Choice between Flights	Choice between Airlines
Time (speed, reliability, etc.)	Major thing liked and disliked about flying. Like in-flight speed; dislike delays, time getting to and from airports, etc.	Speed a major advantage for airlines. But no difference seen in reliability.	Time highly important for all flyers but most important for business flyers. From 60 percent to 90 percent rate time-related factors as very important.	In-flight speed not a factor but airline's reputation for reliability second in importance only to courteous service.
Comfort	Second most frequently mentioned thing liked about flying.	Second major advantage over auto travel.	Not measured.	Not a major factor as such.
Safety	Fear of accidents, etc., ranks second among the dislikes for flyers and ranks first for nonflyers. Women mention this more often than men.	Nonflyers see no significant difference between air and auto in safety. One third of the flyers feel air much safer than auto, but few wives feel this way.	Equal with time and cost in importance for nonbusiness and former flyers. Ranks behind time for business flyers.	Unimportant. Just as many men mention the pretty hostesses as mention safety record as factor dictating choice or airline.
Expense	Expense not one of the first things most people think of in describing their likes or dislikes about air travel. Not highly salient.	Major disadvantage. One third say air is much more expensive than auto travel.	Not as important as time for business flyers; equally important as time and safety for nonbusiness and former flyers.	Not a major factor. Only 1 percent mention it.
Service	Not one of the things most people immediately associate with airlines. Business flyers most likely to mention this. 7 percent give it as what they like and 12 percent as what they dislike about flying.	Not measured.	Of minimal importance. Meal service important to one third of flyers. Drink service unimportant to two thirds.	Courteous service major reason for airline preference. Especially true for business flyers. Meals, drinks mentioned by only a few.

Medwick Carpet Company (A): Investigating Information-Seeking Behavior

The Medwick Carpet Company was organized on August 3, 1950, as the result of the merger of two smaller companies. With the exception of 1951 and 1952, the company's growth has been steadily upward. Sales have increased from $22 million in 1950 to $98 million in 1967.

In the middle 1950s the company embarked on a plant relocation program. Plants in New York and New England were disposed of in favor of more facilities in South Carolina, Georgia, and Virginia. Lower raw material, labor, and tax costs enabled the company to reduce its cost of manufacturing by several million dollars. Many competitors followed similar plant relocation strategies during this period.

The company's financial condition compares favorably with other firms in the industry. Profit margins have been increasing at a modest rate during the 1960s. Net profit as a percent of sales was 4.5 percent in 1967, compared with 3.5 percent in 1963.

Marketing Strategy

Product Line

The company uses various types of construction, fibers, and styles to manufacture several varieties of carpeting. The basic constructions used include tufted, velvet, wilton, and axminister. Fibers used include nylon, acrylics, rayon, wool, and cotton. This enables the company to produce pile, twist, and looped carpeting in plain, textured, sculptured, and figured styles. Each type of carpet comes in a variety of grades, colors, and widths.

The company's broad product line is designed to satisfy the needs of the consumer and institutional markets. With respect to the consumer market, the company does not follow a strategy of market segmentation but prefers instead to compete for the entire market.

Pricing Strategy

Retail prices vary according to the quality of carpeting and the retailers' merchandising strategies. Although Medwick has suggested retail prices, retailer adherence to these prices varies considerably, and the company has been reluctant to push for compliance. While the company offers carpets in a variety of price ranges, as Table 11–15 indicates, there is a somewhat narrower selection in the higher price ranges.

Table 11–15

Number of Carpet Models Offered by Retail Price Range

Price Category (Dollars per Square Yard)	Number of Models
6– 8	12
8–10	12
10–12	15
12–14	7
14–16	6
16–18	5
Over 18	3
TOTAL	60

Distribution

In 1962, Medwick conducted an intensive analysis of its distribution system. The study revealed that 75 percent of its sales were made by approximately 20 percent of its retail outlets. As a consequence, in 1963, the company streamlined its distribution system by reducing the number of retail outlets handling its products and the methods used to service them. It now sells directly to approximately 4000 retailers through its own 120 man sales force. Carpet specialty stores account for 40 percent of the company's sales to consumers, followed by furniture stores with 35 percent, department stores with 15 percent, and all other types of outlets with 10 percent. Commercial and institutional buyers are served by the salesmen of fifteen distributors located strategically throughout the United States.

Promotional Strategy

In the carpet industry, promotional expenditures are typically less than 1 percent of sales, with .3 to .5 percent of sales not being uncommon. Medwick's promotional strategy has historically differed from its competitors in terms of dollar expenditures and media usage. In 1967 the company spent $975,000 on promotional activities that represented nearly 1 percent of sales.

Competitiors tend to invest the majority of their advertising budgets in general and Sunday magazines. Medwick also followed this strategy until 1964. In that year the company decided to expand its use of media to include radio, television, and newspapers.

Like its major competitors, Medwick advertisements usually emphasize the carpet's durability, appearance, and economy. Color is usually used to dramatize the carpet either alone or in a setting with furniture. For the last three years the company has used the theme "Medwick: The Carpet For Those Who Care."

The company also has a cooperative advertising program with its dealers. The terms are fifty-fifty with the company and the dealer splitting the cost of the dealer's advertising, provided that the latter conforms to certain standards established by the company.

Consumer Research Study

In the spring of 1968 Medwick's marketing vice president, William J. Hoffman, was reviewing the company's performance with Richard Baker, the advertising director. Although the company's profit margin had steadily increased in recent years, market share had declined by nearly 33 percent over the last five years to the current level of 5.5 percent. Hoffman was convinced that their promotional programs were a major factor contributing to the diminishing share of market. He questioned the unusually large advertising budget that he felt was largely due to the use of media that competitors were not using. He instructed Baker to take whatever steps necessary to make certain that they were getting the maximum effective impact from their advertising.

After studying the situation further and conferring with the company's advertising agency—Williamson and Grove—Baker recommended that the company engage in basic research to determine the sources of information used in making carpet purchase decisions. The cost of the study was to be divided equally between the company and the agency and was to serve as the foundation for evaluating current and future budgets and media strategies. Hoffman approved the research proposal, and the research began in the late spring.

Research Design

The research team was comprised of Baker, Medwick's research department, and the research arm of Williamson. After considerable discussion it was decided to use a cross-sectional survey consisting of a national probability sample of five thousand households that had purchased carpeting within the last six months. Personal interviews were conducted by a Philadelphia-based research organization with an established reputation for quality research. The necessary safeguards were employed so as to minimize the possibility that respondents would know the identity of the company sponsoring the study.

Findings

Exposure to Sources of Information

A series of questions were used to determine the extent of information seeking and the role and importance of various information sources. After discussing the purchase situation in general terms in order to refresh the respondent's mind, the following questions were asked in this order:

1. *Specific influence questions.* "How did you happen to choose the particular brand of carpeting that you purchased? Who or what suggested this brand to you?"

2. *Assessment questions.* Respondents were then asked to name the influence they considered the main one in their decision to buy a certain brand of carpeting. The question was "Thinking back now, what was the most important thing in causing you to choose the brand of carpeting that you purchased?"

3. *Exposure questions.* No specific medium was mentioned while administering the specific influence and assessment questions. After these questions were asked, respondents were then asked the following about the brand they had purchased:
   a. "Did you hear any one talk about it?"
   b. "Did you see it in anyone's home?"
   c. "Did a sales person suggest it?"
   d. "Did you hear about it on the radio?"
   e. "Did you see it on television?"
   f. "Did you read about it in a magazine?"
   g. "Did you read about it in a newspaper?"

These questions enabled the research team to determine the percentage of respondents who were *exposed* to each medium and the effectiveness of that medium. The term *effective exposure* was used when respondents said that a medium played a specific role and that it was the most important information source in their decision. *Contributory exposure* was used when respondents mentioned a medium and said it played a role in their decision but not the most important role. *Ineffective exposure* was used when respondents mentioned a source but said that it did not play any role in their decision.

Table 11–16 compares Medwick purchases with purchases of other brands, according to the type of exposure to various sources of information. In terms of total exposure, Medwick purchasers were more exposed to salesmen, personal contacts, and magazines than to other sources. The same total exposure pattern appears to exist for purchasers of other brands. The usefulness of various information sources appears to vary considerably, and Medwick purchasers and purchasers of other brands seem to differ somewhat in the value that they place on the information obtained from these sources.

Comparison of Opinion Leaders and Nonopinion Leaders

The research team suspected from previous experience that personal contacts played an important role in the decision to purchase carpeting. Consequently, provisions were made to investigate this information source thoroughly. Respondents were asked whether or not anyone had asked them for advice about carpeting during the last six months. The respondents who answered affirmatively were classified as *opinion leaders* and those responding negatively were termed *nonopinion leaders.*

Table 11–16

Exposure to Sources of Information

Type of Exposure by Type Of Information Source	Brand Purchased	
	Medwick (Percentage)	Average for Other Brand (Percentage)
Personal contacts		
Effective exposure	28	34
Contributory exposure	18	25
Ineffective exposure	16	6
TOTAL EXPOSURE	62	65
Radio		
Effective exposure	1	1
Contributory exposure	2	2
Ineffective exposure	6	4
TOTAL EXPOSURE	9	7
Television		
Effective exposure	3	2
Contributory exposure	7	7
Ineffective exposure	8	2
TOTAL EXPOSURE	18	11
Magazines		
Effective exposure	15	21
Contributory exposure	22	29
Ineffective exposure	8	12
TOTAL EXPOSURE	45	62
Newspapers		
Effective exposure	3	4
Contributory exposure	15	22
Ineffective exposure	11	10
TOTAL EXPOSURE	29	36
Salesmen		
Effective exposure	29	33
Contributory exposure	35	54
Ineffective exposure	37	10
TOTAL EXPOSURE	95	97

Numerous analyses were performed in an attempt to determine the ways in which opinion leaders differed from nonopinion leaders. For the most part, these two types of consumers are similar; that is, opinion leaders are nearly identical in income and demographics to those they presumably influence. They tend to be in the same age category and have similar incomes and social class backgrounds. Their respective family size and education are also nearly identical. Opinion leaders did have a strong tendency to be more involved in social activities than did nonopinion leaders.

Table 11–17

Comparison of Opinion Leaders and Nonopinion
Leaders—Exposure to Mass Media

| Type of Medium | Brand Purchased | | | |
| | Medwick | | Average for Other Brands | |
	Opinion Leaders	Nonopinion Leaders	Opinion Leaders	Nonopinion Leaders
Radio				
Low exposure	47%	52%	48%	50%
High exposure	53	48	52	50
TOTAL	100	100	100	100
Television				
Low exposure	58	55	56	54
High exposure	42	45	44	46
TOTAL	100	100	100	100
Magazines				
Low exposure	41	60	36	55
High exposure	59	40	64	45
TOTAL	100	100	100	100
Newspapers				
Low exposure	34	42	33	43
High exposure	66	58	67	57
TOTAL	100%	100%	100%	100%

Table 11–17 compares the degree to which opinion leaders and nonopinion leaders are exposed to various sources of information. Although there is considerable variation across media, opinion leaders appear to have a tendency to be more exposed to the mass media.

Initiating Conversations

Respondents obtaining information from personal contacts were asked whether they requested information from someone else or whether the other person(s) volunteered the information. For respondents purchasing Medwick

Table 11–18

Type of Information Obtained from Personal Contacts

Type of Information Obtained	Brand Purchased	
	Medwick (Percentage)	Average for Other Brands (Percentage)
Price		
Yes	10	9
No	90	91
TOTAL	100	100
Brand		
Yes	72	88
No	28	12
TOTAL	100	100
Color-pattern		
Yes	8	14
No	92	86
TOTAL	100	100
Fabric		
Yes	15	23
No	85	77
TOTAL	100	100
Durability		
Yes	52	67
No	48	33
TOTAL	100	100
Cleanability		
Yes	64	73
No	36	27
TOTAL	100	100
Where to buy		
Yes	68	87
No	32	13
TOTAL	100	100
Other information		
Yes	86	93
No	14	7
TOTAL	100	100

carpeting, in 49 percent of the instances the respondent requested the information and in 51 percent of the cases it was volunteered. The comparable percentages for purchasers of other brands were 48 percent and 52 percent, respectively.

Information Obtained from Personal Contacts

The respondents obtaining information from personal contacts were asked to indicate the type of information that was acquired. As Table 11–18 indicates, brand recommendations, where to buy carpeting, and cleanability were the most frequently discussed topics. Medwick purchasers appear to differ from purchasers of other brands in terms of the frequency with which these and other subjects were discussed.

Relationship between Brand Recommended and Brand Purchased

In order to get a better idea of the impact of personal influence, respondents were asked what brand of carpeting, if any, was recommended during their conversations with others. In the situations when a specific brand was recommended, comparisons were made between the recommended brand and the brand actually purchased.

Table 11–19

Relationship between Brand Recommended through Personal Contacts
and Brand Purchased

Brand Recommended	Purchasing Behavior
Medwick	35 percent purchased the brand recommended
	65 percent purchased a different brand
Average for all other brands	60 percent purchased the brand recommended
	40 percent purchased a different brand

As Table 11–19 indicates, only 35 percent of the respondents purchased Medwick following a recommendation by someone else. In contrast, when another brand was recommended, 60 percent of the respondents actually purchased that brand.

Although the percentage of respondents who purchased a brand different from the one recommended is important, it reveals only part of the behavior

that is relevant. The statistic net gain or loss includes the respondents who
were advised to purchase Medwick but who actually purchased another brand
as well as includes those who were encouraged to buy another brand but who
actually purchased Medwick. As Table 11–20 indicates, Medwick's net loss
is much greater than the average loss experienced by its competitors.

Table 11–20

Net Gains and Losses Resulting from Switching from the Brand Recommended
through Personal Contacts

Brand	Number of Respondents Switching to Medwick and Other Brands for Each 100 Respondents Switching from the Brand	Net Percentage Gain or Loss
Medwick	45	−55
Average for all other brands	99	−01

Implications for Marketing Strategy

After reviewing the findings of the study, Baker wondered what recommendations he should make about Medwick's marketing and advertising strategies. He was concerned about how much confidence he should place in the
findings of the study. He also wondered whether Medwick's declining market
share was really being caused by nonadvertising policies. He also was undecided about what he should recommend in terms of future advertising budgets
and media strategies.

Questions

1. Put yourself in Baker's position and prepare recommendations about future
   marketing and advertising strategies based on the findings of the study and
   on the other materials presented in the case.

Medwick Carpet Company (B): Analyzing Alternative Evaluation Behavior[5]

The Medwick Carpet Company produces a broad line of carpeting for consumers and industrial users. The sixty lines of carpeting come in a wide selection of colors and fabrics and range in price from $6 to over $18 a square
yard.

[5] The reader is urged to refer to the preceding case, "Medwick Carpet Company
(A)," for additional background information.

The company uses its 120 man sales force to sell directly to approximately 4000 retail outlets located throughout the United States. Retailers handling the company's carpeting include carpet specialty stores, furniture and department stores, and several other types of outlets. Commercial and institutional buyers are contacted by the salesmen of fifteen distributors.

In 1967 the company invested approximately $975,000 in promotional programs. Media used include general and Sunday magazines, radio, television, and newspapers. Advertisements are usually in color, and the copy emphasizes durability, appearance, and economy. During the last three years the company has used the theme "Medwick: The Carpet For Those Who Care." The company also has a fifty-fifty cooperative advertising program with its dealers.

With the exception of 1951 and 1952, sales have increased steadily, and in 1967 they were at an all-time high of $98 million. Profit margins have also increased at a modest rate, particularly in recent years.

Despite these trends, Medwick management was not optimistic about the future. The major cause of concern was the fact that their market share had declined by nearly 33 percent over the last five years. Their 1967 market share of 5.5 percent was the lowest in the company's history.

In the spring of 1968, Medwick's president, Clarence Medwick, challenged his marketing vice president, William J. Hoffman, to take whatever profitable steps were necessary to reverse the downward trend in market share. Hoffman in turn passed the challenge along to the major managers in his department. Each manager was asked to submit recommendations for improving the effectiveness of the marketing effort. One of these recommendations led to a substantial research effort designed to learn more about how consumers purchase carpeting.[6] The results of the study were to serve as inputs into the design of future marketing programs.

Consumer Research Study

Research Design
The research team was comprised of representatives of Medwick's advertising and research departments and research personnel from the company's advertising agency, Williamson and Grove. The cross-sectional survey employed a national probability sample of five thousand households that had purchased carpeting within the last six months. Personal interviews were conducted by a nationally known research organization, and steps were taken to conceal the identity of the sponsoring company. The object of the phase of the study reported here was to determine how consumers evaluate carpeting and how Medwick compares with its major competitors.

[6] See "Medwick Carpet Company (A)" for the information-seeking phase of the study.

Findings

Features Respondents Sought in Carpeting

Respondents were asked what specific things they were looking for, or were interested in, when they purchased carpeting. Table 11–21 compares the re-

Table 11–21

Features That Respondents Were Looking for in Carpeting

	Brand Purchased*	
Type of Features	Medwick (Percent of Respondents)	Average for Other Brands (Percent of Respondents)
Price	62	65
Brand	4	10
Quality	74	93
Color-pattern	78	88
Fabric	41	76
Durability	65	74
Washability	68	79
Other	72	72
No specific features	17	15

* Percentages total more than 100 because many respondents were looking for more than one feature.

sponses of purchasers of Medwick carpeting with those purchasing other brands. Purchasers of other brands most frequently mentioned quality, color and pattern, washability, and durability in that order. Medwick purchasers mentioned color and pattern, quality, washability, and price most frequently.

Evaluations of Selected Features of Carpeting by Brand

Respondents were asked to rate each major brand of carpeting according to several attributes. Table 11–22 compares respondents' evaluations of Medwick carpeting with the evaluations received by other brands. Although the evaluations of all brands were not particularly high, Medwick ranked below other brands on each feature.

Number of Price Ranges Considered

Respondents were asked how many price ranges they considered before making a purchase. As Table 11–23 indicates, purchasers of other brands commonly considered two or three price ranges. In contrast, Medwick purchasers had a greater tendency to consider a fewer number of price ranges.

Table 11–22

Evaluations of Selected Features of Carpeting by Brand*

	Brand of Carpeting	
Feature	Medwick	Average for Other Brands
Reasonableness of price	2.6	3.8
Price ranges available	3.2	3.3
Quality	2.7	4.1
Color-pattern selection	2.9	3.7
Fabric selection	2.8	3.4
Durability	2.2	4.3
Washability	2.4	4.2
Dependability of delivery	1.9	3.1
Helpfulness of salesmen	1.7	3.3

* Respondents were asked to rate each brand of carpeting on each of the above features on the following scale:

Unacceptable	Below average	Average	Above average	Excellent
1	2	3	4	5

Figures in the table are mean scores.

Table 11–23

Number of Price Ranges Considered

	Brand Purchased	
Number of Price Ranges Considered	Medwick (Percent of Respondents)	Average for Other Brands (Percent of Respondents)
One	58	35
Two	25	33
Three	15	24
More than three	2	8
TOTAL	100	100

Number of Fabrics Considered

Respondents were also questioned about the number of different fabrics they considered prior to purchasing.[7] The results indicate that Medwick purchasers tended to consider a smaller number of fabrics than did purchasers of other brands (Table 11–24).

[7] Fabrics refer to wool, nylon, cotton, and acrylics.

Table 11–24

Number of Fabrics Considered

Number of Fabrics Considered	Brand Purchased	
	Medwick (Percent of Respondents)	Average for Other Brands (Percent of Respondents)
One	63	43
Two	32	47
Three	4	8
Four	1	2
More than four	0	0
TOTAL	100	100

Number of Colors and Patterns Considered

Medwick purchasers also differed from purchasers of other brands in terms of the number of different carpet colors and/or patterns that were evaluated prior to the final purchase decision. As Table 11–25 reveals, purchasers of other brands considered a greater number of colors and/or patterns.

Table 11–25

Number of Colors/Patterns Considered

Number of Colors or Patterns Considered	Brand Purchased	
	Medwick (Percent of Respondents)	Average for Other Brands (Percent of Respondents)
One	35	25
Two	42	33
Three	18	29
Four	4	10
More than four	1	3
TOTAL	100	100

Number of Brands Considered

An attempt was made to distinguish between consumers who entered the market with their minds set on one particular brand and who therefore did not consider other brands and consumers who chose between a large number of brands. As Table 11–26 indicates, a large percentage of the purchasers of other brands considered several brands before purchasing. Medwick purchasers, on the other hand, had a greater tendency to consider a smaller number of brands.

Table 11–26

Number of Brands Considered

	Brand Purchased	
Number of Brands Considered	Medwick (Percent of Respondents)	Average for Other Brands (Percent of Respondents)
One	67	43
Two	21	28
Three	10	21
More than three	2	8
TOTAL	100	100

Number of Stores Visited

Finally, an attempt was made to determine the extent to which consumers shopped around for carpeting before making a purchase. Relative to purchasers of other brands, consumers buying Medwick had a greater tendency to shop in a smaller number of stores (Table 11–27).

Table 11–27

Number of Stores Visited

	Brand Purchased	
Number of Stores Visited	Medwick (Percent of Respondents)	Average for Other Brands (Percent of Respondents)
None	12	13
One	63	42
Two	22	28
Three	2	14
More than three	1	3
TOTAL	100	100

Marketing Strategy Implications

In June, 1968 Hoffman was reviewing the findings of the study. He had not decided what the study revealed about the effectiveness of Medwick's marketing strategies. He wondered whether the results suggested further studies were necessary and, if so, what types of things should be investigated. He was also undecided about what marketing programs he should recommend for next year and whether he should plan these programs now or wait until the results of additional studies were available. He knew he must come to a decision quickly because the company's 1969 model year was to begin on October 1, 1968.

Questions

1. Evaluate the methodology used in the study.

2. According to the study, what are Medwick's marketing problems?

3. What are the alternative explanations or reasons for these problems?

4. Should further studies be conducted? If so indicate the areas that should be investigated and how the company should go about studying them.

5. On the basis of the study, what recommendations should be made for future marketing strategies?

CHAPTER 12

PURCHASE PROCESSES

Universal Drugstores, Inc.: Unplanned Purchasing and
Other Dimensions of Shopping Behavior as a Basis
for Merchandising and Promotional Strategies

Universal Drugstores, Inc., operates a chain of forty-five "super drugstores" located in several cities in Michigan. Each unit carries between 30,000 and 40,000 items, contains approximately 7500 to 10,000 square feet of selling area, and generates a sales volume ranging from $500,000 to $1,000,000 annually.

In recent years the company has experienced considerable difficulty in maintaining its market share largely because of increasing competition from supermarkets, variety stores, discount houses, and some promotional department stores. In an attempt to reverse declining profit margins, the company has pursued several strategies designed to increase productivity per square foot and per dollar invested in inventory. The company has changed to a self-service method of operation, made extensive use of gondola-type fixtures, broadened its product line to include such nontraditional drug items as appliances, apparel, hardware and housewares and has pursued aggressive promotional and pricing strategies.

In spite of these changes, in 1967 the company's profit margin continued to decline largely because of high overhead expenses. Management was convinced that the best avenue to increased profits was a higher sales volume a store. In the summer of 1968 several programs were implemented in an attempt to increase sales volume. One of these programs was a research investigation of consumer shopping behavior.

Consumer Research Study

Study Objectives
To date, Universal had not conducted any studies of shopping behavior in their stores. The purpose of this study was to identify the types of con-

sumers who patronize the store, the extent of store loyalty, how consumers shop the stores, the amount spent, the number of items purchased, the items purchased most frequently, and product rates of unplanned purchasing. The results of the study were to be used to better identify the store's target market, to reanalyze, and perhaps redesign, store layouts, and to select items for special promotional emphasis.

Research Procedures

In order to obtain valid results, it was decided to use a seven-by-seven Latin Square design.[1] The seven stores included in the study were chosen to give balanced representation to different-sized stores and the different market segments that management felt were patronizing the chain. Interviews were conducted during each of the store's operating hours. During each of the seven interviewing weeks, interviews were conducted during every day of the week.

Tabel 12–1

Latin Square Design Used to Balance Out Systematic Variation
in In-Store Shopping Behavior*

Day of Week	Interview Week						
	I	II	III	IV	V	VI	VII
Monday	A	B	C	D	E	F	G
Tuesday	B	C	D	E	F	G	A
Wednesday	C	D	E	F	G	A	B
Thursday	D	E	F	G	A	B	C
Friday	E	F	G	A	B	C	D
Saturday	F	G	A	B	C	D	E
Sunday	G	A	B	C	D	E	F

* Where random assignment yields:

A = Store 3   E = Store 6
B = Store 7   F = Store 1
C = Store 2   G = Store 5
D = Store 4

As Table 12–1 indicates, the seven test stores were randomly assigned to Treatments A through G. Interviews were conducted once and only once in any test store during any of the test hours, during any of the test days, and during any of the interview weeks. In this way systematic variations attributable to these factors were thought to be equalized.

Resource limitations and estimates of the heterogeneity of the characteristics

[1] For a discussion of Latin Square designs, the reader is referred to Seymour Banks, "Marketing Experiments," *Journal of Advertising Research,* March 1963, pp. 34-41.

being studied led to a sample size of one thousand. The number of interviews conducted in each store on each interviewing day was proportional to that store's traffic on that day relative to the total traffic of all seven stores during all interviewing days. A unique uniform sampling fraction was employed in each store during each interviewing day in order that the required number of interviews were conducted during all hours that the stores were open.

Interviews were conducted by a highly regarded Detroit research organization. A combination interview-observation technique was employed. Those respondents eligible for the study were first interviewed when they entered the store. The interviewer noted the composition of the shopping party and asked the respondent to indicate the occupation and income of the household head as well as how many drugstores they had patronized during the previous month. Respondents were then asked to itemize what they planned to purchase during the shopping trip. When the interview was completed, the interviewer noted the time that the shopper began shopping, and the interviewer then thanked the shopper for his cooperation. Efforts were made to make respondents feel that the interview was over at this time.

As respondents shopped, they were observed by other interviewers posing as shoppers. These interviewers noted the specific items handled and purchased, the amount spent, and the exact time that respondents left the store.

Findings

Selected Characteristics of Shoppers

As might be expected, considerable variation exists in the composition of shopping parties (Table 12–2). Those that included children were the most common, followed by a shopping party consisting solely of a man under twenty-five.

Table 12–2

Composition of Shopping Parties

Composition of Shopping Party	Percent of Shopping Parties
Male only: Under 25	9.0
Male only: Over 25	25.1
Female only: Under 25	10.2
Female only: Over 25	12.6
Multiple party: Without children	14.7
Multiple party: With children	28.4
TOTAL	100.0

Table 12–3

Annual Household Income (before Taxes)

Annual Income (Dollars)	Percent of Shopping Parties
Under 4000	8.2
4001–5000	7.1
5001–7000	26.2
7001–10,000	32.3
10,001–15,000	11.2
15,001–25,000	7.1
Over 25,000	3.4
No Answer	4.5
TOTAL	100.0

The average shopper had an annual household income of $7344. However, as Table 12–3 indicates, all income groups shop at Universal.

The store also attracts many occupational groups (Table 12–4). Pro-

Table 12–4

Occupation of Household Head

Occupation	Percent of Shopping Parties
Professional, semiprofessional	14.3
Proprietor, manager, official	27.1
Clerical, sales	18.4
Craftsman, foreman	14.9
Operative	14.3
Service worker	3.9
Farmer, farm laborer	1.2
Other	5.0
TOTAL	100.0

prietors, managers, and officials were the most common patrons, followed by clerical and sales people. Professionals and semi-professionals, craftsmen, foremen, and operatives were also important occupational groups.

Number of Stores Patronized

Respondents displayed a considerable degree of store loyalty. Approximately 60 percent shopped exclusively at one Universal store while 2.5 percent shopped only at the present and other Universal stores. Only 37 percent had patronized non-Universal stores during the previous month (Table 12–5).

Table 12–5

Number of Drugstores Patronized during Previous Month

Stores Mentioned	Percent of Shopping Parties
Present store only	60.5
Other Universal stores	2.5
Other stores	37.0
TOTAL	100.0

Time Spent

The average shopping time in Universal stores was slightly over six minutes (Table 12–6). Multiple shopping parties with children tended

Table 12–6

Time Spent in Store

Time Spent	Percent of Shopping Parties	
2 minutes or less	24.2	
3–5 minutes	31.1	
6–10 minutes	26.4	Average 6.25 minutes
11–15 minutes	9.8	
Over 15	8.5	
TOTAL	100.0	

to spend more time shopping than those without children. Of the shopping parties consisting of only one member, males under twenty-five and females over twenty-five shopped longer than males over twenty-five and females under twenty-five. Generally, the larger the shopping party, the greater the time spent shopping.

Number of Items Handled and Purchased

The average number of items handled and purchased was 3.1 and 1.8, respectively (Tables 12–7 and 12–8). Shopping parties comprised of more than one member tended to both handle and purchase a larger number of items than did single-member parties.

Items Purchased Most Frequently

The ten items purchased most frequently are itemized in Table 12–9. Purchased by the greatest percentage of respondents were pharmaceuticals; tobacco products; cosmetics; candies and gum; books, magazines, and newspapers; greeting cards; toys and sporting goods; paper, paper products, and

Table 12–7

Number of Items Handled

Number of Items Handled	Percent of Shopping Parties	
None	5.1	
1	27.7	
2	23.6	
3	14.2	
4	9.4	
5	4.8	Average: 3.1 items
6	2.4	
7	2.5	
8	2.2	
9	2.3	
10	1.7	
More than 10	4.1	
TOTAL	100.0	

school supplies; and liquors and beer. Although these items were purchased more frequently than others, they are not "power" items in the sense of meat, bread, and dairy products in supermarkets.

Amount Spent

The average customer spent $2.07 while shopping in a Universal store. Approximately 10 percent of shoppers did not spend any money, while 7.5 percent spent in excess of $5 (Table 12–10).

Table 12–8

Number of Items Purchased

Number of Items Purchased	Percent of Shopping Parties	
None	10.2	
1	42.0	
2	25.4	
3	9.3	
4	7.1	
5	2.4	Average: 1.8 items
6	1.6	
7	.7	
8	.5	
9	.6	
10	.1	
More than 10	.1	
TOTAL	100.0	

Table 12–9

Items Purchased Most Frequently

Item	Percent of Shopping Parties Purchasing
Pharmaceuticals	19.3
Tobacco products	17.4
Cosmetics	12.3
Candies and gum	9.2
Books, magazines, newspapers	7.3
Greeting cards	5.4
Toys, sporting goods	3.9
Paper, paper products, school supplies	3.5
Liquors	3.3
Beer	2.7

Shopping parties comprised of more than one member spent more money than single-member parties. The amount spent also increased as the time spent in the store increased.

Planned and Unplanned Purchases

Comparisons were made between what respondents said they would purchase during the store-entry interview and their actual purchases. If a respondent indicated that he would purchase a product and if he actually bought it,

Table 12–10

Amount Spent

Amount Spent (Dollars)	Percent of Shopping Parties	
Zero	10.2	
.01–.50	22.3	
.51–1.00	16.4	
1.01–1.50	10.9	
1.51–2.00	9.3	
2.01–2.50	7.4	
2.51–3.00	4.5	Average: $2.07
3.01–3.50	3.7	
3.51–4.00	3.1	
4.01–4.50	2.3	
4.51–5.00	2.4	
Over 5.00	7.5	
TOTAL	100.0	

Table 12–11

Rates of Planned and Unplanned Purchasing

Product Category	Planned Purchases (Percent)	Unplanned Purchases (Percent)
Antipain	84.3	15.7
Antiseptics	82.7	19.3
Baby products	86.4	13.6
Beer	98.4	1.6
Books, magazines, papers	76.0	24.0
Bread	96.2	4.8
Candies	31.2	68.8
Cigarettes	92.3	7.7
Cleaning Supplies	47.2	52.8
Clocks, watches	37.2	62.8
Coffee, tea	81.7	18.3
Cold preparations	91.3	8.7
Cosmetics	62.5	37.5
Dental products	81.5	18.5
Electrical products	73.7	26.3
Facial tissues	64.3	35.7
Feminine hygiene	34.1	65.9
First aid products	40.0	60.0
Foot preparations	71.6	28.4
Gins	67.0	33.0
Glassware	14.3	85.7
Greeting cards	75.0	25.0
Gum, mints	49.0	51.0
Hair-care items	73.0	27.0
Hardware and tools	83.7	17.3
Housewares	91.3	8.7
Insecticides	66.3	33.7
Jewelry	23.5	76.5
Kitchenware	31.4	68.6
Linaments, rubs	44.7	55.3
Men's needs	83.4	16.6
Ointments	87.2	12.8
Potato chips and cookies	56.0	44.0
Paper and paper goods	67.8	32.2
Party goods	53.5	46.5
Patterns	47.6	52.4
Pet supplies	74.6	25.4
Prescription drugs	93.5	6.5
Radio and radio items	73.2	26.8
Record players, records	43.2	56.8
School supplies	87.0	13.0

Table 12–11 (continued)

Product Category	Planned Purchases (Percent)	Unplanned Purchases (Percent)
Shoe care items	57.4	42.6
Soft drinks	62.0	38.0
Soft goods	90.9	9.1
Tobacco products	83.7	16.3
Toilet tissue	96.3	3.7
Toys, sporting goods	34.6	65.4
Vitamins	71.6	28.4
Waxes, polishes	58.2	41.8
Whiskies	89.2	10.8
Wines	63.7	36.3

the purchase was classified as "planned." If a respondent purchased an item but did not indicate that he intended to buy it, the purchase was classified as "unplanned."

Table 12–11 itemizes planned and unplanned purchase rates for fifty-one major merchandise classifications. The unplanned purchase rates vary widely across product categories. The overall level of unplanned purchasing appears to be considerably lower than comparable rates typically found in supermarkets.

Strategy Implications

In the winter of 1968, Universal management was reviewing the findings of the study. Considerable differences of opinion existed among top management as to the implications of the study for future advertising and merchandising strategies.

Questions

1. Evaluate the methodology used in the study.

2. Assume you have been retained as a consultant to Universal. On the basis of the study and of the other materials presented in the case, prepare a report outlining the advertising and merchandising strategies that you propose.

Big-Deal Stores, Inc. (A):   In-Store Shopping Behavior as a Basis for Store Layout Decisions

During the spring of 1968 the management of Big-Deal Stores, Inc., was formulating policies to guide future expansion plans. Big-Deal, with annual sales of approximately $20 million in 1967, operated twenty supermarkets in three major cities in Ohio. In the next five years, management planned to open ten additional stores in Ohio. By 1980 it was anticipated that Big-Deal would be operating a total of fifty stores in the state.

All twenty existing stores used a standardized exterior and interior design. Both designs were developed when the chain was begun ten years ago by a Cleveland-based architectural firm that specialized in store designs. Management had decided to use a standardized design because it increased store identity and made it possible to advertise the stores as a group.

Although management was satisfied with the exterior design, they were not convinced that the interior layout was best. Although the store interiors were esthetically pleasing, management wondered whether the layout was exposing customers to as many items as possible each shopping trip. They felt that unless the layout was maximizing exposure it was not making the maximum contribution to store sales and profits.

For these reasons it was decided to study the in-store shopping behavior of customers in several of their stores. It was hoped that the results of the study could be used to evaluate the effectiveness of the present design and to decide whether or not the same interior layout should be used in stores to be built in the future.

Nature of the Study

Lacking "in-house" expertise, Big-Deal management retained an independent research agency—Walters Research, Inc. (WRI)—to conduct the study. WRI had an excellent reputation as well as extensive experience in conducting the type of study that management wanted.

Because the day of the week, the time of day, the interview week, and the store were all likely to affect in-store shopping behavior, it was necessary to control for the effects of these variables. The six stores included in the study were randomly selected from the total of twenty stores. Interviews were conducted between the hours of 9 A.M. and 9 P.M. during each interviewing day. During each of the six interview weeks, interviews were conducted on all six days that the stores were open.

Table 12–12 depicts the six-by-six Latin Square design that was used to balance systematic variation in in-store behavior attributable to the factors just mentioned. The six test stores were randomly assigned to Treatments A through F. Interviews were conducted once and only once in any test store during any of the test hours, during any of the test days, and during any of the interview weeks. In this way systematic errors due to these factors were equalized.

WRI and Big-Deal management agreed that the overall sample be limited to a thousand. The number of interviews conducted in each store on each

Table 12–12

Latin Square Design Used to Balance Systematic Variation
in In-Store Shopping Behavior*

Day of	Interview Week					
Week	I	II	III	IV	V	VI
Monday	A	B	C	D	E	F
Tuesday	B	C	D	E	F	A
Wednesday	C	D	E	F	A	B
Thursday	D	E	F	A	B	C
Friday	E	F	A	B	C	D
Saturday	F	A	B	C	D	E

* Where random assignment yields:

A = Store 1   D = Store 4
B = Store 2   E = Store 5
C = Store 3   F = Store 6

interviewing day was proportional to that store's traffic on that day relative to the total traffic of all six stores during all interviewing days.[2]

The second shopping party that entered the store after the indicated starting time for interviews was the first interview unless the shopping party was "ineligible." An ineligible shopping party was defined as (1) a shopping party that consisted *solely* of a child or teenager who was, in the interviewer's judgment, not a household member or (2) a shopping party that had previously been interviewed. Whenever an ineligible shopping party situation arose, the next eligible shopping party entering the store was the one that was interviewed. The second eligible shopping party that entered the store after the completion of the previous interview constituted the next interview.

These procedures were employed in each store on each interviewing day during each interviewing week until the required number of interviews for a given store on a given interviewing day were obtained.

Observational-type interviews were used in all instances. Interviewers traced the exact path of each customer's movements on a store layout replica sheet. Interviewers posed as shoppers so as to minimize the probability that shoppers would know that they were being observed. Interviewers also obtained, by observation, the following information for each respondent: (1) specific products purchased,[3] (2) total grocery bill, (3) total number

[2] The procedure used was: (1) Total customer count was computed by adding the traffic count for each store for each day of the week. (2) For each store, the traffic count for each day was divided by the total customer count. (3) The percentages derived in (2) were then multiplied by one thousand to determine the number of interviews in a given store on a given day in a given interview week.

[3] Product purchases were recorded as single purchases regardless of the number of units, sizes, brands, and so forth that were purchased.

of products purchased, (4) sex of shopper, (5) time spent shopping exclusive of waiting time at the checkout counter, and (6) whether a prepared shopping list was used.

Major Findings

The density of customer traffic throughout the test stores is shown in Figure 12–1. Shoppers moving through the store were counted as passing products on either or both sides of aisle only when their attention was focused on the specific merchandise that was displayed.

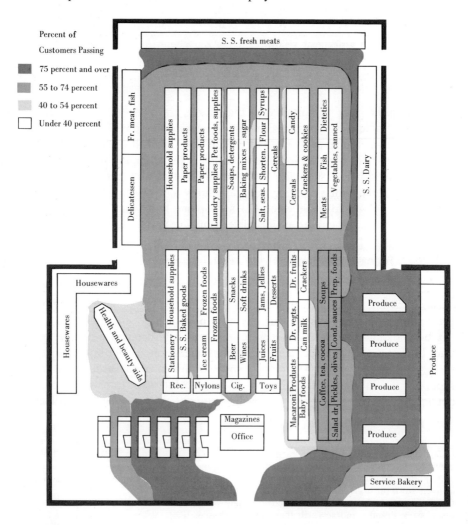

FIGURE 12–1. Big-Deal Stores, Inc.—average density of customer traffic in six test stores.

Passing-buying ratios were computed by WRI to indicate the effectiveness of major product categories in "pulling" customers throughout the store. These ratios are itemized in Table 12–13.

Table 12–13

Big-Deal Stores, Inc.—Number of Shoppers Who Pass and Buy Products in Major Product Categories

Out of 100 customers, 92 *pass and* 77 *buy*		Fresh meats
91	55	Produce
90	75	Dairy products
68	16	Condiments, sauces
67	22	Jams, jellies, spreads
65	30	Frozen foods
64	17	Pickles, olives, radishes
63	35	Paper products
63	15	Tobacco products
63	27	Dish and laundry supplies
63	31	Vegetables
62	27	Cereals
62	16	Household supplies
61	23	Coffee, tea, cocoa
60	12	Ice cream
60	18	Baked goods
60	18	Desserts
59	12	Salt seasoning, spices
58	9	Canned meats
58	12	Dietetic foods
55	15	Baby foods
54	22	Fruit
53	24	Soft drinks
52	14	Snacks
52	27	Baking products
47	13	Health and beauty aids
37	12	Magazines and books
35	2	Stationery
31	6	Housewares
29	1	Toys and records

The other major findings of the study as reported by WRI were.

1. *The number of locations passed affects the number of purchases made.* Customers having grocery bills under $5 passed only 35 percent of the total locations in the store, while shoppers spending over $15 passed over 65 percent of the available product locations.

2. *The number of locations passed affects the amount of money spent.* Shoppers who passed up to thirty of the product locations spent an average of two thirds as much as customers passing seventy or more product locations.

3. *The greater the length of time spent in the store, the greater the number of locations passed.* Shoppers in the store for five minutes passed twelve locations, while twenty-minute shoppers passed fifty-five product locations.

4. *The greater the amount of time spent shopping, the greater the amount of money spent.* Shoppers in the store less than ten minutes spent $3.86, while customers shopping over twenty minutes spent $23.51.

5. *Shoppers using shopping lists spend more time and money in the store than shoppers without prepared lists.*

Questions

1. Evaluate the methodology used in the study.

2. What are the implications of the passing-buying ratios for the interior design of Big-Deal stores? Prepare a new store layout based on the passing-buying ratios.

3. What other merchandising strategies are suggested by the results of the study?

4. Prepare a proposal outlining the way(s) that a food manufacturer distributing a wide variety of products through Big-Deal can use the results of the study to increase its profits.

Big-Deal Stores, Inc. (B): Consumer Perceptions and Shopping Behavior as a Basis for Pricing Strategy

Big-Deal Stores, Inc., with annual sales of approximately $20 million in 1967, operated twenty supermarkets in three major cities in Ohio. During the next five years management planned to open ten additional stores in Ohio, and by 1980 it was anticipated that the chain would consist of approximately fifty stores in the state.

The desirability of these expansion plans were dimmed somewhat by the company's poor profit performance in recent years. Net profit as a percentage of sales had declined for two consecutive years. By 1967 it had reached an all-time low of .5 percent, which was considerably below the national average.

During the company's early years, management was able to increase profits by obtaining more volume a store. However, the rapid expansion of national supermarket chains, cooperatives, and independents had diluted the effectiveness of the volume approach.

In recent years management had relied on operating-expense control as the primary method of increasing profits. This program had been successful. Big-Deal's operating expenses in 1967 were considerably below the national average.

By the spring of 1968, management had concluded that the most promising approach to increased profits revolved around better gross-margin management, particularly a more effective pricing strategy.

Pricing decisions were decentralized with each store manager setting most prices on the basis of his feel for the market. This policy was established in the early years of the company's history and it had not been changed. It was recognized that the individual stores were appealing to different market segments. Hence it was desirable for individual stores to set their own prices according to the characteristics of the market they were serving. Another factor that resulted in the decentralized policy was that, in the early years, management was hesitant to add the additional overhead that would be required if pricing decisions were to be made centrally.

With the company's aggressive expansion plans, management wondered whether or not Big-Deal was becoming large enough to support a headquarters research staff that would coordinate with the merchandising department. By working together, it was hoped that these two departments could play a more active role in formulating pricing strategies, either by establishing prices for all stores or by providing research information and other guidelines to help store managers set their own prices on a more scientific basis.

It was generally agreed that across-the-board price increases were not a viable alternative considering competitors' behavior and the nature and requirements of the market. Management was impressed, however, with the logic of selective price increases. Several executives felt that consumers did not know the *exact prices* of most of the 8000 items carried in a typical Big-Deal store. Although consumers knew the price range for many products, it was suggested that consumers knew the exact prices for only a few products that were frequently purchased or were otherwise of unusual importance. If this were true, management reasoned that it might be possible to establish the desired price image by strategically pricing the products whose exact prices were known to obtain much larger markups on the items whose prices were not so well known. It was hoped that this strategy would allow the company to maintain or increase sales and increase gross margins and net profits.

It was agreed that further analysis of the desirability of this strategy, as well as of its eventual implementation, required better information than was available. Accordingly, management retained an independent research agency—Walters Research, Inc. (WRI)—to conduct several studies.

The Price Perception Study

Nature of Study

The objective of this study was to determine the extent to which consumers were aware of the prices charged for products in Big-Deal stores. The sixty products included in the study were those that Big-Deal executives felt were highly price-competitive and frequently advertised.

Because the stores in the Big-Deal chain appealed to somewhat different socioeconomic groups and because the possibility existed that these groups might perceive prices differently, it was necessary to include several stores in the study. The five stores chosen were selected to yield a balanced representation of the various socioeconomic groups.

It was also suggested that the types of consumers shopping in a store might vary by the day of week and the time of day. For example, working wives would not usually be expected to shop before 4 or 5 P.M. on weekdays. Because different types of shoppers are likely to perceive prices differently, it was considered necessary to interview during all hours of each shopping day.

Finally, it was argued that consumers differ in the frequency with which they shop at supermarkets. Those shopping twice a week might perceive prices differently from those shopping less frequently. In order to include all these types of shoppers in the study, it was considered desirable to conduct interviews during several weeks.

Table 12–14

Latin Square Design Used to Determine Consumers' Perceptions
of the Prices of Selected Products*

Day of Week	Interview Week					
	I	II	III	IV	V	VI
Monday	A	B	C	D	E	F
Tuesday	B	C	D	E	F	A
Wednesday	C	D	E	F	A	B
Thursday	D	E	F	A	B	C
Friday	E	F	A	B	C	D
Saturday	F	A	B	C	D	E

* Where random assignment yields:

A = Store 6   D = Store 4
B = Store 2   E = Store 1
C = Store 3   F = Store 5

Table 12–14 illustrates the Latin Square design that was used to balance systematic variation in price perception attributable to the factors just mentioned. The six test stores were randomly assigned to Treatments A through F. Interviews were conducted between the hours of 9 A.M. and 9 P.M. during each interviewing day. During each of the six interview weeks, interviews were conducted on all six days that the stores were open. Thus, interviews were conducted once and only once during any of the test hours, during any of the test days, and during any of the test weeks, thereby equalizing systematic errors due to these factors.

It was agreed by WRI and Big Deal management that a sample of one thousand customers would yield reasonably accurate measures of price per-

ceptions. The number of interviews conducted in each store on each interviewing day was proportional to that store's traffic on that day relative to the
total traffic of all six stores during all interviewing days.

The fifth shopping party entering the store after the indicated starting time
for interviews was the first interview unless the shopping party was "ineligible." An ineligible shopping party was one consisting solely of a child or
one that had previously been interviewed. Whenever an ineligible shopping
party situation arose, the next eligible shopping party entering the store was
interviewed. The fifth eligible shopping party that entered the store after the
completion of the previous interview constituted the next interview. The
uniform sampling fraction procedure was used to eliminate interviewer bias
in respondent selection and to make certain that interviews were conducted
during all hours of the day.

If an eligible shopping party was willing to cooperate in the study, they were
directed to a trailer located outside of the store. The trailer was partitioned
into two sections. In the rear of the trailer, a female employee of WRI enter-
tained any children present in the shopping party. In the front section, the
sixty products included in the study were placed on a series of tables. Respondents were told by a second interviewer that Big-Deal was interested in
finding out whether or not they knew the prices of products. Respondents
were told that they would receive ten cents every time they correctly estimated
the price of a product. They were then given a form itemizing the sixty
products and were asked to write in what they would expect to pay for each
product. After the respondent finished estimating prices, the interviewer
determined the correct number of price estimates and paid the respondent the
amount due.

Findings

Table 12–15 itemizes the percentage of respondents estimating the correct
price and the percentage estimating the price within plus or minus 5 percent
of the actual price for each of the sixty products included in the study.

Using appropriate tests of significance it was also found that

1. Price perceptions (percentage estimating correct price and percentage estimating price with plus or minus 5 percent of the actual price) did not vary
   (1) by day of week (2) by interview week, or (3) by interviewer.

2. Price perceptions varied across income classes. Respondents having incomes
   less than $5000 and those having incomes in excess of $15,000 were less
   aware of actual prices than were respondents earning between $5000 and
   $15,000.

3. Product usage affects price perceptions. Respondents purchasing a product
   once every two weeks or more frequently displayed more accurate price
   perceptions than did respondents purchasing the product less frequently or
   not at all.

Table 12–15

Big-Deal Stores, Inc.—Comparisons of Consumers' Perceptions of Prices
with Actual Prices for Selected Products

Product	Percentage of Respondents Estimating Correct Price	Percentage of Respondents Estimating Prices within 5 Percent Higher or Lower
Coca-Cola (6 pack)	91	94
Pepsi-Cola (6 pack)	90	93
Wonder bread	88	97
Borden milk	75	83
Big-Deal bread	75	85
Heinz tomato soup	64	75
Big-Deal milk	63	75
Cut-Rite wax paper	31	37
Pillsbury pancake mix	26	33
Post Toasties	21	26
Del Monte peaches	21	25
Big-Deal tomato soup	21	43
Domino sugar, 5 lb.	20	53
Kraft American cheese	20	34
Big-Deal sugar, 5 lb.	20	42
Parkay margarine	19	22
Big-Deal margarine	19	21
Big-Deal peaches	19	22
Kraft mayonnaise	18	34
Del Monte fruit cocktail	16	27
Pillsbury flour	16	47
French mustard	14	32
Big-Deal fruit cocktail	14	21
Folgers coffee (1 lb. can)	14	18
Big-Deal mustard	14	22
Big-Deal coffee (1 lb. can)	14	15
Skippy peanut butter	13	18
Snow Crop orange juice	13	21
Welch's grape jelly	12	20
Heinz catsup	12	24
Big-Deal peanut butter	12	14
Saran Wrap	11	18
Idaho french fries	11	21
Big-Deal catsup	11	17
Armour bacon (1 lb.)	10	16
Big-Deal orange juice	10	17
Big-Deal grape jelly	10	15

Table 12–15 (continued)

Product	Percentage of Respondents Estimating Correct Price	Percentage of Respondents Estimating Prices within 5 Percent Higher or Lower
Green Giant corn	10	29
Maxwell House instant coffee	9	18
Big-Deal bacon (1 lb.)	9	14
Big-Deal french fries	9	17
Borden's ice cream (1 gal.)	8	27
Big-Deal corn	8	22
Dole sliced pineapple	8	23
Cheer (giant size)	7	33
Big-Deal instant coffee	7	16
Big-Deal pineapple	7	18
Comet cleanser	6	25
Lay's potato chips	6	34
Big-Deal potato chips	6	28
Nestle instant tea	5	24
Metrecal	5	18
Kleenex	5	43
Campbells tomato juice	4	37
Uncle Ben's rice	4	12
Big-Deal instant tea	4	14
Big-Deal tomato juice	3	22
Big-Deal rice	3	12
Crisco	3	27
Big-Deal shortening	2	25

Multiple-Unit Pricing Study

Nature of Study

Many experts believe that multiple-unit pricing can increase the sales of an item above the level resulting from single unit pricing. Therefore, as a basis for formulating general pricing strategy, Big-Deal management asked WRI to determine the proper role of multiple-unit pricing.

Consumers' reactions to multiple-unit pricing are likely to depend on several factors including (1) the product, (2) the single-unit price of the product, and (3) the price multiple used. Accordingly, it was considered necessary to include, and/or control for, each of these factors in the research design. Table 12–16 and the accompanying footnote describe the factorial design that was used.

Table 12–16

Factorial Design Used to Test the Effects of Multiple Pricing*

Store	Week				
	1	2	3	4	5
1	A_1	A_2	A_3	A_4	A_5
	B_2	B_3	B_4	B_5	B_1
	C_3	C_4	C_5	C_1	C_2
	D_4	D_5	D_1	D_2	D_3
	E_5	E_1	E_2	E_3	E_4
2	A_2	A_3	A_4	A_5	A_1
	B_3	B_4	B_5	B_1	B_2
	C_4	C_5	C_1	C_2	C_3
	D_5	D_1	D_2	D_3	D_4
	E_1	E_2	E_3	E_4	E_5
3	A_3	A_4	A_5	A_1	A_2
	B_4	B_5	B_1	B_2	B_3
	C_5	C_1	C_2	C_3	C_4
	D_1	D_2	D_3	D_4	D_5
	E_2	E_3	E_4	E_5	E_1
4	A_4	A_5	A_1	A_2	A_3
	B_5	B_1	B_2	B_3	B_4
	C_1	C_2	C_3	C_4	C_5
	D_2	D_3	D_4	D_5	D_1
	E_3	E_4	E_5	E_1	E_2
5	A_5	A_1	A_2	A_3	A_4
	B_1	B_2	B_3	B_4	B_5
	C_2	C_3	C_4	C_5	C_1
	D_3	D_4	D_5	D_1	D_2
	E_4	E_5	E_1	E_2	E_3

* Where:

1. *Regular price* $= 10\cent$

$A_1 = 2/19\cent$	for	Brand X	pork and beans
$A_2 = 4/39$			soup
$A_3 = 6/59$			shoe string potatoes
$A_4 = 8/79$			frozen waffles
$A_5 = 10/99\cent$			small cakes

2. *Regular price* $= 15\cent$

$B_1 = 2/29\cent$	Jell-o
$B_2 = 3/44$	salt
$B_3 = 4/59$	fruit cocktail
$B_4 = 5/74$	pudding
$B_5 = 6/89\cent$	baking soda

3. *Regular price* = 20¢
   $C_1 = 2/39¢$ napkins
   $C_2 = 3/59$ garlic salt
   $C_3 = 4/79$ canned vegetable
   $C_4 = 5/99$ baby food
   $C_5 = 6/1.19¢$ bread

4. *Regular price* = 30¢
   $D_1 = 2/59¢$ salad dressing
   $D_2 = 3/89$ brown sugar
   $D_3 = 4/1.19$ cereal
   $D_4 = 5/1.49$ spaghetti
   $D_5 = 6/1.79¢$ tomato juice

5. *Regular price* = 40¢
   $E_1 = 2/79¢$ rice
   $E_2 = 3/1.19$ syrup
   $E_3 = 4/1.59$ jelly
   $E_4 = 5/1.99$ olives
   $E_5 = 6/2.39¢$ cookies

Five test stores were selected from the total of twenty stores in order to yield a balanced representation of the different socioeconomic groups served by the chain. Five regular single-unit price levels—10¢, 15¢, 20¢, 30¢, 40¢—were selected to determine the impact of multiple-unit prices at several price levels. For each regular single-unit price level, five products were selected that were considered to vary in susceptibility to sales increases attributable to multiple-unit prices. For each regular single-unit price level, five multiple price levels were chosen. The five regular single-unit prices were then assigned to Treatments A through E. The five multiple price levels were then assigned Subscripts 1 through 5 for each of the treatments (A through E), generating a total of twenty-five treatments.

Table 12–16 indicates how the twenty-five treatments were distributed across both stores and interview weeks. Each treatment occurred once and only once in each store during each week. In this way systematic variations in the effect of multiple-unit pricing attributable to store and interview week were balanced.

Normal weekly sales were determined for each product in each of the stores. Researchers, with the cooperation of store personnel, set up the appropriate treatment in each store during each week. Each treatment lasted one week (Monday through Saturday), and unit sales of each product during the week were recorded.

Findings

Table 12–17 summarizes the results of the tests. The percentage of increase or decrease from normal unit sales is shown for the five regular single-unit price levels for each of the five multiple-unit price levels for each of the products included in the study.

Table 12–17

Big-Deal Stores, Inc.—Results of Multiple-Unit Pricing Tests

Regular Price All Items:	10¢	10¢	10¢	10¢	10¢
Test Prices:	2/19¢	4/39¢	6/59¢	8/79¢	10/99¢

Percentage increase or decrease from normal unit sales

Pork and beans	+36	+ 27	+ 16	+ 15	+ 27
Soup	+60	+150	+355	+480	+570
String potatoes	+42	+ 36	+ 18	+ 11	+ 8
Frozen waffles	+25	+ 33	+ 42	+ 13	+ 2
Small cakes	+39	+ 43	+ 5	+ 2	+ .5

Regular Price All Items:	15¢	15¢	15¢	15¢	15¢
Test Prices:	2/29¢	3/44¢	4/59¢	5/74¢	6/89¢

Percentage increase or decrease from normal unit sales

Jell-o	+48	+12	+32	+8	+ 5
Salt	+16	+10	+ 4	+ .2	− 3
Fruit cocktail	+31	+18	+22	+9	+ 2
Pudding	+28	+14	+18	+7	+10
Baking soda	+12	+ 4	+ 5	−2	− 1

Regular Price All Items:	20¢	20¢	20¢	20¢	20¢
Test Prices:	2/39¢	3/59¢	4/79¢	5/99¢	6/119¢

Percentage increase or decrease from normal unit sales

Napkins	+21	+ 31	+ 16	+ 8	− 1
Garlic salt	+19	+ 14	+ 4	+ 1	−12
Canned vegetables	+62	+113	+212	+288	+14
Baby food	+43	+ 72	+122	+265	+ 8
Bread	+27	+ 33	+ 18	+ 12	+ 7

Regular Price All Items:	30¢	30¢	30¢	30¢	30¢
Test Prices:	2/59¢	3/89¢	4/119¢	5/149¢	6/179¢

Percentage increase or decrease from normal unit sales

Salad dressing	+ 8	+14	+5	−4	−14
Brown sugar	+12	+ 8	+ .5	−7	−22
Cereal, corn flakes	+26	+16	+2	−2	− 6
Spaghetti	+19	+23	+4	−1	− 9
Tomato juice	+23	+26	+1	−8	− 7

Table 12–17 (continued)

Regular Price All Items: Test Prices:	40¢ 2/79¢	40¢ 3/119¢	40¢ 4/159¢	40¢ 5/199¢	40¢ 6/239¢
Percentage increase *or decrease from* *normal unit sales*					
Rice	+23	+2	+ .5	− 8	−18
Syrup	+12	−3	− 6	−14	−22
Jelly	+18	+6	+ 2	− 5	−12
Olives	+11	+1	− 3	−18	−24
Cookies	+43	+1	−10	−22	−26

Questions

1. Evaluate the methodologies used in the studies.

2. What conclusions can be drawn about consumers' price perceptions? (Refer to Table 12–15.)

3. What are the strategy implications of the price perception study? Should Big-Deal selectively increase prices?

4. What conclusions can be drawn about the impact of multiple-unit pricing? (See Table 12–17.)

5. What role should multiple-unit pricing play in Big-Deal's overall pricing strategy?

CHAPTER 13

PURCHASE PROCESSES

Columbia Furniture Company: Analysis of Retail Salesmanship

The Columbia Furniture Company is located in a large midwestern city. It is a retail chain consisting of ten units located both in the downtown area and in surrounding suburbs. Sales growth has continued to be satisfactory, although market share has begun to slump. Alarmed about this situation, management retained a consulting firm to analyze company operations and to determine where changes might be required.

Problem

Detailed analysis showed most aspects of company operation to be excellent. There was cause for concern, however, over the performance of the sales force. Sales volume per employee was relatively high, and turnover was low; yet, there were definite signs of customer alienation caused by a lack of sales-force efforts to build future patronage through an attitude of genuine helpfulness. In other words, making the sale is only one aspect of the total job a salesman is expected to perform.

It became apparent that data were needed on salesmens' performance, using criteria other than sales volume and observation by management. Therefore, a two-phase study was undertaken. Phase One concentrated on the entire sales force and generated a rating of total performance for each member. Phase Two consisted of a further analysis of sales performance in the Country Fair store, the largest unit in the chain. This unit, in turn, was the center of most customer complaints and thus warranted further study in order to identify the problems. Each of these phases is discussed below.

Phase One

Salesmanship was defined for purposes of this study as "showing people how they can satisfy their needs, wants, or desires through the purchase of

234

goods or services." It must clearly be distinguished from *order-taking*, in which the salesman often makes no effort to convert a prospect into a customer.

Salesmanship can be detected only imperfectly from sales records, and a specific methodology was needed to analyze salesmanship with a sufficient degree of accuracy. Indeed, a proper evaluation can only be made in terms of whether or not the salesman has convinced the shopper that his needs can be satisfied through purchase. Thus, in this study, the evaluation of salesmanship was made by people who acted the part of prospective customers.

Methodology

A number of young adults were trained to perform the role of active shoppers, and six different selling situations were utilized:

1. A young couple tells the salesman that they are going to be married in a few months and that they will want to purchase furniture at that time. At the present, they are only looking for ideas.

2. A person tells the salesman that he wishes to furnish a specific room in his house.

3. A person explains to the salesman that he is confused concerning different styles of furniture.

4. A customer does not realize that he is having difficulty in choosing attractive color combinations.

5. A couple states that they are just looking around to get ideas, and they become upset when a salesman tries to inject comments.

6. A customer keeps dickering on the price.

7. A husband and wife have differing tastes in furniture. What appeals to one is not pleasing to the other.

No individual salesman received more than six of the seven situations on the above list.

Each salesman was approached at least several times for purposes of evaluation. The person doing the evaluation carried a hidden tape recorder and filled out a detailed questionnaire covering the following items:

1. Appearance
   a. Clothing
   b. Hair
   c. Personal hygiene
   d. Posture
   e. Other factors

2. Personality
   a. Courtesy and so forth
   b. Ability to make customer feel at ease
   c. Other noticeable traits

3. Enthusiasm
   a. Speed of approach
   b. Interest shown in being of help
      (1) Questions to explore needs
      (2) Attempts to get into the home
      (3) Suggestions
      (4) Use of imagination
   c. Control of enthusiasm
   d. "Romanticizing" furniture

4. Product knowledge
   a. Explanation of construction and so forth
   b. Visualization of needs and good suggestions
   c. Explanation of styles
   d. Justification of price differentials
   e. Explanation of warranty
   f. Other related points

5. Human relations
   a. Use of tact
   b. Ability to make customer feel he made the decisions
   c. Creation of impression that "customer is king"

6. Selling ability
   a. Ability to "get in" with prospect
   b. Development of shopper into prospect

7. Contribution to the store
   a. Conveying good store image
   b. Attempts to encourage return visits and future sales
   c. Thorough explanation of management policies

The shopper rated the salesman on each major point using a scale ranging from 1 (excellent) to 9 (poor). The sales volume record of each salesman was later evaluated by company management using the same scale so that comparisons could be made between volume and customer ratings of salesmanship.

The accuracy of the shoppers' ratings was evaluated through use of a hidden tape recorder. This recorder was built into a handbag carried by the shopper, and an objective record was thereby provided. With few exceptions, the accuracy of shoppers' evaluations was verified.

Data were analyzed by computing an average evaluation score along each criteria for each salesman. These data are graphically presented later in this report.

The majority of the salesmen also were later interviewed by one of the investigators. Fourteen selling situations were listed, and the salesman was asked how he would handle each situation. Company management previously had determined the proper response, and the answers given were rated from 1 to 9 in terms of the degree to which the answer correctly reflected company policy and procedures. This rating is referred to as "expected performance."

In summary, the following information was collected: (1) a rating of salesmanship performance, (2) a rating of "expected" performance on 14 selling situations (collected only for a smaller sample of salesmen), and (3) a rating of sales volume.

Data Analysis

Only certain highlights of the findings are given in this section. Two summary figures have been prepared, and they provide a graphic indication of the results. In Figure 13–1, salesmen are listed in terms of sales rank. Sales performance is graphed by the dotted line. Also an average salesmanship rating was computed for each salesman using the arithmetic mean of ratings given by prospects on appearance, personality, enthusiasm, product knowledge, human relations, selling ability, and contribution to the store. Thus, sales volume and salesmanship, as measured in this study, may be compared at a glance.

It will be noticed that the salesmanship performance, on the average, is quite good. In fact, the average score for all salesmen is 3—an unusually high rating. This provides a definite indication that salesmanship is sufficiently high to verify that training is being reflected, for the most part, in perfor-

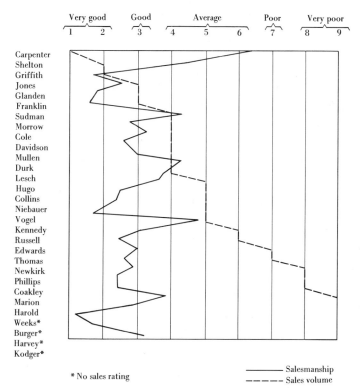

* No sales rating

——————— Salesmanship
– – – – – Sales volume

FIGURE 13–1. A graphic comparison of salesmanship and sales volume.

FIGURE 13–2. A graphic comparison of enthusiasm, product knowledge, and rated selling ability.

mance. There are some low ratings, however, and comments on individuals appear in the next section.

Figure 13–2 provides a sharper measure of sales performance. A review of the data disclosed that enthusiasm, product knowledge, and selling ability proved to be the most meaningful ratings provided by shoppers. Thus, the average score for each salesman on these dimensions was plotted graphically. Once again, salesmen are listed in the order of their sales rank.

Notice that, with the exception of Carpenter and Shelton, high-volume salesmen tend to receive the highest ratings on these three criteria. In turn, the low-volume salesmen also have excellent ratings. The lowest ratings, on the average, are earned by the middle-ranking salesmen, although in few cases are ratings sufficiently low to be of any real concern. The interesting conclusion from this analysis is that the low-volume salesmen may be spending so much time in helping prospects that they are failing to convert them into buyers. In analysis of certain individuals, this tendency seems to be quite apparent.

It is very clear to the investigators that appearance is not a factor that weighs strongly in the prospect's mind. In many instances, the appearance of those rating highest in salesmenship was not felt to be especially good.

It also should be pointed out that salesmen's responses to the fourteen-item questionnaire were, for the most part, excellent. The action they say they would take in each situation closely parallels that specified by management.

There are several implications for sales training that should be noted briefly here. First, enthusiasm and interest in the shopper are the most valued behavior as stated by prospects. If this enthusiasm and level of interest is high, then the prospect, in all probability, will have a high opinion of Columbia as a place to shop and buy. Product knowledge also weighs heavily, and it cannot be emphasized too strongly that the shopper is looking for reasons to buy. If this information is not volunteered by the salesman, the salesmanship rating tends to suffer.

Phase Two

The first phase of this project focused on the manner in which individual salesmen handle complex selling situations. The data, however, did not fully illuminate the problem of treatment of browsers, especially in the Country Fair store. As a result, a further study was undertaken to evaluate whether or not browsers are being approached properly at Country Fair and are being turned into prospects.

Methodology

A total of twenty-two couples served as shoppers for this purpose. They were instructed to visit the store at different times of the day and week and simply to indicate that they wished to browse. At a later point in the visit, however, instructions called for them to begin to show interest in an item in such a manner that it would be observed by an alert salesman. Various data were collected during the visit including the time of first contact by a salesman and the time of any subsequent recontacts. Also of interest were the names of the salesmen, the nature of sales activity during contacts, a record of the number of people in the store, and a general overall evaluation of the extent to which they were satisfied as customers.

Data Analysis

The shopper usually was contacted within the first five to ten minutes after entering the store (over 50 percent reported contact within four minutes). Several went a considerable period before first contact, however, and one left after twenty-eight minutes without seeing a salesman. In 82 percent of the instances the initial contact was made by a member of the sales force. The hostess at the door performed this function only once.

It is disturbing to note that no recontact was made in 41 percent of the visits. Moreover, many shoppers were neglected for as long as a half hour. Finally, the same salesman who made the initial contact returned in only 23 percent of reported instances.

Of the recontacts made, only a few could be evaluated as being real selling where definite help was given based on an awareness of what browsers had been doing and the merchandise they had been examining. In remaining situations the recontact was usually made by a different salesman and consisted merely of a casual offer to help. No salesman, however, followed through on such an offer.

One might expect a problem of neglected browsers in a crowded store. This was seldom the case, however, as it was the opinion of the great majority of the participants that the store was not busy. In addition, idle salesmen were observed in nearly 60 percent of the visits. There were frequent comments about the ideal sales force.

> Four sales personnel, a red-haired woman and three gentlemen, were standing immediately in front of the door conversing with each other.

> There were 20 people in the store. We noticed two salesmen sitting down and talking to each other while two groups of shoppers looked at furniture nearby. Another salesman was sitting talking to the woman at the desk. None of the salesmen made any offer of assistance as we browsed near them.

> Mr. Harvey said, "Believe it or not, there are eight salesmen hidden around here somewhere—sometimes its difficult to give each customer the service they deserve."

Implications

There is no doubt that browsers are being neglected at Country Fair. This neglect, in turn, has led to a predominately negative attitude by participants. Each person was asked to rate the store and its procedures using a seven-point scale. It ranged from 1 (excellent) to 7 (poor), with 4 signifying neutrality. The average rating was 5.1—a strong indication that many shoppers are being alienated. More light is shed on the ratings by consideration of some of the individual comments:

> I receive the impression that the salesman would be happy to wait on a person if he expressed an interest in something but that little would be done to create an interest among browsers.

> I probably never would go back again.

> I counted at least six sales people, and my general impression is that they were not interested in making a sale. The attitude on the part of the

persons was boredom and impatience. No attempt was made to make a sale, to explain the product, or to get me to come back. I was furious.

It should be pointed out that the numerical ratings may be unduly harsh. The participants differed from the typical shopper in that they were alert to certain types of behavior that normally might not have provoked such negative responses. Nevertheless, a good indication is provided of the magnitude of the problem.

The data support these conclusions:

1. The initial contact, as a rule, is made fairly promptly.

2. When a recontact is made, it usually is by someone other than the first salesman. There is a strong indication that salesmen do not stay with shoppers and do not attempt to develop them into prospects.

3. The lack of follow-through is dangerous because the presumption is that salesmen on commission can separate hot prospects from browsers. Yet, what criteria are used for this purpose? A person who appears to be a browser can, in reality, be a real prospect, and it is probable that a significant number of sales are being lost by lethargy.

4. The high number of participants who left with a negative reaction indicate the probability that word-of-mouth communication about Columbia is not favorable.

Conclusions

Management in concerned about these findings, and some felt that perhaps compensation should not be based on commission. Others saw a need to change sales training procedures.

Questions

1. Evaluate the methodology used in this study.

2. What action should management take, if any?

CHAPTER 14

POSTPURCHASE EVALUATION

Alexander Hamilton Life Insurance Company of America: Postdecision Reactions of New Policy Owners

The Alexander Hamilton Life Insurance Company of America has established a remarkable growth record since its founding in 1964. Its product offers a unique combination of life insurance, savings, and investment and thus possesses a distinct competitive advantage. In fact, the program is sometimes considered "too good to be true," thus leading some who have recently purchased a contract to have doubts following their decision. Moreover, the company relies upon names given to salesmen by new policyholders for much of its future business, so management is concerned that any postdecision doubts be overcome quickly or even be prevented entirely by a revised marketing plan.

Company History

The principal founder of Hamilton, E. Keith Owens, served in his early career as regional director for Land of Lincoln Life Insurance Company; as president of Central Illinois Investment Company, specializing in insurance securities; and as an insurance firm consultant. He attained a millionaire status by the age of twenty-nine. Meanwhile, beginning in 1961, he set out to organize a "new dynamic insurance company that would avoid the mistakes of other new companies and would be fast-growing, durable, and profitable at an early stage." An analysis of the ingredients of success and failings of other life insurance companies served as the foundation for these early plans. Three other successful executives were assembled as the initial management team.

Three years of planning preceded Hamilton's entrance into business. The group of four was already aware that the principal problem of many new life companies was because of the success of an early sales effort that can lead to expenses and reserve requirements that exhaust capital surplus. It was axiomatic that this company must have adequate capitalization to support its planned growth.

Every state was next surveyed to appraise the most likely territories for sale of life insurance. Figures in 1962 revealed that Michigan enjoyed one of the highest family incomes in the nation yet averaged only $4800 of life insurance protection as compared with the national average of $10,400. The study also showed that Michigan had the fewest number of domicile companies per capita of any state—fourteen. The group of incorporators grew to fourteen when what is now recalled as the O'Hare meeting was held. In a three-day session near the Chicago airport of the same name, Michigan was selected as a starting base, the name of the company was adopted, and a unity of purpose was established.

The starting date was May 1, 1964. By the end of the first month, Hamilton salesmen had written $15.3 million of life insurance. Five days after charter, eleven regional directors and forty-nine licensed agents were in the field. The first month's sales record surpassed that which most new companies write in their first full year.

The remarkable growth record is attested by the following full-year industry sales records, which were surpassed in only eight months of operation:

1. Year-end insurance in force of $60,331,500 was substantially higher than the previous all-time high of $52,000,000 achieved in a full twelve months by a new company in Hawaii.

2. The traditional first-year heavy operating loss was only $81,500 as compared with an expected cost of $750,000.

3. Only $1.04 was spent for each $1.00 of premium income compared with an average figure of $1.50 in the first year.

4. Hamilton agents received from the National Association of Life Insurance Companies the highest number of individual performance awards based on annualized commissions of any company in the National Association of Life Insurance Companies.

5. Hamilton skyrocketed past most of the 1600 to 1700 life insurance companies in the nation to rank 566th from the top after only eight months in business.

6. The company began with a net capitalization of $8,306,000, the largest starting capitalization in the history of the industry at that time.

7. The company sold stock shares to individuals in nearly every Michigan community, resulting in 8384 stockholders by date of charter.

By the end of the first full year of operation, $102 million of insurance was in force, double the former world's record.

The year 1966 saw a 52.2 percent increase in business to a total of nearly $211 million, a new high in its history. The size of the average policy in force at the end of the year was \$10,304, well above the industry average. The excellent financial position of the company was attested by an A+ rating given by Dunne's Insurance Report.

The Wayne National Life Insurance Company was purchased during 1967, and total insurance in force passed the 330 million mark with \$20 million of company assets. In total insurance volume, the company now has passed more than 1400 of the 1700 life insurance companies in the United States.

Marketing Policies

The company creed appearing prominently on its literature states, "We believe: In God and human dignity; in individual freedom guarded by individual responsibility; and in a free market economy with a government limited to defending the God given rights of man." This Creed reflects the deep religious convictions of the founders and is felt by many to be the primary reason that record-shattering growth has occurred. A distinct customer orientation was adopted from the start, and it is reflected in promotional policies and in the product itself.

Promotional Policies

The company has done little or no advertising and relies instead on its field force and resident advisory boards. Each salesman assembles a group of business and community leaders who serve on his resident advisory board. Their responsibilities range from setting policies to the provision of names for field-force contact. The emphasis thus is placed on word-of-mouth communication generated initially and legitimized by resident advisory board members, each of whom is a respected local citizen. In turn, a policy cannot go into force unless each new policyholder contacts at least six additional people, thereby "opening the door" for a sales presentation. At the beginning of 1967, 173 members served on resident advisory boards, and this figure surpassed 550 by January, 1968.

The company presently operates in only four midwestern states, but it is licensed to operate in most of the remaining states. New territories are opened as experienced field salesmen become available. The backbone of the expansion program, however, lies in the establishment of a strong resident advisory board before operations commence. The success of this policy is attested by the sales growth.

The Policy

From its inception the company was based on the premise that inroads would not be made in this competitive industry unless a product was devised that did more for people than just provide "death insurance" (that is, benefits payable primarily upon death). In addition, a company operating principle was established that the product offered would be designed to allow the policyholder to share in the company's growth. The product was designed to offer "living benefits" in the form of built-in savings and investment provisions along with a competitive insurance program.

A grasp of policy benefits can best be gained from a review of the basic sales presentation that begins with an outline of the facts about company history and growth. The legitimacy of company success is attested to by mention of the members of the company board, which includes such eminent men as S. S. Kresge, president of the Kresge Foundation. The potential customer then is taken through a sales presentation notebook that puts forth pertinent selling points. The salesman, of course, uses it as a springboard for his comments, but the contents of each page will be reproduced here with reference made to additional explanation provided by the salesman only when it is necessary to clarify various points.

Problem

Although it is apparent that the Hamilton contract is unique and has resulted in a pattern of growth that is unprecedented in its industry, some policyholders experience what management refers to as the "postdecision blues" after they sign a contract. The benefits, upon reflection, seem "too good to be true," and some are deeply troubled about whether or not full benefits will be realized. Surprisingly, the facts show that benefits are even greater than anticipated, because minimum dividend projections have understated actual amounts. In addition, company yield rate on its investments (the amount also paid to policyholders on accumulated endowments and dividends) has reached 5 percent and is increasing. The problem, however, is to convince the public of these facts.

Management feels confident that continued company growth will guarantee the attainment of projected policy benefits in the coming years. This judgment would appear to be substantiated by the excellent ratings given the company and its management by such impartial sources as Dunne's Insurance Report. Therefore, there is a need to convince the prospect that the policy is as good as it appears to be, both to win new customers and to reassure the new purchaser. Management is considering changes in the sales presentation as well as other actions to provide this extra element of credibility.

The Policy Presentation

We find that people accumulate money for four reasons:

1. College education

2. Retirement

3. Special dreams

4. Financial independence

Which financial goal is most important to you?
You can reach your financial goal in three ways:

1. Save money

2. Invest money

3. Protect through insurance

But to have the advantages of all three, it would take three separate dollars
—in three different places.

Have you ever had one investment do all three? Alexander Hamilton provides the opportunity to do all three:

1. Gives financial protection through insurance

2. Guarantees savings with interest

3. Makes you money

Alexander Hamilton does all three:

1. Gives financial protection through a tax-free (no income taxes) insurance
    estate ($25,000 maximum policy amount) that guarantees your financial goal.

2. Guarantees savings in two ways compared to only one in regular insurance:
    a. Regular insurance savings in the form of cash value—cash that increases
        yearly. When withdrawn this reduces your insurance estate and must be
        repaid with interest.
    b. Alexander Hamilton insured savings—cash value *and* the flexibility of
        annual endowment that, when withdrawn, leaves your insurance estate
        intact. It need not be replaced, and there are no interest charges.
    Which would you rather have? (*Note:* An endowment fund is built that
    consists of $15 for each $1000 of protection. For example, $375 on the
    maximum-size policy of $25,000. This sum is accumulated yearly.)

3. Makes you money in two ways:
    a. From insurance operations you receive dividends.
    b. From investment operations you receive a special interest rate.

Here's how our *special interest rate* will make you money. All financial institutions have two interest rates: (1) savers receive the depositors' rate; and
(2) borrowers pay a higher rate than the lender's rate. Alexander Hamilton
pays the higher rate. Instead of the depositor's rate, you receive the higher
rate. You make what we make—you get the company yield rate on investments. (*Note:* It also is stipulated that the company will pay 3.5 percent or
the yield rate, whichever is higher.) What does this mean to you? We will pay
you whatever the economy allows us to make on our money. In 1967 the depositors' rate ranged from 4.5 to 5 percent, and the lenders' rate from 6 to 7

percent; you will always receive the higher rate. Do you know any other financial institution that will pay you its yield rate?

In addition to our special interest rate you will make money on dividends from our insurance operation. The size of your dividend depends on the future market potential for our product and the ability of Alexander Hamilton to sell the product. (*Note:* At this point the salesman looks at population and economic projections for the next twenty-five years that show the great potential for the insurance business and reviews Alexander Hamilton's remarkable growth record.) In the world's largest business Alexander Hamilton Life Insurance Company of America is growing faster than any company, anywhere in the history of the industry. Dividend participation allows you to share in this growth. Here are our minimum dividend projections (filed with the state insurance department), and they can be increased depending on the growth of Alexander Hamilton:

Year	Percent
2	7.88
3	9.89
4	11.90
5	13.91
6	15.95
7	17.98
8	20.04
9	22.08
10	24.16
11	25.62
12	27.08

If our dividends are no higher than the minimum projections, could we count on your help? (*Note:* These dividends are based on 1958 mortality projections, and premium rates are set so that the company makes an increasing profit the longer the insurance is in force. Hence, Alexander Hamilton simply is sharing their earnings with the policyholder by paying an increasing dividend on the yearly premium. Example: The dividend on a $1000 annual premium would be $78.80 at the end of the second full policy year [7.88 percent of 1000]; $98.90 at the end of the third year; $220.80 at the end of the ninth year; and so on.)

Now, let's look at what can be earned by placing a $25,000 policy (the maximum allowable amount) on an eight-year-old child. The annual premium would be $825.25. Each year after the first full policy year $375 is added to the endowment fund (15 for each $1000 protection), and this sum is accumulated. In addition, dividends are paid after the first full year in accordance with the projected minimum rates presented earlier. At the end of the second year, for example, you will earn roughly $66 (7.88 percent of $825.25); you will accumulate approximately $82 by the end of the third year (9.89 percent of $825.25); and by the end of the twelfth year you will have earned nearly $223 (27.08 percent of $825.25). This assumes, of course, that the minimum dividend projections are realized, and thus far they have been exceeded.

The amount of the yearly endowment and the amount earned from dividends are added together, and this combined sum earns interest at the current company yield rate. Example: at the end of year two, the endowment is $375 and dividends are $66.00, making a total of $441 that then earns additional interest of 3.5 percent or the company yield rate, whichever is higher. Assuming 6 percent, this means that you also earn the additional amount of $26.46. This can be shown graphically in this way:

Year	Premium	Endowment	Dividend	Total Sum That Earns at Yield Rate
1	$825.00	–	–	–
2	825.25	375.00	66.00	441.00
3	825.25	375.00	82.00	457.00
7	825.25	375.00	108.50	483.50
12	$825.25	$375.00	$222.75	$597.75

Now you can use this contract in two ways: (1) as an investment, and (2) as a limited pay life contract. There are, of course, additional options in the way you can use dividends and endowments, but here is how these two will work:

1. *As an investment.* Let's assume on the above contract that the maximum premium of $825.25 is paid yearly (there are ways in which dividends, etc. can reduce this); the minimum projected dividends are paid; the company has a net investment yield rate (figures following assume 6 percent); and all dividends and endowment accumulations remain in the company and are invested at the yield rate. Here is what we will have at various intervals in the child's life:

	Years the policy is held			
	10	15	20	At age 65
Total premium investment	$8,252.50	$12,363.75	$16,050.00	$ 47,039.25
Total accumulations (endowment and dividends plus interest at yield rate)	$7,476.00	$14,173.75	$23,114.50	$274,604.24

   Accumulations can, of course, be withdrawn at any time.

2. *As a limited pay life contract.* If all endowments and cash values are allowed to accumulate and to be applied against premium, the contract will be paid up in eleven years or at the time the child is nineteen. If dividends are also applied against premium, the policy will be paid up several years sooner.

As one last benefit, Alexander Hamilton also offers the "convertible premium deposit privilege side fund option" to accumulate more money toward your financial goal. Deposits in amounts of $50 or more will be accepted at any time, and you will make what we make on the entire fund. Do you know any financial institution where an initial deposit entitles you to receive the lender's net yield on investments as an interest rate? *Note*: This option works in exactly the same manner as a savings account where the individual invests certain amounts and earns going interest rates. Here he has freedom to invest and withdraw funds while earning the company's yield rate, which in all probability will be higher than the rate that could be earned elsewhere.)

Questions

1. Why might postdecision dissonance occur in this situation?

2. Can it be overcome? What actions, if any, would you suggest for Hamilton management?

PART V

AGGREGATE BEHAVIOR
OVER TIME

CHAPTER 15

DIFFUSION OF INNOVATIONS AND FASHION

Hollywood Vassarette: Predicting Fashion Trends for Women's Intimate Apparel

The Hollywood Vassarette Division of Munsingwear Incorporated manufactures a complete line of intimate apparel. Intimate apparel is also known as lingerie, which encompasses slips, half slips, pants, nightgowns, pajamas, robes and peignoirs, and brassieres and girdles. This division is involved almost exclusively with women as its customers. The company considers some of its products as having a cosmetic function (bras, girdles) but also markets its products with appeals emphasizing comfort, femininity, fit, and (especially with sleeping garments) sex appeal.

Vassarette is one of a relatively small group of marketers that are vertically integrated. That is, the company knits, dyes, and finishes almost all of the fabrics used in its lingerie products and a good deal of those used in bras and girdles also. The company is considered a major producer of intimate apparel, and it uses a wide range of outlets in its distribution, totally refraining from any sales to chains (Sears, and so forth), discounters, or private-label distributions.

As a major manufacturer, Vassarette produces several hundred garment styles each year. In lingerie alone the consumer is offered a wide choice of from fifteen to twenty-five fabrics over the range of these styles, along with a wide variety of lace and embroidery trims. There is also a lot of variety in the colors offered ranging from seven to thirteen on particular styles; and at least six times a year large print collections are also offered in daywear and sleepwear lingerie. A similar pattern of many style and color offerings also exist in the bra and girdle product area, although not to as pronounced a degree. The industry basically has two seasons, spring-summer and fall-winter.

Traditionally the daywear lingerie and foundations markets had been reasonably stable, with not much variation in the fabrics and styles offered to consumers from year to year. The only real variant had been in the area of color. The sleepwear lingerie market had been a little more volatile, but still was somewhat restricted to the same fabrics and general types of trims offered in daywear. All of this contributed to a relatively slow market growth situation, with firms able to estimate their production requirements for an upcoming year on the basis of the previous year's sales, subject to some minor adjustments.

Recently, however, this has changed. Items of intimate apparel have become more and more subject to fashion changes. Increasingly, large groups of consumers are shifting their choices of these products from year to year. Large differences in fabrics, color ranges, styling features such as silhouettes, trimmings, lengths, varieties of fit, and a host of other considerations have made it more difficult to plan production and marketing schedules in advance of the season. Also, a general change seems to be occurring in the importance that consumers place on the "look" of an intimate apparel garment. The problems of scheduling were particularly acute for a manufacturer such as Vassarette, which was vertically integrated and which produced such a wide range of fabrics, styles, and sizes.

To see if marketing research could help on this problem, Vassarette had for some time encouraged Thomas Carlson, director of marketing research for the parent company, Munsingwear Company, to look for methods that would help the company accurately predict shifts in aggregate market behavior and preferences for intimate apparel. Research was authorized that would be adequate to determine the proper "mix" of the merchandise lines of Vassarette for the coming season in time so that production could be scheduled efficiently and that the garments could be delivered to retail stores at the peak of consumer demand for specific styles and colors. Because the problem was expected to increase in difficulty, the authorization specified that a research program be developed on a continuing basis that would allow the firm to anticipate seasonal shifts and major style trends in outerwear that were believed to be instrumental in shaping consumer demand for intimate apparel.

Research Approach

Carlson formulated four broad objectives of the research program that he felt would be mutually beneficial to both Vassarette and its customers, and he stated them as follows:

1. The first is to cover consumer preferences on styling considerations involving colors, fabrics, garment lengths, garment silhouettes, fit, fabric differences, trimmings such as laces and so forth, and garment function when dealing with foundations, pettipants, and the like.

2. A service approach to try to discover items wanted by consumers, but which they have been unable to find in the stores.

3. Complaints about the products these consumers have bought in the past.

4. To discover regional differences regarding the appeals of this styling feature or detail versus other choices for the same garment.

Aside from the existence of one or two consumer panels that could only point up historical shifts in consumer preferences, and some specialized studies conducted by the large fiber companies, there was a very small residue of experience to draw from in the area of apparel consumer research in 1964 to 1965. Customer Preference Clinics (CPC) of New York was almost alone in this field, and in late 1964 Vassarette engaged them to help develop a research program to achieve the stated objectives.

Unlike most other research firms, this firm had specialized in the area of in-store research with active shoppers in an actual shopping situation. Very few firms conducted research in this manner then or now. The majority concentrated more on the general public as respondents rather than active shoppers per se. In addition, CPC put strong reliance in its questioning technique on the shopper's last purchase of the garment on which she was being interviewed. On numerous style features the customer was then asked what she actually found in the last garment she bought, and then what her preferences on these features were for the next garment she was shopping for. In this manner style trends could be discerned from the customer's last purchases versus next garment preferences as well as from survey to survey.

Customer Preference Clinic

CPC president Frederick H. Rahr describes the operation of CPC in the following manner:

1. *Physical facilities.* The consumer's interviews are conducted from an interviewing unit that consists of a counter and illuminated color screen, set up in the departments of the stores retailing the type of merchandise being researched.

2. *Respondents.* Respondents entering or leaving the store department are approached and asked a question such as, "Are you shopping for a swimsuit, or lingerie, or (whatever the item under study is) today?" If the answer is no, the customer is dismissed with a courtesy statement such as "Be sure to come back later whenever this store can serve you." If the consumer states what she is seeking and if it is the item under study, she is invited to walk over to the interviewing counter and to tell us about it so that the store where the research is taking place will be better able to serve her. The usual response is surprised willingness to talk about the item and often is interest in the fact that someone wants to listen to her opinion.

3. *Questionnaire.* Working with Carlson and others at Vassarette, a standardized questionnaire was developed with approximately seventy questions per broad

product category (daywear lingerie, sleepwear lingerie, brassieres, girdles) and approximately five hundred options per product. The interview recording device was a matched pair of IBM mark sense cards, one for the last garment purchased and the other for the next being shopped for, which would facilitate analysis on EDP equipment and so forth.

4. *Sample.* A particularly large sample is required for this kind of research to permit statistical validity on the customer's color preferences for her next garment. On most questions she is presented with three to four choices for an answer to a question. However, when it came to color, the range of choice reached 150 to cover all the colors shown her on the illuminated color screen used with the CPC interviewing unit.

From 1000 to 1500 respondents were interviewed for Vassarette in each of the following stores and branches *on the first study* conducted on intimate apparel:

Altman's (New York)	3 stores
Rich's (Atlanta)	1 store
Hudson's (Detroit)	3 stores
Famous Barr (St. Louis)	2 stores
The Denver (Denver)	1 store
Meier and Frank (Portland)	2 stores
The Bon Marche (Seattle)	1 store
The Broadway (Los Angeles)	2 stores
	15 stores

The research firm states that "these sample sizes will usually provide statistical reliability at a level of 95 percent plus or minus 5 percent" on their color preferences and an even higher level of reliability on other product areas where the choices are not so numerous.

A second advantage of this large sample is the ability to stratify it to permit valid cross-tabulations. For example, customer preferences might be broken down into classifications such as junior-size customers or misses customers, or by geographical regions.

Two studies of this type were conducted. The first was completed in the spring-summer season of 1965 and the second in the fall-winter selling season of 1966. Different stores were used on these two different surveys, and future research will probably involve other stores not hitherto surveyed. The sketches accompanying this report are exact duplicates of those shown to consumers.

Results

In all, over 30,000 customers were interviewed on the two surveys, and, after poring through the very substantial quantity of raw survey data generated by the lengthy questionnaire and respondent samples of this magnitude,

Carlson presented the results of these surveys to his management. Many of these findings were used in planning for the lines for subsequent seasons, a number of which are detailed following.

Age of the Department Store Intimate Apparel Customers

The overriding factor in all the survey work done so far—both in the spring of 1965 and in the fall of 1966 has been the age of the customers surveyed. On a national basis, roughly 40 percent of the pantie girdle or girdle customers have come from the twenty-five-year and under age group. Fifty percent of all the bra customers have come from this age group also, both times surveyed. Fifty percent or better of the daywear customers have come from this same age group. This ranges from 40 to 45 percent of the slip customers, 55 to 60 percent of the half slip customers, and 80 percent of the pettipant customers. Fifty-five to 60 percent of the sleepwear customers have come from this same age group.

This young group of customers, in addition to being very numerous in the population, appears to be shopping more frequently than the other age groups in the population. This younger group of customers, along with the next age group (twenty-five to thirty-five years of age) appears to be leading the way in fashion changes in intimate apparel, particularly with respect to (1) color and color coordination, (2) garment lengths, (3) garment construction, (4) garment-size requirements, and (5) fabric preferences.

Daywear and Outerwear Lengths

The length of slips is determined mostly by the length of outerwear. Since slips and half slips basically have the same function for a wearer, it was commonly believed that the length, silhouette, and fit of the skirts of these garments would be somewhat the same. Figure 15–2, however, shows quite a different pattern. This exhibit shows that the wanted length in a half slip was substantially shorter by an average of two inches than that wanted for a slip. Table 15–3 also shows that the half slip customer definitely wanted a slimmer,

Table 15–1

Preferred Innerwear and Outerwear Lengths 1965 Survey (Slips and Half Slips)

	Slips		Half Slips	
Length Wanted	Innerwear National	Outerwear National	Innerwear National	Outerwear National
4 inches or more above knee	5%	–	10%	–
2 inches above knee	41	8%	48	11%
At knee	41	50	34	57
Just below knee	11	39	6	29
Other	2%	3%	2%	3%

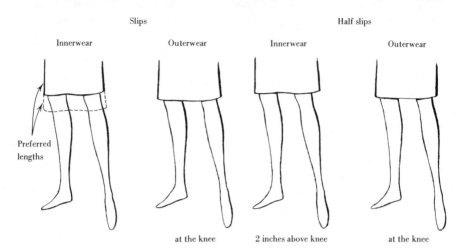

FIGURE 15–1.   Preferred daywear and outerwear lengths, 1965 survey.

tighter skirt than was the case with the slip customer and wanted some type of slit in the skirt.

Hollywood Vassarette was particularly interested in these findings because the savings in fabric cost of shorter slips are substantial when dealing with hundreds of thousands of units, even though the difference in slip lengths might be only one or two inches.

These differences in the wanted slip and half slip length preferences were consistent between the 1965 and 1966 surveys, even though there was a radical shift in preferences for the overall lengths of these garments in this time interval (see Table 15–2 below).

From the first survey taken in 1965 to the second survey taken in 1966, the miniskirt length in outerwear got a firm grip on the consuming public's interest. This swing in length preferences was unusually pronounced and happened a lot faster than had been the case with other historical swings in style preferences. The second survey readily tracked this swing in length prefer-

Table 15–2

Preferred Daywear Lengths 1965 and 1966

	Innerwear National		Outerwear National	
Length Wanted	1966	1965	1966	1965
4 inches or more above knee	26%	6%	2%	–
2 inches above knee	47	49	13	13%
At knee	21	36	48	54
Just below knee	5	7	14	30
Other	1%	2%	2%	3%

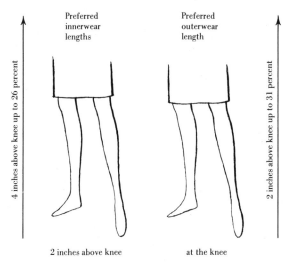

FIGURE 15–2. Preferred daywear lengths (slips/half slips/pettipants combined).

Table 15–3

Even with the Shorter Lengths the Wanted Skirt Silhouette for a Half Slip Still Differed Substantially from That Wanted for the Full Slip

Skirt Silhouette Wanted	Slips		Half Slips	
	1966	1965	1966	1965
Very slim	19%	23%	43%	50%
Moderately slim	70	65	51	42
Full	10	11	6	6
Very full	1%	1%	–	2%

Skirt Slit Treatment Preferences

Slit Treatment	Slips		Half Slips	
	1966	1965	1966	1965
No slits	60%	62%	38%	35%
One slit in front	1	2	3	5
One slit in back	11	8	15	15
One slit on one side	9	8	15	13
A slit on both sides	15	16	23	25
Others	–	–	1%	–

ences so that Vassarette was able to anticipate what was soon to be the norm in the preferred daywear skirt lengths. Figure 15–2 demonstrates these findings.

On the original 1965 survey it has been determined that the skirt silhouette preferences also differed quite radically on a slip as opposed to a half slip.

This particular finding still held up in the later 1966 survey, despite the fact that the wanted skirt lengths of both garments were considerably shorter than in 1965.

1. Although a moderately slim silhouette was preferred by most customers, the very slim silhouette was almost as popular with the half slip customer.

2. Half slip customers were more predisposed toward some type of slit treatment than were regular slip customers.

Slip Front Necklines

In the recent past (up to 1955 to 1965, and so on), almost all the slip styles of major manufacturers featured a standard v-neck treatment. Figure 15–3 indicates that this remains the preferred style but that 23 percent of respondents in the national survey would like a high round neckline and that significant segments of the market want other types. Cross-tabulations revealed that the nonstandard neckline styles were preferred most among women wearing

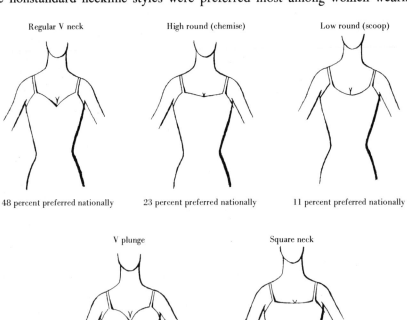

FIGURE 15–3.   The women preferred two general types of necklines for their next slip, 1965 survey only.

junior and junior petite sizes. It was found that there was a significant interest in slip straps in wider widths than those found in conventional slip straps. The subsequent 1966 survey showed an even greater diversity of interest in various types of slip necklines wanted.

Strap Preferences

The daywear respondents were asked three questions regarding the types of straps preferred on slips. The findings on these questions were:

1. There was significant interest in wider strap widths in slips. This preference was trending up.

2. There was a very strong degree of interest in the lace covered type of strap.

3. The all-stretch strap received very little mention.

Fabric Preferences

Vassarette was heavily committed to the knitting of nylon tricot fabrics and thus was particularly interested in the fabric preferences of the consumer. Using five-inch by three-inch plain white unidentified fabric swatches in the questionnaire, Table 15–4 shows that consumers of slips, half slips, and pettipants had strong overall preferences for tricot fabrics, particularly in the fall of the year.

Table 15–4

Consumer Fabric Preferences (The National Fabric Preferences in the Fall Survey Were Substantially Different than Those in the Spring— Running to Much Heavier Denier Fabrics)

General Fabric Classifications	Slips		Half Slips		Petti- pants	
	Fall 1966	Spring 1965	Fall 1966	Spring 1965	Fall 1966	Spring 1965
Tricot-type fabrics	75%	75%	72%	69%	93%	85%
Cotton/taffeta or other woven fabric	20	22	24	28	6	13
Other/ undecided	5%	3%	4%	3%	1%	2%

Specific Fabric Choices Comprising Most of the Preferences

Fall 1966				Spring 1965			
Fabrics	Slips	Half Slips	Petti-pants	Fabrics	Slips	Half Slips	Petti-pants
Woven taffeta/ stabilized tricot	21%	25%	11%	Single-layer Lustrelite	11%	9%	13%
30 denier tricot	13	12	12	30 denier tricot	11	12	11
40 denier tricot	12	13	13	Single-layer 20 denier tricot	10	9	14
Satin tricot	12	9	8	15 denier over Lustrelite	9	7	9
20 or 30 denier tricot	8	9	10	Dacron-cotton-nylon blend	8	12	8
30 denier tricot	6	7	8	30 or 40 denier tricot	8	7	6
Lustrelite	5	4	8	Antron nylon satin tricot	6	5	3
Crepelon	5	3	5	Taffeta	6	11	1
DNC blend	4	3	3	Acetate tricot	6	5	9
Lace over tricot	3	7	15	Crepelons	5	5	5
15 over 20 denier tricot	3%	2%	5%	Lace tricot overlay	Not significant	Not significant	10%

1. Unlike the spring 1965 survey, most of the fabric interest went in the direction of the heavier-weight fabrics such as the 30 denier, the 40 denier, the taffeta and stabilized tricots, and the satin tricot.

2. The taffeta and stabilized tricot taken together were particularly strong on slips and half slips, picking up 21 percent and 25 percent of all the fabric interest, respectively.

3. The choices of the customers wanting the chemise, scoop, or square necklines ran stronger to the tricot-type fabrics.

4. The customers wanting taffeta fabrics seemed to want a little longer garment also.

5. Eighty percent of the slip customers who chose a tricot-type fabric wanted some trim on their next garment. Usually these people also wanted a little more trim on this garment.

6. Among the half slip customers who chose a woven fabric, 55 percent wanted some trim on it.

These fabric preferences indicated substantially different consumer wants in the spring versus fall of the year, even with such similar appearing fabrics as nylon tricot. Most of the market offerings at that time were in one type of tricot the year around, and there had been no attempt to promote these various fabric weights to suit the season of the year.

Table 15–5

Trim Preferences (Except for a Slight Swing to the Untrimmed Type of Garment among the Half Slip and Pettipant Customers, the Trimmed versus Untrimmed Groups Did Not Change Substantially from Survey to Survey)

	Slips		Half Slips		Pettipants	
Trim Preferences	1966	1965	1966	1965	1966	1965
Want trim on garment	83%	84%	72%	77%	76%	84%
Want no trim on garment	16	14	25	21	21	14
Undecided	1%	2%	3%	2%	3%	2%

The Women Reaffirmed Their Preferences for the Lighter Types of Trim Evidenced in the Last Survey

	National		
Trims Preferred	Slips	Half Slips	Petti-pants
#5933 hemline trim—light scalloped lace	22%	18%	27%
#5962 hemline trim—light lace applique	14	16	6
#5909 hemline trim—light floral embroidery	11	11	15
#5941 hemline trim—deep lace	11	12	7
#5914 hemline trim—minimum embroidered chiffon	10	6	7
#5965 hemline trim—moderate scalloped lace	9	11	11
#5990 hemline trim—embroidery lace applique	7	10	17
#5966 hemline trim—deep lace	6	7	5
#5922 hemline trim—double-row lace between fabric	4	2	–
#5914 top of garment—light eyelet floral embroidery	4%	4%	5%

1. The interest in trims was definitely related to the fabric choice, as the no-trim group was much more prevalent among those picking a taffeta fabric.

2. The combined half slip and pettipant groups tended to prefer a little more elaborate type of trim. Their specific trim interests ran to the deep lace of Number 5941, the embroidery lace applique of Number 5990, and the deep lace of Number 5966.

Trim Preferences

For several years, Vassarette had been using the phrase "the understated look" to characterize the appeal of their merchandise. This phrase referred to limiting the amounts and types of laces, embroideries, and other types of trims used on the garments and to moving toward simpler trim treatments.

The 1965 survey figures had shown that there was a strong trend away from the more lavish type of trim treatments characteristic of so many merchandise lines and toward the lighter types of trim treatments.

The 1966 survey further reaffirmed this strong trend to the lighter types of trims. Using actual trim samples taken from certain garments in the Vassarette line and completely disregarding the price of these garments, the clear winner was the trim taken from Vassarette's number-one selling slip Number 5933, now representing better than a third of all this company's total sales of slips.

Daywear Color Preferences

Table 15–6 shows the national color preferences for slips and half slips. Prior to the time of these surveys, standard offerings (other than white) had been black, red, navy, and the deeper pinks. At the time of the survey, light yellow and light green were generally not available in lingerie. The exhibit shows that red (except in the fall), navy, and deep pink were some of the colors that received the most negative or "not wanted" responses from customers.

Table 15–6

Color Preferences

Slips	1965	1966	Half Slips	1965	1966
White	66%	55%	White	51%	50%
Beige	10	12	Black	10	14
Pink	7	11	Beige	9	4
Aqua	6	5	Pink	9	5
Black	5	9	Light blue	8	8
Light blue	3	5	Aqua	7	6
Light yellow	3%	3%	Light yellow	6	4
			Medium red	–	5
Note colors			Light green	–	4%
Light green					
Blue purple			*Note colors*		
Off white			None		

Slip Color Preferences

The trend away from white is even stronger than it was in the spring, going from 66 percent white in the spring to 55 percent white in the fall.

1. Beige was a little bit stronger in the fall (12 percent), with still very little ownership.

2. Pink was stronger in the fall at 11 percent, with still very little ownership. The wanted pinks at both times were closest to our Sachet pink.

3. Black was a substantially stronger fall color, but it still also has a high degree of ownership.

4. Light blue was somewhat stronger at 5 percent—also aqua, but the wanted type of aqua was a little more greenish than it was in the spring.

5. Light yellow has about the same strength (3 percent) as it did in the spring, but it has some ownership now where it did not have before.

6. Except for the yellow green note color, no light green showed up in the fall.

7. Blue purple showed up as a fall note color. It was absent in the spring survey on daywear, only showing up in sleepwear.

Half Slip Color Preferences

1. The interest in white was the same in both surveys, but the ownership was down (more color: 67 percent fall, 75 percent spring) from what it had been in the spring.

2. Black was substantially stronger in the fall (14 percent) than in the spring and also had a high rate of ownership.

3. Beige, the number-three color in the spring, drops way off in the fall from 9 percent to 4 percent, with all the interest centering on the darker beige.

4. The number-three fall color is light blue, with all the interest on the clear light blue shade in this color family.

5. Aqua was about the same as in the spring, with all the interest in the lightest least green variety.

6. Red has good strong interest in the fall at 5 percent, with no ownership, although it was nothing in the spring.

7. There was much less interest in pink in the fall at 5 percent, with all the interest falling on a medium pink shade.

8. Light yellow was a little less strong in the fall (4 percent versus 6 percent), with still no ownership.

9. Light green is much stronger in the fall at 4 percent, versus being a note color last time.

Additional questions were analyzed on color preferences for lingerie, especially in reference to coordination of the wardrobe. The following results were enumerated:

1. A consumer regards a foundation and lingerie coordinated assortment as being a pastel colored or printed item that should be matching in trims as well as in color. White does not constitute coordination.

2. Although the merchandising and promotional emphasis in coordinated selling has been spread over a wide range of intimate apparel, the primary interest is in the bra and the half slip.

3. Brassieres and girdles, which had been traditionally white and black, with an occasional touch of beige, are gradually evolving as fashion items.

Sleepwear Color Preferences

The color preferences for sleepwear are revealed in Table 15-7. Management summarized the most important of these to be the following:

1. Consumers preferred more vivid pinks and blues than the pastels preferred in daywear.

2. The black nightgown may be important as a peace offering for errant husbands or as a desirable gift item for *Playboy*.

3. Although red is a standard offering of major manufacturers, its popularity is in the same category as black from the viewpoint of the user.

Table 15–7

Sleepwear Color Preferences (A Comparison of the Fall 1966 and Spring 1965 Gown and Pajama Color Choices)

Gowns				Pajamas			
Fall 1966	Per-cent	Spring 1965	Per-cent	Fall 1966	Per-cent	Spring 1965	Per-cent
Pink	22	Pink	29	Aqua	23	Aqua	25
Aqua	17	Aqua	19	Pink	22	Pink	25
Lt. yellow	16	Lt. blue	14	Lt. blue	19	Lt. blue	15
Lt. blue	14	Lt. yellow	13	Med. red	13	Lt. yellow	13
White	6	White	12	Lt. yellow	9	White	6
Peacock	5	Blue purple	5	Peacock	9	Blue purple	5
Black	5	Med. blue	2	Med. blue	5	Peacock	5
Med. red	5	Peacock	2			Med. blue	3
Peach	4	Lt. green	2	*Note colors*		Med. red	3
Blue purple	3	Black	2	Peach			
Orange	3					*Note colors*	
		Note colors				None	
Note colors		Mauve purple					
Med. blue		Orange					
Mustard							

A few points regarding the color preferences of the gown customer are

1. The white interest was down from 12 percent in the spring to 6 percent in the fall. In both cases it was heavily oversold, however.

2. *Black* was up from 2 percent in the spring to 5 percent in the fall.

3. *Red* was up from nothing in the spring to 5 percent in the fall.

4. *Pink* still remains the strongest color from spring to fall, but its position drops off from 29 percent to 22 percent. The wanted colors of pink are almost identical at both times, however.

5. The *aqua* family is 19 percent in the spring and 17 percent in the fall. However, in both cases this excludes the greenish type of aquas.

6. *Light yellow* is getting even stronger than it was in the spring, with no interest in the dark yellow shades.

7. The *light blue* colors have maintained exactly the same position they had in the spring. The wanted colors are virtually the same.

8. *Peacock,* but just the bluest peacock (close to medium blue) goes from 2 percent to 5 percent spring to fall. Medium blue is a note color this time.

9. *Peach and orange* (a different stronger orange), which were nothing in the spring, came up very strong in the fall: 4 percent peach, 3 percent orange.

10. The blue purples were a little less strong in the fall (from 5 percent to 3 percent), but the wanted colors are still the same.

Some points regarding the color choices of the pajama customer are

1. The *aqua* and *pink* families are still strong. Again, the greenish aquas are absent from the picture.

2. *White* amounts to nothing, while red comes up as a fairly strong color. Black is never evident.

3. *Light yellow* is still strong, but not as much as it was in the spring.

4. *Peacock* and *medium blue,* like the situation in gowns, were also stronger in the fall.

5. *Peach* (no orange) was only a note color.

Regional Differences

The regional differences in wanted items were numerous, and only a few specific instances are recorded here:

1. Most of the interest in extreme or daring styling details for any garment type included in the survey were confined to New York and to a much lesser degree to California.

2. In areas with a high proportion of Negroes, there was a very definite rejection of the deeper beige tones.

3. Definite patterns exist in garment usage. For example, New York customers preferred half slips over full slips three-to-one while the situation was just the reverse in the Southeast. The pantie girdle was virtually a unanimous preference in southern California, but the regular girdle was much more prominent in certain areas of the Middle West.

Conclusions

These experiences with the Customer Preference Survey were regarded as an eye-opener by the management of Vassarette. They immediately undertook an extensive program to incorporate these findings into their forecasting procedures and prepared to make numerous changes in their merchandise mix.

Questions

1. What changes in the merchandise mix should be undertaken on the basis of this survey?

2. Are the procedures used by Vassarette satisfactory to predict changes in aggregate market behavior?

3. What long-range policy recommendations would you make for Vassarette to allow it to plan better for fashion changes in the intimate apparel market?

Self-Medication: Sources of Influence in the Acceptance of New Products[1]

The direct use of over-the-counter drugs by consumers is an important factor in American medicine as attested by the fact that sales of proprietary remedies reached approximately $1.3 billion in 1964. Self-medication, moreover, is growing rapidly, due to the following factors: (1) rising educational levels; (2) increased availability of information about medicine and drugs in advertising and articles; (3) the declining ratio of general practitioners to specialists and greater consumer reluctance to

[1] Reproduced with special permission from James F. Engel, David A. Knapp, and Deanne E. Knapp, "Sources of Influence in the Acceptance of New Products for Self-Medication: Preliminary Findings," in Raymond M. Haas (ed.). Reprinted from *Science, Technology, & Marketing,* published by the American Marketing Association, Chicago, 1966, pp. 776–782.

call a specialist for treatment of minor ailments; and (4) the low socio-economic level of a portion of the public which leaves only the alternatives of a crowded welfare clinic or the use of home and/or patent remedies.

The pharmaceutical industry has responded to this market need with a veritable flood of new products, but wise marketing planning is severely hampered by the virtual absence of data on how consumers arrive at self-medication decisions. This information gap also has important public policy ramifications. Therefore, a long-term research project is needed to answer such questions as the following: "What information sources are most influential in an individual's decision to pursue a specific self-therapy?" "Are appropriate uses being made of self-medication drugs?" "What is the importance of price in the purchase and use of a home remedy?" This paper reports findings from a pilot study and focuses on the sources of information used in the acceptance of new drug products.

Pilot Study Methodology

An exploratory study was undertaken during Summer, 1965 with the objective of identifying and delineating the motivating factors involved in the self-medication process. Six group interviews were held in the Behavioral Sciences Laboratory of the College of Commerce and Administration at The Ohio State University. In addition, 30 individual depth interviews were undertaken with Columbus, Ohio, housewives. Although a random sample was not utilized, a good socioeconomic cross section was attained.

To shed further light on the sources of information which might be consulted for specific ailments, an attitude scale, referred to as the Disease Scale, was developed to measure the potency of sources of information about health. Seventeen diseases are scaled as to their perceived seriousness and subjects were asked to indicate whose advice would be accepted (i.e., a doctor, friend, and so on) for each. It was not utilized, however, in the pilot study with housewives.

The Self-Medication Process

It was interesting to discover the degree of sophistication shown by most respondents in the use of drugs, although they often lacked specific knowledge. In addition, respondents were concerned about this lack as evidenced by the amount of gossip reported regarding health and the appeal of health articles. Surprisingly, the amount of misinformation exhibited in the interviews was small and, for the most part, inconsequential.

Most of those studied presented unmistakable signs that the absence of specific knowledge about a drug or treatment procedure leads to a significant degree of perceived risk that a wrong decision might be made. As a result, they are quite cautious in pursuing new self-medication strategies and show a strong propensity to search for additional information. Obviously some housewives possess a greater degree of knowledge and hence are less prone to inquire further.

The findings verified the risk-reducing role of well-known brand names. This, of course, is the most widely-cited advantage of brands to the consumer, but seldom has it been verified empirically in such convincing fashion. Many respondents commented that a reputable manufacturer would not put his name on a product which is impure or which might offer dangerous side effects. A new product from such companies, therefore, seems certain to be tried more readily, all things being equal.

For those who required additional information, the following sources were mentioned most frequently: (1) doctors; (2) advertisements; (3) friends and relatives; (4) pharmacists; and (5) articles.

Doctors

It is clear that those interviewed placed their greatest confidence in a recommendation, although most will not call their physician immediately when they have a cold. There is a prevailing fear of being labeled a hypochondriac, and there appears to be a strong reluctance to bother the doctor outside of office hours. This tendency is less evident, however, if a child is sick rather than an adult.

The doctor's impact in recommending self-medication procedures seems to be greatest at times other than when a minor ailment occurs. Many consumers, for example, reported raising questions on the reliability of branded products to their doctor during regular visits. Once verification is given from this source, product and brand loyalty can become deeply imbedded, because the doctor is legitimately regarded by most respondents as being quite authoritative.

Advertisements

As might be expected, great indignation and disapproval was expressed regarding drug advertising, especially overstated television commercials. Yet, the high incidence of brand names mentioned and the reported use of branded products attest to the tremendous impact of advertising. It seemed that those who protested the loudest were most able to give a verbatim playback of copy and also were most likely to be users of the product in question.

The primary effects of advertising were to develop an awareness of the existence of a new remedy and arouse initial interest in its use. Most respondents were reluctant, however, to act on this information alone, apparently because of some doubt regarding the authenticity of the claims. As a result, it was common for respondents to inquire further of doctors, friends and relatives, or pharmacists. Of great interest to the researchers was the amazing impact made by advertisements for a new cold remedy which extends therapeutic usefulness over a relatively long period of time. It has become a market leader at least in part because of the success its advertising had in stimulating great interest which, in turn, led to a remarkable number of inquiries aimed at other information sources.

In some cases, advertising is viewed as having a sufficient degree of authority to stimulate direct action. This was especially true when the remedies were mentioned and endorsed by leading personalities. Arthur Godfrey was mentioned in this context, for example, as were local personalities in the Columbus market.

Friends and Relatives

This communication channel was widely used to verify information about product innovations gathered from other sources. The consumer apparently values the informal channel quite highly and actively seeks reports on the practical results experienced by trusted friends and relatives in treating a specific ailment or in trying a new product. It was encouraging to note in this context that proper precautions were frequently mentioned regarding the advice of others (i.e., what works for one might not work for another).

There were some instances where friends and relatives *volunteered* information, but these were not frequent. Volunteered information was most frequently reported after friends and relatives used the new cold remedy mentioned above. The impetus, however, most frequently lay with the person *seeking* the information as opposed to those who *gave* it.

The relative incidence of use of this communication channel was such that the success or failure of a patent remedy may be dependent in large part upon the evaluation which is given by word-of-mouth.

Pharmacists

As might be expected, the druggist was frequently mentioned as a source for further information, especially once initial interest was given in response to specific questions by the consumer rather than volunteered. There is no doubt that a majority of those interviewed regard the pharmacist as an expert in his field.

A number of housewives, however, voiced concern over the changing role of the pharmacist as indicated by the rise of discount drug outlets. Many indicated that the sharply reduced opportunity for personal contact leads to an unconcern about the welfare of the customer. Many, for this reason, will pay the higher prices to shop at neighborhood pharmacies where they know the owner and trust his professional judgment. The need of this segment of drug users for a pharmacist who knows and understands their requirements and expresses personal concern should not be ignored.

It also is of interest to inquire whether or not pharmacists are willing and able to be a source of drug information. Some preliminary findings from a research project now underway raise some rather disturbing questions in this regard.

Articles

Articles in magazines and newspapers are read with varying degrees of interest and skepticism. Most respondents indicate little faith in reports of "miracle cures," but they apparently are influenced by *negative* reports about remedies. Thus, articles seem to serve as motivators to avoid a product or treatment rather than to try it.

The Disease Scale

While the group and depth interviews indicated an active search for information and the sources used, the researchers also desired to have a more precise indication of whose advice is likely to be accepted if proffered, all things being equal. Therefore, the Disease Scale mentioned earlier was developed, and it consists of 17 diseases which have been scaled as to their perceived seriousness using equal-appearing interval and paired comparison procedures (see Table 15–8). It has proven to be reliable and valid.

Table 15–8

Scale Values for Diseases

Scale Value	Disease
0.000	1. Dandruff
0.989	2. Headache
1.160	3. Upset stomach
1.420	4. In-grown toenail
1.565	5. Common cold
1.694	6. Sunburn
2.513	7. Sinus trouble
2.661	8. Flu
3.111	9. Hemorrhoids
3.420	10. Stomach ulcer
3.608	11. Arthritis
3.835	12. Kidney stones
4.013	13. Pneumonia
5.035	14. Tuberculosis
5.377	15. Heart disease
5.434	16. Stroke
6.209	17. Cancer

The diseases were arranged along a vertical continuum of seriousness at points corresponding to their appropriate scale values (Table 15–9), and the subjects (introductory psychology students) were asked to indicate at what point on the continuum they would no longer accept advice from a given source of health information. The sources rated included friends, pharmacists, physicians, television advertisements, articles by physicians, and articles by pharmacists.

Results are shown in Table 15–9, and it will be noted that, on the average, a physician's advice is accepted for all diseases up to and including stroke. The advice presented by a pharmacist in person or that given in an article written by a physician would be accepted if the ailment were no more serious than "flu." The written advice of a pharmacist, however, would be disregarded if the ailment were more serious than "sunburn." Finally, friends and television advertisements would be regarded favorably for such minor difficulties as "upset stomach." All differences are statistically significant at the 0.01 level.

Table 15–9

Disease Scale and Communicator Rankings

The Disease Scale		Communicator Rankings	
Cancer	–	Cancer	–
Stroke	–	Stroke	– ←——— Physician
Heart disease	–	Heart disease	–
Tuberculosis	–	Tuberculosis	–
Pneumonia	–	Pneumonia	–
Kidney stones	–	Kidney stones	–
Arthritis	–	Arthritis	–
Stomach ulcer	–	Stomach ulcer	–
Hemmorrhoids	–	Hemorrhoids	–
Flu	–	Flu	– ←——— Pharmacist
Sinus trouble	–	Sinus trouble	– Article written by physician
Sunburn	–	Sunburn	– ←——— Article written by
Common cold	–	Common cold	– a pharmacist
In-grown toenail	–	In-grown toenail	–
Upset stomach	–	Upset stomach	– ←——— Friend
Headache	–	Headache	– TV Advertisement
Dandruff	–	Dandruff	–

These results verify the findings of the group and depth interviews. The perceived risk of ineffective or even dangerous treatment no doubt increases with the scale value of an ailment, and the need for authoritative information shows a corresponding rise. Many sources are used, however, for colds and related illnesses, with the degree of perceived risk and information seeking varying widely from individual to individual.

Future Research

These findings, of course, are based only on pilot studies. As a result, they should only be regarded as tentative. Even if more elaborate methodology had been used, however, the limitations of a cross sectional study would remain. No attempt is made in cross sectional research to study behavior "in the act," so to speak, with the result that the opportunity exists for memory distortions of all types. Decision-making processes can be studied with clarity *only* through the use of longitudinal analysis which focuses on individual patterns of change over time.

Questions

1. Appraise the methodology used in this pilot study. What directions should future research take?
2. Assume that you are the marketing manager of a large packaged-drug firm who has the responsibility of launching a new product that has been demonstrated clinically to out-perform any cold remedy on the market in terms of drying nasal tissues. The therapeutic effects last for at least twenty-four hours. What sources of information would you use? How could word-of-mouth communication be stimulated, if this were felt to be desirable?

The Touch-Tone® Telephone: Diffusion of an Innovation[2]

In 1965 the Illinois Bell Telephone Company introduced a new product to their marketing area on a limited basis. This was the Touch-Tone telephone, a phone that utilizes a new and easier method of dialing. Actually, the term *dialing* is used incorrectly because the new feature is a push-button, rather

[2] This case was developed by Professor Thomas S. Robertson in conjunction with the Illinois Bell Telephone Company's Research Staff and under the financial support of the Illinois Bell and Michigan Bell Telephone Companies. Particular help was rendered by Messrs. James N. Kennedy, Edwin N. Asmann, John P. O'Reilly, Ronald J. Hevrdejs, and James B. Cation of Illinois Bell Telephone Company.

than a dial, telephone. Push-button dialing represents an innovation in phone design and is the key to new services that may later be introduced. Its acceptance by consumers was therefore very important to Illinois Bell, and their executives were anxious to take full advantage of marketing research methodology in order to have a better assessment of market acceptance.

Problem

Illinois Bell decided to introduce Touch-Tone service to a "control group" of customers and to obtain feedback data that would prove helpful in later full-market introduction.

The product was introduced into several Chicago suburban communities, including Deerfield, Illinois, an affluent suburb north of Chicago. During the introduction, limited local newspaper advertising and bill inserts were used to promote the product. An interested party could obtain a new Touch-Tone phone by calling the Illinois Bell office and by agreeing to its installation. The customer paid a one-time charge plus $1.50 per line per month, regardless of the number of extensions, above his regular charges, to have Touch-Tone service.

Study

In this study, *innovators* were defined as the first 10 percent of the community's members to adopt the Touch-Tone product. Early in 1966, 11 percent of Deerfield's residents had adopted the Touch-Tone, and thus the community was considered most suitable for the study.

Study parameters were developed by Thomas S. Robertson, then of Northwestern University, working with Illinois Bell's business research people. Professional interviewers were provided by Social Research Services, Inc., of Chicago. A sample of a hundred respondents was systematically selected using a telephone street-address directory. A breakdown of sixty persons who were Touch-Tone innovators and forty persons who had not yet adopted the innovation was secured within the geographic concentrations in which diffusion for the product was most advanced. This breakdown and selection process allowed the best opportunity to study the interpersonal communication flow. Interviews were arranged in advance by telephone, and an 80 percent rate of response was obtained.

Data was collected by in-home personal interviews with the female head of household using the questionnaire in Appendix A. She was chosen as the spokesman for the family consumption unit. The interviews required an average of 1½ hours to complete and resulted in 2500 pages of data. Depth interview material was coded using four coders, and 90 percent consistency was obtained using guidelines established by the principal researcher.

Table 15–10

Measurement Components for Each Variable

Variable	Measurement Components
Predispositional factors	
Venturesomeness	Willingness to buy hypothetical innovations Actual purchases of appliance innovations Attitude toward innovative behavior Self perception on represented innovator characteristics
Social integration	Extent of social visiting Attitude toward neighborhood interaction Self-perception of neighborhood popularity Organizational memberships and offices Attitude toward organizational membership and offices
Cosmopolitanism	Readership of cosmopolitan magazines Frequency of out-of-town trips Choice of friends and activities engaged in with friends Attitude toward the local community
Social mobility	Occupational mobility Locational mobility Organizational mobility Friendship mobility Neighborhood mobility aspirations
Privilegedness	Income level Number and ages of children Self-perception of financial standing in community
Communication factors	
Communication exposure	Exposure to information concerning the innovation under study Exposure to information concerning other innovations Exposure to information sources in general
Affective learning	Knowledge of the innovation under study Favorability of attitude toward the innovation Intention to purchase (noninnovators) Desire for further information (noninnovators)

Table 15-10 (continued)

Variable	Measurement Components
Communication factors	
Legitimation	Information sources chosen to legitimate behavior
	Evaluation of the purchase decision (innovators)
Opinion leadership	Influence of others to purchase the innovation (innovators)
	Extent to which innovation was shown or noticed (innovators)
	Self-designated measure of new product influence

Theoretical Framework of Study

A pilot study consisting of thirty interviews had been conducted in October of 1965. From this pilot study and from a review of literature concerning the diffusion of innovations, a theoretical framework and specific hypotheses were formulated for the study. It was hypothesized that innovative behavior is a function of both (1) predispositional factors on the part of the individual, and (2) exposure and response to the communication flow regarding innovation. The predispositional factors form the predictive part of the model, while exposure and response to communication on innovation are viewed as necessary requirements of innovative behavior.

Predispositional Factors

A consistent finding in diffusion research is that innovators are "different" from later adopters. The composite of factors tested in the present study represents the variables of highest predictive value in characterizing consumer, farmer, and physician innovators. Each variable is hypothesized to be positively related to innovative behavior.

Venturesomeness

Venturesomeness may be thought of as willingness to take risks in the purchase of new products. Risk is involved because the product may not live up to performance expectations and because it may never gain acceptance among members of the individual's reference group. The product purchaser, therefore, risks loss of money and loss of face.

The venturesomeness characteristic, as detailed in Table 15-10, is assessed by four measurement components. The answers to these components are arranged on seven-point scales from *highly venturesome* to *highly nonventure-some*. The mean of the several components then yields an overall venturesome-ness score for the individual. Measurement of the remaining variables is carried out following the same procedure, and the measurement components for each variable are documented in Table 15–10.

Social Integration

Social integration is a variable that may be defined as "the degree of an individual's participation and acceptance within his community." A highly socially integrated person is popular and well accepted while a highly non-socially integrated person is unpopular and poorly accepted.

Cosmopolitanism

Cosmopolitanism may be defined as "the degree to which an individual's orientation is external to a particular social system." One may talk in terms of local and cosmopolitan individuals. The local largely confines his interests and activities to his community. The cosmopolitan is more oriented to the world at large.

Social Mobility

The concept of social mobility refers to movement on the social class hierarchy. In the present study, upward movement in social class is the concern.

Privilegedness

Individuals within a community will differ in how financially privileged they are. The privilegedness concept is actually a refinement in evaluating financial ability to buy. It includes not only income but also number of children, age of children, and the individual's perception of her relative financial standing in the community.

Personality

The Thurstone Temperament Schedule was used to examine four personality factors: impulsiveness, sociability, dominance, and activeness. *Impulsiveness* is thought of in the following terms: happy-go-lucky, likes to take chances, can make decisions quickly. *Sociability* means "enjoying the company of others, making friends easily, and being sympathetic and cooperative." *Dominance* is basically "taking initiative and assuming responsibility." Activeness is thought of as "on the go"—speaking, walking, driving fast, even when it is not necessary to do so.

Communication Flow

The *communication flow* may be defined to consist of marketer-controlled channels of information, including advertising and personal selling, and non-marketer-controlled channels of information, including other people, or "personal influence." It is hypothesized that innovators will be differentially involved in the communication flow regarding innovation.

Communication Exposure
Innovators have been found in prior research to be more exposed to the flow of communication on innovation. Measurement of communication exposure is detailed in Table 15–10. Communication factor components are not combined as was done for the predispositional variables.

Affective Learning
Again, prior findings are that *knowledge* of innovation does not separate the innovator and noninnovator groups. These groups can be distinguished, however, on the basis of the extent of affective learning, or "liking" for the product.

Ability to Legitimate Behavior
The presence of risk in buying new products leads to attempts to legitimate purchase. Innovators, because of greater exposure to communication, are apparently in a better position to legitimate adoption behavior. Personal influence is the most frequently cited communication source in obtaining legitimation.

Opinion Leadership
Innovators exert greater opinion leadership than later adopters. By opinion leadership is meant how frequently the individual is turned to for advice and information.

Findings: Predispositional Factors

Results, as summarized in Table 15–11, indicate the percentages of innovators and noninnovators falling within the high, medium, and low categories for each factor, as well as the mean scores obtained by each group and the significance level of the difference between the means. The mean scores are based on a maximum possible score of 7.0 (most venturesome, most socially integrated, and so forth) while the minimum possible score is 1.0. An overall review of the results indicates that cosmopolitanism is the only hypothesis to be refuted.

Venturesomeness
Innovators are significantly more venturesome than noninnovators (.01 level) and purchase more new appliance products already on the market. Innovators adopted an average of 6.2 other home appliances from a list of 13 while noninnovators adopted an average of 4.5. Innovators for a new product,

Table 15–11

Predispositional Factor Results

Variable	Group	Degree of Variable*			Mean Variable Score (/7.00)	Significance Level of Mean Difference
		High	Medium	Low		
Venturesomeness	Innovators	69%	53%	15%	4.88	.01 level
	Noninnovators	31	47	85	4.12	
Social integration	Innovators	63	44	50	4.13	.05 level
	Noninnovators	37	56	50	3.78	
Cosmopolitanism	Innovators	10	48	58	2.77	.10 level
	Noninnovators	90	52	42	3.03	
Social mobility	Innovators	68	47	35	3.93	.01 level
	Noninnovators	32	53	65	3.20	
Privilegedness	Innovators	70	46	42	3.68	.05 level
	Noninnovators	30%	54%	58%	3.25	

* All results are adjusted for the difference in innovator (60) versus noninnovator (40) sample sizes.

it would appear, are likely to be drawn from past innovators for similar products.

Social Integration

Innovators are significantly more socially integrated (.05 level). Personal sources of information would seem to be of particular importance in appealing to the innovator.

Cosmopolitanism

Innovators are found to be less cosmopolitan, or more "local" in orientation. This finding is at odds with the hypothesized relationship. Coupling of the social integration and cosmopolitanism findings does, however, seem to suggest a logical result, for if the innovator is socially integrated within his local neighborhood, it could perhaps be expected that he would be more oriented toward that neighborhood.

Social Mobility

Innovators are significantly more socially mobile (.01 level). They are moving up in the social class hierarchy. Socially mobile individuals who are going through new life experiences may be drawn toward new product experiences, or new product consumption may be a visible symbol of an advancing status position.

Privilegedness

The privilegedness measure reveals that innovators are more financially privileged than other community members (.05 level). Innovators need not possess the highest absolute income levels in society but may possess higher income levels relative to their associates, at least for certain product categories.

Personality

Innovators score significantly higher (.05 level) on personality traits of "impulsiveness," "activeness," "dominance." The measure of the "sociability" trait does not yield a conclusive finding. Innovators, it seems, can be tentatively distinguished on the basis of personality traits, and further research would seem to be in order.

Composite of Factors

The relative importance of each factor (excluding the personality variables) and the predictive power of the composite of factors were evaluated using multiple discriminant analysis techniques. Venturesomeness was found to account for 35 percent of the difference between the innovator and noninnovator groups, while social mobility accounted for 29 percent of the difference. Privilegedness and social integration had relative contribution values of 11 percent, and localism had 9 percent. Incidental variables accounted for the remaining 5 percent of relative contribution.

The composite of factors resulted in the correct average classification of 70 percent of the innovators and noninnovators. This discrimination was significant at the 5 percent level with a multiple correlation coefficient of .417.

Findings: Communication Exposure and Response

Communication Exposure

General exposure to communication sources is almost identical. Innovators listened to radio approximately 2¼ hours a day while noninnovators listened a little over two hours a day. Innovators watched television 2 hours a day while noninnovators watched 2¼ hours. Both groups subscribed to approximately the same number of magazines. Time spent with other people was approximately the same for both groups, although innovators had a higher *frequency* of interaction. Innovators are considerably more apt to discuss new products for the home (Table 15–12).

Affective Learning

Innovators cannot be distinguished from noninnovators on the basis of knowledge about the innovation. It is found that 90 percent of the noninnovator sample has adequate knowledge and that only 5 percent of noninnovators are unaware of the product's existence.

Innovators are, however, much more favorably inclined toward the product. It can, of course, be argued that measurement of innovator affective learning *after* purchase does not constitute a valid comparison with measurement of noninnovator affective learning *before* purchase. In the after state innovators must justify their purchase behavior and maintain cognitive consistency which would seem to suggest the lesser likelihood of nonfavorable responses.

Ability to Legitimate Behavior

The legitimation stage in the purchase process is the point at which adoption is being considered and must be justified. Noninnovators did not advance as far as legitimation or did not successfully obtain legitimation. Innovators, it was found, were most likely to turn to other people for legitimation and particularly to members of their own families. Because innovators are more socially integrated within their communities and engage more frequently in new product discussions, they are in a more advantageous position to secure legitimation.

Opinion Leadership

Innovator influence in encouraging others to adopt is documented in several ways. It is found that 33 percent of innovators can name at least one per-

Table 15–12

Communication Factor Results

Variable	Group	Degree of Variable*			Mean Variable Score (/6.00)	Significance Level of Mean Difference
		High	Medium	Low		
Communication Exposure–New Product Discussion Frequency	Innovators	61%	41%	40%	3.35	.05 level
	Noninnovators	39	59	60	2.95	
Opinion Leadership–Self Designated	Innovators	49	60	43	3.53	.05 level
	Noninnovators	51%	40%	57%	3.12	

* Results are adjusted for the difference in innovator (60) versus noninnovator (40) sample sizes.

son who later bought the innovation, in whole or in part, because of their influence. Further evidence reveals that 68 percent of noninnovators can mention someone they know who has the innovation. It is also found that 77 percent of innovators either show the innovation to visitors or have it noticed by visitors.

Measurement of opinion leadership for home items in general using a self-designating measure revealed that innovators are more influential, on the average (Table 15–12). Noninnovators scored high on influence just as often, however, suggesting the possibility of negative opinion leaders who persuade others not to buy new products.

Conclusion

The model of innovative behavior tested appeared to successfully identify Touch-Tone innovators. Such individuals were found to be significantly more venturesome, socially mobile, socially integrated, financially privileged, local in orientation, and possessing distinguishing personality traits. The venturesomeness and social mobility factors were most important in classifying innovators and noninnovators.

Analysis of exposure and response to the communication flow revealed that innovators and noninnovators were almost equally exposed to mass media but that innovators engaged in more new product discussions. Innovators were found to be higher in affective learning regarding the innovation, to be better able to legitimate innovative behavior, and to exert greater opinion leadership.

Questions

1. Is the research design described above adequate for decision making by executives of Illinois Bell?

2. Has this study included the relevant information needed to isolate the most likely innovators of the Touch-Tone telephone?

3. Based upon this study, how should Illinois Bell promote the Touch-Tone when it is introduced on a wide-scale basis?

Appendix A: Sample Completed Questionnaire of a Typical Touch-Tone Innovator[3]

Part 1—Northwestern University Touch-Tone Depth Interview

Name ——————— Telephone ————— Interviewer ———————

Address ————————— Date ———— T-T —— Non T-T ————

1. Please tell me how many children you have and how old they are.

    We have three children—two boys and a girl. Jimmy, the oldest, is twelve. Jane's ten and Carol is seven.

2. What are the family interests? What things do you do together?

    Everything. Last Sunday we went bowling, and on Saturday, skiing. Our weekends are taken up by boating, swimming—summer or winter things. We spend most of the weekend doing things, even if it's just a ride someplace. We ice skate, too.

3. How do you feel about belonging to organizations—clubs, social groups, church groups, community groups, and such?

    It depends upon the organization. On the whole, I rather enjoy such activities because I enjoy being with people.
       Sometimes they can be a burden, however, with three children to take care of. I like being out meeting with others. I've belonged to the PTA and been an officer. There's Infant Welfare and, of course, our bridge groups.

4. How do you feel about holding offices in such organizations?

    I don't seek offices, but I'll take my turn. I really just don't have the time necessary to devote to such responsibilities.

5. What about *your* friends and the friends that *you and your husband* have together. Where do you know them from? (*Probe*: How long have you known them?)

    We have friends from the neighborhood, my husband's business, and from college. We haven't lived here very long, but we're all in the same boat and get to know each other. There are quite a few transfers here.

6. What type of people are these friends? How could you best describe them?

    My college friend is out of our league financially, but that doesn't impair our friendship. Our other friends are from the neighborhood and pretty much like we are—suburbanites, husbands in business or professions. We're pretty sociable and make life worthwhile together.

[3] Prepared by Thomas S. Robertson, University of California, Los Angeles.

7.   What types of things do you and your friends do together?

Parties and cookouts in the summer. Share our homes during ice-storms. Last winter we had the Oxfords here for days because they had no heat. We played bridge by candlelight and had a ball. We just socialize, I guess. Friends in Glen Ellyn we've known since 1948. Met them in Virginia, Minnesota. The men met through a meeting of the Junior Chamber of Commerce. Wives were there too, so we really all met each other at the same time. We have parties and see each other frequently.

8.   Tell me about your neighborhood. What's it like?

This is a nice neighborhood. It's very socially oriented. Everyone is sociable and nice. Anyone who could not get acquainted in this area would not be trying very hard. They have a coffee for the new people who move in.

9.   What do you dislike about your neighborhood?

It's rather inconvenient to transportation and shopping. There's a sameness that is sometimes disturbing. The homes, the people, the cars are all the same. It's kind of far from the cultural and entertainment life of Chicago.

10. If you move, what kind of neighborhood would you like to move to? (*Probe*: Why?)

My husband would like to move east of the tracks in Glencoe, and this is very expensive. I would rather find something we could more afford. [Where?] An upper-middle class neighborhood—an older refined elegance, nicely maintained with more conveniences . . . maybe closer to the water, the lake than this, yet close enough to town so the children could walk or bike it.

11. How do you feel about buying new things that come out for the home?

I'm terrible for that. I try everything. I try all the new products—anything that's a work saver. If you don't have them, you miss them, but if you have them, you need them.

12. How often do you talk with people about such new things that come out, and who do you talk with?*

If it's something I think is real great I'll talk to my friends and neighbors about it. It's funny . . . sometimes I sound like an unsolicited testimonial. Top Job Cleaner, Oven Brite oven cleaner and Metal Klean I've really pushed. I've told the girls from Service League about them . . . even some of the girls from high school days.

13. Do people ever come to you for advice about new things on the market for the home? (Who?) (Why?—or why not?) *

Oh, we talk over things we've bought. The Andersons came to ask about

---

* All starred questions require that you probe into the *who*. What are the relationships of the people mentioned or where does the respondent know them from?

our T-T phone. My husband told him about it, and they wanted to try it, but I don't know that they wanted advice.

14. Is there someone you generally look to for advice on new things for the home? (Who?) (Why?—or why not?)*

My husband. He has to pay for it. Oh, the girls in bridge club talk now and then, and I might ask for opinions on one thing or another. If we're thinking of buying something, we generally might ask whoever already has it.

15. Among the women you know, how would you describe the women who are usually first to buy new things?

Whatever I am . . . active, interested in progress, want convenience and comfort, can afford them. Probably the younger ones—thirty to forty—the more outgoing, modern ones. Those who are willing to try anything once.

16. Which of the following items do you have for your home?

X Color television	___ Electric potato peeler
X Electric knife	X Teflon cookware
X Electric toothbrush	___ Snow blower
___ Cordless electric shaver	X Air conditioner
X Touch-Tone telephone	___ Air humidifier
X Electric can opener	___ Electrically operated garage door
___ Electric broom	X Dishwasher

Let's take one of the items that you mentioned and get a little more information from you about it. Let's see, you mentioned having a Touch-Tone telephone. Let's talk about that for a little while as an example of how you feel about new products.

17. What do you think of the Touch-Tone telephone?

I think it's marvelous. It's faster and more fun. Sometimes I almost forget how to use a regular dial phone.

18. What was *the very first thing you* ever heard or saw about Touch-Tone? (*Probe*: When, where? [*exactly*])

It was in one of the neighbor's homes one Saturday night at a party. We had to use it to call home to the children. This was about last year. [When exactly?] Maybe February. But my husband had mentioned it before. He hears of all kinds of new things in his work.

19. What was the next thing you heard or saw about Touch-Tone? (*Probe*: When, where? [*exactly*])

Then everyone was getting one. The girls talked during the card games. [When?] I don't remember. It was two or three weeks before I got mine.

* All starred questions require that you probe into the *who*. What are the relationships of the people mentioned or where does the respondent know them from?

Then they all started asking if we had one. People who come to my house are amazed at it. They have heard nothing of it.

20. How did you get interested in buying a Touch-Tone?

We just heard so much about it. It seemed right. We talked about it at cards with the girls.

21. What finally made you decide to get it? Was it you or your husband that made the suggestion to buy it?

We were remodeling the kitchen and needed a new color, and I thought this is my chance. [Whose suggestion?] Husband, he is often the stimulus. Course, I probably had mentioned I'd like it. He had me change the rest of the phones to Touch-Tone a few days after we put the one in the kitchen and has remarked several times, "That was a good idea you had."

22. Who do you remember having Touch-Tone before you? (Get *names*)*

Mrs. Over, a neighbor. Mrs. Wills and Mrs. Simpson.

23. Do you remember what happened after you got your Touch-Tone? Did anyone you know follow you in getting one? [Who?] [Why?]*

We had a tremendous number of comments on it. A tennis friend stopped for coffee and immediately called home just to try it. They bought one. [Who?] Sue Moore. [Why?] She was remodeling her recreation room and liked it. My girl scout leader got one. [Who?] Mrs. Wrentcher. [Why?] Had three children and thought it would be convenient.

24. Do people know you have a Touch-Tone, or, if they don't, do you show it to them?

Everyone is very impressed. They know it costs money and wonder why we have it. They kid us about it. We're the first to get things. [Show?] No, they just see it.

25. Do you by any chance know how much Touch-Tone costs per month? (How much?)

I have no idea. It seems like 25 cents or 50 cents extra each month. My basic bill is $8.79 and these units which really mount up. It's not very much, I know.

26. What kinds of things do you really like to spend your money on?

Oh, I enjoy buying things. Mostly things for the home, things for the children, and, of course, clothes.

27. What is your idea of what the modern wife and mother should be like?

In two easy words, *oh great*! She should be able to cook, should be interested in everything her husband and children are. She should make a point

---

* All starred questions require that you probe into the *who*. What are the relationships of the people mentioned or where does the respondent know them from?

of keeping herself looking good. She should keep informed on current events in the world. She should keep her house well. She should be alive, not lazy, interested in everything.

28. Here are a group of incomplete sentences. You complete them for me with *the very first thing that comes to your mind.* For example, If I said, "Roses are . . ." you might say "red."

    a. My major interest is . . .
        my home and family.
    b. My home is . . .
        a pleasure.
    c. Success for a woman is . . .
        raising a wonderful family.
    d. My most important goal is . . .
        to live a worthwhile life.
    e. Women should be . . .
        women.
    f. Community activities are . . .
        necessary.
    g. Being a mother is . . .
        difficult.
    h. I wish I could . . .
        fly.
    i. I enjoy . . .
        lots of things.

Interviewer

Describe respondent (age, dress, behavior).
    Middle thirties, slacks and blouse, nice looking, very happy and congenial, very relaxed.

Describe home (type, age, inside and outside appearance, upkeep).
    Split level, relatively new, ten years or so, well kept, nicely furnished, with some mixture of periods and styles.

Describe neighborhood (type, age, upkeep, types of residences).
    Same type of homes. Upkeep of neighborhood was excellent. Attractive area.

Describe interview (length, cooperation, receptivity, pleasantness).
    Very cooperative and receptive. Pleasant and willing to answer questions. Commented she felt like she was back in Psych I. An hour and a half in length.

Part 2—Self-Administered Semantic Differential

1. Decide which side (word) is most appropriate.

2. *How much* or *to what degree* do you feel this way.

There are no right answers. Your own opinion is what matters. Even where you do not have a strong opinion, *be sure to mark a choice.* Otherwise, your opinion can't be counted.

Circle: O — when you feel *very* much this way
         o — when you feel *rather* much this way
        . — when you feel *slightly* this way

A housewife with an electric toothbrush is

Left	very	rather	slightly	slightly	rather	very	Right
young	O	o	(·)	.	o	O	old
shy	O	o	.	(·)	o	O	bold
poor	O	o	.	(·)	o	O	rich
old-fashioned	O	o	.	.	(o)	O	modern
smart	O	(o)	.	.	o	O	stupid
immoral	O	o	.	(·)	o	O	moral
interesting	O	(o)	.	.	o	O	boring
quiet	O	o	.	(·)	o	O	lively

A housewife with a Touch-Tone telephone is

Left	very	rather	slightly	slightly	rather	very	Right
young	O	o	(·)	.	o	O	old
shy	O	o	.	(·)	o	O	bold
poor	O	o	.	(·)	o	O	rich
old-fashioned	O	o	.	.	(o)	O	modern
smart	O	o	(·)	.	o	O	stupid
immoral	O	o	.	.	(o)	O	moral
interesting	O	(o)	.	.	o	O	boring
quiet	O	o	.	.	(o)	O	lively

A housewife with a color television is

Left	very	rather	slightly	slightly	rather	very	Right
young	O	o	(·)	.	o	O	old
shy	O	o	.	(·)	o	O	bold
poor	O	o	.	.	(o)	O	rich
old-fashioned	O	o	.	.	(o)	O	modern
smart	O	o	(·)	.	o	O	stupid
immoral	O	o	.	(·)	o	O	moral
interesting	O	o	(·)	.	o	O	boring
quiet	O	o	.	(·)	o	O	lively

There are many possible ways for people to *find out* about a new item on the market for the home. Some of these ways are listed below. *Tell* us *how important you think each way is* by deciding first whether it is important or unimportant. Then circle to show the degree.

How important do you think each way would be in *finding out about a new item on the market?*

	Very important				Very Unimportant	
Magazine advertising	O	◎	.	.	o	O
Friends	◎	o	.	.	o	O
Relatives	O	◎	.	.	o	O
Television advertising	O	◎	.	.	o	O
Newspaper advertising	◎	o	.	.	o	O
Neighbors	◎	o	.	.	o	O

How important do you think each way would be *in getting you interested in a new item on the market for the home?*

	Very important				Very Unimportant	
Friends	◎	o	.	.	o	O
Newspaper advertising	O	◎	.	.	o	O
Magazine advertising	O	◎	.	.	o	O
Neighbors	◎	o	.	.	o	O
Television advertising	O	◎	.	.	o	O
Relatives	O	◎	.	.	o	O

How important do you think each way would be *in helping you to make a decision to buy a new item for the home?*

	Very important				Very Unimportant	
Relatives	O	o	⊙	.	o	O
Television advertising	O	o	⊙	.	o	O
Neighbors	O	◎	.	.	o	O
Newspaper advertising	O	◎	.	.	o	O
Friends	O	◎	.	.	o	O
Magazine advertising	O	o	⊙	.	o	O

How important do you think each way would be *in helping you to choose a specific brand of the new item for the home?*

	Very important				Very Unimportant	
Television advertising	O	o	⊙	.	o	O
Neighbors	O	◎	.	.	o	O
Newspaper advertising	O	o	⊙	.	o	O
Friends	◎	o	.	.	o	O
Relatives	O	◎	.	.	o	O
Magazine advertising	O	o	⊙	.	o	O

How willing would you be to buy the following items immediately after they come on the market?

	Very Willing					Very Unwilling
A new electric hairbrush	O	o	.	(.)	o	O
A new picture phone	O	o	(.)	.	o	O
A new home dry-cleaning unit	O	o	(.)	.	o	O
A new dishwasher that cleans by sonic waves	O	o	(.)	.	o	O
A new infra-red cooking range	O	(o)	.	.	o	O
A portable radio whose batteries are rechargeable by the sun	O	(o)	.	.	o	O
A new 60-inch screen wall television	O	o	.	.	(o)	O

How satisfied are you with the following items?

	Very Satisfied					Very Dissatisfied
Automatic washers	(O)	o	.	.	o	O
Color television	O	o	(.)	.	o	O
Telephones	(O)	o	.	.	o	O
Vacuum cleaners	(O)	o	.	.	o	O
Toasters	O	(o)	.	.	o	O
Refrigerators	(O)	o	.	.	o	O
Electric fry pans	O	(o)	.	.	o	O

In regard to new products on the market, I am (rate yourself)

bored	O	o	.	.	(o)	O	interested
last	O	o	.	(.)	o	O	first
carefree	O	o	.	.	(o)	O	cautious
a follower	O	o	.	(.)	o	O	a leader
influential	O	o	(.)	.	o	O	noninfluential
calm	O	o	.	(.)	o	O	excited
definite	O	o	(.)	.	o	O	uncertain

Charge accounts to me are

good	O	(o)	.	.	o	O	bad

Credit cards to me are

good	O	(o)	.	.	o	O	bad

How interested are you in the following things?

	Very Interested					Very Uninterested
Movies	O	o	(.)	.	o	O
Furniture	O	(o)	.	.	o	O
Sports	O	o	(.)	.	o	O
Electrical appliances	O	(o)	.	.	o	O
Telephones	O	(o)	.	.	o	O
Community groups	O	o	(.)	.	o	O
Cars	O	o	(.)	.	o	O

Telephones to me are

a pleasure	O	⊙	.	.	o	O	a nuisance
glamorous	O	o	.	.	⊙	O	sensible
a luxury	O	o	.	.	o	⊚	a necessity
too expensive	O	o	.	.	⊙	O	worth the money
practical	O	o	.	.	⊙	O	artistic
dull	O	o	.	.	⊙	O	bright

Part 3—Self-Administered Psychological Instrument

For each question, mark a cross in the square for the answer that fits you best.

	Yes	?	No
a. If your answer is Yes, mark the space under *Yes*.	X		
b. If your answer is No, mark the space under *No*.			X
c. If you absolutely cannot decide, you may mark the space under the question mark.		X	

	Yes	?	No
1. Are you more restless and fidgety than most people?	X		
2. Do you ordinarily work quickly and energetically?	X		
3. In conversation, do you often gesture with hands and head?			X
4. Do you drive a car somewhat fast?	X		
5. Do you let yourself go and have a gay time at a party?		X	
6. Do you often make people laugh?		X	

Part 4—Self-Administered Classification Instrument

1. Is your present full-time occupation as a housewife?

   Yes __X__   No_____ (*If No, then what?*)_____

2. In what year were you born? ____1932_____

3a. Which of the following magazines are received in your home on a regular basis?

American Home	——	Newsweek	——
Better Homes and Gardens	X	Reader's Digest	X
Family Circle	——	Saturday Evening Post	——
Good Housekeeping	X	Saturday Review	——
Holiday	——	The New Yorker	——
House and Garden	——	Time	X
Ladies Home Journal	——	True Story	——
Life	X	T.V. Guide	——
Look	X	U. S. News & World Report	——
McCall's	——	Woman's Day	——

b. How many hours a day do you spend watching television?

Less than 1 hour	_____	About 4 hours	_____
About 1 hour	_____	About 5 hours	_____
About 2 hours	X	Over 5 hours	_____
About 3 hours	_____		

c. How many hours a day do you listen to radio?

Less than 1 hour	_____	About 4 hours	_____
About 1 hour	_____	About 5 hours	_____
About 2 hours	X	Over 5 hours	_____
About 3 hours	_____		

d. How many hours a day do you spend with friends or neighbors?

Less than 1 hour	_____	About 4 hours	_____
About 1 hour	X	About 5 hours	_____
About 2 hours	_____	Over 5 hours	_____
About 3 hours	_____		

e. How many hours a day do you spend with relatives?

Less than 1 hour	X	About 4 hours	_____
About 1 hour	_____	About 5 hours	_____
About 2 hours	_____	Over 5 hours	_____
About 3 hours	_____		

f. How many hours a day do you spend on the telephone?

Less than 1 hour	_____	About 4 hours	_____
About 1 hour	X	About 5 hours	_____
About 2 hours	_____	Over 5 hours	_____
About 3 hours	_____		

4a. What is your husband's occupation?

                    Sales Manager—IBM

                    (Please be specific)

b. What position did your husband hold before this one?

Assistant Sales Manager

_____

1952
5a. How long have you been married? _____
b. Where were you married?   Pittsburgh   Pennsylvania

                           (City)   (State)

                                  2 years
6a. How long have you lived at this address? _____

b. How often have you moved within the last five years?

        Never _____   Twice   _____
        Once   X   More than twice _____

c. Do you own or rent your home?

     Own   X   Rent _____

7a. Do you own one or more automobiles?

     One _____   Two   X   More than two _____

b. What make and year are these cars?

                    Thunderbird   1965
     Make _____ Year _____

                    Falcon   1963
     Make _____ Year _____

8. How many years of formal education have you completed?

    0–6 years   _____   3–4 years college   _____
    7–12 years   _____   More than 4 years college _____
    1–2 years college   X

9. What is your religious preference?

         Protestant   X   Other _____
         Catholic   _____   None _____
         Jewish   _____

10a. What is your approximate family income?

Under $5000 per year	_____	Above $20,000 but under $25,000	_____
Above $5000 but under $10,000	_____	Above $25,000 but under $30,000	_____
Above $10,000 but under $15,000	_____	Above $30,000	_____
Above $15,000 but under $20,000	X		

b. How would you compare yourself to most people in the neighborhood?

Very much richer _____   Somewhat poorer   _____
Richer   _____   Poorer   _____
Somewhat richer   X   Very much poorer   _____

11.   How often do you go out of town as a family or with your husband?

Once a year or less _____   4 times a year   _____
Twice a year   X   5 times a year   _____
3 times a year   _____   6 times a year or more _____

12.   How popular do you consider yourself to be among the neighborhood women?

Very popular   _____   Somewhat unpopular _____
Popular   _____   Unpopular   _____
Somewhat popular   X   Very unpopular   _____

13.   Who do you see most often socially in the neighborhood?

Mrs. Over
_____

(Give full name)

14a. List the organizations, if any, that you belong to—clubs, social groups, church groups, community, and so on—and indicate any offices held.

Organizations   *Offices held*
PTA
_____   _____

Infant Welfare
_____   _____

Country Club
_____   _____

_____   _____

_____   _____

b. How often do you give up one organization and join another?

Once every 6 months _____   Once every 3 years   X
Once every year   _____   Over 3 years   _____
Once every 2 years _____

15a. How often do people stop by to visit you?

Once a month   _____   4 or 5 times a week   _____
Once every 2 weeks _____   6 or 7 times a week   _____
Once a week   _____   8 or more times a week _____
2 or 3 times a week   X

b. How often do you stop by to visit other people?

Once a month	_____	4 or 5 times a week	_____
Once every 2 weeks	_____	6 or 7 times a week	_____
Once a week	_____	8 or more times a week	_____
2 or 3 times a week	X		

CHAPTER 16

BRAND LOYALTY

Ford Motor Company[1]

Early in 1965 Ford Motor Company executives were reviewing the progress of the Mustang, a low-priced sports car introduced in April of 1964. From the day the Mustang had been first displayed and advertised, it had been the most talked about automobile of the year. By the end of May, the first full month on the market, the Mustang had moved to the number-one spot among compact cars and to the number-seven spot among all nameplates. It was not completely clear, however, how much the car had contributed to the Ford's goal of increasing its share of the total automobile market.

Table 16–1 presents sales and market share data for the leading American manufacturers. The automobile industry's market share pattern reflected a variety of conditions. A major consideration was the well-known fact in the industry that automobile buyers tended to remain loyal to a particular manufacturer. Part of this loyalty reflected a relationship with the manufacturer's retail dealer, but it also was based on other factors. An automobile that had been free from service problems brought to the manufacturer, regardless of the dealer, a certain degree of loyalty. As manufacturers had increased their service warranties and had improved the quality of car performance, consumer brand loyalty had been strengthened. In a mobile society like the United States, the manufacturer also enjoyed certain benefits; for a newcomer to a community would tend to turn to the dealer for the car he currently owned. Manufacturer loyalty also reflected the consumer's ability to stay with the line of a particular manufacturer as his income increased and as his preference shifted from lower- to higher-priced cars.

With its long product line, General Motors (GM) had always enjoyed a competitive advantage in this respect. The degree of brand loyalty had been documented through analysis of car buying habits in the state of Michigan

[1] Reproduced from Kenneth R. Davis, *Marketing Management*. Second Edition. Copyright © 1966, The Ronald Press Company, New York, pp. 473–481, 659–673. By permission of the publisher.

Table 16–1

New Car Registrations

Year	Total Registrations	General Motors Percent Share	Ford Percent Share	Chrysler Percent Share	American Motors Percent Share	Imported Cars Percent Share	Studebaker-Packard Percent Share
1964	8,059,235	49.08	26.01	13.81	4.70	6.0	0.32
1963	7,556,717	51.04	24.87	12.37	5.67	5.10	0.85
1962	6,938,863	51.87	26.30	9.61	6.10	4.89	1.12
1961	5,854,747	46.53	28.53	10.79	6.33	6.47	1.23
1960	6,576,650	43.64	26.60	14.01	6.42	7.58	1.61
1959	6,041,275	42.10	28.12	11.30	6.01	10.17	2.21
1958	4,654,514	46.35	26.44	13.92	4.00	8.13	1.03
1957	5,982,342	44.86	30.39	18.33	1.96	3.46	1.13
1956	5,955,248	50.78	28.45	15.48	1.93	1.65	1.76
1955	7,169,908	50.75	27.63	16.82	1.91	0.82	2.06

SOURCE: *Automotive News Almanac*, 1964.

(Table 16–2). Data from this study, conducted for the past fifteen years by the R. L. Polk Company, had been widely used in the automobile industry. As indicated in Table 16–2, it permitted the automobile manufacturer to determine loyalty by brand, division, and corporation. Thus, in 1963, 63.2 percent of the cars one-year-old traded for a Chevrolet division car were cars

Table 16–2
Source of Sales (1963 Sales, State of Michigan)

Make	Percent Trading Same Brand, Division, or Corporation Car, by Age of Trade-in		
	One Year Old	Three Years Old	All Ages
Buick (div.)	73.9%	72.9%	57.0%
GM	92.6	92.4	83.9
Cadillac	93.3	84.4	70.9
GM	97.2	95.4	90.1
Chevrolet (div.)	63.2	67.4	63.8
GM	84.3	84.8	79.6
Chevrolet (std. mod.)	58.6	61.1	54.1
Corvair	19.6	31.8	25.3
GM	79.4	80.5	80.1
Oldsmobile	72.4	69.9	56.6
GM	93.4	91.9	85.1
Pontiac	68.9	65.5	56.6
GM	89.1	90.3	83.5
Ford (div.)	67.9	58.1	57.3
Ford Co.	73.2	63.6	62.8
T' Bird	43.0	29.4	28.6
Ford (std. mod.)	70.1	60.2	57.2
Falcon	24.2	23.2	24.5
Ford Co.	68.2	59.7	63.1
Lincoln	80.9	39.0	33.0
Ford Co.	88.7	57.3	61.7
Mercury	65.9	55.7	43.3
Ford Co.	79.2	72.9	65.7
Dodge (div.)	60.4	43.0	42.0
Chrysler Corp.	73.3	59.4	57.0
Plymouth (div.)	62.6	40.8	34.0
Chrysler Corp.	78.0	56.8	51.0
Valiant	41.0	30.1	31.9
Rambler	55.0	49.1	46.2
AMC	59.5	53.5	51.6
Volkswagen	27.6%	31.8%	32.2%

SOURCE: Research Department, R. L. Polk Company.

from this division of GM. Of all one-year-old cars traded in, 84.3 percent were from GM. In contrast, in 1963, 19.6 percent of the cars one-year-old traded in on Corvairs were Corvairs. Although Table 16–2 does not indicate such data, the study also permitted an analysis of "conquest" sales. For example, in 1963, among cars one-year-old traded for the Chevrolet (standard model), 58.6 percent were of the same brand, 26 percent were other GM cars (including other brands from the Chevrolet division), 10.3 percent were Ford Motor Company cars, and 3.4 percent were Chrysler Corporation cars.

A further factor contributing to the stability of market share was the basic distribution system of the leading manufacturers. Thus, GM, by virtue of the fact that it had 13,800 dealers compared to 8400 Ford dealers, enjoyed a competitive advantage in selling and servicing its cars. Commensurate advantages were reflected in the advertising expenditures of the two firms, with GM spending approximately $160 million in 1963 compared with $101 million for Ford.[2] These differentials in dealer systems and advertising expenditures were related, of course, to the length of each firm's product line. GM was able to present, through its basic divisions, a product line of thirty-four cars as compared to twenty for Ford.

To offset these conditions, Ford had tried a number of approaches. The addition of the Edsel has been based, in part, on the desire to fill a gap in the company's product line. The Falcon and Fairlane car lines represented a further step in tapping major market segments. Numerous promotions and basic advertising campaigns had been directed toward segments of the market that were believed to be in a formative stage in terms of their automobile-buying habits. The desire to gain market share was a major consideration in the introduction of the Mustang, for executives recognized that a low-priced sports car could be the first new automobile purchase of people in the twenty to twenty-nine age bracket. More frequently, however, people in this age bracket purchased a used car (Table 16–3).

Table 16–3

New and Used Car Purchase Rates by Age Group

Age	Percent of Group Buying	
	New	Used
All ages	8.6	16.7
18–24	4.4	26.5
25–34	9.8	22.5
35–44	11.3	21.3
45–54	10.4	16.7
55–64	7.3	8.9
60 and over	3.7	5.0

[2] *Advertising Age* estimates of total expenditures.

Development of the Product Concept

As part of its program for evaluating the acceptance of the Falcon line, including the Futura, the company conducted periodic consumer surveys. In addition, certain special surveys sought to measure the trend of consumer interest in sports cars and the acceptance of possible future sports car additions to the company line. In early 1962, two preliminary personal interview surveys were conducted to determine best size and performance characteristics should the company elect to introduce a new car in the sports car or special model market. These surveys also had as their objective an approximate estimate of the probable volume of a new sports car entry as well as the effect of such an entry on current models in the Ford line.

The first of these surveys compared a single seat, two-passenger car, three sports models of present Falcon-Fairlane cars with varying rear seat sizes, and a fast-back Falcon of conventional performance. Respondents were interviewed in their homes and included (1) owners of Thunderbirds, Corvair Monzas, and foreign sports cars; and (2) their neighbors. Additional interviews with interested car owners were taken at shopping centers. Interviews were conducted only in Dallas, Chicago, and Philadelphia. The total number of completed interviews in the two phases was as follows:

Survey 1	Survey 2
149—1959–1961 T-Bird owners	125—1961 Monza owners
168—1961 Monza owners	127—Falcon sedan owners
140—1958–1961 foreign sports car owners	122—foreign sports car owners, 1958–1961 models
356—neighbors	141—foreign economy car models, 1958–1961 models
706—in shopping centers	

The results of the first survey indicated that a car styled along sports car lines with five or six passenger package size would be most attractive. Results also indicated that the market was interested in both six- and eight-cylinder engine sizes. The survey also indicated that styling of the sports car would have an effect on the sales of the Thunderbird.

The second survey focused more directly on a model designed to be competitive with the Corvair Monza, and here respondents included the owners of Monzas, Falcon sedans, foreign sports cars, and foreign economy models. Results of this survey also indicated considerable consumer interest in a modified sports car package with six- and eight-cylinder options.

The results of these surveys indicated that a sports car styled along these lines would capture a 1 to 2 percent share of industry automobile sales. However, in conducting the surveys, the process of selecting respondents excluded what the company considered to be standard-size car buyers. This exclusion resulted from a desire to focus on people who had a genuine interest in sports cars, as evidenced by ownership of Thunderbirds, Monzas, or foreign cars. At the same time, however, the exclusion of this large proportion of the potential buying market limited the company's ability to project results to the total market. Another limitation in projecting estimated total volume was the fact that the sample used was limited in geographical coverage. Company executives were aware of this limitation but at this juncture felt that a more elaborate survey was not necessary.

In September and October of 1962, the Ford research department again made a survey—this one with 950 prospective new car buyers in a national probability sample of households. This was a personal interview survey of persons planning to buy a new car within the next two years. The questionnaires used in this survey generally followed the format of earlier studies. Pictures of a Ford fast-back Galaxie, the fast-back Falcon, and Fairlane hardtops were used along with a Corvair and other competitive sports cars. The properties used were side views of the test cars and three-quarter front and rear views of the various cars. Specification sheets covering the test cars and other cars currently available, along with diagrams to illustrate shoulder room and clearance, were also used.

While the earlier surveys indicated a potential volume of 50,000 to 100,000 in a 6.2 million car year, the 1962 survey suggested a potential volume between 150,000 and 300,000. Of the T-5 sales (T-5 was the name given to the proposed sports car model), it was estimated that one third would be incremental and that two thirds would substitute for other Ford Motor Company car lines.

Other data from this research pointed to the importance of the "under twenty-five" buyer as a potential market for the T-5. In this age bracket, Chevrolet enjoyed a commanding lead over Ford, largely because of the success of the Monza. Certain attitudinal data suggested that the T-5 would be attractive to persons desiring characteristics not always present in standard American cars. Style was played back as a significant reason for choosing the T-5 more often than was typically found in automobile preference tests. Although many sports-type features (bucket seats, four-speed transmissions, and tachometers) were desired by a higher-than-average proportion of respondents, the majority still desired the conventional car accouterments.

Pricing Considerations

Following these baseline studies of the product concept, Ford's market research department conducted an exhaustive study on possible price levels for the proposed T-5. The study covered 1600 prospective buyers of hard-topped convertibles and other small sports cars in twelve cities.

Inherent in the pricing of the T-5 was the question of substitution. The greater the T-5 volume reflected substitution for other Ford cars, the higher the T-5 price would have to be. Estimates of substitution had to be based on predictions of the action that competitors would take in modifying their cars. An uncertain element in the pricing was the long-run gain of additional Ford owners, particularly in the younger age group.

Promotional Strategy

The Mustang promotional program evolved in several distinct states. Once the division had decided to introduce a new car designed to appeal to younger car buyers, its marketing and advertising executives undertook, with the assistance of its advertising agency, J. Walter Thompson, to formulate the basic copy platform and media plan. Initially, only a small group of Ford advertising executives and agency creative personnel were permitted to view the car's early mockups and photographs. Working under considerable time pressure, as well as maximum security, this group began in April, 1963, to formulate basic advertising strategy, including preliminary rough layouts. At this time, the car was tentatively named Torino. Throughout the development of the prototype and during the product's market research, it was referred to as "the special car" or the "T-5." Initial advertising plans, however, utilized the name Torino and called for copy appealing to the youth market with emphasis on an Italian theme.

Although the sports car appeal of the T-5 was obvious from the outset, company executives believed the potential of the product was much broader. Accordingly, they recognized the importance of emphasizing the practical nature of the car. Figure 16–1 is an early comprehensive ad for the T-5 with the copy emphasis on such product elements as low price, gasoline economy, and four-passenger capacity.

A feature of the early planning for the T-5 was the copy line "brand new import—from Detroit." This line was to be used in all preannouncement and announcement advertising. At the same time, company execut-vies wanted to make it crystal clear that this was a United States car, not an import from Italy. Plans called for taking no photographs in Italy, but advertisements would endeavor to borrow some of the Italian flavor.

As the promotion planning for the T-5 progressed, Ford executives stressed the importance of restricting the number of features to include in the car's copy platform. It had been their experience that advertising or personal selling that tried to emphasize more than three basic product features tended to confuse the prospective buyer. Accordingly, in August, 1963, it was decided that all advertising should emphasize the following product qualities:

1. *Style:* described as Italian flair but usually expressed most eloquently by the illustration of the vehicle itself

2. *Price:* expressed by "$2,368 f.o.b. Detroit"

3. *Universality:* virtually unrestricted choice of options expressed in the "three faces of Torino," to wit:

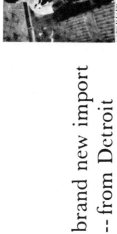

FIGURE 16–1. A Ford ad emphasizing the practical nature of the Torino.

    a.   Economical, practical family car
    b.   Luxurious, sporty, personal car
    c.   High performance car for highway or toughest competitive events

Following up the concept that T-5 was a "universal" car, tentative lists of the features, equipment, and options particularly applicable to the individual faces of the car were developed:

1.   For the economical, practical, family car
    a.   Standard 170-cubic-inch six
    b.   Standard three-speed manual transmission
    c.   Family passenger room
    d.   Roomy trunk in the rear
    e.   GT bucket seats
    f.   Superb ride and handling

2.   For the luxurious, sporty personal car
    a.   Optional 260-cubic-inch V8
    b.   Optional three-speed Cruise-O-Matic Drive
    c.   Power steering and power brakes
    d.   Personal console between front bucket seats
    e.   Air conditioning

3.   For the high-performance car
    a.   Optional 289-cubic-inch V-8
    b.   Four-speed manual transmission
    c.   Rally-pack (speedometer-clock unit)
    d.   Handling package (stiffer roll bar, shocks, and springs)
    e.   Knock-off hubs
    f.   Fourteen-inch wheels (in place of standard thirteen-inch)
    g.   Low center of gravity

Using this basic frame of reference, the agency prepared a number of comprehensive ads and a detailed strategy plan for a conference to be held with Ford executives early in August.

At the same time that the agency was preparing its initial proposals for the T-5 advertising campaign, the Ford marketing research department was analyzing the impact of sports car styling, assessing the potential competitive strength of the T-5 as an entry in the overall automobile market, and conducting final research on the strength of *Torino* and alternative car names. Although the concept of a car with sports car styling was generally agreed upon by agency and division executives, the precise size and character of the market was still subject to interpretation. A name such as Torino and an advertising strategy that stressed the Italian and foreign sports car influence was designed for maximum appeal to the segment of the market that was significantly sports car oriented. Using this approach, the car's name, advertising strategy, media schedule, and advertising copy would follow one pattern. On the other hand, it was recognized that the market for a car like the T-5 could very well call for a somewhat different advertising approach. If the T-5 had an "across the board appeal," *Torino* and heavy foreign car overtones in the advertising could significantly restrict the car's appeal and, in turn, the development of the market.

To study the merits of alternative brand names, the marketing research department had an outside organization conduct a two-phase research project. In Phase 1, group discussions were conducted with seventy-three persons identified as potential prospects. These people were interviewed in groups of five to ten people in Chicago and Los Angeles. A trained discussion leader showed each group photographs of a "special car," a Corvair Monza, a Thunderbird, and other cars. These taped discussions were relatively unstructured, lasting from two to three hours. They covered the group's perception of the car itself, suitability of various proposed names, the group's suggestions of names for the car, the suitability of the car for various kinds of people, and potential uses of the car.

Phase 2 consisted of structured personal interviews with 203 prospects in four cities. The structured interview used was developed from the findings of Phase 1. Individual respondents, rather than groups, were exposed to photographs, and information was gathered on the suitability of names and on the perceived function of the T-5.

Potential names were judged against a variety of criteria: (1) The name should be a word that was liked, that had pleasant associations independent of its suitability as a name for this particular car. (2) The connotations of the word should be suitable as a name for the car, (3) The name should be easy to pronounce, (4) The name should be easy to remember.

As a result of this research, plus other considerations, the decision was made late in August, 1963, to adopt *Mustang* rather than *Torino* as the car's name. The name *Mustang* had been registered by Ford and used on an earlier two-seat prototype sports car. The change in the car's name reflected a basic change in management's appraisal of the size and nature of the market. Estimates of the market were more than double those made a year earlier. At this point, the decision was also made to increase the car's promotional effort and to incorporate in its advertising strategy copy appeals and media plans that would reach a much larger segment of the total automobile buying market.

With the change in name and product concept, three major changes were made in the advertising strategy of the Mustang. Throughout the development of the car, the Ford public relations department had worked with a variety of trade and consumer publications to insure maximum publicity for the car. From this activity, it became apparent that the car would enjoy a substantial amount of free publicity. Consequently, it was decided not to use a "teaser" or preannouncement campaign, where only part of the car or the car covered with canvas would be illustrated. The use of such preannouncement techniques was common practice in the automobile industry. Company executives felt that because they had such an unusual car this approach would be unnecessary. Indeed, the preannouncement technique might put the Mustang too much into the frame of "just another car." Moreover, the car's unique styling could not be effectively featured in a teaser campaign.

Another change centered around the use of a styling award. Walter Hoving, president of Tiffany's, world-famous jewelers, had been invited to Detroit to view an early model of the Mustang and to comment on its style. Subsequently, the Mustang received the Tiffany Award for Excellence in American Design, the first automobile to be so honored. It was decided at this point to feature this award in announcement advertising.

The final major change was the decision to emphasize price in the announcement ad headlines and to spell out the many features that this price included. Inasmuch as the car would have a number of items that were extras on most cars, it was deemed important to say this in very specific terms in the advertising. In addition, the unique feature of being able to select from a extremely wide list of extras, thereby designing the car to meet individual needs, was also considered an important feature—so important that it, too, called for inclusion in the announcement ad.

The final announcement ad featured the car's profile, considered its most attractive styling angle, and carried an accompanying spread that gave essential product details (see Figure 16–2).

The media plan that was developed to carry Mustang advertising was unique in several respects. It was assumed that for such a completely new car concept there would have to be above-normal advertising expenditure rates. Thus, although it was anticipated that the car would represent 10 percent of Ford sales during the introductory period, it was recommended that in excess of 40 percent of all Ford advertising during this period be devoted to the Mustang. This reflected, in part, the fact that the car would be introduced in April instead of late fall, when it could be featured in the advertising of a completely new line of Ford cars. In addition, it was reasoned that the car was so different from former new car concepts that the buyer-education task would be greater. In this connection, it was considered very important to concentrate the car's advertising during the early weeks and months following its introduction. During this period the car would be in short supply and its features could not be communicated by "road exposure." Finally, it was assumed that there would be such a favorable response to the Mustang that its news and publicity value would build dealer traffic and sales of other Ford cars, thereby justifying a higher-than-normal ad budget.

The basic elements of the media plan called for allocating available dollars among the major media as follows:

Media	Percent
Magazines	24%
Newspapers	15
Outdoor	26
Radio	1
Television	29
Direct mail	5
TOTAL	100%

The concentration of effort in the months of April and May is indicated in Table 16–4, which shows the allocation of effect by media, April to August.

One of the highlights of the Mustang's announcement advertising was the simultaneous TV commercials on ABC, NBC, and CBS. The total cost of the three commercial minutes on "Perry Mason," "The Jimmy Dean Show," and on the Ford-sponsored "Hazel" came to $450,000. Tie-in advertising arrangements were also made with four top shows having over 18 million viewers. Mustangs given away on these shows, such as "The Price is Right," were provided free. The use of two hundred billboard showings in major markets and one hundred showings in minor markets was most unusual. Prior advertising campaigns had used only one hundred showings and fifty showings.

In conjunction with the national advertising, the company undertook a number of sales promotion efforts. Mustangs were displayed in 125 Holiday Inns, and the May issue of the *Holiday Inn* magazine featured the Mustang ad on its back cover. Other Ford ads were scheduled for the June and July issues of this publication. The Mustang was featured in the Holiday Inn national advertising travel and safety films and on the cover of 7 million Holiday Inn directories.

Other sales promotion efforts included featuring the car at the World's Fair in New York and at fourteen airport terminals. Seventy special high traffic locations such as shopping centers, bank lobbies, hotels, and motels frequented by business groups were used in cities throughout the United States.

The nationally known suntan lotion Sea and Ski featured a line of new, high-fashion sun glasses through its subsidiary Renauld of France. The new style of sun glasses was called Mustang, and ads for them featured the Ford Mustang. In announcement advertising, a Mustang car was offered for $1. The Mustang was the official pace car for the 1964 Indianapolis 500. A major Mustang consumer promotional program was based upon visits to dealer showrooms. By registering at dealers' showrooms, consumers could enter a contest with a thousand prizes valued at more than $110,000. There were 25 first prizes of Mustangs, 25 second prizes of Philco color TV sets, 100 third prizes of Philco portable TV sets, and 850 fourth prizes of Philco transistor radios.

As the company reviewed the success of the Mustang, it had at its

Table 16—4

Mustang Advertising Schedule by Major Media, April–August, 1964*

Medium	April 5	12	19	26	May 3	10	17	24	31	June 7	14	21	28	July 5	12	19	26	Aug 2	9	16	23	30
Magazines																						
Life	4				1																	
Look	4					1																
Saturday Evening Post	4			4		1																
Reader's Digest									1													
Sports Illustrated		2				2																
Time		2			1																	
Newsweek			2			1																
U.S. News & World Report			2				1															
New Yorker				2		1																
Playbill						2		1														
Better Homes & Gardens								1														
National Geographic					2																	
Holiday							2					1										
Town and Country							2															
Sunset						2																
Palm Beach Life					2				2													
True									2													
Argosy					2																	
Field & Stream						2																
Sports Afield						2																
Outdoor Life						2																
Mechanix Illustrated					2																	
Popular Science					2																	
Popular Mechanics					2																	

Table 16-4 (continued)

Medium	April				May					June				July				August				
	5	12	19	26	3	10	17	24	31	7	14	21	28	5	12	19	26	2	9	16	23	30
Magazines																						
Vogue							2	—	—	—	—	—	—	—								
Ebony											1	—	—	—								
Esquire												1	—	—	—							
Car Buff magazine									2	—	—	—										
Newspaper																						
Basic list	X																					
Sixty markets			X																			
Ten markets (women's page)	X						X															
Outdoor																						
#200 top 50 markets			—	—																		
#100 next 170 markets			—	—																		
Radio (minutes)																						
MBS	1	1	1		1	1	1			1	1	1										
NBC	2	1	2		1	2	1			2	1	2										
Television (minutes)																						
"Hazel"	3	2	1					1			1				1				1			
"Participations"	14	13	4		6	4	4	2			1				1				1			
"T-Bird Golf"										3												
Direct mail																						
Ford owners' newsletter	—	—																				

* Key: 4 = four pages
        2 = two pages
        1 = one page

FIGURE 16–2.   Two Ford ads for the Mustang.

Table 16–5

New Passenger Car Registrations, Compact and Imported Cars

Car	Introduction Date	Calendar Year					1964											
		1960	1961	1962	1963	1964	Jan.	Feb.	Mar.	Apr.	May	June	July	Aug.	Sept.	Oct.	Nov.	Dec.
Falcon	10/59	451,030	436,658	314,247	199,273	182,145	16,186	14,697	16,502	20,053	17,007	16,656	16,664	14,688	11,778	13,647	12,829	11,438
Falcon Futura	4/61	-	45,304	41,639	125,805	103,461	8,847	8,208	9,817	11,623	10,067	9,051	9,098	7,455	6,195	8,779	7,745	6,576
Corvair	10/59	229,985	155,170	82,617	57,263	44,140	3,924	3,374	3,987	4,956	4,786	4,301	4,176	3,570	2,428	2,289	2,320	4,035
Corvair Monza	10/60	-	160,858	207,268	187,451	149,502	11,714	10,255	11,239	14,593	13,956	12,857	11,975	10,997	10,100	12,045	11,562	18,223
Fairlane	11/61	-	5,096	92,260	90,408	71,464	5,861	5,949	6,407	7,250	6,977	6,560	6,608	5,539	4,032	5,734	5,755	4,792
Fairlane 500	11/61	-	15,771	249,443	229,056	181,957	14,922	15,148	16,313	18,460	17,765	16,702	16,825	14,104	10,265	14,599	14,652	12,202
Mustang	4/64	-	-	-	-	248,916	-	-	-	4,564	21,364	27,208	28,723	32,168	33,682	37,363	34,114	29,730
Chevy II	9/61	-	35,250	343,693	312,914	168,372	14,641	12,952	15,752	20,196	19,683	18,785	18,132	15,522	10,477	8,186	4,939	9,122
Chevelle	9/63	-	-	-	57,714	313,616	23,564	21,680	26,081	32,567	34,407	33,978	30,331	28,141	19,643	20,676	14,579	27,979
Valiant (Plymouth)	10/59	192,961	120,795	122,993	178,399	184,951	12,285	11,912	14,377	19,977	19,278	21,474	20,675	17,862	13,548	11,756	10,623	11,184
Dart (Dodge)	10/62	-	-	25,677	156,497	187,469	11,484	10,817	13,992	19,181	19,114	19,164	18,328	16,446	12,754	15,851	15,295	14,043
Lancer (Dodge)	10/60	16,610	63,431	47,566	-	-	-	-	-	-	-	-	-	-	-	-	-	-
Tempest (Pontiac)	11/60	12,335	110,188	138,144	139,313	240,524	15,672	15,578	19,910	27,324	27,269	26,875	24,380	20,020	12,302	12,657	12,271	26,266
F-85 (Oldsmobile)	10/60	17,233	70,813	94,983	121,483	172,071	11,419	11,393	15,564	19,289	19,508	19,614	17,305	14,579	10,356	10,835	6,827	16,382
Special (Buick)	10/60	15,469	91,353	152,312	144,691	180,460	12,948	11,770	14,370	20,623	20,028	20,308	17,097	15,622	9,968	10,664	9,469	17,593
All imported cars	-	498,785	378,622	339,160	385,624	484,131	37,197	29,841	35,759	44,973	41,293	42,452	44,150	42,369	42,384	46,172	39,851	39,356

SOURCE: R. L. Polk Co.

disposal the car registration data for directly competitive makes in Table 16–5. Less direct effects of the Mustang introduction could also be revealed in sales of the leading standard-size models of the Ford and Chevrolet lines (Table 16–6).

Table 16–6

New Car Sales in United States, 1960–1964 (Selected Models)

	1964	1963	1962	1961	1960
Ford					
Custom	95,966	68,553	12,382	–	–
Custom 500	83,799	104,102	153,554	–	–
Galaxie 500	559,734	549,178	411,100	346,434	298,235
Ford station wagon	134,643	128,876	122,914	131,074	166,093
Thunderbird	86,929	63,857	73,975	83,033	81,603
General Motors					
Biscayne	151,763	174,838	169,534	187,822	287,272
Bel Air	282,063	335,863	354,342	342,894	398,518
Impala	820,903	822,128	718,421	523,183	550,680
Chevrolet station wagon	174,449	191,581	186,915	172,916	219,317
Corvette	20,097	21,901	15,239	11,641	11,153

SOURCE: R. L. Polk Co.

Questions

1. Was the Mustang successful in dealing with the problem of brand loyalty?

2. Evaluate the research involved in developing the Mustang product concept.

3. Evaluate the research involved in the development of the promotional strategy.

4. Evaluate the degree to which the Mustang marketing program was consistent with the dimensions of consumer behavior presented in the case.

PART VI

TOTAL PROCESS OF CONSUMER BEHAVIOR

CHAPTER 17

COMPREHENSIVE CASES

City National Bank and Trust Company of Columbus, Ohio: Developing a Comprehensive Consumer Orientation

The City National Bank and Trust Company (CNB) has served residents of central Ohio and Columbus since 1868. As a result of a 1929 consolidation between the City National Bank of Commerce and the Commercial National Bank, City National became the third largest bank in the central Ohio area. It is a member of the Federal Reserve system and offers all general banking services such as savings accounts, investor saver bonds, checking accounts, trust services, safe deposit service, Christmas club, travelers' checks, mortgage loans, and business and consumer loans of many types. It also offers several special services, described in a later section.

Background

Growth and Profitability

By 1968 CNB regularly received acclaim from banking leaders as one of the most progressive and customer-oriented banks in the United States. Its officers are invited to speak at important conferences and were as frequently quoted in journals and other publications as the officers of banks many times its size. Just as important as its progressiveness in achieving this acclaim was its profitability. CNB in the period of 1960 to 1967 was consistently among the five most profitable banks in the nation. In six years its resources doubled, and in 1967 resources increased $55 million, the most ever in a single year and a jump of approximately 18 percent. Net operating income in 1967 reached an all-time high of over $3.5 million. Table 17–1 displays revenues and earnings for the period of 1963 through 1967 and reveals an average ROI of over 15.5 percent.

Table 17-1

Revenues and Earnings, 1963–1967

Year	Deposits	Capital Surplus Undivided Profits	Net Operating Income	Net Operating Income to Average Capital Funds*	Cash Dividend Payments	Net Operating Income per Share†
1967	$335,812,391	$23,000,000	$3,549,560	15.69%	$1,410,750	4.15
1966	282,329,745	21,500,000	3,283,933	15.64	1,282,500	3.84
1965	256,932,201	20,000,000	2,940,553	14.93	1,140,000	3.44
1964	218,378,616	18,500,000	2,754,691	15.14	760,000	3.22
1963	$195,760,551	$16,100,000	$2,573,654	16.52%	$ 620,250	3.18

SOURCE: Annual Report, City National Bank, December 31, 1967.
* This figure has consistently been one of the highest for all U.S. banks.
† Based on 855,000 shares outstanding December 31, 1967.

Banking Objectives

Prior to 1960, City National had been a good, sound bank but had maintained the banking status quo in the community. In 1960, however, a small group of top executives developed a new concept in banking.

The new concept was to organize the bank in a way that would enable it to become a leader in retail banking in Ohio. The idea was to become a marketing-oriented bank that would meet the total financial needs of consumers. This group of executives believed that a bank that truly met the needs of its customers could also be a very profitable bank.

The decision to become retail oriented resulted from an analysis of the role CNB played in the community. It was the smallest of three major commercial banks in Franklin county, with deposits of approximately $100 million in 1960. Although growth had been above average, the future looked much the same unless a new force was introduced in the bank. The executives believed that a new concept of consumer orientation could place City National into the role of a driving force in the financial community of central Ohio.

In order to accomplish the new goal, top management was recruited to lead the bank into creating a financial center that would truly reflect the needs of the customer and that would further the development of the community. In 1959 Everett D. Reese, a man respected for his ability to get things done, was recruited from outside the bank and elected chairman of the board, the top leadership position of CNB.

Marketing Program

The chairman's first action was twofold. He first decided that if the bank was to serve the community and consumer, it had to be where the consumer was. City National had seven branches in 1960, and this number was expanded by 1968 to seventeen, with immediate plans for several more. These branches were strategically placed—primarily in the communities surrounding Columbus having the highest population growth and in the best traffic positions. Each branch incorporated striking architectural features and had unusually high consumer appeal.

The chairman's second step was to choose a man to head up an advertising program that would create a distinctive bank image in the eyes of the consumer. The advertising manager, John Fisher, was recruited from outside the banking industry and was eventually to become head of a comprehensive marketing department.

The advertising manager immediately began to develop a marketing program that would (1) develop a specific image for the bank itself, aside from the overall banking community; (2) identify specific consumer services that would meet unfulfilled needs; and (3) develop and market the varied services of the bank on a carefully planned, predetermined basis.

The bank's advertising soon came to be recognized as among the most

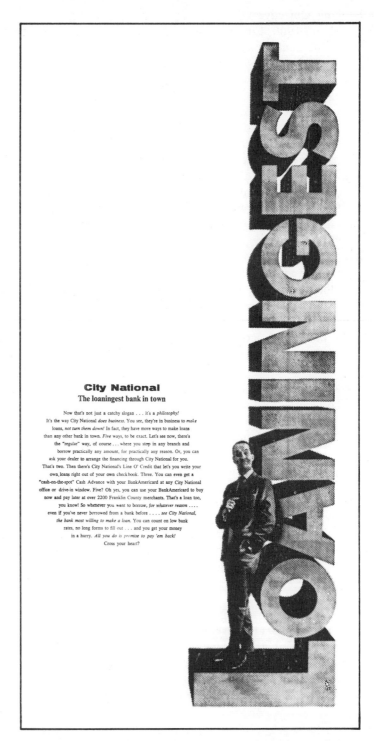

Figure 17-1. Part of City National Bank's "Loaningest Bank in Town" campaign.

Why is a BankAmericard® like a Volkswagen?

**Because
year after year
it looks just the same...
but perfoms
better and better.**

It's not easy to improve some things that are so near perfect. But BankAmericard has done it ... with Line O' Credit.

Now, you get better performance from your BankAmericard. You can go further, buy more, pay for it any way you want. BankAmericard with Line O' Credit lets you pick the way you want to get things ... write a check charge it, pay cash. ■ You can write yourself a loan in your own checkbook; ■ you can charge it at 250,000 places from Boston to Honolulu, in Europe and Great Britain; ■ you can get instant cash at any of City National's 17 offices.

BankAmericard, with Line O' Credit, not only gives you the means to shop anywhere, for anything ... you can pick your own terms. For everything you do, you get just one monthly bill. Pay for it in 25 days, it's the same as cash; or extend payments over several months for just a small service charge.

No, we couldn't improve the way it looks ... but we sure made BankAmericard perform better.

®*Servicemarks owned and licensed by BankAmerica Service Corporation*

Figure 17-2. The dynamic "Line O'Credit" ads helped to identify CNB in the community.

creative and successful of any bank in the nation. In order to develop an image of the bank that was personal and differentiated from banks in general, well-known personalities were used in the bank's advertising, including Phyllis Diller and Shari Lewis. The bank also developed continuing campaigns for its services. One of the most successful campaigns in bank advertising history was the "Loaningest Bank in Town" campaign shown in Figures 17-1 to 17-3. Later research revealed that this campaign not only stimulated loans but also was instrumental in the decision process of new residents in deciding to open a checking account at CNB. Along with the advertising campaign was an effort to simplify application forms and the slogan was used, "All you have to do is promise to pay us back." CNB had been one of the first major banks to aggressively enter the consumer credit field.

The bank's advertising was colorful, artistically advanced, and used a variety of media. Full-page color ads were frequently inserted into local newspapers, and a heavy television schedule was used.

The image of the bank was also affected by a decision of the bank to move into an impressive new twenty-four story office building located in the center of Columbus. On top of the building were large blue neon signs with the words *City National* that could be seen for many miles in all directions. Research conducted for the bank in 1967 indicated that many people in Columbus believed that CNB was the largest bank in Columbus, although it was actually third largest. These people identified CNB with the entire twenty-four story building, even though CNB leased only a few floors of the building. The research performed throughout the period indicated that CNB had the image of a young, progressive, and dynamic bank.

Figure 17-3.   One ad in the CNB's aggressive consumer credit series.

Implementation of the Marketing Concept

In addition to improving existing banking services and to promoting them creatively, CNB executives felt that adoption of the marketing concept indicated a strong role for the marketing department. To give leadership at top management levels in implementing this concept, C. Gordon Jelliffe was brought in as vice chairman, a new position for the bank. He had previously been president of Columbus Coated Fabrics, a division of Bordens, and in that position had developed strength in marketing and a systems approach to attaining management objectives. In 1968, Reese retired as chairman of the board and John McCoy, previously president of the bank, became chairman of the board and Jelliffe became president.

As president of the bank, Jelliffe described the role of marketing in the bank: "The new role of marketing is one of guiding the development of the bank system so that it is responsive to a dramatically changing environment. Marketing can no longer be merely selling or communicating. It should be the *fundamental force in deciding what the bank should offer.*"

In describing the function of the bank, Jelliffe articulated the bank's rejection of a narrow concept of banking:

> At City National Bank, as we presently see it, our business is much more broadly conceived than the traditional business of banking. We believe our business is to analyze the total needs of individual and corporate consumers relating to the making, possession and expenditure of money or money substitutes and to satisfy all those needs which we are qualified to profitably and legally serve.

Jelliffe also commented on the role of top management and its relationship to marketing's role:

> The job of top banking executives is developing systems geared to reaching fundamental management objectives. In our modern conception of a bank as a total service and information system, marketing occupies a much different role. It should be the integrating force which interprets the environment to the bank, defines objectives to guide the entire system, and provides guidelines for long-range corporate development.

To accomplish these objectives, CNB had introduced several new services by 1968, some of which are described below.

Travel Service

CNB management was convinced that travel would become an increasingly large expenditure by the affluent customers of the bank. Also, Columbus was a center of governmental, educational, and consulting personnel who traveled frequently. CNB established a complete travel service in their downtown office and in some branches.

Computer Services

CNB was a leader in computerizing bank services. Beginning in 1962, CNB viewed computerization as a means to "separate the paper work from the people work." A new computer operations center was built to house the bank's NCR 315 installation. CNB management had a strong commitment to seeking new computerized programs, especially those that would help medium-sized retailers compete with the giants and would provide new computerized decision-making tools for management.

Customer Hours

Banks traditionally have been open from 9 A.M. to 2 P.M. CNB, however, was open on several evenings and had drive-in service at most banks each day. In addition, management was receptive to other hours if they could be shown to meet legitimate customer needs.

BankAmericard

Probably the most significant addition to services was the BankAmericard program initiated in December of 1966. It exceeded all expectations of management. This was a comprehensive credit card originally developed by the Bank of America, the world's largest bank. The management of CNB went to the Bank of America with the suggestion that CNB become the first stage in a national franchising program of the BankAmericard program.

CNB developed a much more encompassing concept of the BankAmericard than did most banks for their bank credit card. At CNB, the BankAmericard was promoted as "the billpayer plan" and patrons were encouraged to use the card to pay for almost any product or service in the world. The card was accepted by about 2000 merchants and service establishments in Franklin county. It was also accepted in many other cities on a similar basis where BankAmericard had been franchised to a local bank. Additionally, it was accepted by major airlines and hotel chains and by 1968 was accepted by merchants and other businesses almost throughout the world, due to aggressive promotion of the program by the Bank of America throughout Europe and other countries.

The mechanics of the BankAmericard were simple. Merchants accepted the card and were reimbursed immediately by CNB, less a small discount. Consumers were billed for all their purchases once a month, and, if they paid within twenty-five days, there was no interest charge. If they chose extended payments, customers paid interest ranging from 1 to 2 percent a month, depending on the amount of the balance and the special terms that might be chosen. Experience indicated that at least half of the customers who used BankAmericard in a month left enough balance at the end of the month to incur interest charges.

BankAmericard provided several benefits to CNB. First, it was a profitable service in its own right. Second, it brought to the bank thousands of customers who previously had no relationship to CNB. (The card was originally sent to over 100,000 persons who qualified on a credit basis; many of these were not CNB customers at the time.) Third, BankAmericard became the basis for selling and processing other services provided by the bank. Finally, it was an essential step in CNB's desire to provide a comprehensive credit and management information system for the business clients it served. The management of CNB believed that a bank that could develop a credit system that would enable the medium-size retailer to compete effectively with the giants of retailing would receive the patronage of this important group and would help them remain a vital business force.

CNB management believed that the BankAmericard might be a unifying customer service with which CNB could achieve its total customer satisfaction goal. Reese commented:

> The City National BankAmericard credit card program is a good example of this emphasis on the customer. Now, it may not be the answer for everyone, but it does provide a more convenient way to buy things and pay for things for many people. It does provide a very real and competitive service to most merchants. And it does take banking one step closer to providing customers with a complete bill paying and money management service.

It may be that the credit card will become the major bank service through which all the customer's money business will be handled. The simple little piece of plastic could eventually be used to feed information directly into the computer. They do tie together.

Line-O-Credit

CNB management decided to constantly improve the BankAmericard in line with their policy of adding new services in the Billpayer Plan (see Figure 17–2). One of these was the Line-O-Credit, which permitted customers to write their own loan with their own checkbook, for whatever purpose the money was needed, and at their own convenience. Figure 17–3 shows how the concept was promoted. CNB became the first bank in the nation to include the complete legal agreement for the Line-O-Credit in their newspaper advertising. CNB management hoped to allay some of the fears consumers have of borrowing from a bank.

Color Photo Identification

In March, 1968, CNB became the first bank in the United States to announce that its credit cards would carry a positive identification system featuring a color photograph of the patron on each BankAmericard and a sealed coding system. The management department had approached the Polaroid Corporation and had asked them to work with the bank in developing the system, and the two companies jointly announced the program in Columbus. The event received major segments of time on local news media and received news stories and advertising in the major banking publications of the nation. The implementation of the photographing process was accomplished in the spring of 1968 at the branches of CNB and was accompanied by a creative advertising campaign. The net result was not only to provide a positive identification system but also to give an important promotional push that stimulated usage of the card and brought many new patrons into the branches of the bank.

In assessing the value of the BankAmericard program, CNB management felt that the benefits of the card went far beyond customer service and direct profitability to the bank. Management felt that the program had produced a synergistic effect upon the total marketing and operations activities of the bank.

Proposed New Programs

Banks in general have been conservatively managed and have lacked a consumer orientation. By 1968, however, a few banks were investigating and adding new programs and services in an attempt to develop consumer orientation. The management of CNB believed that in addition to pioneering new services themselves they should be aware of the potential of services being developed by other progressive banks. Some of the services that they were considering or that other banks were already developing are described following. A number of research projects were needed to determine which of these services were important to consumers and which ones could be profitably undertaken by CNB.

Total Financial Servicing

One of the programs mentioned most often by banking officials throughout the United States was a total financial service for customers. This meant that the bank would pay utility bills and insurance premiums and make transfers to systematic savings plans. In addition, the bank would keep records of various types for the customer and would assist in other ways in the development of a complete money management system. In return for a basic fee, the bank would endeavor to provide every financial service and information about the services. This could be incorporated in the BankAmericard and include automatic loans, an overdraft system, and whatever other services the customer needed. The concept of a total financial service had been researched by an Eastern bank using focused group interviews. That bank found little acceptance for the idea, except among high-income executives. Other banks had begun to implement parts of the program, however, and believed that it would be very successful.

Mutual Funds and Insurance

One of the largest banks in the United States announced that it had purchased a mutual fund and had developed plans to market the fund through the branch banking system. This encountered legal difficulties that in 1968 were still unsolved. Other banks, however, were already considering offering mutual funds and other types of investments to their banking customers.

Several banks were developing a comprehensive insurance sales program to be added to the regular services provided by the bank. In Wisconsin, one bank had added a complete service—selling life, casualty, and property insurance. This encountered resistance from area insurance agents, and was withdrawn. Later the service was reinstated and appeared to be on its way to becoming a profitable division of the bank. CNB, like most banks, was already selling credit life insurance and found it to be highly profitable. CNB management wondered if there were psychological variables that would discourage consumers from buying insurance or mutual funds from their banker.

Minibanks

In Boston, a major bank had recently developed a system of satellite or "minibanks." These were banks of less than one thousand square feet manned by a staff of two or three persons. To reduce security problems, they included no safe deposit boxes and included only a small amount of cash. The investment was very small for these banks, and they were viewed by some of the banks considering them as a possible step to an era when there would be no branch banks, at least as traditionally known. At the present time, however, minibanks were used as supplementary to regional branch banks that offered full services. The minibanks could pay off all investments and return a profit of 10 to 15 percent a year within a five-year period. There was considerable question about the effect of cultural trends on acceptance of the minibank.

In-Home Services

A proposal already adopted by some banks was the concept of in-home banking. In its initial stages, officers or employees of the bank would visit customers to determine what services were now unused that might be useful to the customer. There were also numerous proposals that banks establish in-home remote computer stations that would allow customers to check balances, transact business of many kinds, and use the bank's computer for other tasks. The question again was whether the American culture would accept this innovation, and, if so, the question was what would be the speed of acceptance.

Cashless-Checkless Society

Throughout the banking industry, proposals were prevalent for an era when checks would no longer be needed or, at least be needed in fewer instances. The exchange of money would be through electronic credits, and accounts would receive information about transactions and deposits as they occurred. Consumers would simply give their "credit card" to the retailer in exchange for merchandise, the card would be inserted into a computer remote station connected to the bank, and the customer's account would be updated immediately. A national magazine imagined how "electronic" money might affect our lives.

When One Credit Card Fills the Bill[1]

> Here's what life might be like in a world of electronic money and the "third man."
>
> Your whole relationship with your bank has changed; you rarely appear there in person. Your personal credit rating is programmed into the

[1] Reprinted with special permission from "Money Goes Electronic in the 1970's," *Business Week*, January 13, 1968, p. 61.

bank's computer, which keeps tabs on your debt load and makes decisions on additional loans up to the prescribed limits for your rating. The rating is reviewed regularly and upgraded in line with your salary increases and equity positions, or downgraded if you go too heavily into debt or fail to pay your bills.

You pay very few bills yourself. You've arranged for the bank to make many of the big payments automatically—on your house, car, insurance, electric and telephone charges. The computer also pays you your salary and makes all tax and other deductions. It plunks some of the remainder into a savings account, and perhaps another piece into a mutual fund.

Convenient

To find out what's in your account, you slip your bank card into your home videophone data terminal and key in the appropriate code numbers. After a quick identity check, the computer at the other end is ready for your command. You tap out a request to see your accounts, and an up-to-the-minute bank statement flashes on the viewing screen.

Before you is a profile of your entire financial status, from the balance in your savings account and your mutual fund holdings to the residue of your mortgage. Listed, too, are all payments made in the last week, plus the prearranged payments due to be made in the next week, and a projection of deposits, after deductions, from your employer. It looks good. You can afford that badly needed suit.

Pocket money

Finding you have no cash when you leave the house, you stop at the change booth on the corner: You'll need some for chewing gum, to tip the cab driver, and to slip a dollar to the elevator operator who is also a numbers bookie. You insert your card in the change booth slot and tap out the amount of coins and bills you need. Then you head for the men's store.

Meantime, your wife is studying a catalogue of kitchen equipment and decides she is finally going to buy that new laser gadget. At the data terminal she keys in the number to reach the retailer, then the numbers of the item.

The retailer, perhaps through his own bank's computer, verifies your wife's identity against her own card, checks your credit rating, and closes the deal. Your wife decides to pay "cash," so the store's bank contacts your bank, computer to computer, and your account is instantly debited.

At the men's shop, you decide on a suit and the salesman ushers you to the store's data video-phone. The salesman inserts your card and taps out the details of the transaction. With lightning speed, the store's bank contacts your bank to identify you and gets a go-ahead on the sale. You've specified a "cash" purchase to get the discount. But the data terminal lights up bright red, meaning "insufficient funds." You light up, too.

Frustrations

"There's been a mistake!" you shout. You ask for another look at your account. There's been no mistake, of course. There's an outrageously large entry, new since you left home, from a kitchen appliance dealer. Now you must make a credit arrangement for, say, a month.

Perhaps your bank computer will compare the "cash" discount with the interest rates on your line of credit and savings account and advise you on your next move; otherwise you'll have to do the complex calculations in your head.

The salesman might also offer to arrange for you a contractual credit plan with a finance company, but this month his shop would rather extend the credit itself and get the discount. So he keys in the arrangement. Thirty days later, your bank will automatically transfer funds to the store's account. The whole deal has taken no more than a couple of minutes.

The Federal Reserve system in 1968 had already developed test market situations to try to determine consumer reaction to an electronic money system. The executives of CNB felt a definite need for competent appraisals and rigorous consumer research to evaluate the feasibility or time table for entering the cashless-checkless society. There was also the question of whether the "change agent" in promoting these innovations should be an individual bank or some other organization such as the Federal Reserve Board or the American Banking Association.

Central Data Files

One of the problems typically found in banking is that banks do not know how many customers they have. Each account is recorded separately, and generally there is no record of which checking account customers also have passbook savings accounts, trust relationships, loans, and so forth. Sometimes an individual might have a small checking account but may be an officer in a corporation having large balances with the bank. Most banks have no systematic record of such facts, however. In addition, some customers have more than one account of a given type. By the mid-sixties, it was clear to some banks that it would be useful to establish a consumer monitoring system that would permit the bank to know the total banking relationship that existed between a customer and the bank.

In 1968, the National Cash Register Company of Dayton, Ohio, introduced its Century series of computers with a Central Information File (CIF) software package designed specifically for banks. This package made it possible to randomly access a customer account and retrieve, either through an instant video system or through hard copy, the total relationship of the bank with a customer. The files contain almost every conceivable bit of information about the accounts that the customer presently maintains or has previously maintained. In addition, the files permit inclusion of many items of external data. A small sampling of the information available for consumer research includes the following items:

Sex	SIC of employer
Children (number and ages)	Rent or own home
Marital status	Transaction history (all accounts)
Credit rating	Reason accounts closed
Occupation	Dun and Bradstreet rating
Zip code	Income range
Census tract	Interest paid last year
Opening officer	Real estate taxes paid last year
Birthdates of family	

The software package had a complete set of management report options with which a bank could cross-classify the segments of its business by any variable in the CIF. For example, if the bank wanted to know the age distribution of its passbook savings accounts, it could place an inquiry in the computer and receive such a report. If it wanted to determine those accounts with large demand deposit accounts but no other relationships, that could easily be reported. Also, the computer could be programed to produce promotional outputs such as letters addressed personally to each customer on their birthday or on the occasion of his children's entering college or on other special occasions. Another feature of the CIF was the capacity to treat a customer as a "net account"; that is, the balance and profitability of a *customer* could be assessed rather than the balance and profitability of an *account,* which is only a fractional representation of the customer.

From the customer's perspective, CNB management felt that CIF would provide much improved service as well as more efficient marketing research. Reese commented:

> It's this computer opportunity that excites me. Imagine, as a customer, getting a statement every month that spells out all of the things the bank did for you that month. You'll receive a complete report on your family financial status, including a listing of all the bills paid for you, the amount added to your savings, the balance on your mortgage loan, or the status of your income tax deductions.

Although the technical feasibility of the CIF offered no serious difficulties, the problem faced by CNB was how best to use the information contained in the file. They needed to answer the questions of how to gather the external data, how much of the information to relay to customers, and in what ways the information could be used to solve research questions.

Marketing Research Activities

Of the 14,000 banks in the United States in 1968, the number with marketing research departments probably was no more than a few dozen. However, CNB had been conducting research of various kinds of several years and, in 1967, appointed John Russell to take charge of their research activities. The marketing research group consisted of Russell and the assistance of two marketing analysts. These analysts worked on research projects as needed but had other duties. The marketing research group serviced the advertising department, headed by Ron Castell and the planning department, which was under the supervision of John Shea. All these personnel reported to Fisher, vice president in charge of marketing, who reported directly to the president and the chairman of the board. The marketing department was in the process of being enlarged to include additional functions and staff.

Prior to 1968 the marketing research activities had focused upon branch analysis and planning and upon image measurement among various market segments. There was an increasing need by 1968, however, for increased understanding of consumer decision processes as they applied to banking services and to the marketing mix of CNB. Although CNB was possibly the smallest bank in the nation with a major marketing research program, management had already demonstrated its interest and commitment to the research area. The task that lay ahead was to determine the organization and research activities that were needed to prepare the bank for changes in the environment and in the bank's offering.

Problem

CNB in the past six years had built one of the most impressive records of growth and profitability of any bank in the nation. This was accomplished by aggressive and imaginative programs to serve customers better. As top management pondered the future, they recognized that the problem of being customer-oriented would become more and more challenging because of the dramatic shifts in population and income. At the same time, management realized that the rewards would also be greater for the bank that was most effective in developing its consumer offering.

The marketing department of CNB was charged with the responsibility for developing a comprehensive information and planning system for insuring that the bank maintained and improved its consumer orientation. In 1968 they were attempting to answer the question of how this could best be accomplished.

Questions

1. What are the primary reasons a consumer chooses a particular bank in preference to a competing bank?

2. Develop a proposal for a continuing consumer research program for the bank to provide inputs for the marketing decisions that CNB management must make.

3. What new services should CNB provide for its customers? Justify your decision in terms of maintaining the bank's excellent past profit performance.

4. Does the CIF appear to offer enough value to CNB to justify its purchase? Specify in detail the marketing programs that would be affected by the CIF and how CIF would contribute to greater effectiveness in obtaining the bank's objectives.

The Homemaker and Home Furnishings[2]

The objective of this study is to investigate the motivations and behavior that affect the purchase of home furnishings. It shows how the homemaker sees her needs and desires and how she makes decisions in the purchase of home furnishings. Because the housewife is the principal customer for home furnishings, it is important for manufacturers, retail outlets, and advertisers to know how the housewife functions, why home furnishings are important to her, and what brings her to market and to a purchasing decision.

Research Methodology

Research Objectives

This study investigates the following dimensions of motivation and behavior as it relates to the purchase of home furnishings:

[2] This case is based on selected excerpts from a study prepared for the Home Furnishings Marketing & Research Council by Social Research, Inc., of Chicago.

1. *The home environment.* How do families define and utilize their homes? Which rooms are most important and why? What are the overall home environments and life styles that the homemaker is trying to bring about?

2. *Role of advertising.* How do housewives use the communications media in coming to their decisions about home furnishings? What are the functions of the various media? How do women use and evaluate the information they obtain from media?

3. *The shopping experience.* Eventually the housewife comes to the market. Where does she shop? How does she go about it? What does she want in the shopping experience and how does she think it works out?

Research Methods

The study was conducted in several phases beginning in the spring of 1966 and continuing throughout most of the year. Several research methods were employed. The basic approach was personal interviews in which women were asked to tell in their own words what their views and experiences were. All respondents were asked about their homes and their attitudes about furnishing it. Selected subsamples were asked about recent purchases and about the role of advertising.

Sample

A total of 806 women were interviewed. Respondents were selected on the basis of convenience and were assigned quotas in order to obtain representation in a variety of geograhpical areas, communities, social classes, and stages of homemaking experience.

Type of Study

This is a qualitative rather than a quantitative study. With few exceptions it does not indicate the number of women who do one thing or another. Instead, it attempts to define the various points of view that women have, their feelings and wishes, and how they go about trying to satisfy them.

Home Environment

This section presents the general motivations, attitudes, and values that housewives have about their homes and their home furnishings.

The Homemaker Has Great Aspirations for Home Furnishings

To most housewives the home is a major area of concern, of hopes and dreams. Most women aspire to a home and home furnishings well beyond what they currently have. They may not complain, and they may praise their present homes, but typically they think of other objects, other styles, other colors, and so on, that would move beyond the present to that "dream home." When asked to choose between new furnishings, entertainment and recreation, a new or a second car, or new clothes, about half chose new furnishings.

Home Is to Be Loved, Used, and Displayed

The American home is a place that is warmly loved and intensively used by almost everyone in the family. There are some exceptions, of course. The home and its furnishings are often a source of dissatisfaction, and some areas of the home may be distinctly "unlovable" or "off-limits" so far as family use or enjoyment are concerned. Generally, however, homemakers feel a need to emphasize how the home and its furnishings are used and loved by everyone in the family. This is what makes a home a home—it is what characterizes a successful homemaker. It is, in fact, one of the ideals of the American homemaker.

Housewives are aware, however, of another important function of the home; it serves as a showpiece, a thing to behold and display with pride. Although women take pride in their home, they are reluctant to admit they do so for the purpose of making a "display" of it. They tend to feel it is bad to use a home for display purposes if this suggests nagging their families to stay out of certain rooms or not to touch certain furnishings. They deny this quality in themselves primarily because it runs counter to prevailing norms, namely, that the home is to be used, enjoyed, and loved by the entire family.

Thus, there is a real or potential conflict between the housewives' ideal of freely using and enjoying the home and their personal wish to preserve it— clean, fresh, unmarred—as a symbol of worth and beauty to self, family, friends, and the world at large. Homemakers who feel relatively confident of their ability to handle this conflict tend to be the most enthusiastic about the merits of acquiring new and better furnishings.

Homemakers who have a special recreation room feel much better able to resolve this conflict between home-for-use and home-for-display. A family room, a dining room, or a spare bedroom that can be converted into a den does much to reassure the homemaker that she can both meet the family's needs and her own wish to be able to "show off" part of the house.

The Home Symbolizes Success and the Good Life (or Failure)

Housewives look upon a well or nicely furnished home as proof of being able to live the "good life." A woman whose home is well furnished at least by the standards of her friends and neighbors is looked upon as better off and luckier than others. She is felt to be envied and socially sought after. She is seen as enjoying and benefiting from the material blessings that are bestowed by the economy. To be able to participate in this good life by acquiring better furnishings is a strong, underlying motive of many housewives.

Women are generally aware of what would constitute a next-step-up in acquiring "better" furnishings. They acquire this awareness from the stories, articles, and advertisements that they have seen in the mass media, and from the displays that they observe in retail stores.

Some housewives feel that they are making headway toward a better furnished home; others do not. Both, however, show considerable personal involvement with their furnishings and have a tendency to measure their own worth and status in life in terms of the quality and appearance of these furnishings.

Change and Desire for Change Precipitates Buying

Housewives move toward their goals at an irregular pace. Shopping for home furnishings is not one of her regular activities. Occasionally she feels a pressing need for change, for something fresh and new. She feels that something is wrong or missing in the home.

Shopping for household furnishings is one of the more important shopping events in the life of the housewife. It is viewed as an occasion for excitement and hope, fear and uncertainty, discovery and fulfillment. It is a time for reconciling dreams with reality—for realizing some dreams, discarding others, and finding new ones. It is a time for resolving social relationships and for thinking about a way and a style of life involving self and family. It is a time for redeciding what one is to be and to do, and how one is to appear in the eyes of the world.

The sense that something is "wrong" comes gradually and often arises from the homemaker's own feelings, independent of external pressures or events. A particular item becomes insufferably shabby over time or, even when in good condition, so dull and "blah" that the sight of it can no longer be tolerated.

More commonly, housewives attribute the inadequacy of the furnishings to changing external circumstances. Although internal needs may be involved, the decision seems much more justifiable and satisfying if it can be attributed to external circumstances, for it is then no longer a matter of personal whim or "selfishness." These external circumstances most often involve changes of occupants, job, or residence.

New furnishings become more essential when new people come into the household, or leave, or alter their way of life. The prospect of a new baby, the death or departure of a family member, maturing children, a special guest or visitor, a new hobby or recreational activity—all these seem to call for something new in the household to honor, facilitate, or symbolize. In such situations, the housewife is apt to rationalize that such furnishings are really not for her, that they are for the happiness and well-being of the baby, the growing children, her husband, the aging relative, the special guest. Actually, however, she is very much personally involved with these furnishings and brings to bear all her standards and tastes in selecting them; for she perceives them as saying a great deal about what kind of a person she is and how well she performs her various roles—mother, wife, daughter, hostess.

A new job, promotion, or raise in pay are also viewed as a fitting occasion for purchasing new furnishings. It seems right to the homemaker that her husband's success should be translated into a more gratifying standard of living, as exemplified by the furnishings. The entire family can see, use, and enjoy the new possessions. Friends, neighbors, and relatives can be made aware of, and impressed by, this visible evidence of success.

Remodeling or moving is the most compelling reason for buying new furnishings. This kind of change occurs because women tend to firmly believe that household furnishings must be fitted or adapted to the physical layout and mood of the house or apartment.

Change precipitates more change. The purchase of an item—especially if it is thought to represent a step upward in furnishings for the home—causes the older items to be perceived as less adequate, leading to a need to purchase some replacements, in turn leading to a need to purchase still more, and so on, until the area has been fairly completely, or completely, redone.

Shopping Begins at Home

Typically women begin shopping for furniture in the home before they enter a store intending to buy. This in-home shopping takes many forms: referring to media, advertising, brochures and catalogs; consulting with the husband, friends, and neighbors; and considerable thinking about various alternative ways to solve the problem.

Interestingly, many women never stop shopping for furniture. Even when they have no immediate intention to buy, or have definitely decided to do no buying at all, they observe and appraise furnishings in the homes of others, in the store as they walk through the department, in the homes shown in "shelter magazines," television, stores, newspaper ads, and so on. Very often this is the kind of background information and opinion that women first rely on when they begin to decide what they want to attain or avoid in their "active" shopping.

When she feels ready, or nearly ready, to make a purchase, she wants to update and/or reevaluate the information and attitudes resulting from her continuous "fantasy" shopping. Above all, she wants to be able to compare and study alternatives, side by side rather than widely separated in space and time, as most of her previous impressions of styles, colors, and materials have been.

The Role of Advertising

Home furnishings advertising is very important to women. It keeps them informed and up-to-date, it stimulates them, and it often serves to get them to do something about their homes. The various roles that advertising plays in the home furnishings purchase decision process are outlined below.

Women Want to Know

In general, women are very responsive and sensitive to home furnishings advertising. They think there is a great deal of advertising for home furnishings, and they usually notice a lot of it, even when they are not in the market for specific products. This is because many housewives view it as part of their job or role as a homemaker to know what is going on in the home furnishings field. She accomplishes this in part by observing trends in shelter and women's service magazines, and in other advertising. This general outlook or attitude influences her interest in home furnishings advertising and causes her to identify with it.

Home Furnishings Advertisements Are an Important Information Source

Advertising plays a vital role in the shopping process for home furnishings. This is evident from the comments of housewives when they express their attitudes as to what they want home furnishings to do for them and when they react both favorably and critically to many advertisements that they have seen.

Advertising is expected to provide a variety of kinds of information. Because women use them to keep up on what is happening in the area, as well as for personal guidance, they are interested in much more than mere facts about product availability.

Generally, radio is seen as having the least potential for advertising home furnishings—primarily because the medium is nonvisual in its impact, whereas furnishings are so essentially and gratifyingly visual in their impact. Many women dismiss radio on the grounds that they would have to see the furniture to really be interested. Radio does perform a valuable role, however, in terms of communicating about the store and in discussing home furnishings, particularly the historical background of certain styles, the advantages of certain types of construction or material, the ways to clean or maintain furnishings, and so forth. The newspaper is a medium that women take quite seriously and make frequent use of in their shopping activities. However, this medium has some disadvantages for the advertiser. When homemakers were asked to recall some examples of poor advertising that they had seen, they often replied that the only examples that they could think of were newspaper ads. This is the only medium that was singled out for criticism. The shortcomings that women find in newspapers are twofold: (1) They find the quality of the paper and of the advertisement in general to be cheap and unrealistic and generally inferior to what they find in magazines. (2) They look upon the newspapers as the retailers' medium, and for these women this suggests the likelihood of poor home furnishings ads, lacking in eye and idea appeal, quality, and integrity.

Housewives generally feel that magazines do the most to make home furnishings seem especially important and desirable. The quality of the paper, illustrations, and color makes this medium seem preeminent. Also important is the home environment setting and the editorial material of the magazine.

Magazine advertising, however, does not appeal to all women. Some, especially those of the lower class, feel excluded by the wonder and excitement of the advertisements and see it as evidence that it could never rightfully be in their home. Another shortcoming is that magazine advertising often lacks local-price and local-store information.

Television is regarded as a medium that currently has little place for home furnishings advertisements but that has considerable potential for them. Most current advertising in this medium is felt to be unpleasant and high-pressure. One of the reasons why women feel this is a good potential type of advertising medium is that it can demonstrate furniture in action. This is an important dimension of furnishings that is felt to be lacking in the print media. Another potential is that it could help make home furnishings store appeal seem more personal by letting viewers see the store, its owners, sales personnel, and the way customers are treated. Another potential scene for TV is to show furnishings in an attractive, modern, and a full, lifelike setting.

The major weakness of TV is that advertisements in this medium cannot be studied and reexamined at will. Rather, it is a fleeting thing that is inconsistent with the homemaker's need to think and evaluate.

How the Advertisement Looks at First Glance Is Crucial

Homemakers feel that if what they see at first glance is pleasing in appearance they will then look further into the advertisement, but if it is not, they will not investigate further. When something other than the product dominates the advertisement it has a good chance of being rejected by the viewer.

When there are too many things in the advertisement the reader often becomes confused because there does not appear to be anything of importance. Too much effort seems to be required to interpret the message, and often this type of ad will not seem to be worth the bother.

Homemakers are generally inclined to deal with an advertisement with only one or two dominant visual ideas. An advertisement presenting many items and many pictures or many items in print gives viewers the feeling that the store is more interested in quantity rather than the quality of what is being advertised.

The pictorial elements of an advertisement dominate attention. With the picture the prime attraction, women like the explanatory material to be fairly short. Other things being equal, the shorter the amount of written material, the more likely viewers will be to read it.

The overall appearance of the advertisement does much to determine whether the homemaker will turn away or become involved. The manner in which illustrations, type, space, color, and copy are handled, organized, and interrelated all have a subtle but strong impact on the viewer and can lead her to many decisions about the communication before she really evaluates it.

Color is one of the most attractive attributes of an advertisement. Given a choice between color and a black-and-white ad, a woman would generally feel compelled to look at the colored one. Colors lend mood to furniture, and they often do this more powerfully than its other characteristics. Color makes women feel that they are seeing the furniture in its actuality. Without color, they think they are in the dark about how the materials of the furniture would look in their home.

Color needs to be used with care, however. Too many bright colors may evoke too many strong feelings at once and may seem upsetting and exhausting. Clashing colors tend to give the viewer a distressed feeling that she does not want to duplicate in her home. When color is used to highlight or emphasize something other than the central idea of the advertisement, it distracts attention and causes the ad to become confusing and the main featured furnishings relatively unattractive. Therefore, when color is used in a background, it should not detract by its own strength but should serve to highlight and enrich the central picture by blending or complementing it.

Most housewives prefer photographs to sketches. A poor photograph, however, is seldomly preferred to a sketch. For this reason, many women feel that in newspaper advertisements sketches are superior to photographs.

The best illustrations use contrasts to highlight the featured furnishings. A certain amount of shading gives the feeling of depth, but too much shading can interfere with the real picture of the piece. The realism of the illustration is of utmost importance. Although women like advertisements that show beautiful furnishings, they want the pictures to represent the real furniture. Going to a store and finding that the ad was not a realistic portrayal of the furniture makes women furious and builds up resentment toward the store.

Furniture displayed in a room setting helps a woman to picture how it would look in her own home and how it would serve her purposes. It tempts her more strongly to buy it and to plan the things that seem to go with it. The homelike setting also helps the housewife feel that the advertisement is fulfilling a worthwhile, educational function; for a room setting acts much like an interior decorator. She may feel that the purchase of a new piece of furniture means an alteration in the looks of the whole room. Therefore, she needs to know what changes the new item will make in her home and she wants to know how to decorate in accordance with her personality and family needs. She often looks to furnishing advertisements for such guidance. Room settings give her norms and new ideas that can be utilized in her home.

The type of room setting is also important. The most effective type presents the home environment and style of life that is slightly better than the target audience now has—but not too much better. The homemaker wants to improve her furnishings and move up to a better life. However, the implications of a dramatic improvement is likely to frighten her and to make her feel that the featured furnishings would be unusable and unenjoyable in her case.

People in advertisements are an effective way of attracting attention. The person shown affects the perception of the ad in two different ways. First, the person informs the viewer as to whether or not the advertisement is directed to women of her type. If the person impresses the viewer as being similar to herself and to be the people she normally associates with, or as similar to the type of person she would like to be, the advertisement becomes more relevant and the furnishings become more appealing. Second, if the people in the advertisement appear to be looking at, using, or enjoying the item of furnishing, they help to explain and give meaning to the item. On the other hand, if the people are purely decorative, or simply stuck in the ad, then they serve to distract attention and to imply that the furnishings are of little interest or importance to them.

Shopping Experience

The Purchase Decision Is a Personal, Sometimes Painful Experience

Some degree of anxiety is generally involved in purchasing household furnishings. The housewife has to weigh the main things she has seen and heard from family, friends, media, salesmen, and displays in various stores. She has to relate these to her values, attitudes, and aspirations and to the reality of her own home and financial circumstances. This is complicated by the fact that a purchase decision is in its own way a very personal matter. It is, in a sense, more personal than a dress or hat because, if the latter seems dissatisfying, or receives adverse comment, it can readily be buried in the back of the closet. The home furnishings, however, are on display every day for a long period of time, and they are not easily hidden away or forgotten.

Time and privacy are the two major devices the homemaker uses to cope with her anxiety. She wants to take her time in coming to a decision. At some point in her shopping, she is likely to want the salesman, however helpful he may have been, to go away and let her think in private with one or more objects she has tentatively decided upon. She wants to be able to look at these objects critically and lovingly, and in private. She needs to feel free to evaluate all the factors involved, so as to come up with the best compromise or the perfect solution.

For some women this anxiety can be resolved in the store. The salesman makes his presentation, answers inquiries, and is sent away while she evaluates her problem. Other women need or want still more time and help, preferably in their own homes.

Housewives generally use four major criteria in evaluating home furnishings decisions. These are:

1. The elements of style, beauty, and appearance are among the most important factors influencing purchase decisions.

2. Easy care and maintenance are also important. Whatever information the shopper has that suggests a particular style, color, material, or will be easier for her to clean or maintain, guides her as an important reason for deciding on that item. This is especially true if she has children or teenagers about the house.

3. Another criterion is durability and cost, the two being closely related in the housewife's mind. Durability justifies cost. The cost can seem less insurmountable if she can justify it in terms of greater durability.

4. The fourth criterion concerns the compatibility of the new objects with the old furnishings at home. Here the housewife faces a basic dilemma; should she strive for compatibility or should she buy the new item that is incompatible with her current furnishings in the hope that someday the balance of the room will be changed and made compatible with the item that she is considering. The way that a homemaker resolves this dilemma depends on how conservative she is and what she expects the family's future financial state will be. Older women, for example, are apt to feel that this may be one of their last purchases and, therefore, attempt to achieve compatibility with what presently exists. Most women, however, are basically optimistic and expect that their husbands will eventually allow them to buy the additional furnishings that will allow compatibility.

Transaction Should Be Completed Quickly

Once the woman has passed through her ordeal of making the best selection, the tempo of her mood and behavior changes drastically. No longer does she want patience; rather, she wants everything to move at a fast pace. She wants the order written up quickly and wants the credit arrangements taken care of smoothly and unquestioningly.

Housewives are particularly distressed when credit arrangements require them to deal with a third party such as a bank or loan company. They dislike this because it suggests to them some time lag, and they feel apprehensive about dealing with these institutions and coping with what they perceive to be complicated legal and financial matters. Moreover, they dislike having to turn the matter over to their husbands because they are likely to be not too happy at having to deal with a bank, and, as a consequence, the husband may be frustrated enough either to call off the transaction or at least to indicate disapproval of what the wife has done.

Prompt Delivery Is Important

Women become very frustrated when a promised delivery date is broken. Repeated frustrations of this sort can result in a highly emotional, negative attitude that lingers long after the purchase is actually in the home. The housewife has invested so much importance in this event and she has looked forward to it with such hope and anxiety that she finds it very difficult to overlook the big letdown that a broken delivery date provokes.

Payoff: How Does It Look at Home?

After the new item has been delivered and put into its proper place, a period of evaluation and validation begins. The homemaker needs to evaluate her purchase to determine whether, in its intended setting, it does create the impression and image she had hoped and imagined it would. In making this evaluation, she uses the opinions of others—husband, children, friends, neighbors—to validate her taste and judgment.

The opinions of others are very important to her in evaluating her success as a shopper. The new item often becomes a conversation piece when friends visit the home. A woman cherishes the approval of these visitors and often relishes the envy she suspects they have. She seldom reports derogatory remarks by visitors, but, when she does, she feels a need to demolish them.

Thus, the homemaker uses the comments and presumed attitudes of others to cement her own feelings of satisfaction about what she has chosen for her home. One of the most valued opinions she needs at this time is that of her husband. If the husband favors what she has done, if he shares her feelings of pride, then she can relax in the knowledge that everything has gone well. Her taste and judgment, and indeed her entire role as a homemaker, seem to her to be reflected in the new furnishings.

Perceived Attributes of the "Ideal Store"

As housewives talk about the various stores in which they have shopped and talk about the things they find especially pleasing or disappointing, they paint a picture of what the ideal outlet should be like. The ideal store should:

1. Have an extensive selection of goods in stock—a full range of styles, colors, materials, and prices.

2. Have information and illustrations pertaining to items not stocked and indicate a willingness to order these if the homemaker is so inclined.

3. Segregate furnishings by room and by style.

4. Add settings to provide a sense of being at home—for example, carpets, accessories, and draperies displayed along with sofas, chairs, and other living room furniture to give the feel of an integrated home.

5. Provide ample room for moving about so that the shopper can look at and touch furnishings without having to stumble and crawl over various sundry things.

6. Feature on-the-spot and/or in-the-home counseling services—with color charts, samples of fabrics, and so forth, and an interior decorator or specialist who seems like a real professional.

7. Have a convenient location, parking, and shopping hours.

8. Guarantee quick delivery but not make promises that cannot be fulfilled.

9. Have a management that will stand in back of its merchandise, readily replacing any item that is damaged or otherwise unsatisfactory.

10. Provide store financing arrangements that do not require the buyer to deal with an outside loan company.

11. Have a management that keeps its personnel in line, seeing to it that they are more interested in the shopper and her problems than in selling or pushing a particular item.

Store Loyalty

Shoppers do not have a sense of loyalty to any particular store, even when they have been thoroughly satisfied with their purchase and shopping experience. Although they indicate an intention to try the store again, it is usually one of several stores that would be considered.

Questions

1. Evaluate the methodology used in the study.

2. Use the results of the study to recommend marketing strategies for manufacturers and retailers of home furnishings.

Quality Builders: Decision-Making Process in Buying a New Home

Most builders in the Columbus, Ohio, market offer somewhat conventional home designs, and a few build custom homes that can only be described as "far out" contemporary. Therefore, a need existed for new designs that were not stereotyped while, at the same time, attaining a blend of the old and the new. Quality Builders (QB), founded by two young Ohio State University graduates, features what is now known as "full environment design." As such, it is not opposed to any established style but is an approach in engineering and art form that seeks to minimize stylistic restrictions and stereotypes. The essential point of differentiation is that family needs and desires are paramount, and the style recommended helps the family to achieve its goals by reflecting tastes and habits of each member.

---

[3] Qualstan is now building only in Worthington Hills, which was originally their development; several builders are now active there.

The success of QB has surpassed expectations, but management felt the need for definitive survey evidence documenting the type of people who buy QB homes, their life styles, their desires, and their response to their home. Of special importance is assessment of differences, if any, between QB buyers and those who have patronized competitive builders in the Franklin county (Ohio) market.

In more detail, survey objectives focused on the criteria that house purchasers use in making a decision to buy a new home. This gives rise to such questions as the reasons for moving, the time of the house purchase, the relative importance of such factors as location and design, location selection factors, design preferences, builder selection factors, and evaluation of builders in Franklin county.

Methodology

Research Design
The objective of the study was to find what criteria were used in selecting a new house. The exploratory research design was adopted, as it is particularly suited to the search for new ideas or relationships. No formal design could be established because too little was known about the above criteria to permit the drawing of basic hypotheses. The advantage of the exploratory design was that it enabled the problem to be defined and suggested areas to be investigated more thoroughly. The method of attack was a cross-sectional survey of recent home buyers.

Data Collection
The market research information was gathered from primary sources, that is, from formal personal interviews of recent home buyers, using a formal questionnaire. In these personal interviews a series of set questions was asked and various responses secured. This method of data collection is well adapted to somewhat lengthy, detailed questionnaires, such as the one actually used. It is also applicable to exploring a variety of subject matters, including personal attitudes, where other types of questions or observations might be prematurely terminated.

Sampling
The universe from which the samples were drawn was composed of all homeowners in northern Franklin county who had purchased their homes within the past two years. The house and lot valuation ranged only between $20,000 and $50,000. This represented the approximate building area and price range of houses handled by QB.

The sample size for this research was determined by the time and manpower available. A total of 220 homeowners were interviewed, which was a large enough sample to allow statistical analysis to be made.

The total sample was comprised of two subsamples: one subsample was QB homeowners and the other subsample was non-QB homeowners. The sizes of the subsamples were 21 and 199, respectively.

Using the Homeowners Association's records of home purchases as a source, an unrestricted-random-sample method was used to secure the subsample of other homeowners from the closely defined universe. The QB subsample was also considered randomly selected in the statistical analysis inasmuch as twenty-one of the possible fifty-two QB homeowners were interviewed. The random factor occurs in the way that the QB homeowners were actually contacted or not contacted purely by chance. Thus, the QB subsample retains some degree of the randomness required for valid statistical analysis.

Field Work

The length of the interview was limited to approximately twenty minutes to reduce the respondent's anxiety concerning the time involved in answering questions.

When people were not at home, an attempt was made to contact them at a later time. If the recontact was not successful, another sample unit was obtained from a reserve list of addresses created by intentional oversampling, that is, by securing a larger total number of addresses than required for the initial contacts.

Analysis

A frequency distribution was compiled, giving the total number of responses —classified by QB homeowners (QB subsample) and other homeowners (other subsample)—to the various questions and subquestions. An IBM 1620 computer was utilized to secure appropriate preliminary statistical information. A frequency distribution of answers was used to indicate which responses apparently warranted further statistical analysis.

The basis used in this survey for determining whether an observed relationship was statistically significant was that the relationship would not occur by chance more than five times out of a hundred (this is refered to as the "95 percent confidence level"). If a reasonably important relationship was observed between the two samples, occasionally it was incorporated into the findings of this report, even though this difference lacked statistical significance at the 95 percent confidence level. This was considered to be justified because of the exploratory nature of the research.

Limitations

Because of the exploratory nature of the research and the fact that no specific hypotheses were tested, the reader must be cautioned against making unwarranted assumptions based on this report. It should be remembered that the objective of the survey was to discover probable new house selection criteria and to develop specific hypotheses for possible additional research. The data was secured in October, 1967, from recent buyers of $20,000 to $50,000 residences (house and lot) in northern Franklin county; thus the conclusions should not be extended beyond the scope of the survey.

Findings

Because of space limitations, detailed survey results could not be included. Hence, findings are reported in narrative form.

Reasons for Moving

Why do people move? Why do they give up their familiar surroundings to venture forth in the quest of a new house?

Although change of employment location was the most important reason that other homeowners purchased another house, it was the *least* important factor for QB homeowners. This, of course, is a noncontrollable factor so far as any builder is concerned. QB has not had to contend with this situation and thus is able to rely upon other factors to secure house buying prospects to a much greater degree than other builders.

The survey indicated that almost three fourths of the QB homeowners had lived in Franklin county for five or more years and that almost 40 percent of these homeowners looked for a new house for twelve months or longer. It is revealing to find that long-term residents of Franklin county made a somewhat extensive search for their house (and builder) as a considered purchase without excessive time pressures bearing on them. In contrast to this, one third of the purchasers of other homeowners looked for less than one month before they found their builder and/or house, and a cumulative total of over 50 percent of these homeowners looked for three months or less. These findings are reinforced by the fact that almost 72 percent of the QB homeowners purchased their houses before construction began, as compared with less than 43 percent of the other homeowners doing so. Thus, the buying decision process was apparently longer than that associated with other homeowners.

Purchasers of houses in Franklin county indicated that a desired change in home size was another primary motivation for buying a new house. Both QB homeowners and other homeowners ranked this as the number-one reason for moving. Although there is no significant difference between QB homeowners and other homeowners in this measurement, it should not be overlooked. Spaciousness also appears to be a compelling appeal to the total market for new residential housing. Increased spaciousness can be roughly equated with higher costs, so there is considerable relevance in the next most indicated reason for moving, that is "could afford a more expensive home."

QB homeowners were much more concerned with house design and room style than other homeowners. A desired change in these factors was given second and third ranking, respectively, on the moving list. This ranking may suggest that the innovative design approach adopted by QB has considerable merit for securing sales for the company.

Change in the size of family had about equal ranking merit with both QB and other homeowners. This may be a slightly more compelling motivation for QB homeowners inasmuch as they tended to be somewhat younger than the other homeowners and presumably were in a less-advanced growth stage of the family unit cycle. The somewhat younger QB homeowners also were three times more evident in the slightly lower income bracket of $7500 to $10,000 (19 percent versus 6.4 percent).

QB homeowners were somewhat more interested in changing neighborhoods, and pleasing appearance of the neighborhood was considered very important by practically all of the respondents.

Time to Purchase

The building cycle necessarily dictates the builder's approach to the consumer, that is, from one of maximum design discretion during the "before" construction stage to that of a convincing presentation of the speculatively built, finished product in the "after" construction stage. The builder would do well to decide which approach (or balance thereof) should be utilized, because this decision will affect his sales efforts and construction schedules.

The total survey produced a somewhat even split between "before" and "after" construction, giving a bimodel configuration to the building cycle selection time. However, in the case of the QB homeowners, 72 percent purchased their houses before they were built, with less than 29 percent buying speculatively built QB houses. No QB homeowners purchased during the building cycle; either they wanted to start from the ground up or to wait for the finished results.

Speculative building would appear to have less merit for QB than for other builders. It is axiomatic, however, that a builder needs to have some showcase houses to demonstrate his expertise as well as to secure a share of the prospects who do not want to become involved in the construction of their house and/ or do not remain in the market very long before making a house buying decision. Market demand and the individual builder's financial strength would help to establish a reasonable number of completed houses that the builder should have on hand.

Style and design of home the builder constructs was one of the most important builder selection factors indicated by the survey. This presupposes that there are some fully constructed houses that can be seen and evaluated by the prospective buyer. Any house, whether occupied or not, can be judged to some extent simply by driving past it. Interior style and design, however, is quite another consideration. Few homeowners want to be a showroom for subsequent prospects unless this is agreed upon in advance, and then there is usually some financial consideration involved. When consumers are committing themselves to the largest investment in their lifetimes, they are usually interested in close-up evaluation of the finished results of previous builder efforts.

Almost 51 percent of the other homeowners looked for their houses for three months or less, and 28.5 percent of QB homeowners did so. Inasmuch as the minimum house building time is approximately ninety days, if everything goes right, it appears that the majority of these "lookers" would be the ones most interested in the completed house purchase. They do not take the time, for one reason or another, for a long-term buying decision. Considering the fact that almost 50 percent of the total survey respondents looked for their house for a relatively short time period and that design and quality are such important house selection criteria, speculative building appears to have merit for any area builder, including QB.

The used-house market has a bearing upon the total house selection process, too. Over 60 percent of both QB and other homeowners considered used houses during the time they looked for another house. The realtor had a much better chance of dealing with other homeowners by almost three-to-one. This reflects the greater amount of "before" construction purchasing done by QB buyers in that many realtors are concerned only with used house sales.

There appears to be a lack of extensive comparison house shopping, however. Approximately 43 percent of both QB and other homeowners considered from one to four used houses during their search for the "in-house." Over 40 percent of the QB owners responding indicated they had made an offer for a used house to the owner, as compared with 27 percent of the other homeowners. The percentages of "no offer made" were 59 percent and 73 percent, respectively; thus, the QB homeowner appears to have a greater proclivity for negotiation—whether on a new house or old!

Location, Design, and Builder

Each survey respondent was asked to rank in order of importance the three basic selection criteria of location, design, and builder. Although the overall survey response indicated that location was by far the most important consideration, somewhat different results were obtained when a comparison was made between QB and other homeowners. The latter gave a resounding vote to this factor, but QB homeowners gave design first ranking. The innovative design approach expounded and practiced by this company apparently struck a responsive chord with these owners.

Design is given a clear-cut second ranking by other homeowners; thus it is obvious that design has to be an important consideration for any area builder. Although subsequent findings shed a small amount of light upon some of the components of design, additional research might be undertaken to refine the consumer definition of the term so that the builder may be able to better discern how to fulfill this house selection factor.

QB homeowners were so enamoured with design that they gave it second, as well as first ranking. Location was the next most popular choice for second ranking. Perhaps this middle choice can be inferred from the fact that QB homeowners emphatically ranked design first, and even more emphatically, ranked builder last, thus clearing up some of the apparent confusion in the middle design-location factor, with location earning second place.

Location Selection

How can *location* be better defined? What are its components, and what differences exist between QB and other homeowners? All of those interviewed equally ranked the following location selection components as very important:

1. Pleasing appearance of neighborhood
2. Good reputation of the community
3. High quality of schools
4. City utilities
5. Low noise level
6. Price of neighbors' homes

Other homeowners also considered all these factors very important and also added the following three factors: (1) nearness to schools, (2) sidewalks and curbs, and (3) paved streets.

There was considerable agreement between the two groups on the location factors that were "somewhat important." These included:

1. Nearness to grocery stores
2. Nearness to schools
3. Nearness to shopping areas
4. Low noise level
5. Nearness to work
6. Social class of neighbors
7. Streetlights

QB homeowners considered the following location selection components as *not* important:

1. Nearness to public transportation

2. Nearness to playgrounds

3. Sidewalks and curbs

4. Nearness to friends

5. Nearness to relatives

6. Streetlights

Other homeowners were in agreement on the not-important factors, with the exception of sidewalks and curbs, which they ranked as very important.

Some of the location factors on the total list are controllable by the builder, that is, paved streets and city utilities. Others are only semicontrollable and the remainder are noncontrollable so far as the builder is concerned. The real benefit to the builder will be derived from his attempt to develop an optimumly desirable combination of as many of the very important and somewhat important variables as possible. Tract and/or site selection can be used to capitalize on some of these factors, but no one location will probably be able to satisfy the demands of this imposing composite. Nevertheless, a definable goal is better than no goal at all.

The builder should select the factors most applicable to his situation and structure his sales and advertising presentation accordingly. Over a period of time some of the factors can be interchanged to give variety to the builder's consumer appeals. Obviously, the least important factors should receive little, if any, builder attention.

Perhaps the most revealing factor in the entire listing is the resounding approval of distance between the respondents and their relatives, with the obvious inference being, the farther away, the better. The Biblical admonition that "a man (shall) leave father and mother and shall cleave to his wife. . . ." (Matthew 19:6) has apparently been enthusiastically adopted in suburbia.

The relatively low rating of sidewalks, curbs, and streetlights may reflect the *de facto* absence of these features in the various newly developed areas. Although most areas had paved streets, few also included sidewalks or streetlights.

House Design

The frequency with which the design criterion appears throughout the survey reflects its importance to the new house buyer. Design and quality were the top-ranked factors that were investigated in selecting the actual builder, with custom design and special work done by the builder being ranked closely behind. These three factors were emphasized more strongly by QB homeowners, however, which indicates that these owners were perhaps more discriminating in these selection areas. Since 72 percent of the QB homeowners purchased their house before construction began (42 percent for other homeowners), they apparently exercised the maximum design latitude.

The strong desire of the QB homeowner to have a change in home design and room style (following change in home size) also indicates the intensity of these feelings. The survey attempted to define the idea of style and design, at least in part, by having the respondents consider several statements and then express their degree of agreement or disagreement.

The dominant thought distilled from this attitude listing is that a house should reflect the tastes and living patterns of its owners. Because both groups strongly endorsed this supposition, it would be to the builder's advantage to better determine who he is selling to and to attempt to discern, in general, their mode of living. If this reflection aspect could be tangibly expressed to future prospects, any builder would be able more quickly to establish some rapport with them. Only one such indicative statement was presented, that is, "I like to entertain a lot in my home." The use of the home for a social center probably reflects the more informal entertaining generally engaged in by the residents of suburbia. Only fifteen respondents claimed, in effect, that they liked to do little, if any, entertaining in their home. The balance of the replies in both groups was almost evenly split between the more socially minded "somewhat" and "strongly agree" categories.

Less than 10 percent of the entire sample felt that a house with lots of glass looks cheap. Considerably more from both groups had some reservations, however—24 percent of QB homeowners and 45 percent of other homeowners somewhat agreed to the negative appeal of the overuse of glass. Perhaps the admonition of "doing all things in moderation" has application here. Nevertheless, three fourths of the QB homeowners and 46 percent of the other homeowners strongly disagreed with this contention. It appears, therefore, that lavish use of glass cannot necessarily be considered a detriment to acceptable house design.

Few respondents were enamoured with the row and/or assembly-line house concept in that most of them agreed that they liked a house that stands out from those around it. Most of them also felt that a fireplace makes a room look warm. Perhaps a more meaningful question, at least to the builder, would have been, "How much would you be willing to pay to have a fireplace in your home, considering that this feature adds approximately $600 to the cost of a house?"

More other homeowners felt somewhat strongly that natural wood is not attractive, but even more important was the general agreement by this group that natural wood is difficult to maintain. Thus it appears that maintenance is a problem to a greater extent, so far as other homeowners are concerned, than appearance. Outdoor balconies were more strongly defended by QB homeowners, which probably reflects the greater use of this construction feature in their houses.

Some indication of the relative acceptance of the different house styles can be found in the breakdown of a number of dramatic shifts in housing preferences between the homeowner's previous house and the one occupied (and purchased within the past two years). In the case of QB homeowners, split- and multilevel houses achieved a substantial acceptance. This increase was partially at the expense of $1\frac{1}{2}$ story houses, although the large proportion of no answers given make any meaningful determination extremely difficult.

The emergence of the two-story house is obvious from the other home-owners' responses, accounting for over 50 percent of all the style preferences (that is, purchases). Split-level houses have achieved some popularity, too, but not to the degree of the two-story configuration. Perhaps this indicates that further consideration should be given by QB to the development of one or more such floor-plan arrangements that would be compatible with their over-all design approach.

Builder Selection

The mere fact that selection of the builder was the last of the three criteria indicated in the survey (location-design-builder) did not preclude a somewhat thorough investigation of the builder by the house buying prospect. Many of these builder selection factors are controllable by the builder, which allows him considerable latitude in casting his own image. The five most important builder selection factors are all controllable by the builder himself; only his reputation as expressed by others could be considered a semicontrollable variable. A reputation cannot be bought, it must be "built"!

Quality, style, and design can mean many things to many people. It seems as though the progressive builder should attempt to define these terms (from the consumer's standpoint) and then tangibly express them in the houses that he offers.

Within certain bounds, style and design are corollary attributes that the individual builder selects and then projects to the best of his ability. The contemporary stance adopted by QB represents part of the style and design continuum available. Assuming a reasonably profitable capitalization of this approach, the company may conceivably exploit only this area. As previously mentioned, a promising addition to the line might be a two-story floor plan.

The amount of custom design and special work that the builder will do, of course, affects primarily the "before construction" buyer, and, to a much less extent, the "during construction" buyer. In QB's case, no sales were made to the respondents while houses were being built, but almost 72 percent of the sales were made before construction began. In this circumstance custom design and special work assume much greater importance, and the company has apparently been able to capitalize on these desires through its attempt at "full environment design." Unfortunately the communication of this concept has been received and understood by only 75 percent of the QB homeowners and 8 percent of the other homeowners. Although "success" is only relative, it appears that some better projection should be developed for this corporate philosophy.

The continuing concern for proper workmanship is indicated by the buyers expressed interest in warranties. Some builders have attempted to capitalize on this concern through the means of an elaborate guarantee program (for example, Ryan homes). Other, perhaps smaller, builders probably tend to rely more upon personal responsibility as their "guarantee." Whichever approach is taken by the builder, there must be some recognition of this consumer concern for performance and satisfaction.

The other factors only require *de facto* recognition of their existence and importance inasmuch as the builder has primary control over their execution.

Consumer Awareness of the Builder

How does the consumer first become aware of the builder? The answer to this question can have an important bearing upon the basic marketing strategy of the builder. The rank correlation between the two homeowner groups in builder awareness factors is .63, reflecting to a great extent three major differences in sources of consumer awareness of the builder.

Advertising is apparently QB's most productive lead source, with almost three times as many QB homeowners first learning about this builder as other homeowners learned about their respective builders. The two advertising categories can legitimately be combined to give further credence to the importance of this factor to QB. The two promotional projects (that is, the House of Glass and the House of Magic) undoubtedly increased the total consumer awareness of QB as a builder far more than the lack of recognition of the concept of "total environment design" might indicate.

"Driving around" was less than half as important to QB as to other builders, and none of the QB homeowners stated that they knew the area before hand. This eliminates, to a great extent, happenstance selling; it also may reflect the limited operations of QB compared with the total Franklin county housing market, or other related factors.

Salesmen have a definite place in this initial awareness picture. No attempt was made in the survey to determine whether the salesman was a realtor salesman or a direct salesman for the builder. In many cases, the consumer would probably not be aware of this distinction; this ratio could be significant, however, to the builders who maintain their own direct sales organization.

The third-party recommendation appears to have considerable merit, with about one buyer out of six or seven being made aware of the house and/or builder in this manner. Good will becomes a very tangible factor when considered in these terms. The continuing success of the builder could be due, in part, to his follow-through with his previous house purchasers as well as his actual building effort.

An analysis of consumer satisfaction with builder performance is somewhat revealing. Considering the importance of buyer satisfaction and third-party recommendations to the builder, there are some obvious danger signals in this analysis. Less than 43 percent of QB homeowners are very pleased with QB's job performance, compared with almost 72 percent of the other homeowners expressing great satisfaction. The relative dissatisfaction of QB homeowners is even more positively expressed in that almost 43 percent of them indicate some reticence in making any QB recommendations to others. Over three fourths of the other homeowners apparently have no similar reservations, strongly disagreeing with the idea of nonrecommendation. It appears that QB has some "fence mending" to do if they are to expect the same degree of ownership satisfaction evidenced by the other homeowners.

Competitive Builders in Franklin County

Franklin county is an active residential market and represents a substantial sales potential for area builders. Considering that the survey indicated that 86 percent of QB homeowners and 58 percent of other homeowners previously owned houses within the same area, some marketing direction can be deduced. The area builder materially increases his opportunities for additional sales by making himself known, first, to area residents, and second, to prospects moving into the area. Herein lies a logical rationale for consistent advertising and promotion. Multiple exposures of the builder's name to area residents will enhance their recall when, in fact, they become active prospects for a new house. On the other hand, sporadic advertising and promotion efforts can easily miss their intended mark if their appearance does not correspond to the on-the-scene appearance of the out-of-town prospect.

The more successful builders, in terms of the survey, can readily be deduced from the total list indicated in Table 17–2. No compilation of nonlisted builders was made, although the additional names would probably not materially effect the tabular statistics.

While advertising and promotion are especially important for QB, name exposure alone is not sufficient to ensure adequate sales volume. This is dramatically illustrated in Table 17–2 in that several builders, qualifying as being well known, did not qualify particularly well where it really counts— in signing the contract. The moral of the story is that the builder cannot reasonably rely on any one factor as a guarantee of success.

Within the price and purchase time constrictions of the total sample (see the previous section entitled "Sampling"), Ryan Homes emerges as the sales volume leader with twenty-four respondents listing this company as their builder. Ryan's closing percentage is somewhat spectacular, particularly as one moves from the initial phase of builder-talked-with to the final purchase step of actually-built.

Other builders, such as Ernest G. Fritsche and Virginia Homes, generally meet the sampling requirements at the high end of their pricing scale; their closing percentages would probably improve if lower-priced housing had been considered.

Portrait Homes also showed a good closing ratio (on 60 percent less volume than Ryan, however). The apparent high ranking of QB in this respect is due to the purposive (quota) sampling method used to ensure that the maximum number of these homeowners would be available for analytical purposes. A true random sample would have reduced this QB figure, so it is not included in Table 17–2.

Table 17–2

Competitive Builders

	Recognized	Talked	Built
Ryan Homes	211	63	24
Portrait Homes	151	30	10
Betts Built Homes	106	17	6
Qualstan/Worthington Hills	137	48	6
Ernest G. Fritsche	168	14	5
Virginia Homes	163	11	4

Inasmuch as a considerable number of nonlisted builders were given in the total of 220 interviews, no absolute competitive ranking can be determined; however, the most active listed builders in Franklin county who can be considered competitive to QB are:

1. Ryan Homes

2. Portrait Homes

3. Betts Built Homes

4. Qualstan/Worthington Hills[3]

5. Ernest G. Fritsche

6. Virginia Homes

Conclusions

Why do people buy QB houses? Are they different from other Franklin county house buyers? Who are they? What do they like? What do they expect when they buy? These are some of the questions that should be answered if the market research efforts are to be meaningful to management.

Answers to some of these questions can be found as the survey results are analyzed and comparisons are made between QB homeowners and other homeowners. Other answers will require more definitive research to adequately translate them into specific builder goals.

QB homeowners were motivated to move because of their multiple desires for a larger house and a change in home design and room style. Their generally longer residence in the Franklin county area allowed them to choose their houses without a great amount of time pressure. These buyers are more open to imaginative design, and they appreciate QB's unique design approach to contemporary living. Because they are not generally impulse buyers, they plan ahead and look for what they want (that is, the in-house, their practical dream come true).

QB homeowners are interested in an idea, not the finished product, because they want to see their idea(s) transformed from the drawing board into their house. While three out of four purchased their house before construction began, the "after" construction figure (approximately 25 percent) might reflect the lack of sufficient finished houses to meet a potential demand. Some consideration should be given by management to doing additional speculative building, particularly in view of the finding that 40 percent of other homeowners purchased their houses after they were completed.

QB homeowners look first for house style and design, second for the location for the house in terms of area and building site, and third for the builder for their house. The relative importance of these factors for other buyers emphasized location to a larger extent, followed by house design and builder.

QB homeowners want to be conveniently located in the "right" neighborhood, as other buyers do. They are concerned about the usual neighborhood amenities (for example, appearance and reputation of the area and community; schools; and city utilities), but these things can be found in any progressive building area (and so they keep design expression as their primary goal).

Distinctiveness of house design is a desirable goal for each buying group; the QB homeowners, however, are apparently more receptive to incorporating innovative, contemporary design ideas into their houses (for example, large glass areas, outdoor balconies, and natural wood exteriors).

Two intangible factors for builder selection head the choice list for both QB homeowners and other homeowners: (1) quality of houses the builder constructs and (2) style and design of these houses. More tangible factors include the amount of custom design and special work the builder will do, price range of his houses, and warranties on workmanship. Inasmuch as the house purchase represents their most important investment, all house buyers are concerned with the things that contribute to the value and enjoyment of their house.

The third-party recommendation should be contributing one out of six or seven consumer leads that ultimately result in house purchases, as indicated by the responses to the "reputation of the builder as expressed by others" and the "first awareness of the builder." QB should consider doing some additional "fence-mending" with their previous buyers. Too many of these buyers expressed some reluctance in recommending the company to others; this unnecessarily limits the appeal to others who might also desire an uncommon house design.

QB should develop an effective and consistent advertising and promotion program. A great number of their buyers first became aware of them through previous media and promotion efforts, and consumer recognition is a vital factor in continuing sales success.

The QB buyer is interested in his total living environment, but this marketing approach has not penetrated to him in a meaningful way, and even less so to other house buyers. Their real concern is the "in-house," the uncommon house. A sharper focus on this idea by QB should project a more meaningful image to their potential buyers.

Competitive builders have been building a much larger proportion (50 percent) of two-story houses than has QB. For QB homeowners, multilevel living is "in," two-story living is "out," but we wonder if it is because the multistory house has assumed the place of the two-story house, or whether this might indicate the lack of an acceptable two-story floor plan.

The three primary competitive builders in the Franklin county area are Ryan Homes, Portrait Homes, and Betts Built Homes. Perhaps their construction, promotion, and/or sales efforts should be reviewed to determine whether some aspects of their relatively successful marketing approaches might be adapted to the overall QB strategy.

Finally, this extensive market research project points the way for QB to sharpen its focus on their market potential. But the report, just as a compass, only shows "where." It is now up to management to consider, evaluate, and act in their own best interests to establish a profitable market attainment for their imaginative, uncommon, and exciting design concepts.

Quality Builders . . . the uncommon house.

Questions

1. Evaluate the research used by Quality Builders.

2. What action, if any, should management take?

3. What future research should be undertaken for management?

Aqua-Craft Corporation (B): Designing a Consumer Behavior Information System[4]

"I don't know, Jim. Maybe additional information on our consumers won't help us that much. On the other hand, maybe it will."

The speaker was Claude Whipple, the chief marketing executive and co-founder of the Aqua-Craft Corporation, a manufacturer of boats. Seated across from him was Jim Best, the company's new marketing research director. Also present was Bill Whipple, Claude's son and the firm's advertising manager.

"Bill and I have had a lot of discussions about this subject." Claude continued. "It's going to be a real challenge to keep growing the way we have in the past. We need some new ideas."

"Anyway," Claude continued as he got up from his desk, "I want you to evaluate the information system we currently have. I want to know its strengths and weaknesses. If you think the present system is inadequate, I want to know what types of additional information we should have, how frequently we should have it, how we should go about obtaining it, and how it's going to help us sustain our rate of growth . . . . Any questions?"

"No, I think you've made it clear enough," replied Best.

"Good," said Whipple. "I'll expect your written recommendations on this within two weeks. Feel free to consult with Bill or me on this as you see fit."

Claude Whipple, Bill Whipple, and Jim Best had just finished a long meeting in Claude's office. They had spent the last two hours talking about many of the problems facing the company and the role that a consumer behavior information system might play in coping with these problems and in formulating new marketing strategies.

Claude and Bill had often talked about the company's lack of information about the market they were attempting to serve. The issue had first come up shortly after Bill had assumed the position of advertising manager. One of Bill's first tasks was to evaluate past advertising efforts and to submit recommendations for future programs. He quickly became frustrated over the lack of information about the consumers that the company was trying to communicate with.

Bill had mentioned this problem to his father one day during lunch. The conversation eventually developed into a concern over the role and usefulness of consumer behavior information for all types of marketing programing.

---

[4] The reader is referred to the case "Aqua-Craft Corporation (A)" in Chapter 9 for additional background information on the company and its marketing policies.

They were not sure what type of information, if any, should be obtained nor the best ways of getting it. They had decided to seek the views of Best before pursuing the matter further.

Background on Aqua-Craft

Aqua-Craft manufactures a broad line of boats designed for the mass market. The fifty models in the line include cruisers, runabouts, canoes, sailboats, and utility and fishing boats. The company follows a competitive pricing policy with specific prices ranging from $149 for a nine-foot flat bottom to $4495 for an inboard or outboard cruiser. The boats are distributed by the company's own sales force and by the salesmen of 45 independent distributors to more than 1500 dealers located throughout the United States.

The company has enjoyed a remarkable rate of growth. Sales increased from $5.2 million in 1950 to $10.2 million in 1960. Despite a leveling-off trend in industry sales in the 1960s, Aqua-Craft continued to grow, and by 1967 sales reached an all-time high of $21.7 million.

By the summer of 1968, however, management was becoming increasingly concerned over the ability of the company to sustain its past rate of growth. Management felt that their past differential advantages were likely to become less effective in the future.

The company had pioneered numerous technological innovations in boat construction and was generally regarded by dealers and boat owners as a quality builder. However, it was becoming apparent, particularly in recent years, that competitors could match the company's manufacturing expertise. As a consequence, management wondered how long it could rely on its quality image to stimulate increased sales.

The company's other major differential advantage—a strong dealer organization—also showed signs of decaying. In recent years many of the company's independent distributors began carrying two or three other lines of boats. Because there were minimal differences in the profitability of these lines, many distributors were not pushing the Aqua-Craft line to the degree that they had in the past. Although the company was finding it more and more difficult to exert the desired degree of control over distributors, they had decided, at least for the time being, that they would have to accept the system because the investment required to establish company-owned distribution facilities was considered prohibitive.

The growing number of competitors, particularly large firms like Chrysler, was also a source of concern. If a large competitor decided to get into the boat business in a major way, management feared that the company's sales and market share would decline precipitously.

Current Use of Consumer Behavior Information

In the past, the company has made only minimal use of information on consumer attitudes and behavior. Product strategies have been formulated largely on the basis of materials availabilities and prices, metals technology, and production-run considerations. The company has always depended on executive insights and hunches about what consumers want in boats. In the company's early years this seemed to be a workable strategy because the company manufactured only fishing boats and because many executives—particularly Hull and Claude Whipple, the company's founders—were, as sporting enthusiasts, intimately familiar with the desirable attributes of this type of boat.

Several developments in recent years had convinced many executives that executive intuition about consumer attitudes was a risky approach to product strategy considerations. The company had expanded into other lines of boats, and company executives knew less about what consumers were looking for. Moreover, most competitors were producing boats with nearly identical functional features. As a result, product competition was shifting to other product dimensions: styling, color, trim configurations, and so on. It was becoming increasingly difficult to estimate which of these dimensions would be most effective in establishing brand preference. And, the cost of estimating incorrectly was increasing because of the dramatic increase in inventory investment resulting from product-line proliferation.

Pricing decisions were also made almost completely independently of consumer considerations. The company balanced cost and competitive price considerations in setting prices. All models were priced in order to make the maximum contribution to overhead and profit and to still be reasonably close to competitor's prices. In the past, the models not making any contribution to overhead and profit were dropped from the line. The company has done little experimenting with price variations, and executives admit that they did not really know how important price was when consumers were deciding between different brands.

The company has relied mainly on the judgment of the independent distributors in selecting dealers to handle Aqua-Craft boats. In the past, distributors have been fairly successful in achieving broad distribution for the line. In the last few years, however, problems have arisen, as the growing number of boat manufacturers have caused many distributors to become brand indifferent, and many dealers have reduced the number of brands carried in order to minimize their investment in inventory. Management was wondering about such things as whether or not the importance of various types of dealers was changing, whether they had distribution with the right types of dealers, and how intense distribution should be.

The amount to be spent on advertising is determined by applying a fixed

percentage of forecasted sales (1.5 percent). Readership studies of boat
owners conducted by boating magazines are used to select advertising media
and vehicles.

Sources of Consumer Behavior Information Currently Being Used

Aqua-Craft utilizes several sources of information about the behavior of
boat owners. Distributor invoices are used to tabulate boat sales by model,
price, color, style, and geographic location. This information is used along
with comparable data for the entire industry to predict sales and schedule
production and inventory requirements.

The company collects similar information from its warranty program (see
Figure 17–4). The company guarantees its boats against defects in workmanship and in materials, providing certain conditions are met. The information
from the warranty card is used by management to analyze the movement of
boats by model, color, price and geographic location.

Occasionally, the company's advertising agency conducts studies dealing
with various dimensions of consumer behavior. The agency has determined
how sales vary by occupation, and the reasons people buy boats. A few

FIGURE 17–4. Aqua-Craft warranty card.

Warranty

Aqua-Craft Corporation

Name _____

Address _____   _____   _____
            (City)   (State)   (Zip Code)

Model Purchased _____   Color _____   Price _____

Date Purchased _____   Dealer's Name and Address _____

The manufacturer warrants that all parts are free from defects in material
and workmanship. This warranty applies for a two-year period (from date
of purchase), applies only to the original purchaser, and is not assignable
or transferable. It does not apply to any unit that has been subject to alteration, negligence, abuse, accident or to any unauthorized method of use not
specifically recommended by the manufacturer.

months ago, the agency was asked to determine the role of family members in purchasing boats.[5] This study has not yet been completed.

These are the only internal sources of information on consumer behavior that are available to management. Information from external sources is presently limited to publicly circulated industry reports. These studies typically deal with industry sales patterns, by manufacturer and model, and with the reasons people are buying boats.

Question

1. Put yourself in Jim Best's position and prepare the report requested by Claude Whipple. Your report should contain, but not necessarily be limited to, the following:
    a. The specific types of information about consumer behavior that the company should have.
    b. How each type of information can be obtained most effectively and efficiently.
    c. How frequently each type of information should be obtained.
    d. How each type of information can be used to plan, implement, and/or evaluate marketing strategies.

Miss Ritz Cosmetics (B): Comprehensive Review of Consumer Influence on Marketing Strategy[6]

Charles of the Ritz, Inc., is a successful producer of high-quality cosmetics. In 1966 the company introduced a new line of cosmetics appealing directly to the eighteen to twenty-eight age group in an attempt to capture a high growth segment of the total market. The line was of similar quality to the Charles of the Ritz regular line but the promotional effort, packaging, and product line was aimed much more directly to youth preferences.

Problem

The Miss Ritz line was marketed through the same channels as the regular Charles of the Ritz parent company cosmetics (see "Miss Ritz Cosmetics (A)," an earlier case in this book), principally in leading department stores.

---

[5] See the case "Aqua-Craft Corporation (A)."

[6] For a description of the Miss Ritz line of cosmetics, channels of distribution, and the rationale for the present strategies, see the case "Miss Ritz Cosmetics (A)" in Chapter 6 of this book.

In 1967 the management of Charles of the Ritz participated in a study that investigated the consumer decision process involved in the purchase of cosmetics and the specific attitudes toward Miss Ritz. The study encompassed all aspects of the decision process; thus a base existed for a comprehensive evaluation of the firm's marketing strategy. In 1968, the company was looking forward to the future in an effort to determine if any changes should be made in their strategies. This called for detailed analysis of each area of the firm's marketing activities at present.

Specifically, the company wished to

1. Determine the proper Miss Ritz image to meet collegiate norms and preferences.

2. Determine the advisability of modifying the Miss Ritz product line (including the possibility of abandonment in favor of a new brand or line).

3. Generate promotional strategies to support whatever lines are adopted.

4. Evaluate and modify existing distribution policies to accommodate the new marketing mix.

Research

The research conducted for Miss Ritz consisted of approximately one hundred depth-type interviews at a major state university. The university selected as a typical market was The Ohio State University, the residence of approximately 38,000 students, located in Columbus, Ohio. The respondents to the survey were selected to include a representative cross-section of the female students living on and near the campus. The respondents were not selected on a probability basis, however.

The interviewers were trained by a marketing professor at the university and were selected from senior members of a marketing research class. The instructions given to the interviewers were very complete. A copy of the basic instructions is given in Appendix A. The interviewers were instructed that Charles of the Ritz needs to know how female college students feel about cosmetics, how cosmetics relate to the general topic of fashion and appearance, where students prefer to buy cosmetics, and what they know and feel specifically about the Miss Ritz line.

The company particularly wished to probe on questions relating to the distribution policies of the firm.[7] The company has good reasons for its present policy of distributing exclusively through the leading department store, but it was essential that they learn of the acceptability of this policy by female college students. Some of the other specific questions that the company hoped to answer are the following:

[7] For a description of the Columbus area market for women's fashion products, see the case "Flower Power Fashions" in Chapter 8 of this book.

1. What brands of cosmetics do college students prefer?

2. How do they decide which brand to buy?

3. Do they buy cosmetics on campus usually or only sometimes?

4. How do they recognize their need for cosmetics?

5. How many different types of cosmetics do they use?

6. Where or from whom do they get advice about cosmetics and appearance in general?

7. What mazagines do they read for beauty information?

8. What do they think boys think about makeup and cosmetics.

Each interviewer was required to memorize an outline to be used in guiding the interviews. The outline used was the following:

I. Discuss clothing fashions for women (not reprinted in this case).

II. Discuss beauty: what it is, whose opinions are important, how it can be achieved or improved.

III. Discuss cosmetics (probe deeply on this topic).

IV. Discuss Miss Ritz (or Charles of the Ritz). After initial reactions are obtained, give respondent a free sample of Miss Ritz lipstick and probe extensively on her reactions to the product and distribution.

Results

The data generated from the depth study are presented in Appendix B. The study yielded a large amount of information on the decision processes of college-oriented cosmetic consumers. While these data referred only to one test market, they disclosed many items of potential value in overall marketing planning. The director of marketing for Charles of the Ritz had the task of evaluating the interviews, abstracting the information from them, and presenting to top management recommendations for changes in existing marketing strategy.

Research Tasks

1. Evaluate the research strategy used in this problem.

2. Devise a framework for performing a quantitative analysis of the qualitative interviews.

3. Evaluate how this research should be used in planning additional research activities.

Strategy Questions

1. Should the company put extensive resources into promoting a separate brand for young women, or should the company rely on the traditional Charles of the Ritz line to reach young women?

2. What should be the nature of the product line for this product?

3. What should be the channels of distribution for the young women's line that now exists?

4. What should be the promotion policy for the new firm?
    a. Identify the instrumental individual and social influences on decision making for cosmetics (personality, cultural norms, perception, social class, family).
    b. Identify the relevant stages of decision making that occur in cosmetic purchases (problem recognition, information search, evaluation generation and evaluation).
    c. What creative strategy (appeals) should be used in Ritz promotions to young women?
    d. What media should be employed?

Appendix A: Quasi-Nondirective Interviewing

Nondirective interviewing is a subtle form of artistry. It requires skill and creativity to stimulate the respondent to yield useful information. An interviewer's skill is judged by his ability to extract from respondents new hypotheses, feelings toward the subject of the interview, and original insights into the problem.

1. The opening.
    a. Put the respondent at ease. Do not stress how important her ideas are because this may lead her to try to say something that will "revolutionize" thinking on the subject.
    b. Try to convince her you have no ulterior motives without bringing this possibility to her attention. A good opening is, "We're talking to several students to get their thoughts and feelings about campus fashions and appearance in general, and we would like to talk with you about your feelings on campus clothing and beauty. Would you be willing to talk with us a few minutes?"

2. The respondent should be encouraged to talk freely about whatever aspects of the subject seem to interest her. Never disagree with what she says. The interviewer should not voice strong agreement either. The interviewer should nod, smile, murmur an affirmative response, and so forth, which will encourage the respondent to keep talking without biasing results toward views of the interviewer.

3.   Memorize the outline with which you hope to structure the interview. Do not fumble with a paper or create the appearance that there are specific questions you must ask—this will tend to make the respondent say what she thinks you want to hear rather than reveal her own interests and opinions.

   a.   Let the respondent talk freely about any subject that is even only indirectly connected with the subject under investigation—she may give new insights to the problem that the researchers have never thought about.

   b.   If the respondent starts talking at length about a subject of little interest to the researcher, find a way to draw her back subtly to a topic of interest. Refer back to an earlier statement she has made by saying something like, "Now, you say you buy your cosmetics occasionally at Lazarus. . . ." Let the respondent take it from there. Do not ask an outright question unless you simply cannot get the information any other way.

4.   Your job as an interviewer is to keep the respondent talking instead of yourself. You want her to express what she really feels about a subject.

   a.   You should talk hesitantly or slowly so she will be encouraged to do more talking.

   b.   Allow respondent to develop her ideas thoroughly rather than merely to state an opinion or thought and go on to another topic.

   c.   Be especially alert for ways to *probe* further into important questions. You are especially interested in some aspects of the problem, and you may have to ask her to amplify her ideas when she comes to topics of direct interest.

      (1)   Do not ask direct questions if you can avoid it by some other means.

      (2)   A good technique is to restate the respondent's answers to the main question or her last statement. You might say, "So, you like to buy cosmetics primarily at Lazarus," instead of, "Why do you buy your cosmetics at Lazarus?"

      (3)   Try to probe answers that you believe will be ambiguous or difficult to understand—this is a big help to the researcher interpreting your interview.

5.   Recording the interview.

   a.   Recording the interview in enough detail that the results will be meaningful, and yet carrying on a good interview, is a difficult task. You must concentrate on two jobs at the same time.

   b.   Record the statements of the respondent on a note pad. Try to record all the key phrases the respondent uses and certainly all the main thoughts. Write fast! But do not make the respondent nervous.

   c.   If you have an outline memorized, you may code responses under topics for discussion.

   d.   Transcribe the interview—hopefully typed, even if in rough copy—immediately after completing the interview. You will find that you will be able to remember many of the exact words and thoughts of the respondent if you record the interview immediately. Much will be lost if it is done the next day.

e. After the interview is completed, write a short paragraph describing the respondent—where she lives, here physical appearance, her personality, and any other characteristics that may help the researcher interpret her responses.

Appendix B: Nondirective Interviews (Verbatim Raw Data)

Interview 1

Beauty

Personality is Katy's basic requirement for beauty. She feels that a girl with a good personality tends to take care of herself and will present a pleasing appearance. She does not think that appearance is the most important aspect of beauty but that a fresh, natural look is much better than too much make-up. Just as bad as too much makeup is the extremely "washed-out" look.

Katy stated that there is too much conformity on campus. She feels that girls should start wearing clothes, makeup, and hair styles that fit them instead of trying to look like everyone else. The example she used was long, straight hair. Although it is in style, not everyone looks good in it and, therefore, many girls who wear their hair long and straight should change to a more flattering style.

Cosmetics

When asked for her opinions on cosmetics, Katy said that she tries to keep up on what is new through magazines and just looking around. She seemed to think that brand experience is the best determinant of what cosmetics to use. She currently uses Esteé Lauder cosmetics because she has found that they suit her needs better than other brands. Katy obtained most of her knowledge about cosmetics and their use in a charm school course. Makeup that Katy uses includes eye-liner, mascara, blusher, and foundation. She said that she does not use any type of cream because she has an oily skin.

Katy thinks that most coeds buy their makeup at downtown stores. However, she said that lipstick is many times bought at drugstores around campus where coeds might go to pick up incidentals or to cash checks, and they happen to see a new color that they like.

Miss Ritz

Katy's reaction to Charles of the Ritz in general was that it is for older women. When asked about Miss Ritz, she said that she had never heard of it and that she had not seen it advertised. She liked the color of the lipstick that was given her. She said that she likes pale colors in lipstick.

Katy is a sophomore at Ohio State. She keeps up on fashions and buys clothes frequently. She lives in a dormitory on campus. Katy has a good personality and was a willing talker. She is a little overweight, but has a fairly neat appearance otherwise.

Interview 2

Beauty

Carole believes that personality is the basis of beauty. She said that a beautiful girl usually has an appearance that equals her good personality. She thinks that beauty is a natural look; in her words it is a "wholesome cleanliness."

Carole believes that this naturalness is important to men. She thinks that little makeup and the ability to wear clothes are attractive to men. She said that men look at two things: a girl's eyes and her legs. The eyes should show "warmth." In regard to legs, she said that men feel that if a girl has good legs, they will always be that way.

Cosmetics

Carole uses Avon and Cover Girl cosmetics. She uses Avon because her mother works for that company, and she uses Cover Girl because it is medicated. She thinks that other girls usually buy their cosmetics downtown or at home, where they can get them at a discount and where they know just where to go to get what they want.

For daytime, Carole uses a base, powder, blush, eyebrow pencil, mascara, and, instead of lipstick, she uses her blusher, because she does not like to wear lipstick.

Miss Ritz

Carole has used Charles of the Ritz makeup but does not like the face powder. She said that it is too heavy. She had never heard of Miss Ritz cosmetics until recently, when she saw the information about the Sleeping Beauty contest in her dorm.

Carole is a freshman and lives in a dormitory. She does not have a perfect build, but she is not overweight. Her major problem is a very bad case of acne. Carole dresses well and is neat in appearance, but her complexion is a little distracting. She has a very good personality, however, but has trouble getting dates.

Interview 3

Beauty

"Beauty is not how you look—it's the image that you portray to people," said the respondent. She feels that every person has something in them that is beautiful and they should play up this beauty aspect. "Wearing the right clothes and the right makeup will help to bring this aspect out." She relies mostly on her own opinions. "I have to be satisfied with myself." Nevertheless, she does not want someone to tell her that she looks like a clown.

Cosmetics

The respondent thinks that cosmetics can be used to improve the way someone looks. When deciding what brand to buy, she jumps around. "It's a trial-and-error process." She uses the whole array of cosmetics: lipstick, eye-liner, eyebrow pencil, eye-shadow, makeup base and blush-on. She uses cosmetics every day, at almost all times. "I think they make me look better, so why shouldn't I wear them when I go out?" She feels that the colors worn and the type should go along with one's hair color, eye color, and color of clothing. She uses the Fashion 220 brand of cosmetics, which is not sold over the counter but is distributed on a door-to-door basis.

Miss Ritz

She has heard of Miss Ritz but has never used it.

Reaction to lipstick

She likes the color but would rather have a pearl sheen. To her, the lipstick is creamy; has a shine that she likes; does not taste as bad as most; and feels a little greasy, which is not good to her. She indicated she would use it.

Reaction to distribution

She felt that getting to less people makes the cosmetic exclusive, makes people feel that they are getting something special. She indicated that she would travel to Lazarus to buy it.

The respondent is a senior (not in school this quarter) who is now working. She lives alone in a two-bedroom apartment. She is an attractive girl.

Interview 4

Beauty

"*Beauty* is actually undefinable, it is really in the eyes of the beholder," said the respondent. "True beauty comes from within." But she feels that the first impression one makes on someone comes from how someone looks. Therefore, she says it is important to look good. "The people around you— your friends, who you talk to—influence your evaluation of yourself as to how beautiful you are."

Cosmetics

"The main purpose of cosmetics is to hide your faults, and to improve your general appearance. I think that the most important thing in wearing makeup is knowing how to apply it." The decision on what brands to buy comes from "trying it first, comparing it to what you had before, and wearing whatever looks best on for the longest time." She wears eye-shadow, mascara, eye-liner, eyebrow pencil, lipstick, powder, and blush-ons. Mostly, she uses Max Factor but uses some types of other brands also, Revlon particularly. She gets her ideas on what to wear from other girls and from ads but never from parents. She reads *Glamour* and *Seventeen* for information on clothing and beauty and on what is new. When shopping for cosmetics, price is important, but she does not wear the cheap brands that she did in high school. She also feels that guys do not know anything about cosmetics and that they cannot tell the difference between them. She does not wear makeup much, usually only on dates.

Miss Ritz

The respondent is not sure if she ever heard of Miss Ritz. She has never used it. But she has heard of Charles of the Ritz, and she knows that they blend powders to match one's skin color. She thinks that it is is more expensive than most others, but she thinks it is a top brand.

Reaction to lipstick

She does not like pink. She likes orange colors. It felt good and smooth and she liked the taste. She would not wear it, because of the color.

Reaction to distribution

She thinks that Lazarus is a good store but that it is sometimes more expensive and "you don't always get what you pay for." She would travel to Lazarus to buy Miss Ritz if that was the brand she used, but she would not go there just to try it. She thinks it should be sold on campus.

The respondent is an above-average-looking girl. She said, "One of the reasons I don't wear makeup much is because I don't like guys staring at me." She is a junior and lives at home in a suburb of Columbus.

Interview 5

Beauty

About beauty, the respondent commented, "I don't really know what it is. I'm not great looking, but D thinks I'm cute." (She is engaged to D.) She feels that his opinion is the only thing that matters to her, and she does not care too much what other people think. "I suppose you could say it's the way you look to someone else."

Cosmetics

"I hardly ever wear makeup." D does not like too much makeup on a girl, so when she wears it she does not use much. "He thinks I look good enough the way I am." When she does wear it, it is usually only on dates. Mostly, she uses only eye makeup, sometimes powder, and once in a while lipstick. She said she cannot really tell the difference between most brands and that it does not matter too much what she uses. The only differences are the color of makeup and the taste of lipsticks. She now uses Revlon and has used it since she started wearing makeup. She also said, "I don't like girls who wear a lot of makeup. They look too phony."

She reads *Glamour* usually but not too many other magazines.

Miss Ritz

She has never heard of Miss Ritz, but she has heard of Charles of the Ritz. She has never used that brand.

Reaction to lipstick

She likes the color. The taste is okay. "What else can you say about it?"

Reaction to distribution

"I wouldn't go down to Lazarus to buy it." She said, "I think it should be sold on campus if they want college girls to buy it."

The respondent is a junior majoring in home economics. She is an average-looking girl with a very good personality. She lives in a rooming house.

Interview 6

Beauty

 Q. What do you think makes a woman attractive?

 A. Clean healthy look, sparkling hair and teeth, sparkling eyes, nice clean complexion, smooth skin, and things like that. Too many young people around the campus are dressing sloppy. They run around in blue jeans and tent dresses and clothing that doesn't show a girl's shape.

I think beauty indicates a quality one has which makes one attractive to others in a natural state. I guess what I really mean is that beauty is something that comes from a person before getting fixed up for a day or night on the town.

I suppose the opinions of other men are important, but my husband first, of course, and other girls I associate with, but I think my own opinion is most important because I feel so much better when I think I look attractive.

Proper diet, rest, activity, hygiene, and dental care. The proper use of makeup and clothing for one's figure.

Cosmetics

Cosmetics are important to a girl's looks if used in the right way, meaning not too much or too little so that it makes a girl look gaudy or real plain, but different-type girls require various amounts and types of makeup.

Miss Ritz

Q. Are you familiar with Miss Ritz?

A. No.

Q. Do you know anything about Charles of the Ritz?

A. I've never used it personally, but I have heard it was very expensive. Myself, I use Avon because I think it has a lot of body and moisture to it and they give a better selection for my personal needs than do Revlon or Max Factor. I also like the lady that comes around and sells the products to me. I can order what I need and not have to worry about going to a drugstore or downtown to buy a tube of lipstick. I guess what I really like is the convenience and buying enough so I don't have to be concerned for awhile.

The respondent is a social worker. Her husband is a senior in college. Her appearance was very neat. She had a very clear complexion without too much makeup on. She wore a light shade of lipstick and no eye-shadow.

The respondent seemed very concerned with the hygenic aspects of cosmetics and good grooming (possibly because she is also a nurse).

Interview 7

Coming from an Eastern city, the interviewee was surprised to see how fashion-minded many of the coeds at Ohio State were. Fashion and styles she thought "are especially prevalent among the sorority girls. The college stores have all the up-to-date styles that go with the fashion magazines that I read." She also thought Lazarus was quite in line with the large Eastern stores. She had transferred here from a women's college in the East where "clothes and makeup were of little importance" and was surprised at the everyday concern that most people used toward what they wore. She said she found it hard to believe the number of girls that were made-up as if they were going out on a date and thought that it was "horrible" that some girls even wore false eyelashes to class.

Beauty

Although she started talking about beauty in terms of the individual personality, "eyes that smile, eyes sparkling," eventually she began to discuss more fundamental ideas: structure of the face, high cheek bones, and a straight nose were very important to her, and she criticized the "ski slope" nose she had. She said that she was usually open to suggestions from her friends if she thought they did a good job of making themselves up. She often mentioned how "relative" beauty was and that many people had different value judgments. She thought you "either have beauty or you don't. You can't change the way you physically look but you can improve what you have to work with."

Cosmetics

The girl said that she was very conscious of cosmetics and was sensitive in observing other girls that used them. She thought it was worthwhile to go out of her way in buying cosmetics and in paying more because there was a difference in cosmetics. She could not understand how girls could go around with a line between their chin and neck making it apparent where the cosmetics started and ended. Generally she thought that Jewish girls were noted for their heavy use of makeup and thought that all girls who wore too much have a "caked" look about them. She likes makeup with moisturizers in them because she thinks they blend better with the skin. She also thinks one should use a moisturizer under the skin. She was glad that eye-liner was "in" and thought that it nearly always helped the appearance.

Miss Ritz

She had never heard of Miss Ritz but was familiar with Charles of the Ritz and said she was always intrigued with the way they blended powder. "One of these days I'm going to have them make some just for my skin." She also thought Charles of the Ritz was for older women, but she did not recall ever seeing any advertisements for them.

She said she would not be interested in their general line of products, because she does not think they have frosted lipsticks, and she was pretty satisfied with the makeup she was presently using. She used Revlon Ultama for her face and eyes and used Max Factor Ultralucent for lipstick.

After giving her the lipstick, she tried it and said, "I think it's a pretty shade." But she did not think she would like it because it had an odor. If she were going to buy it, she would buy it where she buys the rest of her cosmetics: downtown at Lazarus.

The respondent was twenty-one, a college student in home economics. She was a very talkative, vivacious, young girl, who enjoyed school and was somewhat influenced by what other people did. She was neatly dressed, about five feet, three inches tall, and sort of plump. Her makeup was very light but could be distinctly noticed. She comes from New York City.

Interview 8

Beauty

The interviewee said, "Beauty can be both an inner feeling and an outward appearance. Personally, I think that it is the outward appearance that makes a person pretty or not." She kept reiterating the fact of how important the right clothes from the right shop are and how not just anybody can put on makeup but said that in order to have it look "just right" one should have a beautician show one how "if you had to put it on yourself."

Cosmetics

Cosmetics were the second most important thing. "They have to blend in with the outfit you are wearing that day. Each day you have to use a different kind of makeup. Sometimes you want to wear a lot of eye-shadow and lipstick and other times hardly any at all. That way you never look exactly the same day after day. It gives a contrast to your appearance. I personally use the best you can buy of Revlon." She seemed to think that Revlon offered a better selection of cosmetics in different colors and shades.

Miss Ritz

When asked if she had ever heard of Miss Ritz, her reply was "No," but she had heard of Charles of the Ritz because her mother uses it. "But it is too expensive for me, and, besides, when I go to buy my makeup, I can never find it anywhere." The interviewee thought that a "radiant look" was the thing that suited her best and felt that makeup should be worn so it can be seen by other people, not just a bit here and a bit there. She thought that lipstick should outline the mouth and "be moist so it looks a little bit sexy." She also felt that eye-shadow should be able to be seen and that this makes the eyes stand out. After giving the lipstick to her, she tried it and thought it was okay, but the color was too pale for her. She did not think there was anything outstanding about the product, "but if it is made by Charles of the Ritz it probably is good because that is what my mother buys."

The respondent was twenty-four, in graduate school to obtain her Master degree. She was a very statuesque person who wore considerable makeup.

Interview 9

Beauty

The respondent associates overall beauty with looking natural and having a pleasing personality. She does not like long hair that looks as if it has been dyed, nor does she like heavy makeup because she feels that it detracts from a person's natural beauty. She thinks that heavy makeup gives the impression of "trying to cover something up." She said that clothes can add to beauty if they are well fitted and if they fit the overall appearance of the woman. She does not like to see a particular woman always wearing the same type of clothing. She judges beauty with being able to wear casual, sports, and evening wear, all in "good taste." According to her, the most important factor of beauty for women is their eyes and general facial expressions. She does not like to accept other people's opinions about clothing because she feels that each person looks different in the same type of clothing. She sees a woman that looks "nice" in a particular outfit, but she says that she would have to see herself in the outfit before she would accept it.

Cosmetics

She said that excessive makeup is not good because people know that you do not really look that way. She likes a natural appearance and said that putting on makeup is an art. "You have to experiment with it to find the right blends." She said makeup should be used to bring out a woman's best features and not to cover up her worst features.

She buys all of her makeup at Lazarus because they have the best prices and they have any type of makeup that one wants. She also likes the "experts" that show how to use makeup that brings out one's best points and that, more importantly, show you how to apply it. She said that you must know the proper way to apply makeup and that many women do not know this. She said that she does not associate price with quality. However, she said that the "better" makeup does not cause any type of breaking out of the skin. She said that she prefers Revlon because she knows that they make good cosmetics and that they also have different lines for different-aged women. She does not worry about her makeup while at work, but she does think that a woman should look her best when she starts out in the morning. She does not like to see women always "primping."

Miss Ritz

The respondent had heard of the Charles of the Ritz line but she had never heard of the Miss Ritz line before. She said that the Charles of the Ritz line was for the "higher priced" cosmetic buyer. She felt that, for a lot of the quality cosmetics, one was only paying for the name and not necessarily for the quality of the product. She judges the quality of cosmetics by experience only, for she feels that what is good for someone else does not mean that it is good for her.

The respondent tried the sample after I presented it to her, and her first comment was that it was very moist. She liked the fragrance of the lipstick. She said it does not have a strong smell, but that one can tell that it is good lipstick. In general, her criteria for judging lipstick are the moistness, the length that it will stay on, and if it will not change color, because she likes to put it on to go to work and she does not want to be bothered with it during the day.

The respondent is a secretary in an attorney's office. She is married to a college student, and her dress was like that of a college coed. She wore very little noticeable makeup other than lipstick.

Interview 10

Beauty

Appearance is very important to this person because she believes that her husband wants her to look decent at all, or most, times. When she was in college she made a special effort to conform with the middle-of-the-road dress and did not like the extreme type of dress of some girls. She said that she could tell about another girl by the way she dressed, the length and neatness of her hair, the amount of makeup that she wore, and the "neatness of her clothes." She said that the most important factor of beauty was a girl's hair, and her overall neatness (no extreme makeup).

Cosmetics

She associated beauty with using natural looking makeup. She indicated that no matter what a girl looked like naturally, she would look worse if she went to extremes with makeup. She said that the proper use of makeup was to highlight a girl's natural face, and not cover it up. She said that heavy makeup could be used if the person using it knew how to blend it so as to make it appear natural.

While in college she purchased most of her makeup at a local campus drugstore, due to its convenience. If she were going on a shopping trip (while in college) it would usually be to Lazarus. At Lazarus she would compare the prices of clothing, makeup, and so forth with the prices of the local campus stores. If the prices were not too high, she would buy at Lazarus. Speaking of the store in general, she thought their prices were reasonable, and in the specific case of cosmetics, she said she found their prices slightly lower than the local campus drugstores. She said that if Lazarus were closer to campus she would do most of her buying of clothing and cosmetics there. Now that she is married and working, she does practically all of her shopping at Lazarus (Northland Shopping Center).

When in college, she made a special effort to always have her makeup on and even went back to the dorm to put it on again at noon. Today the most important cosmetic to her is lipstick. She seldom goes out, even to the grocery, without putting on lipstick. She does not like extremely bright lipstick, nor does she like extremely pale lipstick.

Miss Ritz

The respondent had never heard of the Miss Ritz line. She has associated the Charles of the Ritz line with high-priced, high-quality products. She indicated that while in college she bought the best makeup that she could for the least amount of money. She feels that many of the cosmetic products are of the same quality and that one is only paying for the name when she buys the "most expensive." This used to be an important fact to her, but now that she is married she feels that she can afford to pay more for cosmetics and clothing.

While inspecting the sample that I presented to her, she said that she could not judge the quality without trying it. She added that to judge a product she had to try it or hear the reaction of one of her friends to the product. She said the most important things about "good" lipstick were that it did not dry the lips, that it would stay on for a considerable length of time, and that it did not change colors. She will pay a premium price for lipstick that meets these criteria.

The respondent has been out of college for about nine months. She is married to a college student. Her occupation is nursing.

Interview 11

Beauty

Q.   What do you think comprises beauty or what do you think makes a girl beautiful?

A.   The most important thing is that a girl has got to look like a girl. She has to be sexy without trying to be sexy. Too much makeup is repulsive. Short hair styles don't make a girl look like a girl, a girl with a good-looking short haircut is just sort of cute, she doesn't really look like a girl and she isn't beautiful. A girl should dress to flatter the figure without being vulgar. Bearing, posture, and personality have a lot to do with beauty.

Q.   Whose opinions do you consider important on beauty?

A.   Comes from too many persons to recall offhand. Magazines with good taste such as *Vogue, Bazaar, McCalls* and the ads in *The New Yorker* are sometimes very good, also good, reputable movie stars with good taste and females who are public personalities with good taste.

Cosmetics

Q.   What brands of cosmetics do college students prefer?

A.   Cheap ones. You must consider college students don't have much money and the girls usually buy things that can be gotten in a drugstore such as Max Factor, Revlon, Avon fragrances and night creams.

Q.   How do you decide which brand to buy?

A.   Convenience and price.

Q.   Do they [college friends] buy cosmetics on campus usually or only sometimes? [The respondent is not really sure when students buy cosmetics. According to her, town students do not buy very much on campus and usually buy according to shopping habits formed before going to college. Others probably buy on campus because of familiarity, but she does not really know.]

Q.   How many different types of cosmetics do you use?

A.   Makeup base, some sort of blush or powder, eye-liner, eye-shadow, mascara, eyebrow pencil, lipstick, contour shading, night creams, astringents, moisturizers, medicated soap, and medicated creams or pastes (Clearasil).

Q.   How do you decide what you need?

A. Depends on skin, complexion, features, and the girl's overall facial coloring.

Q. Where or from whom do they get advice about cosmetics and appearance in general?

A. Magazines (any fashion magazines, ads, and features), talking to friends and experimenting on your own.

Q. In what stores do college females buy their clothes? [She thinks they prefer to buy in smaller stores: small chains, small privately owned shops catering to college fashion, with charge accounts definitely.]

Q. What magazines do you read for beauty information?

A. The same ones as fashion.

Q. What do you think boys think about makeup and cosmetics?

A. Boys don't like a lot of it, and they don't like it to be obvious (subdued, camouflaged, in tune with the girl's natural looks).

Miss Ritz

Q. Have you ever heard of Miss Ritz?

A. Yes, it is a division of Charles of the Ritz.

I then handed her the tube of lipstick, and she tried it. I then asked her how she liked the lipstick. She said she loved it. She liked the color and the shade (said it smelled good).

I then asked her what she thought of the fact that the Ritz line is only distributed through Lazarus. She thought it was psychological, that it gives Miss Ritz an exclusive, prestigious aura because one can only get it in one place. She said that people who know of it know where to get it (at Lazarus), but that they probably do not realize it is distributed only through Lazarus. She further stated that what hurts Miss Ritz is that people just do not know about it, that one never sees it advertised and that this is important. She does not think Ritz would get that much more sales if the line were sold on campus.

The respondent is sharp, well groomed, well dressed and has long, brown hair.

Interview 12

Beauty

Q. Beauty—what is it?

A. General appearance and face.

Q. How can beauty be achieved or improved?

A. If you are always neat, you can give the effect of being beautiful if you are not.

Q. Whose opinions do you consider important on beauty?

A. A girl who is naturally beautiful herself is the best judge of another beautiful girl because there is no jealousy involved.

Cosmetics

The girl being interviewed had no answer to the question as to what brands of cosmetics all college students prefer.

Q. How do decide which brand to buy?

A. You choose something you are not allergic to. Pick something that is easy to apply. Pick something which is agreeable in shade to complexion. Price is not usually a factor.

Q. Do you buy cosmetics on campus usually or do you go downtown?

A. Go downtown usually.

Q. What different types of cosmetics do you use?

A. Lipstick, mascara, eye-shadow, eyebrow darkener, makeup base, loose powder, pressed powder, and blush.

Q. How do you decide what you need in the way of cosmetics?

A. You have to decide what needs emphasis and what doesn't, and what needs camouflaging.

Q. Where or from whom do you get advice about cosmetics and appearance in general?

A. *Glamour, Seventeen,* from your friends, because this is from whom you learn what to use.

Q. In what stores do you buy your clothes?

A. The department stores downtown. [For college females in general she thought that the town students did most of their buying downtown and in shopping centers, while the out-of-town students did most of their buying on campus.]

Q. What magazines do you read for beauty information?

A. *Ingenue, Ladies Home Journal* and *McCalls.*

Q. What do you think boys think about makeup and cosmetics? [She thinks boys are taken in by makeup that is put on well, that they like it, and that they dislike a poor makeup job.]

Miss Ritz

   Q.   Have you ever heard of Miss Ritz?

   A.   No.

   Q.   Have you ever heard of Charles of the Ritz? [Yes, she had heard that it is very expensive and that it is fairly good. She doubts whether it is worth what one pays for it.]

   I then gave her the lipstick and asked for her reaction to it. "It is too light, it doesn't give enough color, although it is nice, soft, and creamy."
   I then asked for her reaction to the fact that it is only distributed through Lazarus. She thinks it should be distributed through Lazarus because an awful lot of college girls go there. She does not think it would make much difference if it comes closer to campus, because, if a girl likes a particular brand, she will go out of her way to get the brand she likes. She thinks Lazarus is convenient enough to campus anyhow.
   After I showed the Miss Ritz leaflet to the respondent, she was surprised at the reasonable prices.
   The respondent has long, brown hair and is short and cute.

Interview 13
   These two interviews were done together for the interaction between the two girls. The interviewees were Ronda and Marsha.

Beauty

   M.   Beauty is naturalness.

   R.   Beauty is inside; you can improve it through improving your personality.

   M.   Moderation in everything helps beauty.

   R.   Cleanliness, neatness, clothes sense, dress with coordinated colors and taste, good shoes add a lot.

   M.   Lots of sleep, clean hair, natural and not teased; fewer people are bleaching their hair. It may be dyed. It should not hang in your face even if it's long.

   R.   Shouldn't play with your hair; should have good manners, and never chew gum.

   M.   For advice about beauty I watch advertisements.

   R.   Trends come from ads.

   M.   I look them over in drugstores: shades, colors, tones. If I had the time,

I'd spend more time in selection. I buy on what I read when I was younger about makeup and its application.

R. Beauty comes from yourself and your reactions to your self.

M. Beauty is smiling.

R. I read *Seventeen* magazine if I'm reading that type of magazine, and glance over the ads in it.

M. I read *McCalls* when home because I can sew the clothes from the patterns. I also read *Mademoiselle, Glamour* because mother has them.

Cosmetics

M. I buy Max Factor lipstick, compacts, eye-liner, mascara, liquid make-up, Adorn hair spray, Breck shampoo or VO-5, Revlon Aquamarine, 10-06 and Noxema compacts, and perfumes of all kinds.

R. Revlon lipstick, Max Factor eye-liner, mascara, powder, Angel Face liquid makeup, Just Wonderful hair spray.

M. I buy by price a lot. If I've used it long enough I know what I like.

R. I buy what makeup feels best and looks best. Eye makeup is something bad for the eyes. I use what my mother and sister used, since they started before I did. I buy at Lazarus.

M. I buy at Super X, or some other low price place, and I'll wait until I need quite a few things, and then wait until I can get to a lower-priced place.

R. Campus stores are very high priced.

Guys think

R. They don't think anything about it unless there's too much makeup.

M. If you always wear it and then don't, then they think about it, but usually they don't know whether you're wearing it or not.

Miss Ritz

M. I remember seeing it. It's in Lazarus. I always wanted to stop but never had the time or money to do it. They have the ad with the many powders. It's expensive. There's no difference between it and others.

R. There's no difference I know of. I don't buy it because it's expensive. I don't know much about any cosmetics.

Lipstick

M. It's creamy. Makes you feel like you have to put a lot on. It's messy but it feels great.

R. Feels great, but I don't like lipsticks you have to blot. It doesn't make my lips look cracked, which they are.

M. It's pretty. I like it.

R. It's okay if it is where everybody goes, like Lazarus. Who doesn't go there? For college kids, unless I'm really sold on it, I won't go out of my way to get it. I like quality things.

M. The distribution doesn't bother me. I would make a trip to go get it if I were brand loyal. It lends prestige to the product.

R. You'd always make sure you didn't run out.

Marsha is twenty-one, single (no desire to get married right now). She has a fair figure, a cute face. Ronda is twenty-one, has a pretty good figure and a very light complexion.

Interview 14

Beauty

Beauty is esthetic appeal. It's natural things and true things. Ideas can be beautiful too. Literary things too. Kindness.

My opinions are important, my friends and family for clothes. In the beauty area I depend on people in the art area.

For improved physical beauty, it depends on what you think is important. If it's a clear complexion, then soap and water; if it's clothes, then careful selection and care.

For beauty advice I turn to my friends. I never read magazines unless I'm in a beauty shop for a hair-do.

Cosmetics

I buy Revlon, Fashion 220, Max Factor, Helena Rubinstein, Bonnie Bell, Avon. [A roommate sells Avon.]

I decide what brand to buy if a friend is selling that brand, something I've heard of, or if the shop lady tells me what's best. I ask for something good.

Sometimes I buy on campus, but usually it's at home on my parent's charge.

I use Just Wonderful, Aqua Net, Adorn hair spray; Avon, Woodbury, or Prell shampoos; Revlon eye makeup; Avon, Revlon, and Max Factor lipstick; and Revlon powder. Usually what's on sale.

Decision comes from trying someone else's; whatever they're using.

Guys think cosmetics are a good idea, but not in excess.

Miss Ritz

I don't know much about Charles of the Ritz. I've heard they're good but expensive.

I like the creamy feel of the lipstick. It feels good. If I really liked it, I would go out to get it. I don't think there's much difference between brands. I wouldn't go get a brand of lipstick unless they had a special color no one else had. If I got Charles of the Ritz cosmetics, I would get the powder and would go out of my way to get it, but I'd really have to be sold on it first.

The respondent is short and slightly overweight. She has a very cute face and a bubbling personality. She is twenty-one.

Interview 15

Cosmetics

As for makeup, for class she wears foundation; if needed, she uses blusher, eye-liner, mascara, eyebrow pencil, powder, and lipstick. Buying cosmetics depends on where she is, usually at a department store or a discount drug store. At home in Cincinnati she buys at Mabley and Carew's and Low-Mark. She has no favorite brand and usually buys what is convenient. She uses Maybelline, Max Factor, Cover Girl, Helena Rubinstein, Revlon, Coty, and Miss Ritz.

She gets new ideas on makeup from friends and magazines such as *Glamour* and *Mademoiselle*. She feels that boys like to see girls wear makeup because it makes them look better, but many boys are opposed to eye makeup because it creates an unnatural or phony look. The only place she goes without makeup is to physical-education class or the beach.

Miss Ritz

She has seen Charles of the Ritz advertisements in magazines and has noticed their display counters in department stores. Her mother uses Charles of the Ritz, and she feels confident that it is a good cosmetic company. She learned of Miss Ritz several months ago and has used Santos lipstick ever since and is very satisfied with it because she likes coral orange shades. She thinks the channel of distribution is good because selling Ritz products in drug or variety stores would cheapen the quality of the product. She likes a sales person to know all about her product and to be able to advise her. Besides liking the color of Santos, she says it is creamy. She uses the Mask also and thinks it is refreshing and makes her face feel clean.

This respondent is a twenty-one year old junior majoring in elementary education and living in a sorority house. She is a small, dark-haired girl with a pretty complexion and a look of natural freshness. She wears nice clothes and has a neat appearance.

Interview 16

This is a joint interview with a town student named Charlotte and a girl from New Jersey named Barb. Both are independents. Both are dark-haired girls with brown eyes and are attractive. Barb is a senior in education and Charlotte is a junior in retailing.

Beauty

To Barb, a beautiful person is a person who is empathetic, who is not ethnocentric, and who loves other human beings. Charlotte says beauty is something you remember about a person that really pleases you. Physical beauty to both of them is based on their own ideals. Charlotte says it is something you are born with, with good taste thrown in. Through socialization, Barb says, her perceptual categories have been formed for her as to what is beauty. Charlotte feels that to achieve beauty one must play up the good points and hide the bad features, going along with style. Barb thinks that to achieve beauty one must keep up with what's in *Vogue*.

Cosmetics

As for cosmetics, Charlotte thinks they are necessary, helpful, and expensive to give the natural beauty look. Barb says they are fun to play with, and Charlotte feels naked without makeup. Barb has had a complexion problem, and, as for foundation, she wears Liqui-Mat, a medicated makeup. She prefers Revlon lipstick, Merle Norman eye-liner, Clairol shadow, and Max Factor liner. Charlotte also has no brand preference for all of her makeup. She buys a cheap lipstick, Revlon makeup, Revlon eye-liner, and Maybelline mascara. Max Factor eye makeup seems to give her styes.

Charlotte buys her makeup at the Fashion, drugstores, and from Merle Norman, because she can charge there. She likes to pick things up and examine them, and she cannot at Lazarus because everything is under glass (she is the town student). Barb does not buy at Lazarus because she prefers to buy at drugstores when she needs things in a hurry.

Miss Ritz

Barb feels that Charles of the Ritz is for older women because her mother uses it. Charlotte also associates it with old ladies and with money. Barb has seen advertisements for Miss Ritz and knows it is geared to younger girls, but seems still to associate it with expensiveness. They both think it should be sold at Long's (a bookstore just off campus) and at other more convenient places, such as drugstores. Charlotte has seen the blushers in compacts and thinks the compacts are too big and should be smaller to fit into a purse more conveniently. Barb saw many advertisements for Miss Ritz in the *Lantern* (the campus newspaper).

Barb has never used Miss Ritz. She said the sample felt creamy and tasted good. She prefers light orange, peachy shades, and browns. Charlotte had previously received a Miss Ritz lipstick in the dorm, and she likes it because it does not turn colors. It also does not mat. But she does not care for the packaging. She also likes the taste but thinks Portugal is too light (she has used Santos). She prefers a natural color of lipstick that is not too light.

Both said they would buy Miss Ritz if it were obtainable near campus. Barb said she would buy it if it appealed to her. Charlotte said it would depend on the price and color.

Interview 17

Cosmetics

The respondent believes that makeup should be used in moderation, that drawing attention to makeup is bad, and that drawing attention to natural beauty is the purpose of makeup. Cosmetics should make one look as natural as possible.

She buys her cosmetics where she is shopping, as a convenience. She would not go to a certain store to buy cosmetics, but, if she were in a store that sold them and she needed some, she would buy them there.

She gets advice from other girls about what types of makeup to use. She sees how they look on them and then decides how they would look on her. She then experiments to find out what makes her look best.

Commercials build curiosity for her. She thinks, "How will it look on me?"

Miss Ritz

She had heard of Miss Ritz and she was not impressed with the lipstick. It was too greasy for her. She buys products that are not greasy but that still do not look dried up.

This girl is a senior in education. Although she is not naturally attractive, by practicing her idea of "makeup in moderation" and by being well groomed she does present an attractive appearance.

Interview 18

Beauty

To the respondent, beauty is a total appearance concept. No one thing is beauty. Everything has to be just right. A girl has to be neat, clean, and not overdressed or underdressed to be beautiful. A girl's face must appear natural to be beautiful. If makeup is noticeable, then it is not beautiful.

Cosmetics

She buys cosmetics that are recommended by friends and that she sees in magazines. She looks for the "look I want to have" and then buys the products that she thinks will give it to her. She usually buys name brands (Revlon, Max Factor) because she is then sure of the quality. She buys cosmetics as a convenience item while shopping, but she admitted that she would go downtown to get a product that gave the right "look."

Miss Ritz

She was not too impressed with the lipstick. It was a little too creamy, it rubbed off a little too easily, and it looked as if it would wear down quickly. Again, the respondent described the product as "cheap."

She thinks that the product should be more widely distributed so that more people can try it.

This girl is an upperclassman in education. She is not naturally attractive, but with the proper use of makeup and by presenting herself well groomed, she creates the impression that she is a naturally attractive girl.

Interview 19

Beauty

Q. What does beauty suggest to you?

A. A natural, clear complexion, lightly touched up with makeup, highlighting the best features. Is well poised and stylishly dressed.

Cosmetics

Q. How long do you think a "beauty" spends putting makeup on?

A. Around fifteen minutes.

Q. Doesn't fifteen minutes seem rather long?

A. No, I spend about that much.

Q. What cosmetics do you wear?

A. Makeup base, eye-liner, blush-on, lipstick.

Q. Have you ever used powder?

A. Yes, but not very often. I don't really feel right wearing it.

Q. Have you ever heard of blending powders?

A. Yes, but I consider it too expensive and a waste of time. I have never seen a professional makeup man. I associate blended powders or lipsticks as something an older woman would use.

Q. Can you remember any of the names of the brands of cosmetics you use?

A. Marcelle is the base I use. It is a doctor's prescription lotion. Max Factor eye-liner and Revlon blush-on, and I haven't any particular brand of lipstick.

Q. What brand of lipsticks do you usually buy?

A. Buying lipstick is more of an impulse. I see a color I like and I get it. I don't usually spend over $1.50 for a tube, and even over a $1 is rare. Usually a tube will last a long time, so I don't really purchase lipstick very often. I like pastel colors.

Q. Are you willing to try something new?

A. It all depends on my mood and if I have extra money. I have seen the new two-tone lipsticks but I am afraid it would not last long, so I never tried it. I am usually in a drugstore or Lazarus when I purchase makeup.

Miss Ritz
Q. Have you ever heard of Clairol or Charles of the Ritz?

A. No, not Clairol, but I like their hair-coloring shampoos. I have heard of Charles of the Ritz, but I think it is out of my line. A product more for older women who have the money to buy them.

Q. Have you ever heard of Miss Ritz?

A. No, but I suppose it is a line associated with Charles of the Ritz.

Q. (*Giving her the lipstick.*) Do you care for the color?

A. Yes, but I can never tell about a color until I have tried it on. (*After trying it on.*) I don't like it. For one thing it looks purple on and it feels oily on my lips. I am sure I would never buy it if I knew it was this oily.

Q. Did you know Lazarus is the only place you can buy Charles of the Ritz?

A. No, but I really don't think that is too wise. I really don't think girls are going to travel all the way downtown to buy a tube of lipstick. There are so many brands on the market, and I think young girls buy the color, not the brand.

Q. Remember, you said you have heard of two-toned lipsticks but never tried them? Where did you hear about the product?

A. I must have seen an ad somewhere, maybe in *Glamour* or *Bazaar* or some fashion magazine.

Q. Have you ever heard your friends discuss it?

A. Yes, but no one has ever tried it that I know of.

Q. Would that be a hindrance to you?

A. No, I don't think so. I try to be discriminating and individualistic when buying something. Just because they have never tried it doesn't mean that I wouldn't.

Q. What does a limited distribution of goods mean to you?

A. Something very exclusive and expensive.

Q. Do you, in general, think that college girls are status conscious?

A. Everyone is to some extent, but not in makeup. After all, who knows what kind of makeup or lipstick you have on.

Q. After considering the color, in what order do you find the following variables important in deciding to purchase a tube of lipstick?

A. Color, tube design, price, name brand.

Interview 20
Two girls were interviewed at the same time here.

Beauty
"Beauty is nature, the natural look. A beautiful girl is one who looks the same when she comes out of the water after a swim as she did on a date. She can pull her hair back off of her face at any time and look the same—beautiful." Both associated natural beauty with a true person, one who isn't faky; lots of makeup makes a person look faky, false, not true.

Girls' mustaches or "fuzzy" looking lips look very unkept; they were very much against this. They tend to be influenced by what boy friends think and what boys want a girl to be; they also tend to be influenced by mothers somewhat, but also by close friends and sorority sisters. According to them, the tendency to change ways of appearance with age changes as one grows older.

Cosmetics
The two wear little makeup to class. They feel some girls look terrible with makeup but some look terrible without it. A lot of the makeup takes too much time to apply. They liked the lighter shades, like coral. "A little mascara never hurt anyone." Too much makeup looked false to them. Girls should get into the sun whenever possible for the natural look instead of using

a lot of makeup. It is alright to wear makeup "as long as it blends in with your complexion." They felt girls should not wear it in the summer because it tends to cake and run on one's face. They said there are "extremists": some girls will cut class if there is not time to put makeup on. There are tendencies to change ways and uses as one gets older. Women get softer skin with age. Women use more makeup as they get older and are not as active. Women then tend to make hair more mature and to wear older-looking clothes. They felt there is a tendency for younger girls to wear makeup at a lot earlier age today. Younger girls are growing up at a lot earlier age. They have more mature bodies at an earlier age and want to grow up too soon. They are in a "jet set" generation. They want to enjoy the older things too soon. They want to conform to everyone else so they will not be left out of anything.

According to the two, most girls buy their cosmetics at campus drugstores because of the convenience aspect, but it "depends, because they don't have to buy that often."

Some of the types of makeup they used were mascara, eyebrow pencil, eyeliner (brush and cake were the most preferred), lipstick, pancake makeup, blush-on (powder type), and lip gloss.

Some of the magazines mentioned for information reading were *Glamour, Seventeen, McCalls,* and *Mademoiselle.*

Miss Ritz

They had never heard much about the products: no advertising, no counter displays. The one girl had seen magazine advertisements, but the other one had not. They had heard a lot about it on campus lately but not in any of the stores. The girls could not really say much about the line of Miss Ritz products because they had not heard that much about them.

Lipstick

That the lipstick had a "horrible taste," and that it was creamy (both girls thought this characteristic was good) was their reaction to it. They liked the colors, but it was not what they wore. They liked the light shades.

Distribution

"If they want to make any money they better put the product around the campuses." The girls mentioned Revlon and Max Factor products in that they were easily accessible. They said that they could go to Long's and buy those products conveniently. One of the girls had the impression that Ritz products were very expensive, and she said she also knew that they "came from France." The other girl did not know anything about price.

Addition to Discussion on Beauty

The girls thought that boys had the following feelings about desired beauty: "a natural, carefree, nonsticky look," "could run their fingers through hair and not get them tangled," and "they can kiss you on the cheek or lips and not get makeup on their face."

Respondent Description

Both girls were members of the Kappa Kappa Gamma sorority and both were juniors in education. One girl was from Marion, Ohio, and the other one was from Cincinnati, Ohio. The one from Marion was from a quite wealthy family (her father is a doctor). The one from Marion was very liberal in her way of thinking, but the other one was a little more conservative. Both girls were dressed casually and were well groomed.

Interview 21

Beauty

Beauty is really a superficial thing. A person can be completely un-attractive, but when you get to know him, he can become beautiful in your own eyes.

Real beauty is basically Grecian beauty: the fine, thin, upturned nose; the eyes are emphasized (large eyes considered very attractive) and her hair is her crown. A beautiful girl spends more time on her hair than anything else. Clear, rosy complexion gives the "natural looking" com-plexion. Lots of makeup used now is patterned after the Egyptian. This is more of a trend towards the unnatural look—accentuating the eyes, muting the color of the face and lips, and emphasizing naturally straight hair.

My mother has influenced me quite a bit. She is very conservative. Sorority sisters also influence me, because I live with them all the time. I don't read magazines for beauty information as such because I wear the type of makeup that is best for me.

She tries to accentuate her good features and decentuate her bad ones— maybe not necessarily achieving this, but she is constantly trying.

Cosmetics

There is a trend toward the use of light lipsticks. You see what looks good on someone else, ask them what it is, and then you go out and buy it. The most used brands are Chanel, Revlon, Max Factor (the trustworthy products). I use what is "in," what the magazines and ad-vertisements talk about. It seems to me that the cosmetic companies are probably the ones who start the fads. The companies who don't change their assortments are falling by the wayside. They must improve their products or use a gimmick. Some of the poorer companies today are Hazel Bishop and Cutex.

Where you live, personal preferences, background, religious aspects have a lot to do with the amount and use of cosmetics.

Companies try to use "catchy names" to lure customers: nearly nude, creamy ivory, catalina coral, natural frost, persian melon, pumpkin eyes, sunrise tulip, lamb's down puffer, misty rose, or lagoona peach.

Miss Ritz

Respondent has a favorable reaction toward their astringents and skin freshener, but she thinks they "tend to cater to the older women." She had used the eye-liner, but she didn't like it because it ran. She thinks their line in general is supposed to be good, but they are expensive.

She mentioned the on-campus demonstrations. She didn't like them. She thinks they were too extreme, too thick for everyday use. "The basic concepts of what to wear are probably right, but they put too much on—too gooey. They go too much on one particular trend and they make all of the girls up the same way."

Lipstick sample reaction

"Bitter" tasting. It feels like the kind that would change color (pause) But maybe it doesn't. I am not real sure.

Respondent is a very good looking girl, well groomed and wore very little makeup. She is a member of Kappa Alpha Theta sorority. She is twenty-two years old and a senior in education.

Interview 22

Beauty

To make a girl look as good as she possibly can, she must use makeup to show off her good features and hide her bad ones.

I buy most of my clothes at the Fashion and the Northland Lazarus. When I am at home I buy my clothes at some small, private dress shops.

Cosmetics

I buy mainly Revlon and Max Factor. Most of the time I buy my cosmetics at the drugstore. I like these brands because they are known brands and I can trust their quality. I think that most college students buy these brands for the same reasons as I do. They don't like to experiment with any stuff that's way-out. But if a name brand comes up with some way-out stuff, it's safe to try it.

When I was at home this summer there was a beauty consultant at one of the stores, and I spoke to her. She showed me the correct way to apply makeup and she also showed me just what would be the best combination of makeup for me. Most college girls probably use friends as makeup consultants. I do this sometimes myself. I also get a lot of information as to what types of cosmetics to use by looking at ads in magazines like *Mademoiselle* and *Seventeen*.

Miss Ritz

I never use it but I've heard that it is good stuff. I've also heard that it is expensive.

(Gave her lipstick reaction.) It's creamy but it tastes blah. The color is better for blonds than brunettes.

I think that they should have more stores selling the product. Sometimes when I run out of lipstick I can't go downtown, so I run to the drugstore. But, of course, some companies like to only sell their product at a few stores because they think that it makes it appear to be more of an exclusive product.

The respondent is a junior in the college of social work. She is moderately attractive with an average figure.

Interview 23

Beauty

Beauty is making yourself look as good as you possibly can. If an ugly girl makes herself look better than she really does, this is beauty also.

Cosmetics

Your makeup must fit the clothes you are wearing. You don't wear tons of makeup with shorts, and, of course, you should never wear tons of makeup.

I buy a good deal of my makeup at Lazarus. Occasionally, if I need something in a hurry I buy in a drugstore.

For daily wear to classes I usually wear lipstick, powder, and eye-liner. I think every girl needs to wear this much makeup. For a difference, I may resort to fake lashes and more.

I buy Revlon. I like it and that's why I buy it. I don't know exactly why I like it, but I do.

Miss Ritz

I've heard of it, but I never buy it. For one, it's too expensive. I think that maybe if they changed the name and sold it more places than just Lazarus they would be better off. Charles of the Ritz just sounds too stuffy and old fashioned for a name of lipstick that hopefully will be bought by college students.

[Where do you get advice on your clothing and make-up?] We always talk about that at the sorority house. Everyone shows everybody else their new clothes and makeup. I also read magazines like *Vogue*.

The subject is a junior in the college of education. She is in one of the top sororities on campus. She is extremely good looking and has a wonderful figure. I believe that she may be considered an opinion leader in her sorority.

Interview 24

Beauty

There is no such thing as physical beauty. A girl may appear to be beautiful, but beauty is only real beauty when it goes beneath the skin into the soul.

Cosmetics

Q. Do you use cosmetics?

A. I use no makeup. I believe that makeup is just another one of modern man's attempts to make him appear to be something he is not. If all women were meant to be beautiful, God would have made them so.

Q. Do you believe that a girl should play up her best features?

A. A girl's best features are already played up; otherwise they wouldn't be considered her best features. A person does not look to find physical ugliness. I, myself, always notice a girl's good features. It's just too bad that the girl is so busy worrying that her bad features will show up.

Miss Ritz

Q. Have you ever heard of Charles of the Ritz?

A. No.

Q. Would you like this free sample?

A. Sure, maybe I can give it to the Salvation Army.

The subject is very unresponsive to the idea of cosmetics. She has long, brown hair that is very straight. She was wearing Levis and a white shirt. I believe the subject is in what is known as the "Hippie" crowd.

Interview 25

Clothing

Two types of style at Ohio State, the sorority girls, collegiate looking, short skirts, straight hair, nicely made up, but not heavily and giving the overall impression of the basic college girl. The other group is with the stringy hair, arty type blue jeans and sandals. Sorority styles are set by what stores are pushing and what appears in fashion magazines such as *Glamour* and *Seventeen.*

She doesn't know where the arty styles come from.

Beauty
Beauty depends primarily on three different things:

1. face and hair, the picture given by the total

2. posture and carriage

3. overall clothing (should be stylish)

> The natural look is the best, with soft, clean shining hair. Makeup should be applied very well, not heavily made up. Better clothes help but not necessarily so. A girl to look beautiful should not only buy what is stylish but what is stylish for her. She should be able to judge current styles and decide what looks good. Not everyone can be beautiful, but a neat appearance can create attraction. Personality contributes along with a pretty smile (a must). Personal habits such as smoking detract from overall appearance.

Cosmetics

> I don't use as many cosmetics as a lot of people do, but those I use are to try to arrive at a natural beauty type look. Eyes are the most basic, if they are made up correctly a person can get away with less makeup. Should be subtle but can be striking. Eye-liner, shadow, etc. The girl should know different kinds to pick, the color best for her wardrobe, and needs and complexion. Eyebrows are also important, they should not give the impression of being too plucked or heavy. [She uses Maybelline products for all eye-makeup.]

She likes the new iridescent pale lipstick colors, but feels that a girl should only wear them if they look "good." She uses mostly Revlon and Max Factor. Lipstick should be worn at all times to keep the lips from drying out. She judges a lipstick by how long it stays on, color, type of tube (pretty and whether it works well), and if it cakes when on for a long period of time. Foundations should highlight a girl's best features of face. Blusher should always be used because very few people can look good without them. She feels that sales people can sway you when buying cosmetics, for example, a good looking sales woman might say, "This is good for you" or "Lots of people are using this" and often influence you to buy. She makes most of her purchases at Lazarus and the Fashion.

Charles of the Ritz

"Yes, I used to sell it at Lazarus. I like their Sun Bronze tanning lotion."
Her overall impression was just a little more expensive than usual but likes
the way the powders are mixed for each person. She liked the lipstick. Felt
nice and creamy, color looks good. Tube looks impractical and cheap. Name
implies something a lot better than the tube looks although lipstick seems
nice. She did not feel that she would make a special trip downtown to purchase (even though she earlier said that all purchases were made downtown).
Ritz would need either an effective advertising campaign or some gimmick to
bring the customers downtown. She seemed to think that they should have
them on campus for the spur of the moment purchase.

Respondent is a sharp-looking senior, former model and salesgirl at Lazarus. Good personality, twenty-two years old.

Interview 26

Beauty

"Some people have a natural beauty that has nothing to do with the clothing
they wear or the makeup. Makeup has a lot to do with the impression of
beauty, along with hair style and personality. Makeup contributes most
however. It can change you, especially eye makeup. Someone with eyes that
stand out is sure to be noticed by all the boys." She thinks that most girls were
what makes them look good to the guys, but that a girl can achieve beauty
by being clean and neat and above all, by not wearing too much makeup.

Cosmetics

She buys makeup by what looks good in ads and on models in fashion magazines. She experiments with different kinds of cosmetics. Sometimes she ends
up with junk sold to her by a salesman, but usually she buys only well accepted brands. Most of her cosmetics are purchased at drug stores or Lazarus.
Her supply consists of "basics" and some new products. She might buy something that had a good display, but usually sticks with Revlon. Price is not a
determinant (she says she buys what is right for her) and she steers away
from cheap makeup and non brand names. Makeup can change one's whole
appearance. She has had lots of roommates, very few of whom look good
without makeup or use of cosmetics. "You can overdo or underdo application
of any kind of makeup. No eye makeup looks bad as does an overdone facial,
because it gives you an unnatural look." She judges cosmetics by comments of
other people, but looks for the nice feeling and the lasting effect. She does not
like to wear lipstick but does so because everyone else uses it. She experiments more with lipstick than any other cosmetic because she has yet to find
one that is perfect for her, tries to find what looks good, has lasting effect,
tastes good and doesn't cake. Usually uses a lipstick base and another color
of lip gloss over that because she has trouble finding the exact one.

Miss Ritz

Has heard of Charles of the Ritz, never used it, but sounds too expensive. Miss Ritz lipstick tastes good, but she will have to wear it longer to see if it cakes. Said that it felt good. Would expect to pay $1.75 for the tube since it feels like good quality lipstick, but would be more inclined to buy it, if in the campus area. Thinks display helps quite a bit in purchase of cosmetics and that people often buy lipstick in a hurry and would not have time to go downtown.

Respondent is an office worker attending Ohio State at night. Lives in off campus apartment with two roommates. Average looks, fair figure, good personality.

Interview 27

Beauty

"Some people can be beautiful if they only stay neat and clean and dress reasonably well. Others need a makeup beauty. Many girls only look good when they have makeup on. Personality helps to some degree."

Cosmetics

"There is a real art in application of cosmetics, sloppy makeup can make you look fake or phony." She experiments with different kinds of makeup to create an overall effect which she thinks that people will like. Tended to pay most attention to her girlfriends for advice on cosmetics. Some girls need only a little makeup to bring out or hide features, but she thought that many girls used far too much. She buys most of her makeup from Avon (door to door), drug stores, and cosmetic parties. Her most used brands are Avon, Maybelline, and Pond's. She thinks that liquid makeup should not be greasy, and she abhors lipstick which is greasy or "gooey." She feels that lipsticks should not cake, should be creamy and smooth and keep looking fresh after a period of time. Price did not seem to make any difference in that cheaper cosmetics were considered to be of poor quality and not worth buying. She is attracted by appealing display, but she would not be too inclined to buy something that she did not know.

Miss Ritz

Charles of the Ritz, sounds expensive but she has never heard of it or ever used it. She liked the lipstick, color was good, smell was nice, and it seemed creamy but also seemed doubtful that it would last. Would be willing to go to one shop and purchase but said that she would not make any special trips downtown just to purchase lipstick. She did not seem to think other people would make an effort to obtain Miss Ritz when they could buy many other lipsticks in the campus area.

Respondent is a freshman, living at home, fairly attractive figure and face; but seemed unsure of herself at times and other times very dominant.

Interview 28

Beauty

I believe beauty is a combination of many things. I don't believe there are very many beautiful women. Most girls can become very attractive if they learn how. I believe it is a matter of being clean and well groomed, neat, wearing popular clothing styles, and using makeup. Clothes affect appearance greatly. Unattractive clothes can ruin the appearance of an otherwise attractive or beautiful girl. Hair and makeup are also big factors in creating attractiveness. Personality is part of beauty, and a girl will have a hard time being the totally beautiful girl if she doesn't have a personality to match her outer beauty. A girl doesn't need a perfect figure to be beautiful, but I don't think an excessively fat or skinny girl can be beautiful. A keen sense of competition exists at Ohio State which causes girls to dress for other girls as much as for boys. I believe that a girl can achieve or improve her attractiveness by looking around her and finding out what is the current idea of beauty, talking to friends and roommates, reading magazines, and experimenting with cosmetics and clothing to find out which are most complimentary to her. Overweight girls can diet and exercise and wear clothes which are complimentary to their figure. Girls with bad complexions can improve them with better diets and medical attention. A girl can improve her appearance by taking good care of her hair and seeking information from hair dressers and beauty experts concerning the best styles for her.

Cosmetics

I think cosmetics are great. They can make a girl look like a new person. They actually give you more confidence and can make you feel better psychologically. They can actually change a girl's actions and personality as well as her outward appearance. I prefer Revlon and Max Factor cosmetics. I often take friends and roommates' advice on which cosmetics to purchase. I also often buy cosmetics I see advertised. I purchase approximately two thirds of my cosmetics on campus primarily for reasons of convenience. I use about six or seven types of cosmetics. I decide which types of cosmetics to buy based on my assets and weaknesses, and also according to what is currently popular. I obtain advice and information on cosmetics from roommates, friends, boyfriends, advertising, and television and movie stars. I purchase my cosmetics mostly at small campus shops and nearby drugstores, but also occasionally purchase them at large downtown department stores. I read *Seventeen, Glamour,* and *Mademoiselle* magazines for beauty and clothing information. I believe that boys like makeup, but not too much. They like a girl to conform to the popular and accepted values of beauty.

Miss Ritz

I have never heard of Miss Ritz, but I have heard of Charles of the Ritz. I don't know very much about Charles of the Ritz cosmetics but I believe that they are high quality products because I got some as a gift from my wealthy aunt a couple of years ago. I have never known anyone who used Charles of the Ritz cosmetics, and I have never had anyone recommend them to me. I can't remember seeing them advertised too much. My overall impression of them is high-quality, expensive products used mainly by middle-aged and older women.

The girl interviewed is an extremely attractive senior in the college of education.

Interview 29

Beauty

I believe that beauty is more than just one facet of a girl. It is a combination of several things such as figure, complexion, eyes, straight hair, and mod clothes, and a cheerful and pleasant personality. I don't think a girl can be beautiful unless she has straight hair, whether it be short or long. The opinions of roommates, close boy friends, *Seventeen* magazine and *Glamour* magazine are most important to me in determining what beauty is. I believe a girl can achieve greater beauty by seeking advice from roommates, professional people such as hair dressers, skin doctors, and beauty magazines.

Cosmetics

I think cosmetics are the greatest things since guys. I don't know how women ever got along without them. They're one of a girl's best friends. I use several brands of cosmetics such as Revlon, Max Factor, Avon, Helene Curtis, and Clairol. I get advice on cosmetics from roommates, also find out about cosmetics by experimenting with new ones. I also get such advice from advertisements. I buy about half of my cosmetics in stores close to campus and about half in downtown department stores. I use four different brands of cosmetics. I decide the types of cosmetics which are best for me to use according to my hair color, eye color, and skin tone. I read *Seventeen, Glamour* and *Mademoiselle* for information on appearance, clothing, and cosmetics. Boys don't like excessive amounts of makeup because it makes a girl look false. I think boys like the presently popular natural look on a girl.

Miss Ritz

I have never heard of Miss Ritz. I have heard of Charles of the Ritz. I don't know much about Charles of the Ritz makeup. I don't think it is a brand which is used very much by college girls.

The girl interviewed for this interview is a fairly attractive freshman living in a large dormitory.

Interview 30

Beauty

Being beautiful is bringing out the good characteristics in a person and covering up the bad. A person's personality brings out her beauty. When you wake up and feel good, you want to look good; when you feel lousy you don't care how you look, and if you do try and look good you usually don't anyway.

Cosmetics

I think cosmetics are a waste of time. They're bad for your skin. I just wear lipstick, because I have good coloring and that's the reason most girls use makeup—to give a false color. I like to look natural, because I don't want to give anyone a false impression of myself. It's really not necessary for most girls unless they have a bad complexion.

Miss Ritz

That stuff is too expensive. I did read about the contest in the *Lantern*. It doesn't seem like that great a deal.

The lipstick seems okay, but I'll stick to Yardley because it will stick without caking. I knew it was sold at Lazarus, but I figured it was at the Fashion and the Union too.

The respondent is a freshman majoring in education. She appears middle class, not beautiful but attractive. She wears little or no makeup.

Interview 31

Beauty

Beauty is what society says it is at a particular time. The same is true for fashion. First skirts are shorter, now they're trying to lower hemlines. It's a racket to make money for the designers and the clothing stores. Beauty is only good as long as it's in style.

You try to be beautiful to please the people who are close to you. If your friends are doing certain things to be hip or in style, you do it too. If the girls are all wearing their hair down and long, you'd better do it too or you'll lose out. This is why girls go to beauty parlors, read fashion magazines, and wear contacts and get nose jobs.

Cosmetics

I wear cosmetics just to put on finishing touches when I go out. I don't wear lipstick at all because I just don't like it or the way it feels. I use some eye-liner because it's the thing to do. Cosmetics are okay, they give you a healthy look when you don't look your best.

Miss Ritz

I've heard of Charles of the Ritz because I'm from New York and so are they. I understand it's supposedly very good, but I've never tried it myself. It's too expensive. Some of my friends use it, though, and they seem to like it.

Lipstick

As I said, I don't use lipstick, but it seems very creamy and rich. I didn't know about the distribution, but it seems as though they'd sell better to college girls in one clothing store on campus.

The respondent is a junior majoring in education. She is a member of a sorority. She appears quite wealthy from her manner and appearance. She was very smartly dressed and neat.

Interview 32

Cosmetics

Q. Let's talk about cosmetics. . . . Where does a girl start when she sees a new product?

A. Probably the cosmetic department. And from people that are aware of the product. Another place you find out about cosmetics would be beauty parlors, where they could evaluate your coloring or something and tell you what would look best . . . .

Q. You mean specific brands?

A. Yes, like Revlon or Hazel Bishop.

Q. They'll try to coordinate a "look"?

A. Yes, what's right for you.

Q. What are the basic things they recommend?

A. Like Revlon, and Merle Norman, and Coty . . . Helena Rubinstein . . . the big brand names.

Q. Now, do they make everything, or does one just make lipstick and another powder, etc. . . . .

A. No, all the big cosmetic distributors make everything . . . . I prefer Revlon, personally, for most things . . . because of the *quality* of it. It's more expensive, but again, it's more natural looking.

Q. What do you do when you see something new, like a new line, like Charles of the Ritz, or something? Something rather exclusive.

A. I'd experiment with it.

Q. You'd buy it?

A. Oh, yes.

Q. What was the last new thing you . . . .

A. Ultra-Lash, by . . . . I can't remember who makes it. I wouldn't recommend Coty products, because I don't like them.

Q. Why?

A. Too high a price . . . the products aren't any good. Their lipstick, for example . . . should be much creamier, not so waxy.

Q. What makes a good lipstick? Take a look at these new shades in the Charles of the Ritz line.

A. I've never used these . . . like I said, I would prefer buying Revlon . . . because of their quality and their variety . . . and you pay a dollar for a good tube of lipstick . . . there's no point in paying fifty-nine cents and getting . . . .

Q. Well, now, these are from a somewhat exclusive line . . . have you ever tried any of their products?

A. No.

Q. And you wouldn't want to?

A. No.

Q. But you do try new products sometimes?

A. You probably think I'm crazy.

Q. Not at all. It's just a matter of personal preference.

A. They're not too bad. I like that one. The color.

Q. How's it taste? Is taste important?

A.   No. They all taste the same after fifteen years.

Q.   Anything you'd like to add?

A.   No.

The respondent, Karen, is a junior in education. She is attractive and is living in an apartment near campus.

Interview 33

Beauty

Q.   If you were extremely fashion-conscious, where would you find out what was new or stylish?

A.   You mean around here? Around campus? Magazines, I guess. And go downtown—(*long pause*) and advertising.

Q.   So you think fashion magazines are a good source for style news?

A.   Yeah. And other stuff.

Q.   Like cosmetics, or how to be beautiful?

A.   Where to buy certain things . . . like "Villager" clothes. Name brands are very important . . . they're like a status symbol. You don't buy something cheap, you have to buy something with a good name you respect.

Q.   Maybe an exclusive line of accessories or lipstick or something?

A.   Makeup . . . and hair coloring.

Q.   Some people say that housewives basically dislike to see any beautiful woman advertising soap powder because they feel that they're a competitor in some psychological sense . . . .

A.   I don't think a competitor so much as a fake, because housewives just don't look like that, you know, when they're doing their laundry, dressed up in a fancy little dress, with their hair all perfect, you know. Who puts on all that, who goes through a half hour makeup change and gets their hair done at the beauty parlor before they do their laundry? Not too many people. Those kind of people don't do their own laundry.

Q.   Beautiful women?

A.   You should try and improve your appearance. I mean, experiment with makeup.

Q.   How do you know what's right? Friends' opinions?

A.   That's important.

Cosmetics

Q.   What about makeup?

A.   You get a consensus of opinion . . . money's the b-i-g-g-e-s-t factor. It takes a lot of money to . . .

Q.   . . . buy all these beauty aids?

A.   Yes.

Q.   But now, you might go out in West Virginia and find a very beautiful girl, no makeup . . . just like Cinderella.

A.   Very few of them. Very few. Most of the women nowadays that men think are beautiful really work at it . . . .

Q.   Beauty's a business, then?

A.   Right.

Q.   Clothes are pretty much what someone else has brought forth to the market. But cosmetics are more an individual effort which you make yourself. How do you decide what to buy?

A.   There are so many . . . there are very few things I don't like as long as they're good . . . .

Q.   Good?

A.   I mean you can overdo everything. You have to experiment. There's plenty of stuff you can read . . . .

Q.   But, for instance, what makes a good lipstick?

A.   The name. The color. There's Revlon and Max Factor . . . they all have basically the same shades . . . different names.

Q.   When you decide . . . .

A.   A lot of it's advertisement. Like I use one lipstick because I like the taste of it, or the sales clerk. If I think she knows what she's talking about . . . if she's not trying to push it . . . if she's, you can tell, trying to sell it because she thinks it will look good on you.

Q.   What does lipstick cost?

A.   A dollar and a quarter, dollar and a half. You know, you can buy cheap for thirty-nine cents.

Q.   What brands do you have at home?

A.   Oh, Revlon and Max Factor . . . because they have the shades I like . . . they taste good. I buy them at Lazarus . . . or the drugstore . . . .

Q.   Drugstores? Wouldn't those be cheaper?

A.   Oh, no. They don't have cheap lipstick. I bought my last one at Gray Drug Store, University shopping center, Max Factor $1.25, Laguna peach refill.

Miss Ritz

Q.   Have you ever heard of, or tried, something more exclusive, like, maybe Charles of the Ritz?

A.   Have I heard of it? Yeah.

Q.   How do you like it?

A.   It's too expensive.

Q.   What's it cost?

A.   I don't know. That isn't the only thing. I'm satisfied with **Max Factor** . . . they keep up with the times . . . they're constantly changing and bringing out new things . . . and they're good products.

Q.   But doesn't Charles of the Ritz come out with wild new colors, etc.?

A.   Yes, I suppose, but I guess you get used to Max Factor and things like that because you can usually get them any place. Those are the kind of things you can get at drugstores, and the ones that are a little more exclusive, you have to go certain places to get them.

Q.   But don't you like . . . something that's a little bit more exclusive?

A.   It has to be worth it . . . like there's some things I would definitely spend the money for, because to me it's worth the extra money to have it. The makeup I just bought, everything's a dollar more than the same stuff by the same company, but it's new and it's a little bit better . . . to me. Since I've tried it, I think it's a little bit better . . . like blush-on. You don't know what blush-on is . . . it's a powder you put on with a brush. Gives you the effect of rouge, only it's very soft, and makes you . . . glow . . . pink (*laughter*).

Q.   You don't say. Let me show you a new product . . . .

A.   That color is too dark. (*Examines.*) Smells good. Can I taste it?

Q.   What are your reactions?

A.   It's all right, I guess. It's a new line they just brought out. I haven't tried it . . . they got funny names, you can't tell what color they are from the names.

Q.   Like Portugal?

A.   I think that's a disadvantage. I have to look at every single one—it's not like Laguna peach or Hot coral . . . to tell what color I want.

Q.   Otherwise?

A.   It's about average. Maybe the case is a little smaller. It's a refill. Yes, it's a refill. It's okay, I guess.

Q.   Do you think, to sum it up, that men have many misconceptions about cosmetics or beauty in general.

A.   God, yes! These guys, they don't want their girl to use a lot of makeup. They say they hate makeup. Well, they'd be surprised to learn how much makeup girls use, just to get a natural look. They'd really be surprised.

The respondent is a nurse at University Hospital, recently graduated.

Interview 34

Beauty

A person is beautiful who has a nice facial structure, nice teeth, pretty eyes, knows how to accentuate all the good points on her face and body and make the best out of what she has, yet is not overly made up. I also feel that personality plays a big part in a person's beauty.

I feel a girl can improve her beauty by taking care of herself and not being sloppy, by not letting her physical condition get completely out of hand, and by keeping her clothes neat and pressed.

I believe guys' opinions are the most important, as girls do dress basically to please guys; however, I also take hints and suggestions from my girl friends. I also get a lot of information from fashion and beauty magazines. Some of the magazines I read for beauty information are *Vogue, Glamour,* and *Seventeen.*

Cosmetics

I feel that cosmetics are not essential to a girl who has a pretty complexion and a rosy glow except for maybe eyebrow pencil or mascara. However, there are more girls, including myself, who have a rather drab complexion and need a little color. I use Revlon and Max Factor products myself because they are well known, more expensive, and don't clog up my skin. Most of my friends prefer these same brands. I do use fewer cosmetics in the summer than in the winter. Basically, I choose what brands of cosmetics I use through trial and error. If I use a brand of cosmetics and am satisfied with it, I will continue using that brand. Points that I look for in cosmetics are how it stays on my face, whether it changes color in different lights, and whether or not it is oily.

I buy most of my cosmetics at drugstores down here at school because

I can get what I want there. I usually don't want to bother buying cosmetics at home, except in the summer months.

Most of my advice about cosmetics comes from magazines and from any type of advertisement that I might see.

I don't think most guys appreciate girls who come downstairs looking like she has just been run through a paint machine. I feel guys prefer more of a natural look with a little bit of color so she is attractive but not overdone.

I certainly feel that cosmetics relate to fashion and appearance as is apparent from many of my previous statements.

Miss Ritz

I have heard of the Charles of the Ritz line of cosmetics through their advertisements, but I have never, until now, heard of the Miss Ritz line of their products. Although I have never used any Charles of the Ritz or Miss Ritz products, I am very familiar with Charles of the Ritz powder because my mother uses it. I haven't tried it, as I feel that it is a little bit too expensive for me.

I do like the color of the sample lipstick and would consider buying this line of products, as I am willing to give any brand of cosmetics a try. Although I do buy many of my clothes downtown, I haven't as yet seen this product for sale. If I did start using this product, I liked it, and Lazarus was the only place I could get it, I would go there to get it rather than use something else, unless, I was very pressed for time when I ran out.

The respondent is a sophomore in arts.

Interview 35

Beauty

A person doesn't necessarily have to have a pretty face and figure to be beautiful, although it certainly does help. One who I consider beautiful is neat and clean both outwardly and inwardly. She also has a radiant and warm personality.

Beauty can be achieved or improved by a girl watching her weight and figure, wearing the right clothes for her particular build, and trying to maintain personal cleanliness and grooming habits.

I consider most of my friends opinions concerning beauty are certainly very important. Men's opinions are of particular concern to women, and I feel that oftentimes we dress to please them.

The magazines that I read for beauty information are *Glamour, Mademoiselle,* and *Seventeen.*

Cosmetics

I think that cosmetics are basically essential to every girl, and certainly add to their appearance if used in good taste and not overapplied. I use Max Factor and Avon cosmetics simply because I like their products very much. I don't feel that there is any special brand or brands of cosmetics that are especially preferred by my friends. The way I choose my cosmetics is by seeing a particular brand, wondering what it is like, and then finally trying it.

Most of the time I buy my cosmetics at home. However, occasionally I buy them here at school in campus drugstores.

Some of my advice about cosmetics comes when I am home from the Avon lady who stops at our house. I also get some of my information from the fashion and beauty magazines that I read.

I think that generally guys don't like to see a lot of cosmetics on a girl. Guys, I don't feel, have any objection to the girl who uses her cosmetics in moderation with the expressed purpose of emphasizing her good points. I do, myself, dislike seeing a girl who is obviously over made-up.

Yes, I do feel that cosmetics are related to fashion and appearance. Cosmetics are used to achieve, for example, the natural look which has been, and is, fashion.

Miss Ritz

I have heard of the Miss Ritz line of cosmetics through magazines. However, I have never used any of this line of products. There are no special reasons for my failure to try the product.

I would consider buying or at least trying the Miss Ritz line, but the color of the sample lipstick is too light for me. If I started using the Miss Ritz line and liked it, I would probably go to Lazarus to buy it if I couldn't get it elsewhere. However, if I were short on time, needed cosmetics, and were near a drug store, I would forego buying this product and make something else do. Therefore, I feel that I would be more apt to buy this product if it were available at more places within a closer distance of the campus.

The respondent is a junior majoring in elementary education.

Interview 36

Beauty

I feel that beauty is both inward and outward. A girl is outwardly beautiful when she maintains herself as far as not using makeup to extremes but uses it to modification with the purpose of playing up her good points. Also, I feel a girl should know how to dress at the proper time. She should always dress to enhance herself, be well groomed at all times, and try always to carry herself properly.

Beauty in a girl can be achieved or improved through cleanliness habits, keeping the hair properly fitted to the face, wearing clothes that fit properly, proper color combinations in clothing, and the correct use of makeup.

I feel that guys' opinions concerning beauty are certainly very important. However, women's opinions are probably more important because I am in closer touch with them. I read several magazines for beauty information, including *Glamour, Seventeen, Harper's Bazaar,* and *Vogue.*

Cosmetics

I feel that a certain amount of cosmetics is essential to every girl. It is essential for a girl to have a makeup that covers the face, so that if she is pale she can make herself look a little brighter and if she is too red she can tone her skin down a little. I personally use a Revlon product because it's medicated and also I like it. I also use Avon products and a Charles of the Ritz lipstick because it's creamy. Quite a few of my friends use a Revlon makeup, but the brand of lipstick used varies greatly. I decide upon what brands of cosmetics to use through the trial-and-error method, as I feel most of my friends do.

I buy most of my cosmetics at school, in difference to my clothing needs at home. The two reasons for this are that I usually run out of cosmetics before I get home and that I feel Columbus has a better selection of products with stores such as Lazarus.

I get most of my advice about cosmetics from looking through magazines, my roommates and friends and at home.

I feel guys like cosmetics as long as they are attractive on a girl. It's alright if they can't tell that it is there; but as soon as it becomes so evident that it becomes gaudy, then I don't think a man likes it.

I very definitely think cosmetics relate to fashion and appearance. I think makeup relates to fashion in that one year the bright colored lipsticks will go with the dull outfits, and the next year it will be something else. Another example of fashion and cosmetics is two years ago the pale white lipstick was in, and now the color lipsticks are coming back. Makeup also runs in fashion. For example, for a while we wore rouge, then we didn't, and now we wear blush-on.

Miss Ritz

I have tried some of the Miss Ritz products and like the lipstick especially well. I have used their skin lotion but didn't like it because it seemed to have an oily base, even though it claimed it didn't. My face didn't react to it properly anyway. I have also used their eye-shadow and powder. I especially like the powder and feel that it can do a lot for me

if it is blended properly. However, I am presently out of it and don't
have the money or time to get it.

I feel that the present distribution of Charles of the Ritz products may,
to a certain extent, keep me from buying the products because I either
don't feel like going downtown or have the time to spare. However, if
I really like something, I will usually go out of my way to get it, but I
certainly would be more satisfied if it were more readily available.

The respondent is a sophomore with a major in home economics education.
She is an attractive girl with a pleasant personality and a demonstrated eager-
ness to converse.

Interview 37

Beauty

I think that everyone should have their own idea of what's beauty.
Something that may be beautiful for one person won't necessarily be
beauty to someone else. When I want to get information on fashion or
beauty I go to women's magazines, especially for the hair-do magazines.
I like to change my hair style often. I also read *Seventeen* magazine
regularly.

Cosmetics

When I was in high school I was a majorette. We used a lot of makeup then, and I guess that's when I got started. I use pretty much now
because I like it. I like to use good, high-quality makeup. I never use
powder makeup, but always a good cream. I use bath lotion to keep fresh.

There isn't any certain brand or kind of cosmetics that college students
like to use. They use just about any kind. I buy my cosmetics where
ever it's convenient, not any particular store.

I like to try out new kinds when I can. I usually try out the demon-
strators and testers in stores. If I like the product, I buy it; if I don't
like it, I don't buy it.

Most of the information that I get about makeup comes from magazines. I like to go through the magazine just looking at all the advertisements.

Boys think makeup looks good as long as it's put on right and a good
quality is used. If it's real heavy and unnatural looking, then they don't
like it. My boyfriends think it looks good.

Miss Ritz

I have heard of it, but I have never used any of that brand. The lipstick (sample) looks like my shade. I don't buy any certain brand of
lipstick, but whatever is convenient. That is, I buy whatever the store

has for sale that I happen to be in at the time. I didn't know that Lazarus is the only place in town where I can buy Miss Ritz. Why don't they sell it in other places?

The respondent is a sophomore majoring in social work. She belongs to a social sorority on campus and lives in a dorm.

Interview 38

Cosmetics

Girls use more makeup when they go out on a date or a special occasion in the evening than they use during the day. Too much makeup is frowned upon by most girls. People think that the girl is really out to "land" a boy when she uses too much makeup. Besides, it looks ridiculous. Boys like a girl to look natural yet attractive. A little makeup helps a girl's looks, but too much hurts her looks.

The powder that a girl uses should give her a natural look. If it is used too heavily, it doesn't look natural.

Girls like to try new things. If they like a new cosmetic, they will continue to use it; but if they don't, they simply throw it out.

I look to magazines as an authority on the subject of cosmetics. Some of the magazines that I read are *Glamour, Seventeen,* and *Mademoiselle.*

Miss Ritz

(*Reaction to lipstick sample.*) I have a friend that uses that color. I'll give it to her. It looks good, but I don't use lipstick. I have always associated Charles of the Ritz with facial powders. Don't they mix powders for different complexions and skin colors? I have never purchased any of Charles of the Ritz cosmetics. I didn't know that they were only sold at Lazarus. I don't get downtown very often. If the Miss Ritz products were sold at a drug store where I shop and they had a product that I liked, I would probably buy it.

The respondent is a junior, majoring in secondary education. She is active in student government and is an officer in the girl's dormitory council. Pauline resides at Barrett House. She is a religious person and does not belong to a sorority. She is planning to teach mathematics in high school after graduation.

Interview 39

Beauty

A girl can make herself more beautiful by the clothes that she wears and the ability she has in using the appropriate amount of makeup.

I want people to think that I am pleasant looking. I don't care whether they think that I'm beautiful. The only person's opinion that I really care about is my boy friend's.

Cosmetics

I only use lipstick and sometimes a little powder. That is all that I care to use, but it's strictly up to the individual. If the girl likes to use a lot of makeup, she should feel free to use it.

I don't feel comfortable when I'm out and don't have at least a little lipstick on.

I think boys like to see girls with some makeup on, but not overdone. I don't think that they like a girl who uses thick powder on her face.

I would say that my opinions are similar to many other college girls on the subject of clothes and makeup.

Miss Ritz

(*Initial reaction.*) It's okay. I like to try new things. Is it supposed to be good quality?

I've heard of Charles of the Ritz, but I don't know what they make. I haven't used any of their products. I didn't know that they are only sold at Lazarus. Why don't they sell them at more stores? I would probably buy Miss Ritz if I liked it and it was sold at a convenient store. I don't always buy the same brand, but I often buy Revlon.

The respondent is a sophomore studying premedicine. She attends The Ohio State University branch in Mansfield. She works parttime in a local grocery store.

Interview 40

Cosmetics

The respondent uses eyebrow pencil, white cream, powder, lipstick, lip gloss, and perfume to accent certain areas. She does not believe in using eye makeup indiscriminately, but prefers to use it at night. Her firm belief is that the use of cosmetics is increasing, but to achieve more of a "natural" look. She feels that some fashion models, especially Twiggy, have had a definite influence on the cosmetic industry. Although she is prone to touch-up her hair, she does not advocate a radical change, and, except for seasonal changes, her use of cosmetics does not vary much. She believes that lipstick darkens with time, and she prefers a moist appearance.

Due to her particular avocation, she reads glamour and fashion magazines regularly and is influenced by advertisements. For basic cosmetics, lipstick and eye makeup, she prefers the most convenient place whether on or off campus. She feels she does not have time to go shopping at Lazarus, and rarely does so. Her responses implied that most types of makeup were set by the time a girl enters college. The most impressionable stages were as a teen-ager. Advertisements made the biggest impression on her regarding choice, and friends' recommendations followed this. She feels most boys are unaware of cosmetics in particular, but that they occasionally acknowledge when they like something worn by a girl.

Miss Ritz

The respondent has heard of Charles of the Ritz and has bought some powder on occasion, but very infrequently. She never heard of Miss Ritz. She thought the tube of lipstick was pretty but made no other signs of interest. She recalled that she had not seen any advertisements relating to these products. She felt the word most closely associated with Charles of the Ritz was powder, not cosmetics. She also associated an expensive image with Charles of the Ritz and assumed that Miss Ritz products were expensive also. She indicated she was satisfied with the products she was using and that she did not know whether easier availability of Miss Ritz products would induce her to buy some.

The respondent is an attractive twenty-two year old senior studying home economics, with a clothing major. Karen is not affiliated with any sorority, and she lives in an off-campus apartment.

Interview 41

Beauty

The respondent indicated that appearance is a major concern with her be-cause people generally correlate an attractive appearance with other qualities attributed to a cultured, sophisticated person. She believes beauty is an ap-pearance one generates and can be accentuated with cosmetics and the right attire. Attractiveness should not be aimed at specific people, but its fulfillment should be inherent because of self-pride. The improper use of cosmetics can be destructive to a girl's appearance, and Joyce believes that many girls do not seem to be conscious of this. She likes to accentuate features that she feels are her best and to deemphasize others not as appealing, mainly through the use of cosmetics. She feels that cosmetics are appropriate at any time.

Cosmetics

She uses lipstick, eye-shadow, perfume or cologne, and occasionally a skin tone because her face is not very conducive to a powder. The brands most often used are Max Factor mascara, and Clairol, the latter mainly because of the advertising. She uses different cosmetics for different seasons or for different social affairs. She relies a lot on the advice of roommates and friends and advertisements in such magazines as *Glamour* and *Mademoiselle.* She is attracted to set-up displays, especially if color charts are present. Most of her cosmetic buying is at the Wendt-Bristol Drugs because of convenience, and occasionally at larger department stores. She feels that the same perfumes are not necessarily appealing on all girls and that many girls do not apply perfume properly. She prefers Windsong. She said that boys, as well as girls, prefer the natural look and that most boys are not opinionated with respect to cosmetics unless there is an overabundance. She believes that certain fashion styles dictate a general trend toward the use of some cosmetics. Twiggy is an example of a general trend toward eye makeup.

Miss Ritz

The respondent has noticed the displays of Charles of the Ritz at Lazarus. She mentioned that she knew one girl who used the powder but discontinued its use because she could not apply it the way it was done by the sales personnel. She indicated she did not believe most girls knew how to apply face powder. With regard to the display at Lazarus, she indicated she did not like the appearance of the salesman because he seemed to wear the powder also. She stated that the location of the display was also detrimental because it was near the escalator and people do not like to be observed applying face powder. Charles of the Ritz presented an expensive image and one that older ladies would wear.

She never heard of Miss Ritz and was not especially impressed with the choice of the name. She thought that a wider distribution would be advantageous in that it might help destroy some of the image that Charles of the Ritz gave it. She felt that her cosmetic buying habits had changed since she was in high school in that she believed she knew what would accentuate her features more favorably now.

The respondent is a twenty-one year old senior in the college of education, majoring in Spanish and English. She is not affiliated with a sorority, although she lived at the Spanish House.

Interview 42

Two girls were interviewed: Eileen and Sue.

Beauty

They stated emphatically that they wanted to appear attractive to other people and that cosmetics were very appealing to them as nurses because their dress and, to a certain extent, their hair styles were dictated by school regulations. According to them, girls tend to be much more critical of another girl's appearance than do boys.

Cosmetics

Eileen stated that a "special" boy's opinion was very influential in her use of cosmetics. She said she felt better if her appearance was pleasing and usually was in a bad mood if she had a disheveled look. Sue agreed that one's appearance had a lot of influence on one's behavior.

Sue uses face powder, medicated makeup, lipstick, a few kinds of perfume, plus other accessories. She does not use eye-shadow at all. Again, she tries to achieve that undefinable "natural" look. She states that the proper use of cosmetics applied in a conscientious manner achieves a "natural" look.

Eileen uses lipstick, a base, eye-shadow and pencil, and various perfumes. She says she does not switch makeup very often but uses the same type regardless of where she is going.

Both of them state that they use Revlon and Max Factor cosmetics. They also agree that convenience dictates where they will buy a certain product. They know what type they want to use and will go to the nearest place available to get it, which is usually near campus. The shades of lipstick are very significant in choosing what brand they will buy. Most of the opinions on what types of cosmetics to buy are because of advertisements and opinions of sales clerks. Eileen stated that, while living in the sorority house, she became exposed to many varied types of cosmetics and that the unique ones tended to be quite popular. Neither of the girls reads many fashion magazines regularly but will glance through many other magazines and remember the attractive ads. Colorful, eye catching displays at cosmetic counters influence both of these girls. Eileen states that some of the more attractive sorority members wield a large influence on the use of certain types of cosmetics in her sorority house. Sue said that certain girls can wear cosmetics a lot better than others and that she knew which ones accentuated her best features.

Miss Ritz

Both Eileen and Sue have heard of Charles of the Ritz, and Eileen uses the deodorant. Both feel that it presents a very expensive and very exclusive image. Eileen said that she felt that she had to buy something if she went to their counter because of the intense atmosphere, whereas, at other counters, she could leisurely look at all of the products and felt more comfortable because of a more relaxed atmosphere. She also said that she felt uncomfortable at the Charles of the Ritz booths. Sue said her mother used the face powder occasionally, but she, herself, had never tried the product. It did not portray a young image in her mind.

Neither had ever heard of Miss Ritz. Both thought the tubes of lipstick were pretty but not appropriate for their complexions. Both thought that Miss Ritz should advertise more and distribute through more channels, especially around a college campus. They thought that most girls will not travel very far for cosmetics, and their principal interest in department stores was for buying clothes, not cosmetics.

Respondent Sue is an attractive twenty-three year old senior, majoring in nursing. She is not affiliated with any sorority, and she lives in an apartment very near the campus. Respondent Eileen is a very attractive twenty-two year old senior who also is majoring in nursing and who is a roommate of Sue. Eileen is affiliated with a well-known sorority on campus, but she is not as active in it as she once was.

Interview 43

Beauty
Facial beauty was regarded as "enhancement of the most attractive features," especially eyes, hair, and coloring.

Cosmetics
For lipsticks, the subject stated that she would buy a tube and try it if her interest were aroused and if it were in her medium price range ($2 or less). She stated that the lipstick outlets were as follows: beauty salons, grocery stores, and dime stores, drugstores, and department stores. Her purchases were usually made at Lazarus. When at a large department store, she wanders through the beauty department, buying on the basis of preconceptions (magazine readings and friends' recommendations) and on occasion on the basis of availability and attractiveness of clerks.

Dislikes and associated brands:

1. Breaking off in the tube—Revlon
2. Too dry—John Robert Powers, Max Factor
3. Ugly case—Yardley
4. Ugly colors—Bonnie Bell
5. Poor variety—Avon

Likes and associated brands:

1. Taste and smell—Milkmaid, Charles of the Ritz
2. Nice colors and variety—Revlon, Max Factor, Clairol
3. Attractive cases—Charles of the Ritz, John Robert Powers
4. Oily—Revlon, Max Factor, Avon
5. Long-lasting on mouth—Avon

Orders of likes:

1. Most important—oily, right colors
2. Next important—do not break in tube, taste and small good
3. Least important—long on mouth, attractive cases.

Last three purchases and type of store:

1. Max Factor—drugstore
2. Helena Rubinstein—department store

Three "common" types:	*Three "status" types:*
1. Cutex	1. John Robert Powers
2. Revlon	2. Faberge
3. Max Factor	3. Charles of the Ritz

Miss Ritz

The respondent was then given the sample tube of lipstick. She stated she was familiar with the Charles of the Ritz line but not with Miss Ritz. She added that distribution should be through one or two good stores to retain the status image and claimed that she would travel out of her way to get it if she wanted a tube.

The interviewee is married, attractive, very stylish, and articulate. She is a senior, 25 years old, lives in an apartment, and has access to an automobile.

In a discussion of current Ohio State fashion, the second respondent seemed to indicate that neatness (grooming and so on) was important, along with coordination of dress and accessories for a pleasing image. The values she used to judge clothes and beauty aids were derived from her mother; for current information, the subject placed magazines (*Glamour, Vogue, Bazaar, Mademoiselle*) as most important; observation of other women was next important; then observation while shopping.

Beauty was seen to revolve about figure, face, and hair. The single most important factor seemed to be facial features, complexion, and coloring.

When it was suggested that girls sometimes become tired of lipsticks, the respondent agreed and replied that the best place to go would be Lazarus or the Campus-Neil Drug Store. When asked why, she indicated that Lazarus has the best wide variety of all brands, and that Campus-Neil has good variety and it is close to campus. Accessibility, therefore, seemed to be important on the subject.

As different brands of lipstick were discussed, it became clear that the subject had two favorites: Max Factor and Revlon. She was loyal to these because they did not change colors, they were nice colors, and they lasted longer on the lips. She seemed to abhor some of the cheaper ones such as Cutex and Westmore.

Her recent purchases were Clairol, at a drugstore; Helena Rubinstein, at a department store; and Tussy, at a discount store. While "name-dropping" with brand names, the respondent classified lipstick images as follows:

The "common lipsticks	*The "status" lipsticks*
1. Revlon	1. Esteé Lauder
2. Max Factor	2. Jacqueline Cochran
3. Helena Rubinstein	3. John Robert Powers
4. Clairol	

The subject was given the sample tube of lipstick, and her response was that she was familiar with both Miss Ritz and Charles of the Ritz and would include them in a prestige list. When probed about distribution, the subject felt that status was probably enhanced by limited outlets but that sale in a drugstore would not lower the image if the price remained high.

She liked the color of the sample, disliked the cheap case and the cheap-looking tube, and also disliked the fact that it was sweating (I had kept it in my pocket).

The subject is a single girl, a senior who lives in an apartment. She is very attractive and from a large metropolitan area.

Interview 44

Beauty

As the interview began on the subject of fashion, it was very obvious that the respondent was being sincere, for she chose her words well and tried to convey the thoughts she had concerning the discussion. She felt that fashion was dependent upon personal hygiene (grooming, neatness) and upon the clothes. The clothes, however, depend on the girl, because her physique dictates her styles. Attractiveness was perceived as different for men and women. Men are attracted to women for reasons of physical appearance, while women were attracted to other women for reasons of rapport, feeling of ease, or sympathy.

Cosmetics

Cosmetics were viewed as a means of "playing up the most important feature," usually the eyes. The respondent turned to how, where, and why cosmetics were obtained, and she stated that price was not important because most items were fair traded. Accessibility seemed to be very important, especially if a drugstore was close and the total amount of purchase during the shopping trip was small. Otherwise, a department store was recommended.

Beauty information was gathered from magazines (*Glamour, Mademoiselle*) through ads and pictures. Some news came from other media (newspapers, TV, radio), while more came from direct observation of others.

A good exhibit, a novel product, compliments on past usage, and good experience with the product were cited as being reasons for purchasing lipstick. The subject stated that she had purchased Revlon and Esteé Lauder, all at Lazarus, for her last three purchases.

While talking about lipsticks, she thought that Revlon stayed on for a long time, Esteé Lauder did not change color but Max Factor did, Revlon was too waxy, Revlon offered many types and colors, and Esteé Lauder and Charles of the Ritz had only small lines, but good ones. An overall image projection seemed to be:

The "common brands	The "prestige" brands
1. Max Factor	1. Charles of the Ritz
2. Revlon	2. Channel
3. Avon	3. Estée Lauder

Miss Ritz

When given the sample lipstick, she was probed concerning Miss Ritz, and she replied that she thought that they were paler lipsticks, less expensive, and would appeal to younger girls. She added that she liked the product but was loyal to the Esteé Lauder line.

The interviewee is married, lives near the campus, was previously a sorority member, and was very well dressed.

Interview 45

Beauty

The respondent felt beauty was being well groomed, having clean, neat hair, a clear complexion, and attractive hands. She felt having attractive clothes that are up-to-date and dressing with a certain element of taste were important. She felt it was especially important to have a hair-do and makeup that are currently in fashion. The respondent felt there is a vogue in hair-do and makeup just as in clothing.

Cosmetics

She felt sloppy makeup is "wretched." She very much likes the current ideas of the natural look. She likes the natural sun-tan look and the getting away from the "paste-look." She said no matter how good looking a girl is, she can be more so with attractive makeup. She felt girls must be very conscious of makeup fashion. The respondent reads *Glamour, Vogue,* and *Bazaar* and says they all warn about keeping makeup in tune with the times. They are all pushing the natural look. Again, she stated that there is a vogue in makeup. Everyone should be open to what is new.

She stated that because of financial conditions she is unable to buy the makeups that she would like and stated she would buy blended makeup (Esteé Lauder or Charles of the Ritz) if she could afford them. She felt the blends offer women more.

She has used Maybelline, Revlon, and DuBarry but prefers Revlon. She uses foundation, eye-liner, and shadow. She feels Revlon has good ideas like under-eye-cover cream for accents and contours. She said she also likes Max Factor. She chooses different items for different reasons. Foundation first for the color, second for the way it treats her face, that is, how it reacts with her body chemistry. She said there is no decision on eye-liner. She always buys Revlon. She also buys little extras if they interest her.

The respondent usually purchases at drugstores. If she is in a department store, has the money, and sees something that interests her, she buys. She likes the department store because she likes the attention of the sales clerks. They give her confidence because they usually seem fairly competent. Indicated sometimes they try to push their ideas too much. She also liked the better selection in the department stores. But she further indicated that she only buys about 10 percent of the time at a department store. She usually buys around campus or at home. It is more convenient. She usually buys new make-up about every three months.

She felt she is influenced by advertisements in particular. She sees a good-looking girl in an ad, observes her, and tries some of her gimmicks. She also indicated that the more often she sees an item the less is her resistance. She indicated that she notices girls on campus and tries some of their tricks. She added, again, that magazines, particularly the advertisements, influence her. She said her roommate always flips through the ads but that she always observes them.

The respondent felt men think beauty is being well groomed and natural. They do not object to makeup. They are concerned about a girl's appearance. She felt men feel makeup is popular and want girls to wear it, given the limitation of good application. They appreciate a girl's spending time on herself. She gave an example of a girl in her art class who had never worn makeup all quarter, and who came in the other day with eye-liner, foundation, and eyelashes. The respondent indicated the makeup was well done; the girl looked fresh, healthy, and wide awake. The respondent noted that three guys mentioned how good the girl looked.

Miss Ritz

The respondent again said she knew of Charles of the Ritz and said she has seen the ads in either *Vogue* or *Bazaar*. She said she has always been interested in the makeup, but unfortunately it is sold exclusively in department stores. She mentioned having talked with a Charles of the Ritz sales clerk in Cleveland and felt that the clerk was well informed and trained, as well as very courteous (said the woman took time with her). The respondent said she had never used any of their products because she cannot afford them and because it is inconvenient to go to a department store every time one wants foundation.

The respondent indicated she had seen ads for Miss Ritz. "It's for the jet set."

"The lipstick is a good color, in tune with what I use and like." (She put it on her hand.) "Good consistency. But if it turns dark or come off easily I won't use it. I like the scent very much. If a lipstick tastes or smells bad, I won't use it. This is one of my objections to Cover Girl. I like my makeup to have a scent (fresh and clean), so you'll be pleasant to people around you. This is one of the reasons why I like Revlon."

She is a very attractive girl, an art major, blonde. She was dressed in grundies (art clothes), but the makeup was very well applied. (She herself commented that because one has to wear grundy clothes for art classes, the only way a girl can look good is by the way she applies her makeup.)

Interview 46

Beauty

She thought there was a big difference between being beautiful and being cute or pretty. A person is born with beauty, it cannot be acquired through hair styles and cosmetics. Many girls make themselves attractive by the way they wear their hair or by the way they dress. She always consults her mother on matters of physical appearance. She said her mother is a good-looking woman and she knows how to dress herself so as to bring out the "woman" in her.

Cosmetics

She uses Yardley, Maybelline, Max Factor, and some other expensive cosmetics. She thought her mother was the biggest factor in helping her decide which brand to buy. She thinks there is a big difference in the different brands. She never buys cosmetics on campus unless she absolutely needs them immediately. She goes to Lazarus to purchase many of her cosmetics. She liked their large variety of cosmetics. She always uses the charge account. The different types she wears are dictated by where she is going. Eye-liner and mascara are always worn no matter where she goes. Lipstick, eye-liner, mascara, blush-on, and powder are worn on a date. Most boys like some makeup, in her opinion. Excessive makeup is not favorable to anybody. Magazines are important to her in familiarizing her with new brands. She reads *Glamour, Mademoiselle,* and other magazines for information on cosmetics and fashions. She always tries to buy her clothing from specialty shops. The idea of having the only dress in her size in all Columbus appeals to her. She thinks "you get what you pay for." Money did not seem to be a deterrent to her buying.

Miss Ritz

She has heard of the Charles of the Ritz, but never of the Miss Ritz line. She has never used any Charles of the Ritz products. The Portugal shade of lipstick appealed to her. When told of the limited distribution, she thought it (Charles of the Ritz) would do well by only distributing in department stores like Lazarus. Bringing the line on campus did not appeal to her. She said she would not buy her cosmetics there except under emergency conditions.

The respondent is a sophomore. This was her fifth quarter in school. When asked what she was majoring in, she said she had changed her major four or five times already. It appeared she came from a family that was quite well-to-do. Money seemed to be no problem to her. She was better-than-average looking, although her personality was somewhat snobbish. She lives in an apartment, is nineteen years old and comes from Cleveland.

Interview 47

Beauty

There is a big difference between being beautiful and being pretty. There are many girls that are pretty and still not beautiful. You either have beauty or you don't. Nothing can be done to make you beautiful, whereas, it is possible to achieve "cuteness" through attractive hair styles and through makeup. Beauty is something more than just physical appearance. It is something deep down inside of you. If you want someone's opinion on beauty you should go to someone you admire or someone who is beautiful. It is possible to get advice on "prettyness" from someone who has achieved it through makeup and cosmetics in general.

Cosmetics

College students prefer the big names in cosmetics such as Max Factor and Revlon. There is a big difference between brands of cosmetics. Some do the job a lot better and are cheaper than other brands. Both Max Factor and Revlon have a wide variety from which to choose. The best way to decide which brand to buy is by trying as many as possible. Advertisements are important initially in familiarizing you with a specific brand. A good source of information in deciding upon which brand to buy is by trying your friends. Very often it is possible to try one of your roommate's brands. Cosmetics are bought only on campus when you run out.

Before school starts each fall she stocks up heavily on cosmetics. "The book stores and drugstores on campus are important only for replenishing your supply under emergency circumstances." She goes downtown to Lazarus on the weekends to buy cosmetics if she so needs them. Since she lived near Cleveland she went to Higbie's to get a specific brand that couldn't be bought anywhere else. During the day she wears three kinds of cosmetics—lipstick, powder, and foundation. During a date or when she is going out to a place of importance she wears eye-liner, eye-shadow, rouge, and mascara, plus the ones mentioned above. The boy she is going out with is an important factor in what she wears. If she especially likes the boy she will try hard to impress him with the type and amount of cosmetics she thinks he likes. "Lazarus is an important and good place to buy cosmetics because of their wide variety and charge account." She never reads any books on beauty or glamour because she is too busy with other things, specifically school work. TV is not very important because of the lack of time. "There are many boys who don't like cosmetics at all. Also, there are many who don't know that you are wearing cosmetics." She thinks a boy should appreciate it when she puts on cosmetics because it takes her from twenty to thirty minutes to do this for a date. "Most boys are against excessive makeup."

Miss Ritz

The girl has heard of Charles of the Ritz but she has never heard of the Miss Ritz line specifically. She liked the Portugal shade of lipstick, the shade was soft and appealing to her. She has never tried any of the Charles of the Ritz products. She thought that lipstick and some of the more frequently used cosmetics should be stocked in drug stores. She thought the idea of limited distribution was good for some of the cosmetics.

The girl lives in an apartment. She is twenty-one years old, and she is majoring in mathematics and physics. She is a senior and plans to graduate next fall. She is better-than-average looking, has a good build, and is fairly cute. She is conservative in her dress and hair style.

Interview 48

Beauty

Marcia, a blonde-haired, blue-eyed coed, defines *beauty* as "the state of a person playing up their best features, having simple lines without being plain, and having elegance." She mostly uses her own judgment so as to beautify herself. She says that one can achieve, or improve, beauty by living up to this definition.

Cosmetics

Marcia believes that cosmetics today are fine but that the use of them is abused: many girls seem to use too much, which detracts from their beauty and general appearance. She prefers Maybelline for eye makeup and Pond's for general facial makeup. Marcia usually buys cosmetics at discount stores near Cleveland. She considers men's opinions somewhat important. If a boy friend extremely objects, she would take his advice. She usually buys cosmetics about two or three times a year. Marcia believes that proper application is important.

Miss Ritz

Marcia sat in on a demonstration of the Miss Ritz line of cosmetics and was not impressed. She said that the demonstrator used the makeup too extensively on the models. She also said the point that it was exclusive for the college girl was a gimmick and that selling it only at Lazarus only hurts sales. Her reaction to the lipstick was nil.

Marcia is a very sweet girl and is conservative in clothing. She is a member of Alpha Delta Phi sorority and is a junior majoring in commercial design in fine arts.

Interview 49

Beauty

The respondent felt that beauty in itself is insignificant and that personality is of primary importance. Men's opinions as to beauty were stated to be of greatest importance. The characteristics that a beautiful person has are a clear complexion, a good figure, and good grooming habits. She felt that beautiful women are not in a superior position unless they are able to develop a good personality to go along with the beauty. This respondent stated that a beautiful girl was born and not "made." She feels that many people can be made *attractive* through the proper use of cosmetics but that they cannot be made *beautiful*. This individual buys most of her clohing from campus stores because they are so convenient. She buys from no special stores and feels that a very conservative approach to the use of makeup can many times be helpful.

Cosmetics

Many points under this section have previously been mentioned, but she feels that most girls are at an extreme in the use of cosmetics. She stated that many use too much makeup and also that there are many who use too little. She feels that men do not like girls to use a lot of makeup. It was stated that one's peer group and a person's home training are the most important determinants in the use of cosmetics.

Miss Ritz

She had the image of Miss Ritz as being sophisticated, old-fashioned, and very proper. She pictured the line as being advertised in some type of "high class" magazine, and she associated it with very mature people. She stated that she knows no college students who wear it and believes that it certainly does not have the college "image." She has a very definite attitude toward Miss Ritz. She stated that she uses other types and is happy, so why change? This individual works for the Fashion and consequently had a knowledge of Miss Ritz distribution. She felt that it should be distributed through all types of stores, as are Revlon and Max Factor, because many people try lipstick just because they see it and like it. She uses little makeup and feels that men's opinions, other girls' opinions, word of mouth, and advertising are important in deciding what cosmetics to use. Her reaction to Miss Ritz was one of indifference, and, as stated before, she did not feel that it had the college image. She felt that most lipsticks offered about the same colors and that there was really little to differentiate different types.

The respondent is a senior in commerce and is a marketing major. She does not belong to a sorority and is better-than-average looking. She has had some problems with her complexion.

Interview 50

Beauty

The respondent felt that *beauty* is only as society defines it. She stated that it is nice to have "but that the majority of people get along pretty well without it." She felt that commonly listed traits of beauty were irrelevant because everybody's standards are different, although she admitted that there were certain generally accepted characteristics, but she mentioned none. She felt that beauty is important and nice if one is so gifted but that personality and other factors are of greater importance. She feels that too much emphasis is put on a person's "looks" today and that all too many girls think only in terms of beauty contests. She feels that very few people are really beautiful and, that, when they are, it is an inborn characteristic rather than one that is created or developed. She feels that her opinions are most important concerning beauty and that the peer group and opinion-makers are second and third.

Cosmetics

The respondent appeared to be using a medium amount of cosmetics and stated that she liked to use them. She felt that she was neither a heavy nor a light user of cosmetics but rather fell somewhere in the middle range. The respondent stated that she liked to use cosmetics because it gave her a fresh look and greater security. (I was unable to determine what was meant by the word *security*.) She mentioned that she felt many girls did not know how to properly use makeup and that most overdid it. Nothing was mentioned as to what she felt men thought about makeup at this time. The respondent said that she buys the same cosmetics continually and that she never really thought about changing because she was satisfied, so there was no reason to change. She believes that color is the primary determinant in the purchase of lipstick because price (unless unusually high) is usually not an important factor because most students are being put through college by their parents. She stated that when she finds a cosmetic she likes she buys it regardless of brand name and also that she tries new products very seldom.

Miss Ritz

She stated that she had heard of Miss Ritz but that she had never used it and did not really know why. Her attitude was again one of indifference, and she was aware that it was distributed solely through Lazarus. She felt that it was a foolish method because there are many people who do not shop downtown. She stated no particular image that she associated with the product but said when she thinks of lipstick it is in terms of Revlon "or some other type that you see all the time or is sold everywhere." She was unaware of Miss Ritz variety but did believe that it was a good name. She thought that practically all lipsticks were the same and that a person would buy pretty much by what they got started on. In talking of advertising, she did feel that it has much effect but that she had seen very little advertising by Miss Ritz, if any. In speaking of advertising, she stated that she reads mostly *McCalls* and *Better Homes and Gardens,* as well as most of the weekly news magazines. She was glad to get a free package of lipstick but said she felt that by the time girls were in college they had already decided what kinds were to be used and that very few were likely to change.

This student is a sophomore in education and is not a sorority member. She is a girl of average looks.

Interview 51

Beauty

Both of the respondents felt that the manufacturers of beauty aids had a lot to do in determining today's beauty, although they advertise in magazines. They also felt that some of the well-known people such as Jackie Kennedy, Twiggy, and others had a lot to do with setting trends for today's beauty.

Cosmetics

Both girls used magazines to see what they would look like with some types of cosmetics. They compare themselves with the models in the magazines (as those just mentioned). They both use a variety of brands when buying cosmetics, the ones they feel best in. The phrase "what they feel best in" was mentioned several times. Price was mentioned, but they felt that cheaper brands were only chosen on the bases of what it was used for, such as eyeshadow which they would not pay as much for. They both would go off campus, if need be, to find the things they want—from discount houses to Lazarus. For information, the trial-and-error method, along with magazines, was used.

Miss Ritz

Both have heard of Charles of the Ritz and use the blend face powders. Both feel that the image is very high for Charles of the Ritz, but neither ever heard of Miss Ritz until recently, when a demonstrator came to their sorority. Both had slightly negative views toward the demonstration. They felt that the makeup used on a couple of their sorority sisters did not look good. They also feel that the image is not as good for Miss Ritz as for Charles of the Ritz. It did not mean the same as Charles of the Ritz.

In summary, both girls used certain phrases throughout the interview such as what they "feel best in" and what the "guys like to see" them in. Other things such as magazines were used extensively as sources for information. Some ads were mentioned such as Summer Blonde and the Dodge Girl.

Interview 52

Beauty

The respondent feels that style is a casual-type dress. She feels that styles are set by the underclassmen and the stores on campus. Because of a lack of transportation, she does most of her shopping on campus. Magazines such as *Seventeen* and *Glamour* she uses for information on styles. She also feels that there is a difference between dorm girls and sorority girls as far as dress and that, to a large degree, the different colleges on campus set styles and the way girls dress. She feels that when she dresses she is actually competing with the models in magazines. She feels that guys do not determine a girl's dress by what she feels good in. She does not feel that celebrities set the style or that they set any type of beauty styles. She feels that beauty is also set by models. She did not know how many different brands she had, but she would go to the store that had what she wanted. Price was a consideration in her choice but that it would not be if she liked a particular brand or color.

Miss Ritz

She has heard of Charles of the Ritz but does not use the products continuously. She has tried the eye makeup because her roommate used it. She believes the image of Charles of the Ritz is high, more or less above her. She has also heard of Miss Ritz but does not use it. Her image of this is "it's for little girls." She feels herself in the in-between stage for both products.

The respondent is nineteen years old and her major is education. She lives in a dorm and dresses well.

INDEX OF CASES